ENGLAND
& WALES
Walks Planner & Guide

The Wharfe near Grassington.

bridge near the village of Hebden. Further on, ancient stepping stones enable walkers to cross the River Wharfe when it is low. Linton church can be seen nearby. Following the river to Grassington, one of the most popular centres in the Yorkshire Dales, and the base for this guide's Yorkshire Dales section. The Way then heads for Kettlewell, veering away from the riverbank. Crossing New Bridge, on the edge of the village, the Dales Way returns to the Wharfe as it meanders through Upper Wharfedale. At times the path runs very close to the water's edge, giving fine views of the rapids and swirling current.

Heading now for Ribblehead, the route encounters windswept hills and tracts of rugged moorland deep in Pennine country, a harsh environment of wild summits and high, breathtaking fells that seems a world away from the softer, more intimate surroundings of the lower dales. The Ribblehead Viaduct, its graceful arches blending perfectly with the dramatic landscape, remains a lasting tribute to the skill of the Victorian engineers who built it.

The Dales Way now follows the River Dee as it winds lazily through Dentdale. With its quaint, whitewashed cottages and winding cobbled streets, the village of Dent has long been a mecca for tourists and visitors. These days, the village economy relies mainly on farming and tourism but in the 17th and 18thC Dent echoed to the sound of clicking needles and spinning wheels. In those days daily life centred on this thriving cottage industry and gloves and stockings were mass produced. Dent, the only village in Dentdale, has the highest main line railway station in England, located on the Settle/Carlisle railway line.

The Dales Way makes for Sedbergh, a busy little town generally acknowledged as the western gateway to the Yorkshire Dales. Sedbergh used to be part of Yorkshire but was embraced by Cumbria as part of the 1974 county boundary changes. Once a centre for knitting and cotton spinning, the town has strong Quaker links and the nearby meeting house dates back to the late 17th century, thought to be the oldest of its kind in northern England. The undiscovered Howgill Fells, rising steeply behind Sedbergh, give the town a spectacular setting.

Crossing the M6 motorway, the walk skirts Kendal before making for Burneside and the River Kent which is followed for a few miles. At this point, the route branches off and heads for Bowness-on-Windermere. There are tantalizing glimpses of the lake on this final leg and when you eventually reach it, a stone seat overlooking the water beckons. The inscription reads: 'For those who walk the Dales Way'. You will find this a memorable and satisfying moment.

223

List of walks in this guide with page numbers

ENGLAND & WALES

Walks Planner & Guide

David Hancock & Nick Channer

PASSPORT BOOKS
NTC/Contemporary Publishing Group

This edition first published in 1999 by
Passport Books, a division of
NTC/Contemporary Publishing Group, Inc.,
4255 West Touhy Avenue,
Lincolnwood (Chicago), Illinois 60646-1975 U.S.A.

ISBN 0-8442-9485-3

Library of Congress Catalog Card Number: 98-67 238

Conceived, edited, designed and produced by
Duncan Petersen Publishing Ltd.
31, Ceylon Road
London W14 OPY

Typeset by Duncan Petersen Publishing Ltd
Originated by SX Composing, Rayleigh, Essex
Printed by G.Z. Printek, Zamudio, Spain

Every reasonable care has been taken to ensure that the information in this guide is accurate, but the routes described are undertaken at the individual's own risk. The publishers and copyright owners accept no responsibility for any consequences arising out of use of this book, including misinterpretation of the maps and directions and those arising from changes taking place after the text was finalized. The publishers are always pleased to hear from readers who wish to suggest corrections or improvements.

Please remember that the countryside changes frequently and that landmarks, especially stiles, can disappear or be renewed in a different form to what may be described in this guide.

Editorial director Andrew Duncan
Assistant editors Nicola Davies and Sarah Barlow
Art director Mel Petersen
Design Beverley Stewart, Chris Foley
Maps Eugene Fleury

Photographic credits
David Hancock, Nick Channer, Derek Forss and Wales Tourist Board Photo Library

Illustrations
Peter Hayman

Contents

The editors and authors are especially grateful to those who helped to research
and check-walk the 12 regions:

South Hams and Dartmoor	**Steve and Fran Dunford**
The New Forest	**Andrew Duncan**
The South Downs	**Bonita Toms**
The Marlborough Downs	**Jill and Les Ward**
The Cotswolds	**Steve and Fran Dunford**
Suffolk	**Derek and Evelyn Hancock**
Welsh Borders	**Steve and Fran Dunford**
Snowdonia	**Richard and Sally Rhodes**
The Norfolk Coast	**Bonita Toms**
The Lake District	**Ron Smith**
The Yorkshire Dales	**Douglas Cossar**
Northumberland	**Georgina and Christopher Leyland**

Introduction

They only know a country who are acquainted with its footpaths. By the roads, indeed, the outside may be seen; but the footpaths go through the heart of the land.

– Richard Jefferies, 19thC writer and journalist

Over the past two decades, the simple activity of walking has grown into Britain's most popular outdoor pursuit. With more than one hundred thousand miles (160,934 km) of public footpaths and bridleways criss-crossing England and Wales, walking is truly a national pastime, binding all kinds of people together.

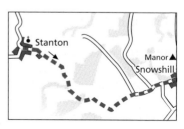

On our maps *an arrow locates the starting point and gives the direction of travel.*

Wherever you go in England and Wales, you are never far from a footpath or bridleway which will take you to the heart of the countryside.

This guide

– Is for the 'ordinary' walker of any age who wants to enjoy the wonderful diversity of countryside in England and Wales opened up by the footpath network. Scotland we leave to another volume: one cannot do justice to the whole of mainland Britain in a book of this length.

The book has also been devised very much with overseas visitors in mind. It will introduce them directly to the cream of Britain's walking country, with all the information needed for planning walks or walking holidays integrated where it is needed.

As the title suggests, it is not only an occasional walking route guide, containing a hundred fully described and originally devised walks to be done as and when you want, but also a guide for planning walking holidays and breaks. We believe that this represents a long overdue departure in walking guides. See under *Planning*, next page.

This is also an original walking guide in the sense that the authors have devised the routes from scratch, hoping to entertain, and to open peoples' eyes. They explore most of the sensationally beautiful areas of England and Wales defined by the National Parks; but they also introduce many little-known and under-appreciated areas such as the Norfolk coast and the Marlborough Downs. (Along the way, they have deliberately left out some over-walked areas such as the Peak District.)

They hope that with the *Walks Planner & Guide,* even those who consider themselves well-travelled in England and Wales will be in for a few pleasant surprises.

Walks for all

Each of the carefully chosen 12 regional sections offers a choice of six fully described, mostly circular, routes graded in length from 4 to 14 miles (6.4 to 22.5 km). These can all be completed within a day, many in less than half a day. The most complex routes are illustrated with maps; otherwise they are described in detail, virtually step by step. However, it is strongly recommended that on any route you carry not only this guide but the appropriate Ordnance Survey map, as specifically suggested in the text of each walk.

The final two walks in each section are relatively ambitious undertakings: although they can mostly be done as two separate day walks, they come into their own as two-day walks, ideal for weekends, using the overnight accommodation suggestions, and convenient public transport back to the start.

Planning

For every route in the book we give all the information you need to organize yourself for a satisfying expedition: not just directions to the starting point, and on where to park, but also the time likely to be taken, and where you could stop for food and drink. There is often information on how to reach the start by public transport as well as by car. And there are notes on the interesting things you can see, and do, along the way.

The guide also describes a 'walking base' for each of its 12 main sections: the villages or towns chosen lie usually within easy reach of most of the walking routes in that section. They are attractive and often interesting places in their own right, and they offer a range of hotels, inns, bed-and-breakfasts, youth hostels and camp sites. Base yourself in one of these places – with this guide – and you are set to enjoy a perfect walking holiday, long or short.

Although having a car will make using this guide easy, we have also tried to please those who don't have, or don't want to use, a car. All the walking bases can be reached by public transport, and within each section more than few of the walks start either at the walking base, or a shortish walk from it.

Transport, national and international
Eurostar trains from mainland Europe arrive at and depart from Waterloo Station in central London.

Airports serving the regions covered by this book are Heathrow, Gatwick, Luton, Leeds/Bradford, Manchester and East Midlands; train services will then get you right to the walking areas. Local bus and some train services operate within the regions, but expect some rural services to be very infrequent.

One or two areas offer enterprising local travel schemes, such as Rover tickets, aimed at walkers and cyclists., enabling them to explore the country between railway stations or to travel further afield by means of free bus links to towns and villages not served by trains.

For times of trains throughout England Wales, call the 24-hour National Train Information line on 0345 484 950.

The Train, Bus and Coach Hotline is open daily 6 am to 9 pm on 0891 910 910.

Long-distance section

At the end of the book is a section describing six of England's most spectacular long-distance paths: The Two Moors Way (West Country), the Macmillan Way (East Midlands and The South-West), the Wealdway (The South-East), the Thames Path (follows riverbank for most of the way), the Dales Way (Yorkshire Dales and Lake District) and the Cleveland Way (North York Moors). They are described in general terms – the object is to provide no more than a taste of each route. A detailed path guide can be purchased for each walk, including precise route-finding instructions – title and publisher are given in each case.

These are by no means all of Britain's long-distance paths. They were chosen as an interesting and representative selection, one from each corner of the country, some of them lesser known and recently established.

Many of the long-established and well-known long distance paths are used as parts of the walks within our main regional sections.

All are ideal for a holiday, taking anything between seven days and three weeks to complete.

Rights of way

England and Wales enjoy access to the countryside that is the envy of the world. Many of the paths are ancient tracks or 'roads', etched into the landscape. Some date back to prehistoric times and were established as lifelines between neighbouring communities. Successive generations used them to travel to church and to market, and to work in the fields and the factories. Every route has its own story to tell from a different age, reflecting the social and economic changes that have taken place in the countryside.

Some footpaths were essential trade arteries or packhorse trails, while others were drove roads established to convey sheep and cattle. Pilgrim tracks and green lanes steered medieval pilgrims between the great centres of Christianity – Winchester and Canterbury. The Agricultural Revolution and the Enclosures Act were responsible for much change and upheaval in the English countryside, producing a new, virtually unrecognizable rural landscape bringing with it many new paths and tracks.

Footpath law

Please bear in mind that the countryside is a living, working environment and should be respected accordingly. Remember, too, that the term 'public rights of way' means exactly what it says – a right to cross private land by following a designated route shown on the Ordnance Survey map and based on the definitive map held by each local authority in England and Wales.

The law relating to rights of way is quite complex, but to simplify it, footpaths, bridleways and byways can be briefly defined as follows:

Footpath A footpath is a highway over which the public are permitted on foot only.

Bridleway May be used by walkers, pedal cyclists and those on horseback.

Byway A minor road, sometimes a metalled lane, sometimes a rough track, but open to all traffic.

Rights of way are defined by signposts, waymark discs and arrows; yellow for footpaths, blue for bridleways and red for tracks that can be legally used by vehicles.

Some areas have what are known as 'permissive paths'. These are not statutory rights of way but are opened at the discretion of the landowner. The Countryside Commission publishes an information booklet entitled *Out in the Country* advising you where you can go and what you can do in the countryside.

Weather

Britain's climate is uniquely fickle and changes constantly. Sunshine, rain, wind and snow can follow close on each other's heels. They will spoil your enjoyment of walking unless you take precautions.

The South of England tends to be warmer and drier than Wales and the North where it is colder, wetter and generally more unpredictable.

Clothing

A stout pair of walking shoes or boots are now accepted as essential for all but the shortest, most casual walks. In winter warm trousers, some form of head gear to avoid heat loss, a windproof annorak, thick socks and a woollen sweater or thermal jacket are recommended – especially on the longer walks and the exposed moorland stretches of Wales, the West Country and the North of England.

Several layers of clothing are essential. Aim for a compromise – don't weigh yourself down with unnecessary items, but wear enough to ensure comfort. It is better to be over-protected than insufficiently prepared when exploring on foot. A small rucksack is useful for carrying extra clothing, as well as a camera perhaps, some bottled water, a hot drink in winter and maybe a light snack.

Weathercall
For an up-to-date report on the weather where you are planning to walk, dial these numbers for a recorded message:

South Hams and Dartmoor 0891 500 404
New Forest 0891 500 403
South Downs 0891 500 402
Cotswolds and Marlborough Downs 0891 500 405
Welsh Borders 0891 500 410
Snowdonia 0891 500 415
Suffolk and Norfolk 0891 500 407 and 408
Lake District 0891 500 419
Yorkshire Dales 0891 500 417
Northumberland 0891 500 418

Golden Valley, in the Welsh Border country – see pages 128-9.

Safety on the hills

The higher the ground, the more severe the conditions: take great care when out on open moorland or in mountainous or hilly country: these are dangerous places if not properly respected. As well as a compass for the undefined stretches, take emergency food rations – chocolate, biscuits or dried fruit. A flask of hot tea or coffee is also recommended and it is advisable to take a whistle and torch – just in case. Also:

• Tell someone where you are going and what time you anticipate returning before setting out. Check the weather forecast carefully and try to avoid going out alone. A group of walkers is always much safer than a single walker. Go at the pace of the slowest. Always allow a margin of time to complete the walk before nightfall.

• If you get into trouble, use the whistle to attract attention by means of the recognized distress signal: six blasts of the whistle, followed by a minute's pause, then repeated.

• If the cloud comes down, walk in single file with 20 yards (18 m) between each of you. The last walker uses the compass, directing the leaders.

• If you get lost in poor visibility and cannot find the way down, stop until the weather clears. Find shelter or build a windbreak from branches or rocks. Put on spare, dry clothing. Sit on something dry. Eat part of the emergency rations and drink something hot. Build an emergency bivouac from anything suitable – a groundsheet, a plastic mac or cape. If cold, keep the limbs moving. Stay awake. Loosen laces and cuffs; huddle close to companions.

Fitness

All the walks in this guide are graded easy, moderate or strenuous. The easy routes should not pose a problem for anyone. The moderate and strenuous walks are best attempted by those who have some degree of experience and know what to expect. The two-day rambles are also aimed at those used to more demanding hikes; if undertaking the entire route, you will need to take a rucksack for an overnight stay. The six long-distance walks are different altogether and should only be undertaken by backpackers and those who are used to completing up to 20 miles (32.1 km) of sometimes arduous trekking in a day.

Maps

Ordnance Survey (OS) Landranger, Pathfinder or Outdoor Leisure maps are the standard maps for walkers in Britain. The last two are large-scale: 1:25 000 (two-and-a-half inches to 1 mile/4 cm to 1 km) and depict the routes covered by this book in minute detail. Landranger maps, at 1:50 000, are less detailed, but usually adequate, especially when accompanied by the directions given in this guide.

Harvey Maps produce similar, very detailed waterproof maps covering popular walking areas in England and Wales and include practical information in English, French and German. All these maps show statutory public rights of way and are available from bookshops and specialist outdoor shops.

The Country Code

Enjoy the countryside and respect its life and work.
Guard against all risk of fire.
Fasten all gates.
Keep your dogs under close control.
Keep to public paths across farmland.
Use stiles and gates to cross fences, hedges and walls.
Leave livestock, crops and machinery alone.
Take your litter home.
Help to keep all water clean.
Protect wildlife, plants and trees.
Take special care on country roads.
Make no unnecessary noise.

Useful Addresses

The British Tourist Authority and English Tourist Board
Thames Tower
Blacks Road
Hammersmith
London W6 9EL
Tel. 0181- 846 9000

The Youth Hostels Association (England and Wales)
Trevelyan House
St Stephen's Hill
St Albans
Hertfordshire AL1 2DY
Tel. 01727 855215

The Ramblers Association
1-5 Wandsworth Road
London SW8 2XX
Tel. 0171-582 6878

Camping and Caravanning Club
Greenfields House
Westwood Way
Coventry CV4 8JH
Tel. 01203 694995

South Hams and Dartmoor

J ohn Leland, the 16thC scholar and
antiquarian who spent much of his
time travelling the English countryside on
horseback, once described the South
Hams, Old English for sheltered or
enclosed area, as 'the frutefullest part of
all Devonshire'. He may well have been
right. Lying to the south-east of Dartmoor,
this is a delightfully rural farming district
where gently rolling hills sweep down to
Devon's spectacular coastline. Here, the county's rivers reach the sea
between sheltered coves and beneath towering cliffs whose breezy
summits rise, in some places, to more than 400 feet (120 metres).
Tourism in this district has expanded significantly in recent years –
though, thankfully, the character and spirit of the South Hams remain
largely intact.

GETTING THERE
You can travel to
Totnes, our walking
base for this region, by
train via Exeter or
Plymouth. Dartmoor
and the South Hams
district are served by
connecting buses. By
car the most direct
route is via the M5 or
the A380/A381.

Kingsbridge and around
The banks of the expansive Kingsbridge Estuary,
dotted with small boats and pleasure craft, are
ideal for walking, particularly for those who want
undemanding outings. Between Salcombe, which
boasts one of the finest natural harbours in the
West Country, and the old port of Kingsbridge,
known as the 'capital' of the South Hams, there are
tantalizing glimpses of peaceful creeks and
winding tidal inlets. To the north of Kingsbridge
there are also many miles of easy public rights of
way which link some of Devon's prettiest villages.
There are also designated forest walks and
pleasant paths cutting through peaceful river valleys.

The South West Coast Path
One of the area's most impressive walking routes, especially for scenery, the
South West Coast Path crosses National Trust land from Bolt Tail, above Hope
Cove, to Bolt Head and then descends through glorious woodland into
Salcombe. The stretch between East Portlemouth and Start Point, to the east
of Salcombe, also offers stunning coastal views. This most southerly outpost of
Devon enjoys one of the mildest climates in the country, and even in the depths
of winter its sheltered, favourable position helps many flowers – including the
famous Devon violet – to remain in bloom.

Dartmoor
Dartmoor, which was designated a National Park in 1951, has a unique and
deceptive character. Consisting of two high, boggy peat plateaux separated by
the River Dart and surrounded by a prehistoric land of stone outcrops, this is
adventure country. There is a timeless quality about Dartmoor – justly earning
its tag as the last untamed wilderness in southern England. In high summer it
basks gloriously in the baking heat, its rolling uplands, granite tors and

meandering rivers shimmering in the sunshine: Dartmoor's friendly face.

During the long, cold months of winter, though, it is a different place altogether: hostile, featureless, often shrouded in mist and rain and seemingly cut off from the rest of civilization.

Manaton Walk 3

Bellever Walk 5

Totnes Walk 6

Loddiswell Walk 1

Slapton Walk 2

Bigbury-on-Sea Walk 8

Salcombe Walk 7

Start Point Walk 4

Dartmoor National Park

With the weather on your side, however, Dartmoor is perfect for walking – dramatic and exhilarating and offering something new and unexpected at every turn. The 368 square miles (954 square kilometres) of the Dartmoor National Park, rising to over 2,000 feet (600 metres) in places, represent some of the most beautiful country in Britain. Numerous paths and tracks weave their way to the very heart of this land of contrasts – where you may catch sight of Dartmoor's famous ponies, step over picturesque medieval clapper bridges, stroll across open heather-clad moorland and through deep wooded ravines.

Chagford and Widecombe-in-the-Moor

Walking is the most popular outdoor pursuit on Dartmoor and some of its easiest and best walks are close to the National Park boundary near Chagford, a picturesque village and tourist centre to the north. Here, there are more formal facilities to attract walkers and families – including waymarked forest walks and nature trails. Haytor Rocks and Hamel Down, which harbour red grouse in spring and summer, are popular local landmarks near Widecombe-in-the-Moor, one of Dartmoor's most famous villages, probably best known for the song Widecombe Fair. As well as a variety of routes ideally suited to the less adventurous walker, there is also plenty of scope for the hardened hiker – particularly in the uncultivated, exposed North and South Moors where a compass is essential.

The North Moor is used as firing ranges by the Ministry of Defence, who publish details of when firing is not taking place. This is the bleakest and most inaccessible part of Dartmoor. South of Okehampton, an old military road runs across the moor, heading towards High Willhays – Dartmoor's highest peak and a popular destination for more intrepid walkers. Despite its wildness and isolation, Dartmoor also bears the stamp of human influence. Many Bronze and Iron Age hut circles have been discovered in the area, and the remains of granite quarrying and tin mining can still be seen – the last mine closed just before the Second World War.

WEATHER
In high summer, Dartmoor can bake in the heat; in winter it has some of the harshest weather in England. In some years there is snow on the tops in late May.

But the real issue is the changeability of the weather. Dartmoor's height, and closeness to the coast, combine to produce wet and suddenly changing conditions. Fogs can descend in minutes, adding to the danger of the bogs, which can be a yard to a mile across. (To avoid bogs, look for vivid green *Sphagnum* moss and keep clear of where it grows.)

WALKING BASE:

Totnes

This bustling town, well disposed to holidaymakers and full of blue-chip facilities, lies just outside the Dartmoor National Park's south-eastern boundary and has a long, colourful history spanning more than a thousand years. It is England's second oldest borough and it makes a charming base if you want to stay in the area in order to walk.

Situated on a steep hill in the glorious valley of the Dart, often described as the loveliest river in England, Totnes quickly evolved as a port of considerable significance, attracting travellers and traders from many parts of the world. By the early 16thC, Totnes was the twentieth richest town in the country with much of the local economy based on the export of local wool cloth and tin.

A fascinating self-guided heritage trail allows you to stroll around the medieval streets of Totnes, where many of the town's charming Elizabethan buildings can be seen. Some of the wealthiest merchants in the district lived here. Visitors to Totnes usually make a point of discovering the Butterwalk, an arcaded walkway in the High Street, where, in medieval and Tudor times, there were sheltered, open-fronted market stalls selling meat and dairy products. Reminders of the town's fascinating past can be seen around every corner, and each Tuesday in summer Totnes brings its history to life when local members of the Totnes Elizabethan Society dress in Tudor costume to run a charity market in the town.

To the north of the High Street is the beautiful red sandstone Church of St Mary. Built in the 15thC, it includes a splendid, intricately carved rood-screen of Beer Stone which is reminiscent of the screen in Exeter Cathedral. Behind the church, located on the Ramparts Walk, is the town's famous Guildhall, dating back to the mid 16thC and built on the site of an old Norman priory. The Guildhall includes a courtroom with a gold-leafed list of mayors going back to 1359, and, on the ground floor, a 17thC jail with one cell looking into the courtroom.

At the top of the High Street are the remains of Totnes Castle, founded in the 11thC and widely acknowledged as a perfect example of a Norman motte and bailey fortification. From the ramparts, there are magnificent views across to Dartmoor and the South Hams.

No visit to this delightful West Country town is complete without a tour of Totnes Museum, housed in a wonderfully restored Elizabethan building. On display are many exhibits illustrating the town's customs and traditions. There is also an authentic Tudor herb garden and a fascinating exhibition dedicated to Charles Babbage, a 19thC mathematician who is generally regarded as one of the founding fathers of the computer age.

Totnes may be justly proud of its rich heritage, but as a town it is also firmly established in the present, with a strong appeal for those who enjoy arts, crafts, music and drama. The town includes a variety of bookshops, boutiques and antique shops and is also a centre for handmade musical instruments, designer knitwear, pottery, bespoke shoes and other forms of traditional workmanship.

Fore Street is one of the town's main shopping thoroughfares, leading down to the 19thC stone river bridge. The scene here is charming, and with the broad Dart fully navigable between Totnes and Dartmouth, there is usually much to see in the way of boating activity. From the bridge there are pretty views of picturesque quays and warehouses and here you can complete your short walking tour of Totnes by taking a leisurely stroll along the delightful Riverside Walk.

ACCOMMODATION AND FOOD

Being a popular West Country destination for holidaymakers, the South Hams, especially the area around Totnes, offers a wide choice of accommodation. Whether you want farmhouse bed-and-breakfast, a convivial inn, an upmarket guest house, or a secluded country hotel and restaurant, you will not be disappointed.

Recommendations in every price band are listed opposite. If you want a comprehensive accommodation list and information, contact the Tourist Information Centre, The Plains, Totnes, Devon TQ9 5EJ; tel. 01803 863168.

SLEEPING AND EATING

HOTELS AND INNS

TOTNES
Royal Seven Stars;
The Plains, Totnes; tel.
01803 862125. Former
coaching inn located at the
foot of the historic town's
main street, dating back to
1660. Well-equipped
bedrooms and buffet bar
serving snacks all day.

ASHPRINGTON
Waterman's Arms;
Bow Bridge, Ashprington,
2 miles/3 km S of Totnes;
tel. 01803 732214.
Historic riverside inn
located at the top of Bow
Creek, offering quality
overnight accommodation
in tastefully decorated and
furnished bedrooms, some
enjoying tranquil rural
views over the small river.
Open fires; delightful
beamed bars, real ales and
hearty home-cooked food.

DARTINGTON
Cott Inn; 2 miles/3 km N of
Totnes; tel. 01803 866629;
closed Christmas Day.
Delightful 14thC stone- and
cob-built inn boasting one
of the longest thatched
roofs in the country.
Beamed bar serving local
ales and varied food,
notably an impressive
lunchtime buffet and
varied evening fare, in
particular local fish and
game. Tucked beneath the
thatch are six pine-
furnished bedrooms.

DITTISHAM
Fingals; 6 miles/
10 km S of Totnes; tel.
01803 722398; closed Jan to
Easter. A 17thC manor
farmhouse set in a
secluded valley, close to the
River Dart, offering plenty
of charm with a stylish
interior, relaxed

atmosphere and country
house party style four-
course dinners. Swimming
pool and tennis.

STAVERTON
Sea Trout Inn;
3 miles/5 km N of Totnes;
tel. 01803 762274. A
welcoming 15thC village
inn, peacefully positioned
in the Dart Valley. Beamed
bars, open log fires and
pretty, well-equipped
cottage-style bedrooms,
ensure a comfortable stay.
Extensive bar menu with
emphasis on home-cooked
food, especially fish dishes,
and interesting restaurant
menu of carefully cooked
dishes.

BED-AND-BREAKFAST

TOTNES
Old Forge; Seymour Place;
tel. 01803 862174. Modern
comforts in a delightful
600-year-old stone building
with walled garden and
blacksmith's workshop.
Individually furnished and
decorated cottage-style
rooms, splendid breakfasts
and afternoon teas served
in Tudor-style dining room.

Great Court Farm; Weston
Lane; tel.01803 762368; no
credit cards. Large
Victorian farmhouse
overlooking the town and
surrounding countryside,
situated on 400-acre (160-
hectare) farm running
down to the Dart. Spacious
bedrooms. Evening meal by
arrangement.

BERRY POMEROY
Old Vicarage; 1¹/₂
miles/2¹/₂ km E of Totnes;
tel. 01803 863169; no credit
cards. Listed 15thC
building set in 2 ¹/₂ acres (1
hectare) of mature
gardens; high standards of

service and hospitality,
imaginative cooking.

LITTLEHEMPSTON
Buckyette Farm;
1¹/₂ miles/2.¹/₂ km N of
Totnes; tel. 01803 762638;
closed Nov to Easter; no
credit cards. Homely
Victorian farmhouse in a
lovely country setting. Good
value en suite bedrooms.

STAVERTON
Kingston House;
3 miles/5 km N of Totnes;
tel. 01803 762235; no credit
*cards.*Superb early
Georgian country house in
13 acres of grounds; en
suite bedrooms, one with
four-poster, elegant candlelit dining room –
reputation for good food.

CAMPING AND HOSTELS

Award-winning campsites
with splendid locations and
offering excellent facilities:
Woodland Leisure Park at
Blackawton, near
Dartmouth (01803 712598)
and *Ramslade Touring*
Park, overlooking the Dart
Valley near *Stoke Gabriel*
(01803 782575). Value-for-
money hostel accom-
modation at *Dartington*
Youth Hostel, *Dartington*
(01803 862303).

FOOD

In addition to the above
hotels and inns, the
following are worth seeking
out for reliable food:
Kingsbridge Inn, Totnes,
tel. 01803 863324; the
Durant Arms,
Ashprington, tel. 01803
732240; *Start Bay Inn,*
Torcross, tel. 01548
580553; *Millbrook Inn,*
Southpool, near
Kingsbridge, *tel. 01548*
531581

15

Loddiswell Loop via the Primrose Line

Although only a few miles from the popular coastal regions and towns of Kingsbridge and Salcombe, you will meet few other people on this walk, and the relative freedom from cars on the road sections will give you that miles-from-anywhere feeling. The views across a patchwork quilt of fields are typical of the South Hams.

Start *Loddiswell, signposted off the A381 (Totnes to Kingsbridge road) and the A371 (Kingsbridge to Plymouth road), 3 miles/5 km north of Kingsbridge; SX720486. Small free car park in centre of village.*

Avon resident at Hatch Bridge.

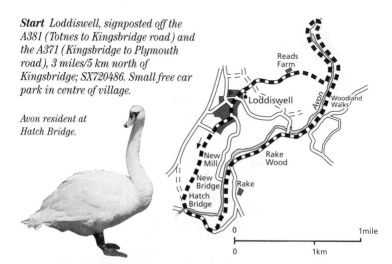

Essentials

Easy 4½ miles/7 km; 2½ hours; mostly flat, but a with a steep finish into Loddiswell; **map** Ordnance Survey 1:25 000 Outdoor Leisure Map 20, South Devon.
Terrain Field, riverside and woodland footpaths (muddy in places), interspersed with comfortable level walking along old railway route; various road sections.

Route directions

Walk down main village street taking 'No entry' side of one-way system. Shortly, turn right along Town's Lane, then at Higher Greystones Farm cross stile and follow footpath along field edge, via two more stiles. On reaching open meadows descend steeply, maintaining direction through two gates to partly hidden stone stile leading to hedged track. Follow stony track downhill to lane and cross bridge over River Avon. Follow peaceful lane beside river for ¼ mile/0.4 km, then just beyond junction take waymarked footpath left over stile. Bear right around boggy ground, cross small wooden footbridge visible 100 yds/90 m ahead, then proceed along riverbank path for ¼ mile/0.4 km to reach road bridge. Cross road (not river bridge) and continue beside river to road at New Mill. Along road for ¾ mile/2 km, passing under old railway bridge to reach Loddiswell Station (private residence). Take footpath alongside former railway yard, then in 200 yds/180 m join old railway track (private path open to public, except first Monday in January). After ¾ mile /1.2 km pass through small cutting, then cross river via stone railway bridge and immediately take path left to double back along riverbank. Ignore footpath right and follow river downstream past weir, then through woods and alongside old leat for ¼ mile/0.4 km to reach open grassy area. Turn right away from river, follow path uphill beside stream, soon to pass Read's Farm and join farm road, which steeply ascends for ¼ mile/0.4 km back into Loddiswell.

• **LODDISWELL** Referred to as 'Lodeswilla' in the Domesday Book, the name probably originating from 'Our Lady's Well', one of the many natural springs and wells in the village. The Church of St Michael and All Angels dates from the 13th and 16thC and contains a Breeches Bible printed in Geneva in 1568.

Nearby are the Blackdown Rings which form a large earthwork with a motte and inner and outer baileys.

• **RIVER AVON** At Hatch Bridge it is possible to take a short detour right down a cul-de-sac footpath along the riverbank. In spring and early summer the riverbank scene will be a riot of colour from celandines, wild daffodils and garlic – a great spot for a picnic.

• **PRIMROSE RAILWAY LINE** Single-track branch line of the Great Western Railway which ran from South Brent on the edge of Dartmoor to Kingsbridge, via Loddiswell. The picturesque line opened in 1893 and closed 70 years later in 1963, but evidence of the fine Victorian engineering can be still be seen at some of the remaining railway bridges and at Sorley Tunnel, a 660-yard (600-metre) tunnel constructed between 1891 and 1893.

> **FOOD AND DRINK**
> Pubs in Loddiswell; Anne Lowe's Mill Coffee Shop at the Avon Mill Garden Centre in the Avon Valley, just off the walk.

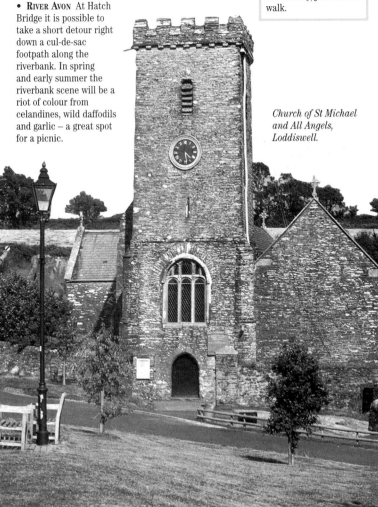

Church of St Michael and All Angels, Loddiswell.

Slapton Ley and Sands

This route is packed with interest: unspoilt coastline; a fascinating stretch of inland water – Slapton Ley – now a nature reserve and a birdwatcher's paradise; and Slapton itself, a sleepy pretty village with much to appreciate; an old chantry, a fine church, charming cottages and two pubs.

Start Torcross, on the A379 between Dartmouth and Kingsbridge, SX824423. Main pay-and-display car park beside Slapton Ley, plus a few free spaces in village centre.
By bus Totnes to Torcross, via Kingsbridge Quay, Western National services 164 and 93, Monday to Saturday only; tel. 01392 382800.

Essentials

Easy 5 miles/8 km; 3 hours; mostly flat;
map Ordnance Survey 1:25 000 Outdoor Leisure Map 20, South Devon.
Terrain Shingle beach, grassy coast path, well-defined paths and tracks and some boardwalks over the marshes through the nature reserve, plus sections of very quiet country lanes.

Route directions

From Torcross either walk alongside beach, or on more sheltered footpath beside Slapton Ley for 1¼ miles/2 km. Just before stone obelisk turn left, signposted Slapton. Cross bridge then immediately turn left on to nature trail footpath, a twisting, often awkward path alongside the Ley. In ½ mile/0.8 km reach an open area – once a quarry. Disregard path left and continue ahead, signposted Slapton Village, path soon curving away from Ley through coppiced woodland. On reaching gate to Southgrounds Farm (do not go through), turn left on to boardwalk which wends its way between reed-beds and lichen-festooned trees to reach crossing of tracks. Take route signposted Deer Bridge and follow often muddy track (Marsh Lane) for ½ mile/0.8 km to metalled road. Turn left, then immediately right before Deer Bridge along quiet lane leading to sheltered and charming hamlet of Start, passing old watermill. At crossroads, turn sharp right up steep hill then after ½ mile/0.8 km turn left at road junction, soon to reach crossroads on edge of Slapton. Go straight across past white-washed cottage, descend steeply taking a right, then left fork to reach village

centre. Pass the church and Queens Arms pub, then bear left signposted 'To the Beach' and follow road for ½ mile/0.8 km out of village, passing Field Study Centre and campsite, back to Slapton Sands. Turn right and retrace to Torcross.

• **TORCROSS** A storm-battered yet pretty little fishing village lying along Slapton Sands. The Sherman tank in the car park was recovered from the sea in 1984 and stands as a memorial to hundreds of American lives lost in 1944 to German torpedo boats during Operation Tiger, a training exercise for the Normandy landings.

• **SLAPTON LEY** Separated from the sea by only a long, narrow shingle bank, this is the largest natural freshwater lake in the South West and an internationally important nature reserve, attracting many migrating birds and wintering wildfowl. In summer the marshland area of the reserve is dotted with wetland plants in flower. The Field Study Centre in Slapton provides useful leaflets and information about the reserve; tel. 01548 580466.

• **SLAPTON VILLAGE** Well worth exploring, this attractive village comprises mainly 14thC cottages lining narrow, twisting streets, the dramatic remains of an 80-foot (24-metre) tower which belonged to a collegiate of chantry priests, consecrated in 1372, and the Perpendicular parish church which features some 14thC windows. A booklet about the history of this ancient village can be obtained from the church.

FOOD AND DRINK

Café and pubs in Torcross, notably the Start Bay Inn (fresh fish) and the Tower Inn and Queen's Arms in Slapton.

Bovey Valley and Becky Falls

A woodland walk centred on the Bovey Valley, with occasional views to the high tors. The spectacular Becky Falls and the delightful village of Lustleigh are worth exploring. Although the paths in the immediate vicinity of Becky Falls and the picture-postcard village of Lustleigh are likely to be busy with visitors out for a short stroll, you will soon escape the crowds to find peace and quiet in the deep, wooded valley.

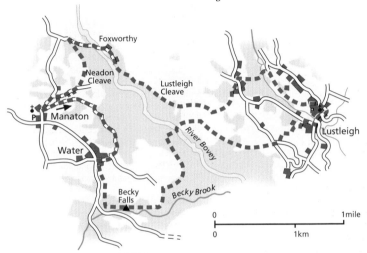

Start *Manaton, on the B3344 between Bovey Tracy and Moretonhampstead, SX750812. Small car park (honesty box) near church.*

Route directions

Walk through village with church and village green on left, then immediately beyond house called Fernstone, turn right through gate on to bridleway. Descend for 880 yds/800 m to crossing of tracks and turn right, signposted 'Water ½ mile', gradually ascending to thatched farmhouse. Turn right, arrowed Manaton Direct, around house to road, then past charming thatched cottages to T-junction. Bear right to reach B-road by Kestor Inn and turn left. In 100 yds/95 m take footpath left, waymarked Becky Falls. Keep to right-hand side of

meadow, following path into woodland to cross stile. After 50 yds/45 m proceed straight on at crossing of tracks, and keep to main track when Blue Trail A bears off right. At a fork (Trail Point A12), go right downhill to reach boarded walkway (refreshments and WCs on right). Follow path signposted Bovey Valley, soon to take path right to view Becky Falls – a worthwhile detour. Proceed along undulating top path, then at Red Trail Point B3, do not descend, but continue through woods. Cross stile, then go straight across junction of tracks, waymarked Bovey Valley. After 440 yds/400 metres take left fork on to narrow path which climbs and meanders past Nature Area board, before dropping steeply through woods to T-junction. Turn right, signposted Clam Bridge, descend steeply to

Essentials

Moderate *7 miles/ 11km; 4 hours; undulating, with some steep hills;* **map** *Ordnance Survey 1:25 000 Outdoor Leisure Map 28, Dartmoor.*
Terrain *Mainly forest trails or narrower woodland paths, in places rather overgrown, occasionally rocky and slippery on the steeper sections.*

19

Bovey Valley.

left. Ascend on track/drive, then descend around left-hand bend into dip and take the track left, opposite field gate, up into forest. As track levels out, look for footpath right, signposted Manaton. Climb wall stile, turn left to next gateway, cross stile, then bear half right uphill across grassy, boulder-strewn meadow to a metalled lane. Turn right, then left at T-junction back into Manaton and car park.

cross River Bovey, then climb path for 440 yds/400 m to take right fork marked Lustleigh via Pethybridge. Follow hillside contour for 880 yds/800 m and keep ahead at next junction signposted Lustleigh. Climb gradually, ignoring gate right to Woodland Trust. Pass through gate further up (Heaven's Gate). Descend on track to road, turn right, then shortly left down lane marked Pethybridge, then next right by phone box and descend for further 880 yds/800 m to centre of Lustleigh. Up past church, then left at war memorial, and next left along track to Cleave. At end of track, bear right along path to kissing gate then go straight ahead across small meadow to further kissing gate. Bear left on unmarked path (not Old Manor House), enter woods and soon go through kissing gates beneath huge boulders to follow narrow footpath for 650 yds/600 m to gate and lane by large white house. Turn left past house, go through gate ahead and shortly cross a stream, then follow rocky woodland path which climbs, sometimes steeply, to a stile and road. Turn left and in 25 yds/24 m bear right on to bridleway. At next gate turn left, head uphill, then start to descend, taking right fork signposted Foxworthy Bridge. Continue 1,760 yds/1500 m through Lustleigh Cleave, eventually descending close to river. Ignore path left to Manaton and continue to pass Foxworthy Mill (on left) to reach gate and track. Proceed along track past Foxworthy hamlet, then bear left over river bridge and immediately turn left on to footpath. Within 100 yds/95 m rejoin track and continue uphill passing footpath to Manaton on

• **MANATON** Pretty thatched cottages and the 15thC Church of St Winifred's, with its fine carved rood-screen, cluster around the green in the heart of this scattered community. Wingstone Farm, close to the church, was once the home of the novelist John Galsworthy, who wrote the sagas about the Forsyte family.

• **BECKY FALLS** Created by the picturesque Becka Brook, these waterfalls plunge 70 feet (20 metres) down rounded granite boulders and are best seen in the winter after heavy rain. Woodland walks, visitor centre, café and WCs.

• **BOVEY VALLEY WOODLANDS** One of the few areas of semi-natural oak and hazel woodlands in the Dartmoor National Park, lying in a deep, unspoilt valley carved out of granite. Belonging to the Nature Conservancy Council, it provides an important habitat for a wide range of animals and insects, notably dormice, woodland butterflies such as the high brown fritillary and white admiral, and some uncommon birds – dipper and pied flycatcher.

• **LUSTLEIGH** Quintessential English village grouped around its green and a fine 13thC church. There's a delightful mixture of architectural styles, from 15thC granite and thatched cottages in the village centre to grand Victorian houses, and some modern dwellings, scattered around the wooded slopes.

FOOD AND DRINK
Kestor Inn at Manaton and the thatched Cleave Inn in Lustleigh. Café at Becky Falls and a pleasant tearoom in Lustleigh.

Start Point

This section of the coastal path is not as undulating as further west, making it relatively easy walking. Even so, there are great views of the rocky headlands in each direction.

Start Start Point, best reached from the A379 (*4 miles/6.4 km south, signposted*) at Stokenham, between Dartmouth and Kingsbridge; SX821376. Private car park (*charge in season*) at end of the public road.

Route directions

From car park, go through white gate and take footpath right, downhill towards Great Mattiscombe Sand, turning right along coast path, signposted Lannacombe. One mile/1.6 km of easy walking leads to this sparsely populated sandy cove. From there keep to the coast path, which becomes rocky and more difficult beneath crags at Woodcombe Point, and past Ballsaddle Rock after ³/₄ mile/1.2 km. The path levels out as you walk across meadows on a raised beach, close to Maelcombe House. Round Langerstone Point, then on nearing coastguard cottages at Prawle Point, leave coast path and take track, waymarked East Prawle 1¹/₄, uphill to metalled lane. Continue ascending, then at right-hand bend, just past barn, turn left on to track which narrows to a footpath as it descends towards rocky outcrop (Gammon Head). Within 100 yds/95 m of rejoining coast path bear right at fork of paths (under a towering rock) and proceed uphill away from sea, affording fine views left to Bolt Head. Cross stile, then in 100 yds/95 m, turn right at a crossing of paths to follow track for ³/₄ mile/1.2 km to road and continue uphill into East Prawle. Cross village green, go down road past Pig's Nose pub and take first turning right by bungalow. On nearing phone box turn right along lane, disregard turning to Maelcombe House, and keep to track which soon becomes footpath. Descend into

valley, cross stream and climb along field edge to reach stony track and footpath diversion (no longer possible to walk past Woodcombe Farm). Turn right along track, follow it round left-hand bend, then where it bends right, keep straight ahead on bridleway through gate and along grassy track to further gate. Turn left over stile, proceed straight across field to rejoin farm road below Woodcombe. Turn right, then at crossroads of tracks carry straight on past Borough Farm and take path towards Lannacombe Green, passing through gate to green lane. Shortly, where track drops down left go through gate ahead and follow arrowed bridleway downhill through series of gates, keeping to field edges. When valley opens up ahead, path becomes unclear. Descend steeply down 'V' on grassy slope between gorse bushes, bearing slightly left further down to join path above river and follow it down to road. Turn right, cross river and shortly turn right, then left steeply uphill, signposted Start Point. At Hollowcombe Head turn right and follow road past masts back to car park.

● **START POINT** The almost sheer cliffs here are over 100 feet (30 metres) high and from the car park there are magnificent views across Start Bay to Slapton Sands and beyond towards Dartmouth. To the north is Hallsands, a ruined ghost-village, where 37 houses on a rocky ledge were washed away in a severe storm in 1917.

● **PRAWLE POINT** is the southernmost tip of Devon, its name deriving from an old English word meaning lookout hill. The raised beach near Maelcombe House was created when the sea level was several feet higher.

Bellever and the heart of Dartmoor

Encapsulates Dartmoor: granite, water, forest and the moor itself.
Explore rugged tors, ancient cists and stone-hut rings, clapper
bridges and the grey stone houses and farms that typify the area.

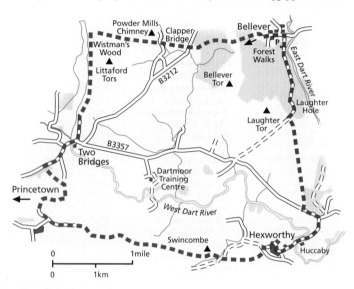

Start *Bellever Forest – signposted off*
the B3212 at Postbridge between
Moretonhampstead and Two Bridges,
SX656722. Free car park (picnic
tables, WCs) beside the East Dart
River in Bellever.

Route directions

Walk back to road, turn left and keep
straight on at next junction passing Youth
Hostel. Shortly, take bridleway ahead,
arrowed The Lichway, up steep stony
track. Enter forest, turn right, and
proceed uphill, keeping straight on at two
crossings of tracks to reach clearing
(Bellever Tor visible left). Continue ahead
through clearing and more forest to stile
and descend to Cherrybrook car park and
B-road. Cross road, pass through gate
opposite, and head towards the old
Powder Mill chimney. Footpath meanders
to right of this line due to boggy
conditions, even in the
driest weather, so pick
your way as best you can.
On reaching mill complex,
pass chimney, cross
clapper bridge, then leave
complex via two gates.

Cross small meadow, keeping parallel to
belt of trees on left to reach unmarked
gate and open moor. Maintain direction
and gradually ascend to rocky outcrop,
below and to left of three tors on horizon.
Skirt to right, then ascend more steeply to
stile in wall ahead. Continue up to ridge to
reach Littaford Tors, then descend other
side to top edge of Wistman's Wood. Turn
left on grassy path and descend to stile.
With river on right, continue for 1,350
yds/1,250 m to pass house, then follow
gravel drive to Two Bridges. Cross B3357,
pass in front of hotel, and go over old road
bridge to rejoin B-road. Take road
signposted Princetown, walk uphill (take
care), then on reaching woods, turn left
on to bridleway after 50 yds/45 m. Follow
track through trees to gate, then proceed
straight across meadow to signpost in wall.
Pass through gate (house down on left),
then bear half-right downhill following
blue and orange markers
on rocks to further gate
and descend track to cross
footbridge over river. Turn
right and continue along
river bank for 650
yards/600 m, then near

FOOD AND DRINK
Two Bridges Hotel (bar
meals and cream teas)
and the Forest Inn at
Hexworthy.

concrete bridge cross stream and turn left up grassy track. Pass stone buildings of Batchelor's Hall (on left) and follow stony track ahead, signposted Peat Cottages. On reaching concrete drive, turn left, pass house and go through gateway on to open moor, then in 100 yds/95 m take left fork, waymarked Hexworthy, on stony track. Ignore track right after 880 yds/800 m, and proceed ahead for 1,350 yds/1,250 m to pass untidy spoil area. Track becomes grassier and rougher, but peaty plateau provides easy walking for 1,350 yds/1,250 m to gate. Maintain direction, gradually descending grassy, boulder-strewn terrain to another gate, then shortly bear left, track becoming more defined between gorse bushes, then stone walls. Pass ruins of Swincombe to river and cross, via bridge or stepping stones, then go over unmetalled road to follow line of sunken bridleway. Pass through two gates, cross road, and continue down track through edge of Hexworthy, descending past thatched cottages to reach another road and Forest Inn. Turn left downhill to humpback bridge over West Dart River, then climb steep hill to B-road (Hexworthy Cross). Bear left on footpath parallel to road for short distance, then cross road and continue past house on right to take bridleway through gate marked Huccaby Newtake. Make for post (just visible) and gate at top corner of plantation. Emerge on to open moor and maintain direction across heather-covered slope to summit (glance back to stay in line with plantation edge behind). Continue across summit plateau until Laughter Tor (nearer rocky outcrop) and Bellever Tor come into view with Bellever Forest on their right. Look for

Essentials

Strenuous 12 ¹/₂ miles/20 km, 8 hours; undulating, with several steep uphill sections; **map** Ordnance Survey 1:25 000 Outdoor Leisure Map 28, Dartmoor. **Terrain** Mostly open moorland, mainly on stony or grassy tracks and on springy peat – plus some road walking. Can be boggy. *Warning* Do not attempt this walk in poor visibility. The higher parts of the open moor can become covered in mist, making navigation impossible without a compass as there are no defined paths. Changes in the weather can take place suddenly so, if, on reaching Huccaby Newtake gate the mist has come down, do not attempt to cross the moor but continue along the road for 1 mile/1.6 km to Dunnabridge Pound Farm, turning right along the track for 1 mile/1.6 km to reach the gate into Bellever Plantation, where you can resume the route.

line of track in hillside opposite, below Laughter Tor. Descend into dip and climb other side to join track and turn right to enter Bellever plantation. Continue for 25 yds/24 m, then fork right down past Laughter Hole Farm and proceed straight on through two gates, following stony forest track for 1,350 yds/1,250 m back to car park.

- **BELLEVER** Planted in 1921, Bellever Forest covers 1,000 acres and is one of the largest on Dartmoor. The track through the forest to Littaford Tors is known as the Lich Way, because those living on Dartmoor were included in the parish of Lydford and corpses (liches) were taken along this route to reach Lydford's church.

- **POWDER MILLS** These ruins were originally a gunpowder factory, built in 1844. The Cherry Brook powered the machinery and the isolated position made it a very safe site. The gunpowder was used to blast stone in local quarries, until the invention of dynamite in the 1890s made it obsolete.

- **LITTAFORD TORS AND WISTMAN'S WOOD** The tors give wonderful views across the vast wilderness of the high moor and, to the south-west, to the forbidding Dartmoor Prison at Princetown. Wistman's Wood is a nature reserve of rare, wizened oak trees, stunted because they grow in such a high and exposed place.

- **SWINCOMBE** is one of many sites, now abandoned, where people used to live on the moor. The river bridge is approached by huge blocks of granite, suggesting that it was originally a clapper bridge. These sturdy bridges, with their massive clappers (granite slabs) date from the Middle Ages.

Totnes to Dartmouth

*A roller-coaster walk. From tranquil river banks to hilltop villages,
then back down to quiet creeks, this varied ramble incorporates ever-
changing scenes. There are distant views from the hilltops and birds
and boats beside the river, culminating in the delights of Dartmouth.*

Start *Totnes town
centre, SX805603.
Ample car parking.*

Planning

An early start is
recommended to allow
time to explore Dartmouth
and to ensure that you
catch return transport.
Return There are three
options for the return trip
to Totnes.
By river between April
and October take a river
cruise (75 minutes) back
to Totnes. Times are
determined by the tides.
Find out the time of the last sailing, which
rarely leaves later that 5.30 pm, but can
be as early as 12 noon. Consult timetable
before setting off: available at Steamer
Quay, or from the Tourist Information
Office, tel. 01803 863168.
By bus direct service to Totnes, Western
National No 89: last bus leaves 4.45 pm
(Sun and bank holidays 5.50 pm).
By bus and ferry cross to Kingswear on
the frequent ferry, then take Bay Line bus
22 to Brixham, changing to service 100 for
Paignton, and then Western National X80
back to Totnes. Leave Dartmouth approx
8 pm to catch connecting buses, last bus
arrives Totnes 9.50 pm.

Route directions

From the Tourist Information Office in
The Plains, go south along New Street.
Follow signposted detour round new
development on river's edge and soon
enter factory yard. Keep to right-hand
side, climb wooded steps to stile and
continue along lower edge of pasture with
river left. Walk through woodland and
more fields, close to river for 880 yds/
800 m to quarry, then ignore path left and
continue (yellow arrows) up steps, bearing
left to gate and field, Descend into dip,
climb to track and continue left along
track to cross stile and brook, then in 440

Essentials

Strenuous 11 miles/17.7
km; 7 hours; very hilly;
map Ordnance Survey
1:25 000 Outdoor
Leisure Map 20, South
Devon.
Terrain Mostly meadow
and woodland footpaths
(overgrown in places),
with short sections of
stony track and
shoreline, and some
country lane walking.
Paths tend to be muddy.

yds/400 m take footpath
right, signposted
Ashprington. Climb steeply
to wood, fork left to road
and turn right down into
village. Pass church and
post office and descend
towards Bow. At low tide, a
short cut is to turn left at
Stepps Cottage to cross
Bow Creek via stepping
stones. Otherwise,
continue to Bow Bridge,
cross Harbourne River and
follow creek past
Waterman's Arms. Enter
Tuckenhay, then beyond
Millhouse Farm turn left to
cross bridge. In 50 yds/45 m follow path
left alongside Bow Creek for 440 yds/400
m to a T-junction of tracks. Drop down left
to proceed along shoreline for further
880 yds/800 m. Leave creek, bearing right
up wooded valley, path becoming a track
and, shortly, curve right to reach
Cornworthy Court. Pass through farmyard
to road, bear left past church, then head
steeply uphill, signposted East
Cornworthy. At Longland Cross turn left,
then in 1,350 yds/1,250 m descend into
village. Walk past East Cornworthy Barton,
then almost opposite steps in stone wall,
cross stile on left to follow shady path to
further stile. Keep ahead across hillside,
cross stile in hedge, descend steps and
cross driveway and stream to road and
turn left. After 220 yds/200 m you have
choice of routes to reach Red Lion,
Dittisham. If low tide, take footpath along
creek edge (may be slippery), locating
slipway on reaching moored yachts, which
climbs between walls to join Lower Street.
Turn left by cottages, walk up steps past St
George's church to pub. Otherwise,
country lane into village and pub. From
Red Lion, walk along The Level towards
Lower Dittisham; at Manor Road turn
right up Rectory Lane. At Old Rectory
(tarmac ends) turn right up steep track,
then left over stile in 220 yards/200 m to

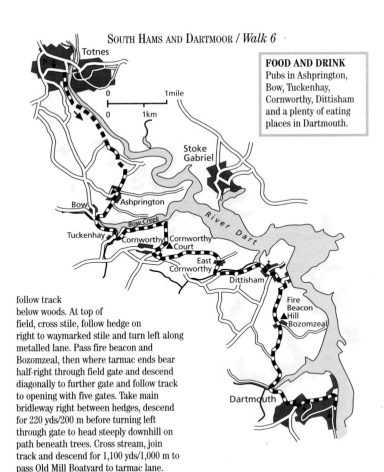

Totnes

Stoke
Gabriel

Bow
Ashprington

River Dart

Bow Creek
Tuckenhay
Cornworthy Cornworthy
Court
East
Cornworthy
Dittisham

Fire
Beacon
Hill
Bozomzeal

Dartmouth

follow track
below woods. At top of
field, cross stile, follow hedge on
right to waymarked stile and turn left along
metalled lane. Pass fire beacon and
Bozomzeal, then where tarmac ends bear
half-right through field gate and descend
diagonally to further gate and follow track
to opening with five gates. Take main
bridleway right between hedges, descend
for 220 yds/200 m before turning left
through gate to head steeply downhill on
path beneath trees. Cross stream, join
track and descend for 1,100 yds/1,000 m to
pass Old Mill Boatyard to tarmac lane.
Proceed to T-junction, turn left across
bridge, walk up steep lane (Old Mill Lane)
to outskirts of Dartmouth. Proceed through
housing estate along Mill Crescent, turn
right along Archway Drive, then left to
main road. Cross over, walk down to
quayside and turn right for pleasant stroll
along promenade to town centre.

• **ASHPRINGTON** A beautiful old village
boasting two fine mansions, picturesque
cottages and a 15thC church featuring an
ancient font and a famous chalice in
constant use since 1275.

• **BOW BRIDGE** A charming spot where
the Harbourne River enters Bow Creek –
the largest creek on the Dart. The
Waterman's Arms served as a prison
during the Napoleonic Wars and was once
a smithy and brewhouse. Lime kilns litter
the banks of the creek, the lime being
quarried at Tuckenhay, which once had
two paper mills and was a thriving trading
port in the 19thC.

• **DITTISHAM** Thatched stone cottages are
scattered through plum orchards and
daffodil fields down to the River Dart in
this attractive riverside village. The 15thC
church houses a contemporary 'wine glass'
pulpit and Dittisham Mill boasts the
largest waterwheel in Devon.

A ferry crosses the Dart to Greenway
Quay, above which stands Greenway
House, the birthplace of Sir Walter
Raleigh. The fire beacon above the village
was one of coastal chain which warned of
the arrival of the Spanish Armada.

• **DARTMOUTH** Famous for its Naval
College, this historic fishing port and now
popular resort is rich in buildings of
historic and architectural interest,
including the 17thC arcaded Butterwalk
and the castellated Royal Castle Hotel. A
lively little town, delightfully sited beside
the Dart estuary with a bustling quay,
noted eating establishments and a 600-
year-old castle guarding the harbour
entrance (open).

Salcombe to Noss Mayo

An exhilarating two-day walk along a section of the beautiful South Devon Coast Path, which forms part of the 560-mile (896-km) South West Way, the longest of England's long-distance footpaths. Day 1 heads west from Salcombe to Bigbury-on-Sea; Day 2 continues along the coast path to Noss Mayo. (From here you have to get public transport into Plymouth to connect with a bus or train to the walking base of Totnes.) You'll explore the outstanding South Hams coastline, incorporating Salcombe, a bustling fishing port and resort; attractive sandy coves and charming seaside villages; and wild stretches of cliff path, with great views. With the sea to your left and a patchwork of rich farmland to your right, you undulate along cliff tops, across flooded estuaries and beside peaceful coves. As well as Salcombe, notable places of interest along the way include Sharpitor, Bolt Head, Hope Cove, Bantham, Burgh Island and Noss Mayo.

Start *Salcombe, SX735390. Due to limited public transport for the return from Plymouth to Salcombe, it is best to approach Salcombe by bus from Totnes. Western National service 30 leaves Totnes at 7.30 am arriving in Salcombe at 8.22 am.*

Planning

The route can only be walked at Easter and between May and August due to the necessity of using the River Avon ferry at Bantham. The ferry operates between 3 and 4 pm, so you have to plan Day 1 accordingly, and in order to reach the overnight stop at Bigbury-on-Sea. Contact Hugh Cater, tel. 01548 560593 to confirm ferry times and charges.

In planning Day 2, it is essential to know when low tide will be at Erme Mouth: you have to wade the river, only possible one hour each side of low water. Contact the local tourist offices, tel. Salcombe 01548 843927, or Modbury 01548 830159, both seasonal, or Totnes 01803 863168, or see *Western Morning News* for daily tide table.

Route directions

As this two-day walk follows the extremely well-waymarked South West Way along the South Hams coastline, a detailed route description is not necessary. Much of the coast path is well worn and the complete trail is signposted with yellow arrows accompanied by acorn symbols. Here is a brief outline of the route.

Day 1

From Salcombe town centre the coast path follows the often busy (especially summer) and narrow road to South Sands and Sharpitor (NT). However, in the summer months it is possible to take the occasional boat service from Salcombe to South Sands. Just beyond Sharpitor (Overbecks Museum and Garden) the main coast path begins, heading south as a high-level path (Courtney Walk) with superb views across Salcombe's estuary to round Bolt Head. The stunning cliff path from here to Bolt Tail is a delight, the worn path wending its way through heather- and gorse-clad slopes and dipping down to charming sandy cove – Soar Mill Cove – ideal for a swim and thankfully free

> ### Essentials
>
> **Moderate** Day 1: 13 miles/20.8 km, 8 hours; Day 2: 13 miles/20.8 km, 8 hours; undulating coast path; a few sharp climbs; *map* Ordnance Survey 1: 50 000 Landranger Map 202, Torbay and South Dartmoor and Map 201 Plymouth and Launceston.
>
> **Terrain** Broad cliff-top paths and bridleways, estuary-side paths and some stretches of tarmac through quiet coastal hamlets. Generally dry underfoot.

from the usual beach 'attractions'. Ascend Bolberry Down (NT, refreshments), round Bolt Tail with its Iron Age earthwork and descend to Hope Cove, where the coast path levels out, linking a string of popular sandy bays, seaside hamlets and hotels. Skirt Thurlestone and its coastal golf course, then, with views to Burgh Island, reach Bantham Sands (bathing dangerous) and the Avon estuary. Take the ferry across the river to Cockleridge to reach Bigbury-on-Sea and fascinating Burgh Island, reached at high tide by a sea tractor.

Day 2

Beyond the family resort of Challaborough, the coast path undulates across cliffs with some strenuous walking in parts. However, this section is delightfully unspoilt, with few coastal settlements, just sheltered coves and breezy headlands affording pleasing sea views. An interesting signposted diversion inland can be made along the Smugglers Path, once used by donkeys for bringing contraband inland, to visit the attractive village of Ringmore. The roller-coaster path eventually reaches the Erme estuary, where you head inland beside the river to the low tide crossing point in Wrinkle Wood. Having waded the river, the trail to Noss Mayo traverses rich agricultural land along the cliff tops with views down to peaceful coves, over Bigbury Bay to Bolt Tail and the previous day's ramble, and inland to Dartmoor on the horizon. Having rounded Mouthstone Point, with views across Wembury Bay, the final stretch heads inland alongside the Yealm estuary, passing the ferry to Warren Point, and beside Newton Creek to enter Noss Mayo.

Return to Totnes Plan to reach Noss Mayo before 6 pm so that you can catch the last bus (service 94) at 6.15 pm to Plymouth, arriving 7 pm. From Plymouth take the X80

> ### ACCOMMODATION
> **Rosbank Guesthouse**, 01548 810724; **Henley Hotel**, 01548 810240; **Burgh Island Hotel** (unique and expensive art deco hotel), 01548 810243 – all in Bigbury-on-Sea. **Journey's End Inn** at Ringmore, 1 mile north of Bigbury. Try **Slade Barn**, 01752 872235 in Noss Mayo; **Maywood Cottage**, 01752 872372, and **Crown Yealm**, 01752 872365 in Newton Ferrers, if you want to stay overnight at the end of Day 2.

> ### FOOD AND DRINK
> **Day 1**: Hope Cove, Thurlestone and Bantham. **Day 2**: pub at Kingston, 1½ miles/2.4 km off coast path, east of Erme Estuary; shop near Stoke House and caravan park, otherwise take your own provisions.

service at 7.35 pm to Totnes, arriving at 8.35 pm. Alternatively, take the train back to Totnes.

• SALCOMBE Sheltered at the head of a south-facing creek, this popular sailing and fishing centre luxuriates with palms, fuchsias and other warm-weather plants. There's a bustling maze of narrow streets and delightful views across the boat-filled river estuary. At Sharpitor (NT) there is a fine sub-tropical garden and in the Edwardian house is a fascinating museum of maritime history, among other exhibits.

• STAREHOLE BAY As you look into the bay, you may pick out the dark outline of of the four-masted Finnish barque *Herzogin Cecilie* which struck the nearby Ham Stone in April 1936.

• HOPE COVE One of the most photogenic fishing villages in Devon, featuring two small squares of fishermen's cottages set around patches of grass and cobble.

• BURGH ISLAND Well worth exploring: it has an inn – The Pilchard – dating from 1336 and once the haunt of fishermen and smugglers; and an art deco hotel built in 1929 where Agatha Christie wrote one of her novels.

• WESTCOMBE BEACH The ruins of a stone building close to the path was once part of the Flete Estate and used as a tea house by the family. A path leads inland to the village of Kingston and its historic church.

• NOSS MAYO and NEWTON FERRERS Old fishing villages in an idyllic setting, lying opposite each other on a tidal creek a mile inland from the mouth of the River Yealm. Popular with sailors and much loved by artists.

Introduction
New Forest

'Like Scotland, but transplanted to Southern England'; 'too many tourists' ; 'beautifully varied'; 'timeless and serene'; 'flat and empty'. People either like or dislike the New Forest; they are rarely indifferent. Whatever your view of the landscape, it's superb walking country, because of its extensive network of paths and tracks, and because the whole area is managed by the Forestry Commission for leisure as well as profit. Access points are frequent and clearly marked; the public is permitted to roam at will unless otherwise stated. So walkers are uniquely free to take advantage of its key attraction: variety.

Timeless

The New Forest consists of several types of woodland: there are the great mixed woods of oak and beech, notably Bolderwood, right at the centre, some hundreds of years old; there are mature conifer plantations, and very recent ones; and, as a contrast to the dignified woodlands, there are casually scattered stands of stunted birch and willow.

Forest', by the way, means a Royal hunting ground (as opposed to a chase, which is a nobleman's hunting ground). The New Forest was especially favoured by the Norman kings for the sport of chasing deer; but its history as a place lived in, and worked in, stretches back much further, with evidence of occupation in Roman times, and before.

And of course, the Forest is much more than woodland. The heaths, mainly heather and gorse, account for at least half the total acreage. People who like the New Forest find the heath wild and beautiful, untouched by, and independent of, man: a genuine survival of ancient landscape into the over-manicured modern world. Lowland heath is a rare habitat, home to a specialized flora and fauna including the adder, Dartford warbler, hobby, honey buzzard – and of course the ponies. Please heed the signs asking you not to feed them: feeding encourages them to stray on to the roads, where a surprising number are killed by cars. Both ponies and donkeys can be aggressive if approached – young children are particularly at risk.

GETTING THERE
The New Forest is served by trains on the Waterloo/Bournemouth line. By car from the north and east the M27 is the best route in, leaving at Junction 1. The region is about 1.5 hours from London by road. From the west the A35 and the A31 give good access.

The heaths lie over an impenetrable geological layer, and many parts never dry out. The bogs, often betrayed by cotton grass, are highly deceptive: you can take a step or two into a boggy area without sinking very deep; one more lands you on what looks like a firm, dry foothold, but is in fact a floating island of moss. You sink to your knees, or even your thighs.

The final ingredients of the landscape are the 'lawns' – grassy spaces, often surprisingly large, grazed short by the ponies; and the cultivated pockets – agricultural land such as the Beaulieu Estate in the south and at Minstead in the north.

New Forest ponies.

Improvised walking

The New Forest has an impressive network of paths and tracks, and it is quite easy to devise your own routes. Do ensure, however, that you are armed with the Ordnance Survey Outdoor Leisure Map of the area at a scale of 1:25 000. The 1:50 000 Landranger maps are not detailed enough. Once among the trees, you can lose your sense of direction quickly; one woodland path can look much like another. For those who are new to walking, the New Forest is a perfect training ground. Although in places paths can be wet and muddy, any walking you do will be fairly undemanding. Now and again, you may come across a short climb, but nowhere will your physical strength be put to the limit.

Heritage

The New Forest is still administered by the Verderers, an old 'private parliament' that sits in open court every two months in the Verderers Hall in Lyndhurst, the forest capital. Their duties are essentially political and judicial – concerning conservation issues and the implementation of local bylaws – among other topics.

Indeed, The New Forest has a rich history, including some interesting literary associations. Captain Marryatt, who wrote *Children of the New Forest*, set his story in the countryside around Sway, and Sir Arthur Conan Doyle, creator of Sherlock Holmes, lived at Bignell Wood near Cadnam and is buried in Minstead churchyard.

Rufus Stone marks the spot where William Rufus, who succeeded William the Conqueror, was accidentally shot by an arrow, and Bucklers Hard on the Beaulieu River is where, for 500 years, oaks were used in the building of some of Britain's greatest ships. There are so many places to see and things to do in the New Forest that visitors are spoilt for choice. A visit to the New Forest Museum and Visitor Centre at Lyndhurst is recommended, providing the opportunity to learn about the region, its culture, history and heritage, as well as its role in the modern world as a living, working community. Between 7 and 8 million people visit the New Forest each year, with tourism playing an essential role in the local economy. But much of this enchanting corner of southern England, particularly those more remote parts of the region that can only be reached on foot, lies silent throughout the year, undisturbed and undiscovered. This is where the real New Forest weaves its own distinctive brand of magic.

> **WEATHER**
> In summer, this is one of the sunniest regions of the U.K. Winter temperatures are often more moderate than elsewhere.

29

Brockenhurst

Fordingbridge Walk 2

Brockenhurst Walk 1

Lymington Walk 3

Brockenhurst, more of a residential village than a town, is surrounded by some of the loveliest woodland scenery in the New Forest. With a choice of places to stay and a railway station with train services to London, it is not surprising that Brockenhurst began to expand during the second half of the 19thC and continued to develop during the 20thC, establishing itself as a convenient and popular inland resort within the boundaries of the Forest. Parts of the original village remain and the partly Norman parish church of St Nicholas, which stands on a mound just outside Brockenhurst, is reputedly the oldest in the region. The churchyard, dominated by an enormous yew tree which may well date back 1,000 years, contains the grave of 'Brusher' Mills, a renowned local character and snake catcher who died in 1905. Brusher earned his name by sweeping loose snow off the ice on Brockenhurst pond to make it easier for skaters. He

lived a solitary life in the woods and is reputed to have caught more than 3,000 adders in his time. Note the intricate carving on the gravestone, depicting Brusher Mills standing outside his hut.

FOOD AND ACCOMMODATION

The beautiful expanse of the New Forest and, more especially, our base town – Brockenhurst – in the heart of the Forest, is a favoured holiday destination, notably for weekend breaks due to easy access from London. As a result, the area is geared up to accommodating the growing number of visitors and a wealth of places to stay, from well-organized camping grounds and humble B&Bs to upmarket inns and large hotels, exist in the Brockenhurst area. Here we highlight a select few in each category. For more comprehensive information on where to stay, including self-catering options, contact the New Forest Tourist Information Centre, High Street, Lyndhurst, Hampshire, SO43 7NY; tel: 01703 282269.

SLEEPING AND EATING

HOTELS AND INNS

Rhinefield House Hotel, *Rhinefield Road*, *Brockenhurst; tel. 01590 622922*. Splendid mock-Jacobean mansion built in the 1890s and set in the heart of the New Forest with ornamental gardens, an impressive interior.

New Park Manor, *Lyndhurst Road*, *Brockenhurst; tel. 01590 623467*. Former royal hunting lodge surrounded by parkland with its own equestrian centre, leisure facilities, well-appointed bedrooms and imaginative cooking.

Carey's Manor Hotel, *Brockenhurst; (on A337) tel. 01590 623551*. Set in five acres of landscaped gardens, this elegant country house has a health club, an informal French-style café and a noted restaurant.

Montagu Arms, *Palace Lane, Beaulieu; tel. 01590 612324*. Creeper-clad hotel with cosy winter log fires, a conservatory overlooking the pretty walled garden and individually decorated bedrooms, one with four-poster. Good restaurant. Wine Press bar open all day.

Master Builder's House Hotel, *Bucklers Hard, nr Beaulieu; tel. 01590 616253*. 18thC house located in an attractive former shipbuilding village, with gardens running down to the Beaulieu River. Main building bedrooms are full of charm.

Rose and Crown, *Lyndhurst Road*, *Brockenhurst; tel. 01590 622225*. 18thC coaching inn with friendly pub atmosphere.

BED-AND-BREAKFAST

Thatched Cottage Hotel, *16 Brookley Road*, *Brockenhurst; tel. 01590 623090*. Pretty, 400-year-old thatched cottage near the village centre. Antique furnished bedrooms and a relaxing restaurant serving lunches, afternoon teas and dinners.

The Cottage, *Sway Road*, *Brockenhurst; tel. 01590 622296; closed Dec and Jan.*. Former forester's cottage featuring oak beams, a welcoming atmosphere and attractively decorated bedrooms. Dinner by arrangement.

Nurse's Cottage, *Station Road, Sway; Tel 01590 683402; closed mid Nov-mid Dec*. Comfortable B&B in a former district nurse's cottage. Well decorated bedrooms. Half-board only.

Caters Cottage, *Latchmoor, Brockenhurst; tel. 01590 623225; closed Christmas*. In the heart of forest, this whitewashed building offers simply furnished accommodation and forest views. A peaceful spot.

Buckler's Spring, *Bucklers Hard, nr Beaulieu; Tel. 01590 616204*. Comfortable accommodation overlooking the Marina and Beaulieu River.

CAMPING AND HOSTEL

The Forestry Commission (01703 283771) owns ten campsites in the New Forest, all with tranquil settings. Sites close to Brockenhurst offering full facilities include *Hollands Wood* on the edge of the village and *Roundhill Campsite*, both open between Easter and September (booking advisable in high season). *Setthorns Campsite* at Wootton, near New Milton, is open all year but offers few facilities. The nearest *youth hostel* is at Burley (6m/10km west) – 01425 403233.

FOOD

Reliable pub food can be found at the oldest pub in the New Forest, the thatched **Fleur de Lys, Pilley** (*01590 672158*), the **Red Lion Boldre** (01590 673177) and the **Hobler, Battramsley** (01590 623291). Restaurants with claims to good food include: *Le Poussin, Brockenhurst (01590 623063)*, or *Gordleton Mill, Hordle*, near Lymington (*01590 682219*) – an idyllic setting in a converted 17th-century water mill – or the *Chewton Glen Hotel, New Milton (01425 275341)*. Also worth trying are *Rocher's, Milford-on-Sea (01590 642340)*, *Whitley Ridge Hotel, Brockenhurst* and *Parkhill Hotel, Lyndhurst.*

Hincheslea Moor and Rhinefield

*Samples the full range of New Forest scenery, from rolling moor to
fine old woodland, and lets you appreciate it to the full through long
views: it's hardly hilly, but the high points open up some fine vistas.
The route is within walking distance of Brockenhurst and gives
access to the Rhinefield Ornamental Drive.*

Start *Forestry
Commission
Hincheslea Car Park &
Picnic Place clearly
signposted on
unclassified road
leading W from
Brockenhurst,
direction New Milton
and Burley, on right
1.5 miles (3 km) from
Brockenhurst centre.*

Essentials

Easy 5 miles (8 km);
two gentle climbs; **map**
Ordnance Survey 1:25
000 Outdoor Leisure
Map 22, New Forest.
Terrain Tracks and
paths over heath; wood-
land paths. Very muddy
sections after rain.

Route directions

From the car park take the track leading
out across open heath – it starts from the
Car Free Area barrier, very muddy after
rain for first few yards. Track soon
becomes a path; head for gentle rise – Red
Hill. Descending, ignore paths branching
right; soon, at fork, go left past lone holly
tree, following path ahead towards pines
and road. At trees leave car park to right
and skirt left round trees to join road via
short gravelly section. Left along road to
Puttles Bridge; then in 50 yards (40 m)
right into Puttles Bridge Car Park and
Picnic Place. Continue to car parking
area, past barrier and in 90 yards (82m)
locate obvious path leading left into wood.
Follow it, ignoring crossing paths, keeping
straight ahead. In 800 yards (730m) pass
stone with inscription Seaton's Passge
1991. Cross footbridge and follow path left
towards road: indistinct for a few yards,
but soon a wide track with felled trees
either side. Just before road note huge
Wellingtonia on left. Turn right along road
and in 90 yards turn left over fence into
wood. Follow fairly distinct path roughly
parallel with fence on right, Rhinefield
House coming into view. At
junction of paths keep
straight ahead, not left
back to road. Continue
until Rhinefield House is
just past (grassy mound on
right). Some 50 paces after
end of Rhinefield House, at

crossing of paths, marked
by Wellingtonias on left
and right, turn left.
Continue gently downhill
to fence/gate. Through
gate, follow track down to
footbridge. Cross and
continue on obvious track
uphill, bearing right.
Follow the track, always
well defined, across the
heath; it generally bears
right. Ignore crossing
tracks. As you reach high ground, road
comes into view ahead. Where track meets
wide grassy space, continue towards road.
At road turn left and follow it back to
Hincheslea Car Park and Picnic Place –
about a mile (1.6 km).

RHINEFIELD ORNAMENTAL DRIVE If you want
to explore it, continue along the road after
reaching it via the woods from Puttles
Bridge Car Park and Picnic Place. There
are stands containing descriptive leaflets,
which describe short exploratory trails.
Perhaps the main feature are the huge
Wellingtonias. These are actually giant
sequoias, natives of California, and
planted on many British estates after
being 'discovered' in the U.S.A. in the
1850s. There is a particularly impressive
avenue of them at Stratfield Saye, the
estate of the Dukes of Wellington – which
is how they got their English name. They
are amazingly long-lived: in California,
specimens 3,400 years old are recorded,
and they grow to great heights – up to 150
feet in Britian. The the wood is brittle, but
it contains chemicals that preserve it.
There are other trees and shrubs of
interest at Rhinefield, notably
rhododendrons – so May
June is the ideal time to
visit.

RHINEFIELD HOUSE see
page 31.

RHINEFIELD HOUSE see
page 31.

FOOD AND DRINK
Rhinefield House, half
way through the walk.
Nearest shops for picnic
provisions:
Brockenhurst.

Turf Hill and Woodgreen

Explores one of the lesser-known corners of the New Forest.

Start Turf Hill Inclosure free car park on the B3080, north-east of Fordingbridge, GR212177.

Route directions

Make for the far end of the parking area and join a path between posts. Follow it through bracken, passing a small pond on left. Carry on along the main path as it curves left and down the slope. At the bottom, beside fence post, turn right and keep trees on your right. Further on, there is a gentle upward slope; continue in a westerly direction to top of incline and then down the other side as the path heads out across a delightful expanse of heath. Avoid turnings on the left and right and continue ahead. The path makes for a distant curtain of trees. As you approach them, veer left to join a wide grassy ride. Soon it drops down to provide glorious views ahead; descend the slope, do not veer right with the trees but continue ahead down to the floor of the Millersford valley. Look for a distinctive clump of pine trees, a useful landmark, over to the left and cross a little stream. Continue towards a gap in the trees and bushes ahead. Follow the well-worn path as it bends right. After several yards, reach a gate. Bear left in front of it and follow a muddy track up to the road at Densome Corner. Go forward for a few yards, then turn left just before the trees and a gate leading into them to join a grassy path running along woodland edge. Pass a gate on the right and continue. Further on, reach the parking area at Godshill Inclosure. Look for Gate 4 situated among the trees on the right. Follow the wide path into woodland. Cross a track; immediately the path forks. Take the right fork and continue through trees. Go over a crossing

Essentials

Easy; 6 miles (9.6km); 2.5 hours; essentially flat with several short, undemanding climbs; *map* Ordnance Survey 1:50 000 Landranger 184 (Salisbury & The Plain) or 1:25 000 Outdoor Leisure 22, New Forest.
Terrain Well-defined paths and tracks across open expanses of valley and plain; some sections are wooded and can be wet after rain.

track. Further down the slope, the route merges with another path and continues ahead. On reaching another path, on a U-shaped bend, continue ahead. Avoid path running off half left. When you reach a gate, emerge from the trees, cross the green at Woodgreen and bear left at the road. Walk down to the Horse and Groom and Woodgreen village hall, then return to Godshill Inclosure. Follow the path beyond the U-shaped bend, avoid the right turning from earlier and continue ahead, now covering new ground. Go straight ahead at crossing track and when you reach another track, turn left, continuing about 70 yards (64 m), then bearing right to join a woodland path. Follow the path all the way to the road at Densome Corner. Retrace your steps down the muddy track and recross the Millersford stream. Once over, veer to the left and follow a path quite close to the trees. Continue across open heathland and soon you reach some wooden posts. Pass between them and follow woodland ride. Go over a junction, follow the ride as it curves left and, at the next junction of tracks, bear right and take the path up the slope. Merge with another track and cut between plantations and felled trees. Beyond them, with a line of pylons up ahead, swing right by some silver birch trees. At the corner of the trees, veer left and return to the car park.

WOODGREEN is famous in the New Forest for its community hall, which boasts walls covered with fascinating murals depicting life in this sleepy village. The hall was built in the early 1930s and it was then that two young artists, Ted Payne and Robert Baker, hit upon the idea of creating a unique social record of the time.

FOOD AND DRINK
The Horse and Groom at Woodgreen, conveniently placed at the halfway point of the walk, offers meals at lunchtime and in the evening.

Lymington to Beaulieu along the Solent Way

A tremendous day's outing through an area not much walked by visitors to the New Forest. The route uses one of the best sections of the well waymarked Solent Way, and makes an interesting change from the heath- and woodland walks elsewhere in this section, proving the amazing variety of scenery in the New Forest.
Roughly the first half of the route goes not along the Solent shore but through pleasant agricultural land generally a mile or so inland. The second half is along the banks of the Beaulieu River, sheltered and beautiful. Access to the Beaulieu Estate for walkers is limited and this walk remains one of the few ways to see this charming corner of the New Forest on foot.

Start *Lymington Town Station. Regular service from Brockenhurst – consult timetable at Brockenhurst Station. Be sure to get off at Lymington Town, the stop before the pier.*

Planning

This is a straight-line route, devised with public transport in mind: you can start from Brockenhurst or Lymington. If Brockenhurst is your base, take the eight-minute train ride to Lymington Town Station, where the walk begins.

It's well worth leaving time to view Bucklers Hard and its historical attractions.

From the walk's end at Beaulieu there's a meandering 40-minute bus ride back to Lymington – see end of route directions for details. **Be sure to plan your walk so that you arrive at Beaulieu in time for a bus back to Lymington.**

Route directions

Just outside station forecourt right into Waterloo Road. Continue to T-junction. Right towards level crossing, continuing over Lymington River by bridge. Right at sign for I.O.W Ferry, along Brickfield Lane – sign inconspicuous. In 300 yards (270 m), almost opposite Old Ferry House,

---

Essentials

Easy 11 miles (17.5 km); 4-5 hours; no climbs; **map** Ordnance Survey 1:25 000 Outdoor Leisure Map 22, New Forest.
Terrain Country lanes and paths; riverside path.

FOOD AND DRINK
Pubs at Bucklers Hard and at Beaulieu village, the end of the walk. Shops for provisions at Lymington, Bucklers Hard and Beaulieu.

---

left on to gravel road, bearing right immediately: locate, in 35 paces, on left, post and stile marked Solent Way. Cross and follw waymarks all the way to Bucklers Hard, some 7 miles (11 km). From Bucklers Hard continue, following waymarks along Beaulieu River to Beaulieu village. Reaching village, Montagu Arms Hotel and pub on left, turn right for the village green, an ideal spot to rest your legs. Or turn left, towards the fork: the village main street is up the left fork (souvenir and craft shops, village stores, gallery); the bus stop is down the right fork (following sign All Through Traffic), on the left, just before the garage.

Return to Lymington Buses leave 10.01 (not Sat); 10.12; 12.02 (not Sat); 14.12 (Sat only); 15.00 (schooldays only); 17.29. *No service on Sundays or public holidays.* Information tel. 01722 336855 or 01202 673555.

- **LYMINGTON RIVER** The top (salt water) reach looks attractive, but further down it is a teeming yachting port with two marinas and the Isle of Wight Ferry ploughing through.

  Lymington is a pleasant town, with an especially attractive cobbled

pedestrian thoroughfare leading from the
bottom of the High Street to the Town
Quay. A short walk up the High Street is a
supermarket for picnic provisions. But
before diverting, check your timing.

• THE SOLENT WAY, Hampshire's coastal
long-distance path, links Milford on Sea,
the village west of Lymington, with
Portsmouth. This section is one of the
most rural.

• BUCKLERS HARD Visit the Maritime
Museum to learn about this tiny
settlement's extraordinary role as one of
Britain's major naval shipbuilding centres
in the 18th and 19thC. Be sure to see the
tiny chapel, and the reconstruction of
master shipbuilder Henry Adams' work
room on the river end of The Master
Builder's Arms. This is an average pub,
with an unexciting range of beers, full of
yachties and tourists, but serving a useful
range of meals. There is a village stores for
provisions.

• BEAULIEU RIVER You have beautiful and
much-changing views all along its middle
reaches between Bucklers Hard and
Beaulieu. Easily sighted birds include

Bucklers Hard.

curlew, oystercatcher and (summer only)
common tern.

• BEAULIEU VILLAGE seems to get busier
and busier, with tourists apparently just as
keen to saunter the street and look at the
crop of shops as to spend time in the
nearby National Motor Museum and
Palace House. These sights deserve a
separate trip.
   From the village green you get a fine
view of the serene topmost salt water
reach of the river. At low tide, the river is
a large expanse of mud. John Betjeman,
fromer poet laureate, immortalised both
the serenity, and the mud, in his poem
Beaulieu Water, which describes a
headstrong local girl of the Twenties who
would go rowing on a falling tide, and got
stuck on the mud far from her jetty.
   The stone seat around the tree was a
present from appreciative Beaulieu
residents to the redoubtable Pearl
Pleydell-Bouverie on her hundredth
birthday in 1995. Formerly Lady Montagu
of Beaulieu, mother of the present Lord
Montagu, she died 1996, in her hundred-
and-second year.

Introduction
The South Downs

Designated an Area of Outstanding Natural Beauty, the South Downs represent some of the finest walking country in the south of England. The 90-mile (145-kilometre) chain of hills, stretching from Winchester in Hampshire to Beachy Head in East Sussex, is a perfect natural playground. Not only walkers, but kite flyers, model aircraft enthusiasts, cyclists and hang-gliders love these windswept chalk uplands.

WEATHER
Comparatively mild; often windy on the tops of the Downs.

GETTING THERE
The South Downs are well served by trains. There are regular services from London Victoria to Chichester, Arundel, Brighton, Worthing, Bognor and Littlehampton. The main A27 runs east to west along the southern boundary of the South Downs and the A23, A24, and A29 link the area to London and the M25.

Long-distance
The South Downs Way, one of Britain's premier national trails, runs like a thread for 80 miles (130 kilometres) along the ridge of the South Downs, attracting not only walkers but cyclists and horse riders. The trail illustrates the true character of the South Downs – wooded in the west, bare and exposed in the east – and there is no better way to discover this delightful region than to follow the waymarked route across the hills.

The South Downs also offer a safe and extensive network of footpaths and bridleways for walkers of all ages, taking you to the heart of this magnificent rolling country. It makes relatively easy walking which can be safely undertaken at any time of year.

Views and viewpoints
There is much more to the South Downs than bracing hilltops and wide open spaces. Devil's Dyke, one of a number of popular local attractions, is a spectacular downland combe or cleft 300 feet (90 metres) deep and half a mile (0.8 kilometre) long. According to legend it was dug by the Devil in an effort to flood the area with sea water, thus destroying the churches of the Weald. The Devil, disturbed by a woman carrying a candle, which he mistook for the light of dawn, supposedly disappeared, leaving his work unfinished.

Rising to over 600 feet (180 metres) this famous beauty spot north of Brighton is also a magnificent viewpoint where the downland views stretch for miles in all directions. Among other landmarks, the 19thC Clayton windmills, known as Jack and Jill, can be glimpsed from here. Built on the site of an Iron Age hill fort, 677 feet (607 metres) above sea level, the windmills edge tantalizingly into view as you make the climb from nearby Clayton village. To the east lies Ditchling Beacon which soars above the village of Ditchling, and, at over 800 feet (240 metres), is the third highest point on the South Downs. From here, with good visibility, you can see as far as the Ashdown Forest and the North Downs. Now in the care of the National Trust, Ditchling Beacon was the setting for one of a chain of fires lit to warn of the Spanish Armada in 1588.

Chanctonbury Ring near Steyning is another famous landmark in the area. Rising to 783 feet (238 metres), this isolated clump of beech trees has stood

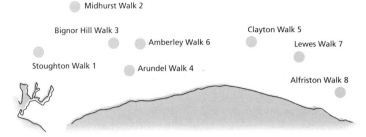

Midhurst Walk 2

Bignor Hill Walk 3   Clayton Walk 5
                    Amberley Walk 6   Lewes Walk 7

Stoughton Walk 1   Arundel Walk 4

                                        Alfriston Walk 8

out for years on the ridge of the hills and is visible up to 30 miles (50 kilometres) away. For centuries, sailors would mark it from their ships; today walkers on the Surrey hills search for it on the distant horizon. Formerly an Iron Age circular rampart and the site of a Roman British temple, it was here that Charles Goring, heir to the nearby Wiston estate, planted a number of beech trees in 1760. Goring faithfully carried bottles of water up the hill until the seedlings reached maturity. Sadly, the site was badly damaged by the storms of 1987, but new trees have been planted.

Landscapes and landmarks
A walk on Harting Down at the western end of the South Downs is also recommended. Here, the landscape has never been intensively farmed and as a result much of it survives as a perfect example of unspoilt, natural chalk downland. Harting Down is managed by the National Trust and West Sussex County Council as a nature reserve. From this lovely spot you can climb up to Beacon Hill, which, at almost 800 feet (240 metres), is one of the highest points on the South Downs. During the Napoleonic Wars this was the site of a semaphore station, one of a chain conveying messages between Whitehall and Portsmouth.

South of Harting Down lies Stoughton Down, a popular picnic and recreational area in the care of the Forestry Commision. From here there is a pleasant walk to Bow Hill where various Bronze Age barrows, known as the Devil's Humps, can be seen. There are superb views from this spot towards the south coast, and on a good day you can even pick out the Isle of Wight in the distance. Nearer, the creeks and channels of Chichester Harbour and the imposing edifice of the city's famous cathedral can also be identified. Below Bow Hill is Kingley Vale, one of Britain's first nature reserves and acknowled-ged as the finest yew grove in Europe, covering more than 200 acres. At Cuckmere Haven, close to the eastern boundary of the South Downs, you can visit the Severn Sisters Country Park and then follow the river as it snakes south towards the sea, climbing up to the windswept 282-feet (85- metre) summit of Seaford Head where there are magnificent views of the English Channel. Here are the famous white-walled chalk cliffs known as the Seven Sisters.

Villages and valleys
In contrast to the spacious downland expanses, there are hidden villages and sheltered river valleys where you can take a leisurely stroll beside, say, the Arun and the Adur. With the coast a short drive away and a host of other attractions – including the delights of Chichester and Arundel, Alfriston church – known as the 'cathedral of the South Downs' – the great houses of Goodwood and Petworth and the fascinating Roman villa at Bignor, the region really has something for everyone.

WALKING BASE:
Arundel

Historic Arundel has a dignified air. Located at the southern edge of the South Downs, only a short drive from the coast, it is a place of great charm where you can take a leisurely stroll along quaint streets of Georgian buildings, gift shops and tearooms.

Approaching Arundel from the south is sure to leave a lasting impression on first-time visitors. The great battlemented castle and grandiose French Gothic-style Roman Catholic cathedral can be seen dwarfing all the other buildings.

There has been a castle here since the 11thC, though much of the present fortification is Victorian. Arundel Castle, built to defend the Arun valley, is the principal ancestral home of the Dukes of Norfolk, formerly the Earls of Arundel, and the second largest castle in the country. There are various family portraits of the Norfolks inside the castle, some of them understood to date back to the Wars of the Roses. Also on show are examples of the family's fine furniture, clocks and tapestries. The Norfolks have lived at Arundel since the 16thC. According to the plaque at the bottom of the High Street:

Since William Rose and Harold fell,
There have been Earls at Arundel.

The castle, first mentioned in the Domesday Book and open to the public during the summer months, was attacked by Parliamentary forces during the Civil War. However, it was extensively rebuilt and restored in the 18th and 19thC.

It was the 15th Duke of Norfolk who funded the building of Arundel's

SLEEPING AND EATING

Accommodation is not in short supply in the Arundel area. There is a varied range of places to stay that will suit all requirements, from charming old coaching inns, thatched cottages, isolated farmhouses and modest B&Bs. Here we list just a few, but for more detailed lists contact: *Tourist Information Office, 61 High Street, Arundel, West Sussex BN18 9AJ. tel. 01903 882268.*

HOTELS AND INNS

ARUNDEL
Norfolk Arms; High Street; tel. 01903 882101 18thC coaching inn built by the tenth Duke of Norfolk. Set under the battlements of the castle, it retains a traditional atmosphere within the cosy sitting room and two bars. Main building bedrooms are spacious and well equipped; more

modern and uniformly decorated rooms are housed in a detached wing to the rear.

Swan Hotel; High Street; tel. 01903 882314. Restored to its former Victorian splendour, this popular small town hotel has a lively taproom bar (Arundel Brewery beers), well appointed and attractively furnished bedrooms and a candlelit restaurant serving an extensive range of freshly prepared dishes.

AMBERLEY
Amberley Castle; tel. 01798 831992. A splendid country-house hotel set within a 900-year-old castle that oozes history and promises complete peace behind its massive stone battlements. Immaculately decorated and antique-filled bedrooms are charming, offering every comfort from video-players to spa

baths and views of delightful gardens. Excellent food served in the barrel-vaulted Queens Room Restaurant.

BURPHAM
Burpham Country Hotel; 01903 882160. Former hunting lodge dating from 1710 set in a peaceful village at the base of the South Downs. Comfortable bedrooms are well equipped and enjoy good views. Elegantly decorated public areas include a candlelit dining-room with an interesting daily menu. An ideal walking base.

SUTTON
White Horse Inn; near Pulborough; tel. 01798 869221. Thoughtfully equipped and attractively furnished accommodation in a pretty Georgian inn situated in peaceful village at the base of the Downs. Imaginative daily-changing menus and real ale.

Cathedral of Our Lady and St Philip Howard. This historic building was originally a church, becoming a cathedral as recently as the mid 1960s. St Philip Howard, the 13th Earl of Arundel, was condemned to death during the reign of Elizabeth I for being a Catholic, though he died in jail before the execution could take place. His bones lie within the cathedral, which includes a shrine dedicated to his memory.

The Norfolk Arms is well worth a visit whilst touring Arundel and from the nearby bridge over the Arun, at the bottom of the High Street, is a memorable view back towards the castle, rising majestically above the rooftops of the town. From here you can begin a delightful circular walk along the Arun to the Wildfowl and Wetlands Centre, home to some of the rarest birds in the world, including Carolina ducks, mute swans, Hawaiian geese and white-faced whistling ducks. The site also has a visitor centre

Author David Hancock at work in the South Downs.

and butterfly walk.

Further on, the route brings you to Arundel Park on the outskirts of the town. One of the 1,000-acre park's greatest attractions is Swanbourne Lake. Beyond the lake, the scenery becomes wilder and more undulating before the walk brings you back into the centre of Arundel.

BED-AND-BREAKFAST

ARUNDEL
Dukes; 65 High Street; *tel. 01903 883847.* Elegant Grade II listed Georgian house offering comfortable B&B. Licensed restaurant with carved walnut ceiling and home-cooked food.

Bridge House; 18 Queen Street; *tel. 01903 882779; closed Christmas week.* Located by the bridge and overlooking the river Arun, this homely guest house offers well-equipped bedrooms, including some in an adjoining 16thC cottage. Sitting room residential bar and evening meals.

WALBERTON
Beam Ends; Hedgers Hill; tel. 01243 551254. Charming thatched cottage enjoying a peaceful setting in 1 acre of wooded gardens. Comfortable B&B and big views.

YAPTON
Bonham House; tel. 01243 582277. Attractive period house with stables, elegant Victorian sitting room and well furnished bedrooms.

SLINDON
*Mill Lane House; tel. 01243 814440.*17thC house in a beautiful National Trust downland village. Comfortable centrally-heated bedrooms and log fires in public rooms. Magnificent views to the coast.

OFFHAM
Offham House; tel. 01903 882129. Elegant Victorian house in a tranquil setting in open countryside close to the River Arun and only a mile (0.8 km) from Arundel Castle.

CAMPING AND HOSTELS

Recommended campsites in the area include the delightfully simple *Camping and*

Caravanning Club Site at *Slindon (01203 694995),* the *Ship and Anchor Marina* site beside the Arun at *Ford (01243 551262),* and *White Rose Touring Park* at *Wick* on the edge of *Littlehampton (01903 716176).* Cheap, hostel accommodation is available at *Arundel Youth Hostel (01903 882204).*

FOOD

Good pub food can be found at the *George and Dragon, Burpham (01903 883131* – also noted restaurant). Reputable restaurants within easy reach of Arundel include *Manleys (01903 742331)* and the *Old Forge (01903 743402)* in *Storrington, Bailiffscourt Hotel* (also upmarket accommodation) at *Climping (01903 723511),* and *The Chardonnay Restaurant, Washington (01903 892271).*

39

Stoughton Down & Kingley Vale Nature Reserve

Delightful short walk that steadily climbs through woodland on well-defined tracks and waymarked bridleways to the top of Bow Hill, a glorious viewpoint with ancient barrows and through Kingley Vale Nature Reserve, one of the finest yew forests in Europe, rich with orchids and unusual butterflies. It then drops steeply into Stoughton, a typical brick and flint downland village with a fascinating church dating from the 11thC. Easy route-finding.

Start *Stoughton Down Forestry Commission car park, SU815127. Located 2 miles (3.2 km) off B2146 Chichester to Petersfield road, 7 miles (11.6 km) north-west of Chichester.*

Route directions

Walk round double wooden gates on to gravel track beside woodland. Track soon bears right into wood, gradually climbing round Lambdown Hill, then at junction leave track, keeping straight ahead along waymarked bridleway. Steadily climb through beech woodland to crossing of tracks and clearing (splendid downland views right). Continue ahead on good track for 100 yds (90m), then bear off left with bridleway fingerpost to follow stony path uphill to crossing of paths. Turn right and keep ahead at crossing to pass triangulation point on right, then soon emerge into clearing with ancient barrows and stunning views. Keep right of barrows to join defined chalky track and soon follow wide grassy swathe through dense woodland (Kingley Vale Nature Reserve). Eventually reach clearing and follow grass-centred track right. Descend into woodland, then steeply down stony track into Stoughton Vale. Turn right along road through Stoughton (turn left to visit St Mary's Church), pass Hare and Hounds, then in 600 yds (540 m) take arrowed footpath left. Climb hedged path to woodland fringe. Turn right with waymarker

Essentials

Easy 5 miles (8 km); 2$\frac{1}{2}$ hours; one steady climb and a steep descent; *map* Ordnance Survey 1:50 000 Landranger Map 197, Chichester & The Downs.

Terrain Good tracks, woodland bridleways; well-signposted paths. Sections can be muddy after rain; stout footwear advisable.

along edge of wood and keep to defined path through scrub along contour of hill to T-junction of paths. Bear right and follow path downhill, passing house (right) to reach lane. Turn right back to car park.

- **Bow Hill** A group of Bronze Age bowl and bell barrows are clear landmarks on top of this hill, which gives magnificent views across Chichester Plain to the sea from a clearing just to the west near the trian-gulation point. The area has a number of other prehistoric sites, including an Iron Age farmstead and Goose Hill Camp.

- **Kingley Vale Nature Reserve** is the finest yew forest in Europe with some 30,000 trees. The dense evergreen canopy lets in little light, creating an eerie atmosphere. According to legend the forest was planted in AD900 to mark the defeat of Viking marauders. Among the 200 species of chalk-loving plants that thrive here are 12 species of orchid, including the bee orchid which flowers in June.

- **Stoughton** nestles in a quiet valley beneath rolling downland and comprises a scattered collection of brick and flint barns, attractive cottages and the ancient Church of St Mary. Standing on a hillside above the village it features tall aisleless naves and chancels that date from the 11thC.

FOOD AND DRINK
Hare and Hounds Inn at Stoughton.

Midhurst to Petworth

*An enjoyable straight-line walk linking the attractive small
towns of Midhurst and Petworth. There's much to see, so allow a
whole day, especially if you plan to visit Petworth House. Return to
Midhurst by bus.*

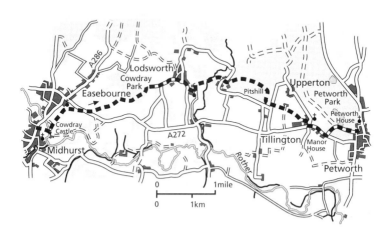

Start Midhurst. Small country town
at junction of A272 and A286
midway between Petersfield and
Petworth. Free car park, SU888229,.
on North Street by Tourist
Information Office (01730 817322)
and bus terminus.
Return: Hourly buses from Petworth
(service 1) on weekdays; every two
hours (service 1B) on Sundays.

Route directions
Go through kissing gate in
left-hand corner of car
park and bear right along
track towards ruins of
Cowdray Castle. Cross
River Rother, turn left in
front of ruins along tarmac
access drive. Where it
curves left, take track right
(arrowed post) and keep
ahead at crossing of routes
through gate. Head north
on track, then at
waymarker post bear right
to stile with Cowdray Park
polo ground right. Keep

Essentials

Easy 6¹/₂ miles (10.8
km); 3 hours; gently
undulating; few
demanding climbs; **map**
Ordnance Survey
1:50 000 Landranger
Map 197, Chichester &
The Downs.
Terrain Field and
parkland paths;
woodland bridleways;
short stretches of
metalled road.

right-handed along fencing and cross field
to stile. Follow defined path as it curves
left uphill across field to A272. Turn right
along grass verge and shortly cross busy
road on to sandy track. In 30 yds (27 m),
at fork of three paths (fingerpost), take
middle grassy track and gently climb
across golf- course fairway. Pass further
marker post, walk beneath bough of
leaning tree and keep to left side of
fairway, eventually passing tee 15 and
tiled-roof shelter. Cross sandy track,
descend through clump of
trees and follow grass
track left – (Steward's
Pond visible ahead). Cross
further track, go through
small gate and cross
pasture, following pond
fence round to fingerpost.
Bear right through pasture
across base of hill to stile
flanking gate. Keep left
alongside scrub and trees,
soon to follow field edge to
reach junction of paths on
edge of Heathend Copse.
Turn left, then
immediately bear right at
fork on wide track along

THE SOUTH DOWNS / *Walk 2*

woodland fringe to lane beside Heath End Farm. Turn left and follow lane into Lodsworth, keeping right at fork (village sign) and descend to junction by Hollist Arms. Turn right along main village street, pass Polo Shop and turn right in front of timbered house (Old Nursery), signposted to church. Pass church, follow lane left, then bear off right (waymarker) opposite gates to St Peters Well Cottage. Go through gate near ancient well, keep left through pasture and shortly turn right at junction of paths (marker) to cross centre of field on worn path, eventually crossing Eel Bridge into River Wood. Bear left immediately beyond bridge, gradually climb through trees to main track and turn left. Remain on defined route, keeping left along woodland fringe to stile and continue beside garden and cottage to lane in hamlet of River. Turn left (views), then in 100 yds (90 m) take arrowed path right and climb through trees, via stone steps to stile. Cross old track and continue on narrow path (can be slippery) that traverses side of steep hill through beech wood. On reaching bridleway and crossing of paths, turn right and bear left in few yards along tarmac drive to Pitshill (visible right). Keep right at fork, cross cattle grid, then where driveway swings left, bear off right along arrowed path and keep right of telegraph pole to stile. Go through coppiced woodland to lane and turn left. At T-junction, go through gate almost opposite and follow worn path along right-hand edge of field. Ignore waymarked path left, keeping ahead towards Tillington church. At village edge follow footpath through graveyard to village street near Manor House. Shortly, bear left along raised pavement, pass Horseguards Inn, then cross road into churchyard and follow path alongside wall to A272. Walk left along pavement for ¹/₄ mile (0.4 km), then enter Petworth Park at lodge. Follow track to lake and bear right towards house. Bear left in front of house to locate main pedestrian access gate and reach road near church. Turn right into town centre (bus stop by hall in Market Square).

FOOD AND DRINK

Choice of pubs, hotels and tearooms in Midhurst and Petworth, notably the Angel Hotel in Midhurst and Petworth House Restaurant (National Trust – Apr-Oct only). Hollist Arms in Lurgashall and Horseguards Inn (good food) at Tillington. Picnic in Petworth Park.

• **MIDHURST** Standing on the south bank of the River Rother, Midhurst is an attractive small market town boasting many historic buildings and some fine old inns. Of particular note is the partly 15thC, half-timbered Spread Eagle Hotel, and the delightful Angel Hotel whose 19thC façade hides an ancient interior.

• **COWDRAY HOUSE** Midhurst's main draw is the imposing ruins of Cowdray House, a Tudor mansion built in 1492 and destroyed by fire in 1793. Well-known for its polo ground.

• **LODSWORTH** takes its name from the River Lod, a small tributary of the Rother.

• **TILLINGTON** Charming estate village positioned on a ridge with splendid downland views. The Church of All Hallows has an unusual Scots Crown tower dating from 1807. Its four graceful arms support a weather-vane and this distinctive church was featured in landscape paintings by Turner, some of which can be seen in Petworth House. The impressive stone-built former Manor House dates from 1600.

• **PETWORTH** Picturesque little town dominated by Petworth House and Park whose walls encroach into the town. Narrow streets and alleys, lined with attractive half-timbered or tile-hung buildings – most housing antique shops – radiate out from the market square with its stone Town Hall, built in 1793. (Tourist Information – tel. 01798 343523).

• **PETWORTH HOUSE** Owned by the National Trust, this magnificent late-17thC house in set in 700 acres of beautiful parkland with lake and pleasure grounds landscaped by Capability Brown. State Rooms contain one of the most important collections of art in the country, including paintings by Turner, Van Dyck and Gainsborough. Open Apr-Oct (tel. 01798 342207).

Bignor Hill and Roman Villa

Lofty chalk bridleways and gently undulating field paths are the staple of this route, which links three attractive settlements at the base of the Downs. It explores the Roman influence on the landscape in this area, and crosses Stane Street, a former Roman road linking Chichester to London. You can visit the remains of one of the largest Roman Villas in Britain. Peaceful villages – Barlavington, Sutton, Bignor – with their pretty cottages and historic churches, are absorbing places in which to linger. The tracks and the South Downs Way in the immediate vicinity of the car park are likely to be popular at weekends and in summer.

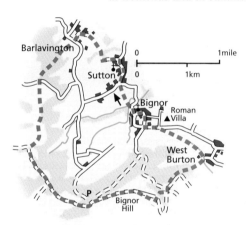

Start *Bignor Hill. National Trust car park, SU973129, on top of South Downs, 7 miles (11 kilometres) north-west of Arundel. Turn left off A29 at Bury, signposted Bignor, go through West Burton and at edge of Bignor turn left and drive up narrow road to car park.*

Route directions

From waymarker post in car park follow South Downs Way (defined track) towards transmission masts. Just beyond Stane Street (information board) leave SDW and follow bridleway with stunning views, soon to pass dew pond, right. Disregard arrowed bridleway left beyond masts, leave NT land and continue along open grassy track. Pass through old gate, descend chalk track alongside scrub, then bear right with fingerpost before gate. In few yards cross wooded track diagonally to follow bridleway – views along escarpment. Go through small gate, climb steadily to further gate and follow established path across field to junction of route. Cross track, ignore footpath right, then almost immediately follow arrowed bridleway right into woodland and drop steeply on delightful path off down to lane at Barlavington. Cross into dead-end road, sign-posted to church, and soon follow waymarked path opposite estate office through churchyard (bench by church door makes ideal resting place). Leave churchyard via gate, join farm track and follow it left around barns and farmyard. Turn right along arrowed path along field edge, drop towards woodland and climb stile right into pasture. Bear half-left downhill to fingerpost, follow field

Essentials

Moderate 6¾ miles (11.4 km); 3½ hours (longer if visiting Bignor Roman Villa). undulating; one steep descent and one sharp climb; **map** Ordnance Survey 1:50 000 Landranger Map 197, Chichester & The Downs.
Terrain Chalk tracks, including South Downs Way, along escarpment; clear field paths and bridleways. Sections can be muddy after rain; walking boots essential in winter.

43

The Old Shop, Bignor

edge to stile, then cross footbridge and bear left, then right uphill through copse to stile. Turn right, soon to follow worn path uphill along field edge. Climb stile left, join defined path and merge with drive to house, following it into Sutton. Turn right, pass church to reach junction by White Horse Inn. Bear right towards Duncton and turn immediately left up drive towards timbered cottage, along waymarked path for Bignor. Shortly, cross open field to stile, descend into valley and follow well marked route round pond and uphill to lane by cottage. Turn left uphill into Bignor. Bear right at junction opposite church, walk through hamlet and follow lane left at junction towards Roman Villa. In 200 yds (180 m) enter broad field on right (fingerpost) and bear diagonally left across it. (To visit Roman Villa keep to lane.) Follow field edge on far side, cross footbridge over dyke and keep left, eventually reaching lane by timbered house. Shortly, turn right on to arrowed bridleway in front of Hatchetts and steadily climb wooded scarp face of South Downs to track and junction of routes. Cross straight over and bear immediately right with SDW. Climb steeply, keep right at junction and follow SDW for ³/₄ mile (1.4 km) back to car park.

• **STANE STREET** Roman road constructed in AD70 to connect port of Chichester

with London. It was metalled, cambered and in most places 20–25 feet (6–8 metres) wide; its southern portion lies on NT land and comprises a high embankment bounded by side ditches 85 feet (26 metres) apart. A branch terrace breaks off near top of escarpment and leads to the Roman Villa at Bignor.

• **DEW POND** A traditional hill pond used for watering sheep before piped water in troughs. These oases provided an important habitat for wildlife as well as being significant landscape features. Formed by putting non-porous clay into chalk depressions to stop water seeping away.

• **BIGNOR** Nestling below the South Down this attractive village is famous for The Old Shop, a 15thC thatched and half-timbered yeoman's cottage which once served as a grocer's shop; and of course, for one of the largest Roman Villas in England (open Mar-Oct – tel. 01798 869259). Uncovered in 1811 and first excavated in 1827, it contains a magnificent mosaic, the longest in Britain (82 feet/25 metres); various finds from excavations are on show. The restored Church of the Holy Cross contains remnants of the 11thC building and a fine 13thC chancel.

FOOD AND DRINK
White Horse Inn (good food and ale) in Sutton (halfway); café at Roman Villa.

Arundel Park and the River Arun

*A lovely walk taking in the historic buildings and monuments of
picturesque Arundel and traversing magnificent rolling parkland to
a downland viewpoint with a superb prospect across the beautiful
Arun Valley and Chichester Harbour to the Isle of Wight. By contrast,
the level return leg of the walk follows the meandering course of the
River Arun from the charming hamlet of South Stoke back to the
formidable fortress of Arundel castle. Bird-lovers should allow time to
visit the fascinating collection of ducks, geese and swans at the
Wildfowl and Wetlands Trust near the end of the walk. Easy route
finding. Dogs are restricted to footpaths in Arundel Park.*

Start Arundel, just off
A27 between Chichester
and Worthing, 9 miles
(14.4 km) east of
Chichester. Park in Mill
Lane car park,
TQ020070 (fee),
opposite Castle
entrance and beside
River Arun. Alternative
car parks in town if
full.

Route directions

From car park turn left
and then turn right on
reaching High Street.
Continue uphill, passing
Town Gate entrance to
castle, and bear right
towards cathedral. Pass St Stephen's
Church, the Roman Catholic cathedral
and primary school, then bear right along
metalled access road towards Arundel
Park. Enter park by lodge, keep to tarmac
road and soon bear right (not arrowed)
across grass towards castellated Hiorne
Tower. Keep right of tower, cross horse
gallop and descend narrow worn path to
track and gate. Turn left and follow track
gently downhill through trees into deep
dry valley (Swanbourne Lake visible
right). At fingerpost in bottom, keep
ahead and climb steeply through pasture
towards Duke's Plantation. Nearing top,
keep left with grassy track, soon to join
chalk track beside woodland (Dry Lodge
Plantation) leading to gate. At woodland
edge bear half-right with marker and
descend grassland with splendid downland
views to waymarked stile flanking gate
(views across Arun valley). Head downhill

Essentials

Moderate 7 miles (11.6
km); $3^{1}/_{2}$–4 hours;
undulating parkland;
level riverbank path;
map Ordnance Survey
1:50 000 Landranger
Map 197, Chichester &
The Downs.
Terrain Combination of
well-waymarked
footpaths across rolling
parkland and downland
and level riverside
bridleways. Wet and
muddy after rain, or
exceptionally high
tides.

through trees and scrub to
T-junction and turn right.
Shortly, at old gateway,
bear off left beside fence,
following it downhill
through woodland fringe
and alongside flint wall to
go through gap right
(waymarked), near River
Arun. Turn right along
bridleway which dips and
climbs through rich
woodland close to
riverbank to stile by gate.
Keep left alongside broad
field, descend to stile and
follow wide track uphill
and along field edge
towards barn. Keep right
of barn to reach drive to
South Stoke Farm and turn
immediately right with fingerpost along
bridleway to right of brick barn. At
metalled lane turn left to peacefully
situated church. Proceed along footpath at
end of tarmac to White Bridge. Turn right
before bridge to join raised riverbank
path. Remain on this delightful and
undemanding path as it meanders south
beside the Arun to reach Black Rabbit pub
at Offham. Just beyond pub turn almost
immediately left off lane to continue
beside Arun (Wildfowl and Wetlands Trust
right – entrance along lane $^{1}/_{4}$ mile /0.4
km). Keep to riverbank path, as it follows
wide meander back to car park by castle.

- **ARUNDEL** See page 38.

- **ARUNDEL PARK** 1,000 acres of rolling
parkland (free unlimited access),
complete with deer and an attractive lake,
surrounding the castle. Near the castle is

one of the prettiest cricket grounds in the country.

Classic South Downs prospect.

• **SOUTH STOKE** Consisting of a few farm buildings, an old rectory and an unpretentious little church, this tiny hamlet enjoys a tranquil position at the end of a lane close to the River Arun. St Leonard's Church has a Victorian wooden tower and is still illuminated by candlelight.

• **WILDFOWL AND WETLANDS TRUST** Over 55 acres of open water, wet

grassland and landscaped pens and lakes harbouring more than a thousand ducks, geese and swans from all over the world. It is also a sanctuary for wild birds, including numerous breeding species and various passage and winter migrants. There are hides overlooking different habitats, as well as a viewing gallery and educational complex. Special events. Open daily all year (01903 883355).

> **FOOD AND DRINK**
> Range of cafés, pubs and hotels in Arundel; the Black Rabbit at Offham (riverside terrace with view of castle).

46

Jack and Jill Windmills and Ditchling Beacon

A longish ramble that captures the essence of the downland landscape, from peaceful dry valleys to lofty scarp tracks with far-reaching views. You can shorten the walk to five miles (8 kilometres) by omitting Pyecombe and Wolstonbury Hill. Starting on the top of the Downs, above the beautiful village of Clayton, at two distinctive windmills, the walk follows the South Downs Way east to Ditchling Beacon, which at 814 feet (248 metres) is the highest point in East Sussex. Beyond, the route follows established bridleways and tracks through dry valleys and meadows before crossing the A273 to reach the attractive, scattered village of Pyecombe, noted for its little flint church. From here the walk gradually climbs to the summit of Wolstonbury Hill (NT) with its Iron Age fort and magnificent views across southern England. After a steep descent, a short section of metalled lane brings you to Clayton, where the simple, mainly Saxon church is well worth visiting. A final sharp climb up the scarp face of the downs brings you back to the start.

Start *Clayton, TQ304134. Small village located close to the junction of the A273 and B2112 at the base of the Downs between Brighton and Burgess Hill, 3 miles (4.8 km) south of Burgess Hill. Car park at the top of the South Downs by Jack and Jill windmills.*

Essentials

Moderate 9 miles (14.4 km); 4-5 hours (shorter option 5 miles /8 km); undulating with a few steep climbs; *map* Ordnance Survey Landranger 1:50 000 Map 198, Brighton and The Downs.
Terrain Mainly dry, chalky tracks and bridleways, following the South Downs Way in part; also some meadow and woodland paths; short section of metalled road.

Route directions

From car park follow track uphill to junction with South Downs Way and fork left, gradually climbing to top of Downs. Keep to SDW along good escarpment track for 1 mile (1.6km) towards Ditchling Beacon (NT). Just before Beacon and car park, turn right along chalky track, heading south gently downhill to Heathy Brow and into lovely dry valley. Follow it right into North Bottom towards Lower Standean Farm. Before farm, cross to right side of valley, go through gate by trough and soon follow track diagonally uphill. Go through gate and drop down to bypass

farm and meet bridleway on west side of farmyard (waymarker). Turn right up track, aiming for lone flint and brick barn in meadow. After barn, track passes through gap in hedge. Next, zigzag beside hedges to where Sussex Border Path crosses route at top of rise. Keep ahead along field edge, the bridleway soon bearing sharp left to reach farm track. Turn right, skirt Pyecombe Golf Course and shortly reach junction with South Downs Way.
Shorter Walk: keep ahead with SDW, passing New Barn Farm to reach Jack and Jill windmills and car park.
Main walk heads west along SDW, downhill to A273. Cross busy road to join bridleway that runs parallel with road into Pyecombe. Turn right along School Lane towards church and just before it, turn right up track called The Wyshe. Gradually climbing, it soon narrows to become bridleway (can be muddy). Keep ahead at crossing of paths, then on reaching wide bridleway cross to small gate and bear left towards Wolstonbury Hill. Pass through

47

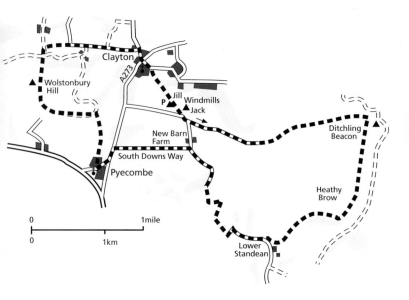

further gate near top and in 100 yds (90 m) bear right up to summit and triangulation point. Head due north to locate footpath (ill-defined at first through earthworks), that steeply descends scarp slope to stile at bottom. Go through belt of trees to track and turn right. Follow track which soon bears right to reach New Way Lane. Keep straight ahead, passing Jack and Jill Inn to reach A273. Turn right, cross railway bridge, then cross road to Underhill Lane. Pass church and take arrowed bridleway right by farm buildings. Climb track up scarp slope via gates, aiming for windmills, back to car park.

• **CLAYTON WINDMILLS** Jack and Jill sit side by side on the Downs. Jack is a black tower mill erected in 1866 (private); Jill is a white post mill that was moved from nearby Patcham by a team of oxen in 1821. Jill stopped working in 1907 and is open to the public on summer Sundays and bank holidays.

• **DITCHLING BEACON** is the third highest point on the South Downs and traces of ramparts and ditches of an Iron Age fort can be viewed on the north scarp. It was the site of one of the fires lit to warn of the approaching Armada. The National Trust own 4 acres and the typical chalk

grassland has many rare flowers and butterflies.

• **PYECOMBE** Once the centre of the crook-making craft, this scattered downland village possesses a tiny, partly Norman, flint church which has a beautifully ornamented, 12thC lead font within its simple interior. The elegant Tapsell gate into the churchyard has a shepherd's crook as a handle.

• **WOLSTONBURY HILL** At 670 feet (206 metres) this stands clear of the Downs and is a landmark for miles. Its summit is en- circled by an Iron Age fort, regarded as one of the earliest in Sussex (5th/6thC BC). The ditch inside the rampart is unusual. Prime Minister Lloyd George, who rented the fine Elizabethan house (Danny) at the base of the Downs, often spent time on the hill reading important papers. The far-reaching views are magnificent.

• **CLAYTON** is noted for its little old church. The humble exterior is deceptive for it contains some of the finest wall paintings in southern England, dating from the 11thC. Much of the unspoilt interior dates from Saxon times.

> **FOOD AND DRINK**
> The Plough Inn at Pyecombe and the Jack and Jill Inn in Clayton.

48

Amberley, Parham Park and Arun Valley

Delightfully varied ramble with fine scenery, incorporating the South Downs Way. More peaceful, less well-walked paths across the beautiful deer park at Parham, where you can take time out to view the impressive Elizabethan manor. The route then explores Greatham Common and the level, wildlife-rich meadows of Amberley Wild Brooks. The charming, predominantly thatched village of Amberley is worth strolling around for its fascinating church and castle. The route then follows the course of the River Arun to Amberley Station, passing Amberley Chalk Pits Museum, an interesting open-air industrial history museum, before climbing steeply for a final breezy 2 miles (3.2 kilometres).

Start *Kithurst Hill Car Park, TQ070125. Parking area on top of the South Downs, ¹/₂ mile (0.8 km) south of B2139 between Storrington and Amberley, 2 miles (3.2 km) west of Storrington.*
By train *from Arundel catch train to Amberley Station (one stop), turn right along verge beside B2139, then in ¹/₂ mile (0.8 km) turn right along metalled lane, signposted South Downs Way, joining route at (A) – see page 50, 19 lines down column one.*

Route directions

From car park entrance (near sign board), follow bridleway left through scrub to gate. Descend rough field to next gate and head steeply downhill off scarp slope through woodland. Pass beside coniferous plantation, then bear left along rutted track which curves right and soon reaches B2139 beside Paygate Cottage. Turn right along verge, then cross to follow narrow unsigned lane north. In ¹/₂ mile (0.8 km), at T-junction with A283 at Cootham, turn left and soon bear left along drive to Parham House. Go through gate beside lodge, walk along drive through deer park, then where it curves left bear off right with fingerpost along defined path – views of manor with South Downs as backdrop. (Keep to drive if visiting manor.) Rejoin drive and keep ahead, signposted 'footpath to Rackham'.

Pass pond, go through gate by lodge and turn left along road. In 100 yds (90 m) turn right along Greatham Road. Almost immediately bear off left with waymarker to follow meandering path through trees to drive. Turn right, pass house, then keep ahead at junction of paths by footbridge, eventually following path back through woods to rejoin Greatham Road. Turn left and left again at T-junction (church ahead) in Greatham. Follow lane (can be busy – care needed) for ³/₄ mile (1.4 km) and climb stile just before river bridge to join Wey-South path beside River Arun. Proceed along raised dyke, cross stile and follow hedge line round to gravel track. Cross cattlegrid, turn right to reach modern house and follow waymarker left to pass farm buildings. Soon fork right (arrowed) along winding track to wooden barn and continue along

Essentials

Moderate 11¹/₂ miles (18.6 km). Mainly level in river valley; one steep descent and long steady ascent of South Downs scarp slope; **map** Ordnance Survey 1:50 000 Landranger Map 197, Chichester & The Downs.
Terrain Downland tracks; good bridleways; parkland drives; water-meadow footpaths (can be wet and boggy in winter); narrow and quiet county lanes. Walking boots essential.

Teal – seen at Amberley Wild Brooks.

17thC manor and a restored Norman church with a simple, oil lamplit interior. The author D. H. Lawrence completed his novel *The Rainbow* when he stayed at a cottage here during the First World War.

field edge and over plank bridges. Keep to straight line, following ridge where possible, for about 1 mile (1.6 km) across Amberley Wild Brooks into Amberley village. At village lane, turn left for pub and shop, otherwise bear right, then right again at T-junction to church. Lane soon peters out to track below castle walls. Where it curves left, keep ahead on path to stile by gate. Remain on path through water-meadows to banks of River Arun and turn left along raised path. Pass footbridge, join SDW and shortly bear off left through gate to join fenced path leading past barns to B2139. Turn right (SDW sign), then cross road and turn left up metalled lane (A). (For railway station and Amberley Chalk Pits Museum keep to B-road for ¼ mile/0.4 km). Gradually climb downs. Keep right at junction, pass house (Highdown), then bear left up steep stony track to gate. Continue to climb on worn path with glorious views unfolding all round. Path levels out on top of Amberley Mount and continues along crest for 1¼ miles (2 km) back to car park.

• PARHAM HOUSE AND PARK Beautiful Elizabethan house with fine gardens set in deer park beneath the downs. It houses an important collection of paintings, furniture, carpets and rare needlework. Its 16thC church features box pews and an unusual 14thC font. Open Easter–early Oct (tel. 01903 744888).

• GREATHAM comprises a small cluster of cottages, a

• AMBERLEY WILD BROOKS An area of water-meadows (often flooded in winter) in the Arun valley, now a nature reserve with a rich bird and plant life. Among the species to be seen are teal, Bewick's swans, redshanks and a wealth of marsh-loving plants. The composer John Ireland, who lived nearby, captured the beauty of the area in a fine piano piece written in 1921.

• AMBERLEY is one of the most picturesque villages in Sussex. Pretty brick and flint thatched cottages line a square of tiny lanes that lead to St Michael's Church. Dating from the 11thC it houses a fine 14thC chancel arch and some remarkable traces of wall paintings dating from 1200. There is a memorial window to the 19thC artist Edward Stott who lived in the village. Also buried in the churchyard is Arthur Rackham, illustrator of children's books, including *Peter Pan*.

• AMBERLEY CASTLE Originally a manor house built for the Bishops of Chichester in the 12thC, its great curtain wall towers above the water-meadows. The splendid half-timbered house (now a luxury hotel) inside the walls has a 14thC Great Hall.

• AMBERLEY CHALK PITS MUSEUM Fascinating working open-air museum situated in 36 acres of former chalk quarry and reflecting the industrial history of southern England. Visit various craftsmen – blacksmith, potter, printer – and experience the sights, sounds and smells of their workshops. Narrow-gauge railway and vintage buses. Open all year daily (tel. 01798 831370).

FOOD AND DRINK
Tearooms at Parham House (when open) and Amberley Chalk Pits Museum; Crown Inn at Cootham and the Black Horse in Amberley; civilized afternoon teas (and lunches) at the upmarket Amberley Castle Hotel.

Along the South Downs Way – Lewes to Eastbourne

Starting from the historic market town of Lewes, this two-day expedition follows a dramatic 23-mile (36.8-kilometre) section of the South Downs Way, from Lewes to Eastbourne via Alfriston and the Seven Sisters. There is overnight accommodation in Alfriston, the halfway point; or, alternatively, each day can be undertaken as two separate day walks, with a bus service returning you either to Lewes or Alfriston.

Planning

Day 1 traverses open grassy hilltops, and the lush valley of the River Ouse to the charming village of Alfriston. **Day 2** (Walk 8) follows the Cuckmere River to Cuckmere Haven before climbing the towering white cliffs of the Seven Sisters and Beachy Head, eventually reaching the large resort of Eastbourne. Quaint villages with welcoming pubs and interesting houses nestle at the base of the downs and make for interesting diversions along the way, although the climb back to the ridge track is rather demanding. As good bus services exist in this area, it is possible to undertake each day as a separate day walk, if so desired.

Essentials

Moderate / strenuous
Day 1 – 12 miles (19.2 km); 6–7 hours.
Day 2 – 11 miles (17.6 km); 5–6 hours; numerous steep climbs, especially on the latter half of Day 2; *map* Ordnance Survey 1:50 000 Landranger Map 198, Brighton & The Downs and Map 199 Eastbourne & Hastings.
Terrain Mainly downland tracks and bridleways; some valley walking, concrete tracks and quiet metalled lanes. Generally dry underfoot and well waymarked.

On the South Downs Way.

Start **Day 1** *Lewes, off the A27 between Brighton and Eastbourne, 8 miles (12.8 km) north-east of Brighton. Easily reached by car from Arundel via the A27, or by taking the regular train service along the south coast via Worthing and Brighton to Eastbourne. The latter is the best option as you can return direct to Arundel from Eastbourne by train on completing the two-day walk. Day walkers arriving by car should park in the long-term car parks at the railway station or Mountfield Road (next to Sports Ground near station).*
Day 2 – *Park in Alfriston village car park (pay and display).*

51

Route directions

Day 1

From station head south (away from town centre) along Station Road and turn right at mini-roundabout (Mountfield Road car park left) along Priory Road. Keep ahead at next roundabout, soon passing Anne of Cleaves Museum. Bear left by Swan pub and then turn right into Juggs Lane (bridleway), following narrow metalled lane to footbridge; cross A27. Climb steeply to end of tarmac road and waymarker post. Continue ahead along bridleway, then on entering field keep right along rutted track (can be muddy) through field, soon to become metalled, leading to Kingston village. At crossroads (village left), cross into private road (bridleway arrowed Rodmell), then at end continue ahead up chalk track that soon climbs sharply up scarp slope of downs. Keep left at fork for long climb to top. Bear left to gate and join firm chalk track along crest (SDW). Go through small gate and turn left at arrowed post on to concrete track. Gradually descend, eventually crossing concrete track to follow bridleway along field edge. Cross further track, gently climb to gate and shortly reach end of tarmac road (Rodmell left). Keep ahead through gate (SDW marker), follow defined grassy path and descend into dry valley to track (barns right). Turn left, then on nearing road bear off right (fingerpost) to gate and climb steeply to further gate and road junction. Follow main road ahead, then in few yards take left turn, signposted Southease. Pass round-towered church, keep ahead by green and cross bridge over River Ouse. Stay on road, cross railway line to reach A26 at Itford Farm. Cross, follow SDW marker right along verge for 100 yds (90 m), then turn left for long climb back to summit of downs. Keep left at fork of tracks, following grassy path to gate at top. Remain on well-defined and well-waymarked route (SDW), passing communication masts and parking area (road down to Firle village –

ACCOMMODATION
A range of places in Alfriston: the old timbered **Star Inn** (Forte Hotel – tel. 01323 870922); **Riverdale House** (tel. 01323 491849); **George Inn** (tel. 01323 870319); **Deans Place Hotel** (tel. 01323 870248); **Wingrove Inn & Hotel** (tel. 01323 870276). Budget accommodation at **Frog Firle Youth Hostel** (on village edge – tel. 01323 870423). Contact Eastbourne Tourist Information Office (tel. 01323 411400) for more details.

shop/pub/Firle Place) to reach top of Firle Beacon. Keep to SDW, passing farm, parking area onto Bostal Hill and remain on main track (paths off to reach Alciston and Charleston Farmhouse) for approximately 2 miles (3.2 km) down into Alfriston village.

Return to Lewes Catch the bus (Rider 125) from the Waterloo Square in Alfriston at 3.05 pm and 5.10 pm (last bus Sat 1.05 pm; no services Sun).

Day 2

Locate footpath to church and Clergy House between Methodist chuch and antiques shop, then, having explored both, keep to left side of green to cross White Bridge over Cuckmere River. Immediately beyond, go through gate on right and follow meandering riverbank path south. On nearing next bridge, bear off right (SDW marker) through gate and along tarmac path into Litlington. Turn right along lane, passing Tea Gardens and pub, then turn left up private drive beside Thatch Cottage. In few yards bear right through kissing gate and climb field to stile (views). Continue on worn path, cross two further stiles and keep to right-hand edge of field, soon to descend towards Charleston Manor and Friston Wood. Cross stile, turn left along bridleway (can be muddy), then bear right up steep wooden steps (SDW) into wood. Keep ahead at top on wide forest track and fork right where track curves left. Continue left at next fork, following woodland path to T-junction. Turn left downhill to gate and enter hamlet. Keep ahead at lane (church left) and where it bears right before green, continue ahead (SDW), soon to climb steps into woodland. Cross stile in wall at top and descend field to gate to reach Exceat (Seven Sisters Country Park Visitor Centre and Tea Rooms). Cross busy A259 (great care), go through gate and join level concrete track along Cuckmere Valley bottom (not SDW), through Country Park. Just before second gate cross stile on left (SDW) and start long climb up on to Seven Sisters cliffs. Remain on coast path as it undulates severely to Birling Gap (refreshments). Continue roller-coaster walk towards Eastbourne, passing old cliff-top lighthouse and then climb to top of Beachy Head. Opposite pub pick up SDW. Follow along wooded ridge, then descend to B2103 on outskirts of town. Keep ahead downhill towards town centre, soon to merge with Promenade to reach pier.

Return to Alfriston Locate Terminus Road (by the Arndale Shopping Centre and Tourist Information Office) and catch bus service Rider 126 (3 pm and 5.30 pm Mon–Fri only – tel. 01273 474747).
Return to Lewes Regular daily train service between Eastbourne and Lewes; also through trains or connecting trains to Arundel via Brighton and Littlehampton (tel. 0345 484950).

- **LEWES** Historic county town of East Sussex attractively situated on a spur of the Downs overlooking the Ouse valley. A natural defensive site since Saxon times, it was one of the first towns to be fortified after the Battle of Hastings in 1066. As well as the ruin of the 11thC keep and well-preserved 14thC barbican (Living History Museum), the town has many charming steep streets lined with Georgian houses. Of particular note is the early-16thC, timber-framed Wealden hall-house, once belonging to Anne of Cleves and now housing a fascinating folk museum.

- **RODMELL** Downland village containing Monks House (NT), once the home of Leonard and Virginia Woolf (tel. 01892 890651).

- **SOUTHEASE** Former herring-fishing village and one of the prettiest settlements in Ouse valley.

- **WEST FIRLE** Tucked away at the base of Firle Beacon, this timeless estate village has a feudal atmosphere. Dominating it is Firle Place, whose Georgian façade hides a Tudor interior. Home to the Gage family

---

FOOD AND DRINK
Day 1 Plenty of places in Lewes for pre- and post-walk refreshment. Short diversions off the South Downs to village inns at Rodmell (Abergavenney Arms); Firle (Ram Inn); Alciston (Rose Cottage); Berwick (Cricketers Arms) and a range in Alfriston – Badgers Tea House, The George Inn, Star Inn, Old Sadlers Tea Shop.
Day 2 Litlington Tea Gardens and Plough & Harrow, Litlington; Farm Café (good teas/lunches), Exceat (Seven Sisters Country Park); Birling Gap Hotel (bar & café), Birling Gap.

---

for 500 years, it houses an outstanding collection of English and European old masters and Sèvres porcelain (tel. 01273 858335).

- **CHARLESTON FARMHOUSE** Charming 17th/18thC manor house. Formerly the home of Bloomsbury artists Vanessa and Clive Bell and Duncan Grant, it houses the artists' decorated furniture and murals (tel. 01323 811265).

- **ALFRISTON** Popular picturesque village located at the base of the Downs beside Cuckmere River. Delightful main street and tiny square lined by a jumble of timber-framed and tile-hung 18thC buildings. Overlooking the river and village green (The Tye) is St Andrew's Church, which dates from 1360, and the Clergy House, a charming, thatched and half-timbered 14thC former priest's house. It was the first building acquired by the National Trust in 1896 and houses an exhibition on 'Wealden Houses' (tel. 01323 870001).

- **WEST DEAN** Tucked away at the end of a No Through Road, this peaceful hamlet comprises a cluster of cottages around a pond, a dovecot and the ruins of a medieval house (AM). The Rectory dates from the 13thC and stands close to the fine Norman church.

- **SEVEN SISTERS COUNTRY PARK** Covering some 700 acres of the Cuckmere valley, this lovely park is a unique blend of unspoilt coastline and peaceful countryside on either side of the Cuckmere River, including salt marsh, meadow, shingle and chalk cliffs. The converted 18thC barn at Exceat Farm houses a Visitor Centre and the fascinating Living World Exhibition of small creatures.

- **BEACHY HEAD** At 536 feet (163 metres) this magnificent chalk headland commands stunning views over the Seven Sisters cliffs and to Eastbourne – you might see up to 30 miles (48 kilometres).

53

The Marlborough Downs

T he Marlborough Downs lie at the heart of Wiltshire, one of England's loveliest but possibly most underrated counties. Perhaps too many people speed through it on their way to the West Country, without fully appreciating its stark beauty and spacious landscapes. After the clutter of the Thames Valley and the home counties, these breathtaking Wessex downs inspire a sense of freedom and timelessness, for everywhere there is evidence of early human habitation. In addition to prehistoric sites, the monoliths and barrows, there are great houses, belts of richly-coloured woodland and forest, snug villages – many recorded in Saxon times – stretches of canal and undiscovered river valleys of more gentle beauty where, in places, there are few reminders of life in the late 20thC. It is hardly surprising that more than half the county has been designated an Area of Outstanding Natural Beauty.

Those who have yet to discover the delights of Wiltshire tend to associate it with Salisbury Plain, that Stone Age landscape now used as a military training area. But the bare Marlborough Downs to the north of Salisbury Plain, the subject of this section, are altogether more peaceful. Hard to believe it now, but this entire region was once one of the most populated areas in the country, inhabited by the people of the late Stone Age and Bronze Age.

The downland

Squeezed between Devizes and the Vale of Pewsey to the south and Swindon and the M4 to the north, the downs offer five-star walking. Probably one of the best times to visit is autumn or early spring when the weather is often dry, crisp and invigorating.

For those who are new to walking, the Marlborough Downs are perfect – dramatic yet not too daunting. A long hike into the heart of this wild open country brings its own rewards and here, at any time of the year, you are more likely to encounter only occasional, scattered groups of walkers. The Marlborough Downs offer a network of ancient paths and tracks which enable those on foot to devise their own circular route, and witness at first hand some of the county's great antiquities. Only by getting right away from the well-trodden tourist trails can you appreciate the true character of the downs, savouring their timeless atmosphere. Barbury Castle, between Marlborough and Swindon, is a perfect example of what you will find. It is a circular Iron Age hill fort of about 12 acres, named after Bera, a tribal chief. Wiltshire County Council has created a popular country park here and many visitors use it as the starting point for

GETTING THERE
Wiltshire is easily reached from many parts of the country. The M4 runs east to west along the northern boundary of the Marlborough Downs. The A4 runs parallel to the motorway, providing easy access to Marlborough. Swindon, Great Bedwyn and Pewsey can be reached by train from London Paddington.

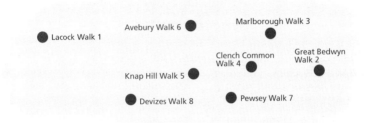

walks. Nearby is Hackpen Hill, a prominent ridge where you can see one of Wiltshire's distinctive white horses carved into the hillside.

Avebury
Being a World Heritage Site, Avebury attracts an international array of visitors, up to 500,000 a year, who come here to inspect and photograph the legendary stone circle that has stood here since 2,500BC. Avebury's true origins are unknown, but some historians believe the site, described by John Aubrey, a 17thC archaeologist, as 'as much surpassing Stonehenge as a cathedral doth a parish church,' may have been chosen as a burial ground for tribal chiefs. There is even a theory that it was built by aliens to remind them of a crater on the Red Planet.

Cobbett's clay country
The A4, once one of the great coaching routes, running between London and Bath, cuts across the Marlborough Downs and south of the road there is great potential for treks into the countryside. It is here that you can explore the great chain of hills rising up to form a formidable natural wall of defence where the rolling downland and spectacular scarp scenery give way to the low-lying clay country of the Vale of Pewsey, bisected by the Kennet & Avon Canal and described by the writer William Cobbett as 'my land of promise'.

Many manageable walks on the Marlborough Downs are included in self-guiding leaflets and other publications available from tourist information centres. However, for something a little more ambitious you could complete several sections of that most famous of prehistoric routes, the 85-mile (135-kilometre) Ridgeway, now a National Trail, which starts at East Kennett, south of the A4, and then makes a wide sweep to the east before heading for the Thames Valley and ultimately the Chiltern Hills.

The Wansdyke
Another popular route follows the remains of the Wansdyke, a bank and ditch probably built by the Britons as some kind of defence against possible Saxon attack. The path is 14 miles (23 kilometres) long and runs from Marlborough to Morgans Hill near Calne. Looking at what remains of the Wansdyke today – a low, crumbling, grassy bank enclosed in places by the trees of West Woods – it is hard to believe this was once an important frontier.

Another waymarked route is the Tan Hill Way, a spectacular 7-mile (11-kilometre) path running along the south-facing escarpment of the Marlborough Downs, parallel to the Wansdyke at its eastern end.

> **WEATHER**
> The weather in this part of Wiltshire is fairly unremarkable. The Marlborough Downs can be breezy in summer and bitterly cold in the depths of winter. Walkers are advised to take appropriate clothing.

Marlborough

B ehind the graceful half-timbered buildings and handsome shopfronts of Marlborough High Street, visitors can explore a fascinating rabbit warren of back alleyways and quaint narrow lanes. The tree-shaded south-western end of the main street is more residential, with lines of picturesque cottages and period houses watched over by one of the town's two main churches – the 15thC St Peter's.

Just round the corner from this church lies Marlborough College, dominated by its two mansion houses and attended by John Betjeman and William Morris – among others. According to legend, Merlin, King Arthur's magician, is buried on the site of an old Norman castle, now swallowed up by the college buildings but still identified on maps and records as a prehistoric, man-made mound. Merle Barrow or Merlin's Tomb later gave the town its name and deer antlers dating from neolithic times have also been discovered here.

The era of the stage coach really put Marlborough on the map. Being on the main London to Bath road, it became an established staging post and the town's surviving coaching inns still serve as a reminder of those great pioneering days of early public transport. Sadly, Marlborough, which was granted its charter by King John in 1204, has witnessed troubled times over the centuries. There was fierce fighting here during the Civil War, when Royalists attacked the town, and no sooner had the townsfolk licked their wounds, than a terrible fire swept through Marlborough in 1653, destroying at least 250 buildings. Two more fires broke out before the end of the 17thC and eventually a regulation was introduced to prohibit the long-established tradition of thatching.

Marlborough Town Council has produced a useful and comprehensive town trail leaflet, available from the tourist information centre, which includes a considerable amount of historical information about Marlborough's most notable buildings. For example, the Merchant's House, in the High Street, is being developed as a museum of 17thC town life and is worth a closer look as you stroll around the streets.

The Green, situated in the north-east corner of the town, was originally a Saxon village which later became part of Marlborough, linked by the High Street to the settlement near the site of the castle. At one time it was the rough, working-class area of the town, with an assortment of rowdy taverns. Nearby is Marlborough's other church – St Mary's – which contains a striking Norman doorway. The church achives include a letter from Cromwell calling for more money to be made available to help rebuild St Mary's and the rest of the town after the fire.

The Town Hall can also be seen on this tour. Dating back to the turn of the century, it is a distinguished building characterized by its carved stonework, oak panelling, decorated plasterwork, leaded-light windows with stained glass and exterior wrought iron. A quaint story emerged recently concerning a one-time Mayor of Marlborough who borrowed £20 from the Mayor of Stratford – father of William Shakespeare – and never paid it back.

The River Kennet flows prettily through Marlborough and a stone's throw from the town centre lies the vast expanse of Savernake Forest, once a royal hunting ground. After completing the town trail, you can escape here into a peaceful haven of woodland trails and glades – a blaze of colour in autumn.

ACCOMMODATION AND FOOD

Nestling in the unspoilt Kennet Valley and surrounded by sparsely populated, open rolling downland, the attractive small town of Marlborough, or one of the charming nearby villages with their abundant thatched cottages, make an ideal base from which to explore the area. Here we highlight some of the best hotel accommodation, upmarket B&Bs and eating places in the area. For more information on places to stay, especially self-catering options, contact the Tourist Information Office, Car Park, George Lane, Marlborough, Wiltshire SN8 1EE; tel. 01672 513989.

SLEEPING AND EATING

HOTELS AND INNS

MARLBOROUGH

Ivy House Hotel; High Street; tel. 01672 515333. Formerly Marlborough Academy for Boys, this personally run, Grade II listed Georgian house offers modern comforts in tastefully decorated and furnished bedrooms. Elegant restaurant serving interesting dishes.

HUNGERFORD

Bear Hotel; Charnham Street; tel. 01488 682512. One of England's most historic inns, once owned by Henry VIII, providing modern bedrooms and comforts in evocative surroundings.

CHISELDON

Chiseldon House; near Swindon (7¹/₂ miles/12 km north); tel. 01793 741010. Former manor house with modern extension set in 3 acres of lawned gardens. Individually designed and well-equipped bedrooms (some 4-posters), elegant sitting rooms and good food.

LITTLE BEDWYN

Harrow Inn; tel. 01672 870871. Only 200 yds (180 m) from the Kennet & Avon Canal, this welcoming country inn offers home-like accommodation, real ales and imaginative pub food.

AXFORD

Red Lion Inn; tel. 01672 520271. Attractive 17thC brick and flint inn overlooking the lush Kennet Valley. Clean and comfortable accommodation in well-equipped main building rooms and adjoining cottage.

BED-AND-BREAKFAST

OGBOURNE ST GEORGE

Laurel Cottage; Southend; tel. 01672 841288, closed Nov–Mar. High standards of comfort and service are guaranteed at this charming 16thC thatched cottage, set in a peaceful village north of Marlborough. Well-equipped bedrooms, including one that is a converted coach house.

WEST GRAFTON

Rosegarth; (7 miles/11 km south); tel. 01672 810288. Built in 1580 as four servants' cottages, this splendid thatched cottage stands in 3 acres of gardens in a quiet hamlet. Comfortable bedrooms and guest sitting room, and pleasant farmland views.

BURBAGE

Old Vicarage; (6 miles/10 km south); tel. 01672 810495; closed Christmas and New Year. Substantial Victorian house located next to the parish church in the oldest part of the village. Two-acre garden, relaxing drawing room with open fire, books and flower arrangements, well-equipped bedrooms and a warm welcome. Dinner available.

ALTON BARNES

Newtown House; (6 miles/ 10 km south-west); tel. 01672 851391.; closed Christmas & Feb. Late-19thC farmhouse situated high up on the Marlborough Downs overlooking the Vale of Pewsey. Principally a restaurant, it has three comfortable bedrooms and an attractively decorated reputable restaurant.

MARLBOROUGH

Vines Guest House; High Street; tel. 01672 516583. Tastefully decorated and well-equipped accommodation in a characterful property overlooking the high street. Residents have use of the sitting rooms and dining areas at Ivy House Hotel across the road.

CAMPING

The Forestry Commission site set in the heart of Savernake Forest (*Postern Hill Camping and Caravanning Site* – tel. 01672 512520), 1 mile (1.6 km) south of Marlborough, occupies 20 acres and has full facilities. *Hill View Park, Oare* (5 miles/8 km south-west) is an attractive level and partly shaded site.

FOOD

The area is rich in good country pubs offering above-average food, notably *Seven Stars, Bottlesford* (Anglo-French cooking – tel. 01672 851325); *Bell, Ramsbury* (tel. 01672 520230); *Woodbridge Inn, North Newnton* (tel. 01980 630266); *Royal Oak, Wootton Rivers* (thatched and close to Kennet & Avon Canal – tel. 01672 810322). Restaurants worth seeking out, in addition to the hotels and inns above, include *Stones Restaurant, Avebury* (good vegetarian cooking – tel. 01672 539514); *Raffles Restaurant, Aldbourne* (tel. 01672 540700). One of the best and most successful tearooms in the country is in Marlborough and must be experienced – *Polly Tea Rooms* (tel. 01672 512146)

Lacock

The world-famous Saxon village of Lacock (originally 'Lacuc' or little stream) is one of Wiltshire's most popular attractions. Preserved by the National Trust, little has changed here since the Middle Ages. The charming stone cottages, narrow streets and welcoming pubs and tearooms, Lacock Abbey and the Fox Talbot Museum of Photography are all well worth exploring. The area around the village offers the walker a variety of footpaths and byways where sheep graze in pasture bordering the River Avon, surrounded by wonderful scenery. This interesting ramble crosses National Trust land between Lacock and the imposing Bewley Court.

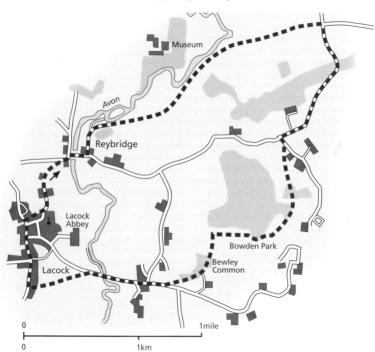

Start *Free car park in Lacock, 50 yds (45 m) from the abbey and village centre, ST916685. Signposted off the A350 between Melksham and Chippenham.*

Route directions

From car park take footpath opposite, signposted to Lacock village, which joins road passing abbey and museum. Keep ahead into High Street and turn right along West Street at end. Pass George Inn, turn left into Church Street and turn left at St Cyriac's Church, crossing Bides Brook to follow path to narrow lane which bends left uphill between cottages. At top, turn right

Essentials

Moderate 5½ miles/8.8 km; 3 hours; hilly in places; *map* Ordnance Survey 1:50 000 Landranger Map 173, Swindon and Devizes. **Terrain** Metalled lanes, gravel and grassy tracks and paths across pasture and cultivated fields.

Church Street, Lacock.

through waymarked kissing gate and follow tarmac path across pasture to Reybridge. Beyond further gate keep to path between houses to metalled lane. Turn right, then immediately right again to cross river bridge and go through gate on left in to field. Follow path diagonally right across field to stile in fence, before gate and house. Cross private drive, follow footpath beside security fencing to private estate to reach stile, beyond which lie several fields. Cross first field diagonally left to gate, enter small field and keep to left-hand edge to gate, the path bearing half-right through pasture to river in far corner. Cross fence, turn left along riverbank to reach fence which prohibits way forward. Turn right, climb left-hand edge of field soon to pass through kissing gate on left. Turn right on to wooded footpath, cross stile and head uphill to open field. Turn left along field edge (if ploughed up) to gate and continue along left-hand edge to gate and farm track. Follow this to lane, turn right and climb steeply to a copse (good views). Continue along lane to junction, just beyond farm entrance on right, and turn left soon to go through gate just before house on right. Keep left along field edge to stile in paddock fence, turn right along fence to further stile, then cross corner of two fields via stiles to woodland. Follow grassy path through copse, then along right-hand edge of field beyond to stile leading into Bowden Park. Keep right, soon to descend to gate and stile, then continue downhill on grassy path to further gate and stile. Bear diagonally left across open field on defined path to farm track leading to Bewley Common. Bear right across common to lane and turn right (turn left uphill for the Rising Sun ¹/₂ mile/0.8 km), following it back to car park on edge of Lacock.

• **LACOCK** Owned by the National Trust, it offers a pleasing mixture of architectural styles, including mellow stone cottages, half-timbered houses, a 14thC tithe barn, a 15thC inn and a gen of a church – St Cyriac's – which dates from the 15thC.

• **LACOCK ABBEY** Set in the heart of this carefully preserved village, the abbey was founded by Ela, Countess of Salisbury in the 13thC. Now a grand home, only the cloisters of the original convent remain and other historic features include half-timbered gables and an octagonal Tudor tower. It was here in 1835 that William Fox Talbot conducted a series of innovative photographic experiments, leading to the world's first photographic negative being made. A museum devoted to his work is housed in an old barn.

• **LACKHAM GARDENS, MUSEUM AND WOODLANDS** Just outside the village, this College of Agriculture houses a fascinating farm museum in thatched and refurbished farm buildings, as well as featuring a walled garden, riverside and woodland walks, a major rose collection in an Italian garden and numerous rare breeds of animals.

FOOD AND DRINK
Wealth of places in Lacock, namely The George and Red Lion pubs and several tea- rooms. Up the hill from Bewley Common towards the end of the walk is the Rising Sun at Bowden Hill (ale, food and stunning views).

Great Bedwyn

The main reason visitors come to this area is to enjoy the sights and sounds of the Kennet & Avon Canal, but, as this walk will demonstrate, there is much more besides – lovely scenery, peaceful woodland alive with birdsong and wildlife, a little-known windmill, the fascinating beam engines at Crofton and an unusual stone museum in Great Bedwyn. The traditional basket-makers' shop, just outside Great Bedwyn Wharf, is also worth a visit.

Start *Great Bedwyn Wharf, SU281644. Free car park on the south side of the Kennet & Avon Canal, opposite Frog Lane. Village is located 6 miles (10 km) south-east of Marlborough, signposted off the A4 and can be reached by bus – Bedwyn Link Service between Hungerford and Marlborough.*

Route directions Turn right from car park along lane, then in 100 yds (90 m) take grassy footpath on right, waymarked Bedwyn Brail. Head uphill between gardens of houses, then keep to right-hand edge of two fields to reach farm track. Turn left towards woodland (Castle Copse), the entrance to copse being through gap in hedge by footpath sign to Bedwyn Brail. Follow path through trees (can be muddy), soon to emerge on to

The Kennet & Avon.

wide grassy track, which becomes gravelled in 200 yds (180 m) as it bears right through open clearing to reach woodland (Bedwyn Brail). Remain on wide track for 1½ miles (2.8 km) to gate at woodland edge. Turn right along grassy path (blue markers), keeping Hillbarn Farm on left, to reach metalled lane and turn right towards Wilton Windmill. Continue along narrow lane, heading downhill into Wilton village, keeping left where lanes merge. Opposite the duck-pond, turn right along grassy track and follow it past Wilton Water (wildfowl lake). Track soon becomes narrow path leading to towpath of Kennet & Avon Canal, opposite Crofton Pumping Station. Turn left, then on reaching lane turn right across canal bridge and take path right leading past the Pumping Station (housing

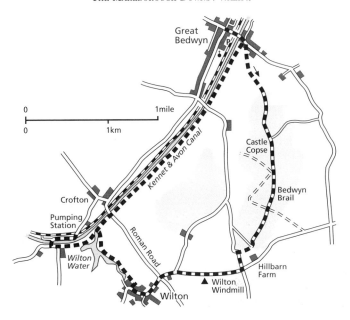

two beam engines). Recross canal by weir and turn left to follow towpath for two miles (3.2 km) back to car park at Great Bedwyn Wharf.

• **KENNET & AVON CANAL** Once a working waterway which, from its conception in 1788, took 22 years to complete, the Kennet & Avon Canal eventually became redundant – thanks to the dawning of the railway era. Restored over a period of many years, the waterway is now run by the Kennet & Avon Canal Trust and is used by colourful narrow boats which ply between Bath and Reading.

• **GREAT BEDWYN** The name Bedwyn possibly derives from the Wiltshire dialect word 'bedwine' or 'bedwind', a term used to describe the wild clematis which is native to the county. It has also been linked to a Celtic stream name of obscure meaning: 'bedwindan' in the Saxon charter dated 778 evidently refers to the small tributary of the Kennet which runs here. Worth investigating are the

Essentials

Easy 6½ miles/10.8 km; 3 hours; mostly flat; *map* Ordnance Survey 1:50 000 Landranger Map 174 Newbury & Wantage.
Terrain Level towpath, gravel forest tracks, grassy paths and some metalled lane walking.

large flint Church of St Mary the Virgin (tomb of John Seymour, Jane Seymour's father) and, along Church Street, the small but special open-air museum explaining the secrets of the stonemason. Here, you can see monuments, gravestones and sculpture dating back to the 18thC.

• **WILTON WINDMILL** is famous for being the oldest working windmill in Wessex. It was originally built in 1821 following the loss of five local watermills when the canal was constructed. Restored in the 1960s, it is open on Sunday and bank holiday afternoons between Easter and September.

• **CROFTON BEAM ENGINES** Designed by Boulton and Watt, the two beam engines, one dating from 1812, operate a huge cast-iron beam and were used to pump water up the canal. Beautifully restored and powered by steam, they can occasionally be seen working.

FOOD AND DRINK
The Swan Inn at Wilton, as well as pubs in Great Bedwyn.

Marlborough, The Kennet Valley and Savernake Forest

For the walker this is an unusually varied area, regarded locally as a favourite haunt of casual strollers as well as more seasoned ramblers. After leaving Marlborough, you go through the peaceful Kennet Valley via Mildenhall and pleasant riverside meadow paths, before climbing into the ancient Savernake Forest, with its easy walking along wide gravel tracks.

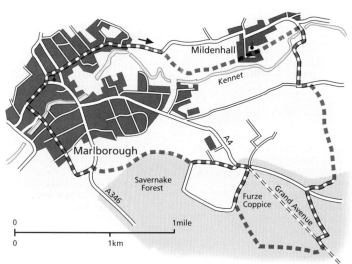

Start *Main car park (pay and display) in Marlborough town centre (Tourist Information Area) SU191685. Heading west along the High Street turn left into Hilliers Yard, signposted Car Park and Council Offices. Alternatively, park in the High Street – if there is room.*

Route directions

Return to the High Street, turn right along left-hand pavement and shortly pass the old Town Hall. Keep left to sign for Ramsbury and Aldbourne and turn right into Silverless Street and soon cross A346 Swindon to Salisbury road, keeping straight on past Queens Head pub and downhill out of town. Cross river bridge, then turn right along footpath, waymarked Werg, with river away to right. Head diagonally across pasture to gate in corner and soon climb steeply (handrail) through wooded area to cross Chiseldon & Marlborough Railway Path. Descend into field and turn right along edge to join farm track. Bear right with track for short distance, then turn left to follow right-hand edge of large cultivated field to reach series of stiles (yellow arrows). Cross two paddocks, enter yard and soon join lane opposite Mildenhall church. Proceed through churchyard to kissing gate and follow diagonal path (can be indistinct) across pasture to kissing gate, then cross cricket ground to take path between house and tall hedge to reach metalled lane. Turn right, cross bridge and proceed uphill

Essentials

Moderate 7 miles/11.2 km; 3½ hours; hilly in places away from Kennet Valley; *map* Ordnance Survey 1:50 000 Landranger Map 173, Swindon and Devizes and Map 174, Newbury & Wantage. **Terrain** Interesting combination of metalled lanes, gravel forest tracks and grassy paths and byways.

to T-junction. Turn left, then take arrowed footpath right alongside drive to bungalow and soon climb rutted track through woodland. On reaching gravel path, cross straight over to follow footpath (can be overgrown in summer) along wooded ridge between fields. In ½ mile (0.8 km), turn right at T-junction of paths, heading downhill to barrier and A4. Cross road on to grassy track that bears left uphill into Savernake Forest. At junction of several tracks (½ mile/0.8 km) with Grand Avenue – the main gravel forest track – turn right on to grassy track, then at third crossing of paths turn right and head downhill to Furze Coppice and the metalled lane leading back to A4. At the main road, turn left past gravelled track on to footpath running parallel with fence and A4, then on reaching entrance to Marlborough Cricket Club turn left along drive, keeping left through gate marked Slow Children and Animals. Skirt cricket ground, walk through car park and make for gap in fence behind clubhouse to join path through woodland. Bear right downhill over wooded common, then keep left on merging with path from right (views of Marlborough right). Keep right at next merging of paths and head steeply downhill to cross A346 on to tarmac lane. On reaching end turn right along footpath, passing

Marlborough's wide main street.

pumping station to stile. Continue past flats and entrance to St John's School to reach residential road, then make for zebra crossing at its end, passing garage to enter car park from where you started.

• **MILDENHALL** pronounced 'Minal', lies at a junction of three Roman roads running through the Kennet Valley; from Bath, Winchester and Cirencester. At this point a thriving trading community grew up; known as Cunetio by the Romans, it survived into Anglo-Saxon times as a small market.

• **SAVERNAKE FOREST** Comprising more than 2,000 acres, this medieval hunting forest features many walks and rides that radiate out from the Grand Avenue, a magnificent 4-mile (6-kilometre) drive lined with stately beech and oak trees, and designed by Capability Brown in the 18thC. Jane Seymour's family home was in the forest and it was here that Henry VIII courted her. The area is a haven for wildlife, notably migrant warblers and fallow deer. Walkers strolling this way in spring or early summer will see carpets of bluebells and primroses, as well as rare orchids.

> **FOOD AND DRINK**
> None along the route, but the thought of an excellent cream tea at the famous Polly Tea Rooms on your return to Marlborough should keep you going.

The Giant's Grave and Huish Hill

*The attractions of this walk include a stretch of the Tan Hill Way;
Martinsell Hill, part of an area of surviving chalk downland; the
famous hilltop landmark, the Giant's Grave; the villages of Oare and
Huish; a remote downland track to the edge of West Woods, renowned
for their daffodils and bluebells and a stretch of the Wansdyke Path;
and Huish Hill, which has superb views across the Vale of Pewsey.*

Start *Martinsell Hill
free car park SU183645.
Follow the A345 between
Marlborough and
Pewsey; take the minor
road (signposted
Wootton Rivers) at
Clench Common; the car
park is on the right in
about 1 mile (1.6 km).*

Essentials

Moderate 9 miles/14.5
km; 4 hours; mainly flat
with several reasonable
climbs; **map** Ordnance
Survey 1: 50 000
Landranger Map 173
Swindon and Devizes.
Terrain Paths and
bridleways; downland
tracks and woodland
byways; one stretch of
quiet country road.

Route directions

Keep road behind you,
cross stile and follow Tan
Hill Way with woodland on
right. At its corner keep ahead, following
lower slopes of wooded hillock, curve
gently left and make for wrought-iron gate
against skyline.Take path to next junction,
turn left towards West Wick, go straight on
at next junction over Martinsell Hill. Pass
dew-pond and bear right at sign for Giant's
Grave. Keep right of remains of old barn
and left of fenced copse and head down to
stile and gate. Follow grassy path over
Giant's Grave, pass triangulation point and
descend steeply with fence on right. Cross
stile, take next right gate, go straight
across field, with cottages of Oare over on
right, turn right at track and make for
village centre. Turn right at A345, pass The
White Hart, take left turning for Huish and
follow lane for about 1 mile (1.6 km). Pass
rows of thatched cottages and beyond join
No Through Road as lane bends left. Pass
Huish's tiny Norman church, where British
film actor David Niven was married during
Second World War, and continue on track,
following it right, then left by corrugated
barns. Pass hard tennis court and keep on
track. Climb quite steeply and continue
over junction of paths at top of slope. Avoid
turnings left and right, veer a little right
and keep going between
fences, trees and bushes to
line of the Wansdyke. Bear
right here up slope and

follow byway for more than
1 mile (1.6 km), with West
Woods on left. At next road
junction, turn right towards
Bayardo Farm. Bear left at
outbuildings and follow
right edge of field. Make
for top right corner, cross
into next field and turn
right. Go down to gateway
in field corner, continue
ahead along boundary, pass
track and hedge on left and
then bear immediately left.
Follow hedge along field
edge, cross through gap
into next field and keep ahead. Make for
line of trees in top boundary, cross stile in
corner and continue ahead with fence on
left. Look for gate on left leading you out to
track. Turn left and follow it past Huish
Down Farm, then across Huish Hill to
A345. Go straight over to join bridleway;
bear left just beyond corrugated barns and
continue on track for about third of a mile
(½ km). Turn left, opposite gateway, and
follow sunken path between trees. Keep
going through wood to signposted junction.
Go straight across and retrace steps to car
park at Martinsell Hill.

● **THE GIANT'S GRAVE**, on Martinsell Hill, is
chiefly associated with a charming legend
which claims that anyone who runs along
this unchambered long barrow seven times
will wake the sleeping giant.

● **WEST WOODS** comprise about 600 acres
of mostly beech woodland. The woods are
renowned throughout the area for their
wild daffodils and hazy carpet of bluebells
in spring. Some of the paths within West
Woods are public rights of way, while
others fall within the jurisdiction of the
Forestry Commission and
are therefore open to the
public at its discretion.

> **FOOD AND DRINK**
> The White Hart at Oare.

Knap Hill to the Kennet & Avon

This walk explores the southern fringes of the Marlborough Downs before meandering along the towpath of the Kennet & Avon Canal to the peaceful villages in the Vale of Pewsey.

Start Knap Hill free car park, SU115636, on the unclassified road between Manton, 1 mile (0.6 km) to the west of Marlborough, and Alton Barnes.

Route directions

From car park cross road and follow Tan Hill Way ahead, keeping fence on left. Cross two stiles and follow rough track to line of the Wansdyke. Turn left on reaching it (signposted Ridgeway Link Path), pass through gate and follow field edge with earthwork on immediate right. Bear right in field corner to join track, veer left and follow it down between fences. Continue over main junction and follow track as it begins a gradual sweep left. Pass several barns and continue to road. Cross over and take turning for Stanton St Bernard. Walk down lane, pass church on left and then swing right to Pewsey Vale Equestrian Centre. Turn left here and follow broad track to Kennet & Avon Canal. Bear left to join towpath, following it for about ³/₄ mile (1.2 km) to The Barge Inn at Honeystreet. Turn right, pass main door and follow drive until it curves to left by sign for the inn. Go straight on along waymarked path, cross stile, continue for a few yards, then bear right into adjacent field and immediately left. Cross stile and follow field edge with fence on left. Head diagonally across next field to stile in left corner. Join path, cutting between hedgerows, which soon becomes a drive. Follow it to sharp left bend and climb several steps up bank. Beyond them the path forks. Bear right and make for stile in field corner. Turn immediately left in adjoining field, continue into next field and keep alongside wall. Bear left through gate just beyond it and follow lane through Woodborough. Go straight over at crossroads, passing

Essentials

Moderate 10 miles/16 km; 5 hours; flat in the middle, strenuous at start and finish; *map* Ordnance Survey 1: 50 000 Landranger Map 173, Swindon and Devizes.
Terrain Field and downland paths, tracks, canal towpath.

FOOD AND DRINK
The Barge at Honey Street (on the canal bank) and the Seven Stars in Bottlesford.

footpath on right which leads across fields to inn, the Seven Stars, and continue for about ¹/₂ mile (0.8 km) to turning on left for Woodborough church. Follow road to church, bear right through churchyard and left at green lane. Pass farm and continue for about ¹/₂ mile (0.8 km). Bear left on reaching Kennet & Avon Canal again and follow towpath for about 1 mile (1.6 km) back to Honeystreet. Pass under road bridge, turn immediately left and left again at road towards Alton Barnes. Just beyond phone box, take right turning for St Mary's Church (Saxon) at Alton Priors and follow road down to turnstile on left. Join paved footpath here, cross several footbridges and head for church. As you draw level with church, veer left and cross field keeping alongside thatched wall. At road, turn right, then left to join Ridgeway. Follow it to next road and turn left. Descend slope; in 300 yds (275 m) take next path right, running up to stile. Go straight ahead across top of downs to Adam's Grave, a chambered long barrow with deep-sided ditches, and the summit of Walkers Hill. The car park at Knap Hill is seen from this superb viewpoint. Veer diagonally right, down to stile and out to road. Turn left and follow right-hand bank back to car park.

• **KNAP HILL,** one of Wiltshire's lesser-known treasures, is the site of a 4-acre neolithic causewayed camp dating back to around 2,760BC.

• **ALTON BARNES AND ALTON PRIORS** Alton is Anglo-Saxon for 'farm or village by the springs'. These can be seen very clearly bubbling away on the bed of a pretty little stream near the Church of All Saints. The Alton Barnes White Horse was cut in 1812.

Avebury Stone Circle and Windmill Hill

This superb walk is littered with Wiltshire's historic remains and famous antiquities. Beginning in Avebury, the path runs across country to Silbury Hill, one of Britain's great unexplained landmarks, before following the course of the River Kennet and then the route of the Ridgeway. The peaceful village of Winterbourne Monkton includes a well-sited pub and from here the walk heads for the open downland country of Windmill Hill before returning to Avebury.

Start *Free car park, SU101699, opposite village post office in Avebury's high street. Follow the A4 and take the B4003 or the A4361 north to Avebury.*

Route directions

Turn right on leaving car park and follow high street to sign for Avebury Museum, manor and National Trust shop. Bear left at this point and follow path with Avebury Stone Circle on left. Pass sports field and head for another car park. Make for A4361, then just beyond it, turn right; in a few steps left at sign for West Kennett Long Barrow. Go through two gates in quick succession and follow grassy path alongside the Kennet. Silbury Hill stands out clearly ahead. Pass track and bridge on right after about half a mile (0.8 km) and cross several stiles. Continue beside Kennet, following right-hand edge of field to the A4. Turn left for several steps, then bear right at sign for West Kennett Long Barrow. Pass through wrought-iron kissing gate, veer left and walk to junction of paths by oak tree. To visit the ancient site, turn right here; to continue walk, keep straight on. Skirt field, pass through gate and continue to lane. The river is to your left. Go straight across lane and enter field via stile. Follow path with fence and hedge on right. Pass remains of old stile and keep to path as it curves right. Look for stile ahead and follow enclosed path between trees and hedgerows – this can be a little overgrown in summer. At next junction, turn left and

Essentials

Moderate 11 miles/18 km; 4½ hours; level ground with a few undemanding ascents; **map** Ordnance Survey 1: 50 000 Landranger Map 173 Swindon and Devizes.
Terrain Field and valley paths; downland tracks; some stretches of quiet road.

FOOD AND DRINK

Red Lion pub and Stones Tea Room and Restaurant (excellent vegetarian food – open all day) in Avebury. New Inn at Winterbourne Monkton.

immediately right. Bear left at junction with track and follow it down to farmyard at East Kennett. Keep along village street, passing various thatched cottages, and turn right at next main junction, by phone box. Pass school on right and turn sharp left for West Overton. Soon road bends right; continue ahead at this point and follow route of Ridgeway. Pass over Kennet to byway/bridleway sign on field edge. Turn left and follow path round field perimeter, making for higher ground. Cross A4 again and follow Ridgeway for about half a mile (0.8 km). Branch off left at byway sign and head for clump of beech trees. Curve right here and continue across open downland. The famous Stone Avenue (B4003) can be seen over to left. Keep parallel with road, heading north. Pass through several gates and beside buildings of Manor Farm. Turn left at junction, then right for Winterbourne Monkton. Pass over drive and keep to left of farm outbuildings. Follow track up slope and at next junction, go straight over to continue on track alongside hedgerow. When you see some old ruined farm buildings 150 yds (140 m) ahead, turn left and follow track beside Windmill House. Continue along lane between high hedgerows and straight over at next junction for Winterbourne Monkton. Bear sharp left at No Through Road sign and pass New Inn. Look for footpath on right, just beyond pub and cross field by heading diagonally left to next stile. Follow path through woodland, cross stream to junction with

Avebury's stone circle.

sizeable outer bank and inner ditch, this is recognized as one of Europe's most important megalithic sites. The standing stones, which weigh up to 60 tons and are 8 ft (2.4 m) tall, make up one of the largest remaining henge monuments, even older than Stonehenge. The only way to appreciate its unique atmosphere is to visit the site, which is in the care of the National Trust, perhaps avoiding summer weekends and bank holidays. Avebury Manor (NT), a splendid Elizabethan manor house, is open to the public and well worth a look.

tarmac path, turn right and cross bridge. Go straight ahead on reaching road, passing Winterbourne Monkton church. Follow lane round several bends, merging very soon with track which runs straight out across fields. The slender obelisk on Cherhill Down can be seen on far horizon. After about 1 mile (1.6 km) reach clump of trees and slurry tanks. Turn left to join grassy track, following it for half a mile (0.8 km). As it curves right, cross stile and climb to summit of Windmill Hill. Keep to right of mound and go straight on towards gate in perimeter fence of next mound. Keep left of mound and follow fence to gate by National Trust sign. Follow left edge of field down to gate and continue along next boundary to next gate. Turn right at stile just beyond gate and go straight across elongated field to two stiles with ditch between. Cross next field to stile close to left corner. Go straight across to stile in next boundary and head for bridge over Kennet stream. Turn left and head for next stile leading on to tarmac path. Turn left, avoid path on right, recross Kennet and at Hunters House, a thatched cottage, bear right for high street. Turn left on reaching it, pass church and return to car park.

• **Avebury Stone Circle** Consisting of a

• **Silbury Hill** Built 4,600 years ago and dominating the surrounding area, Silbury Hill is the largest man-made mound in prehistoric Europe. Constructed on a spur of natural chalk, this vast engineering project involved millions of hours of labour, though its true purpose still remains a mystery. Access to the mound is now prohibited – mainly due to erosion. However, the adjacent car park offers good views of the site. Information panels illustrate its history.

• **The Sanctuary**, Overton Hill. In the care of English Heritage, this site dates back 5,000 years and was originally a timber shrine which was rebuilt and enlarged several times. The shrine was eventually replaced by a double stone circle linked to Avebury by the Stone Avenue, seen during the middle stages of the walk. The circle was destroyed early in the 18thC when the top of the field was ploughed; it was rediscovered in the 1930s.

• **Windmill Hill** The rounded hill includes the remains of three concentric lines of earthwork dating back to about 3,250 BC. Later it became a causewayed camp where animals were brought for slaughter. From the top there are magnificent 360-degree views over the entire region.

67

Exploring the Kennet & Avon Canal

The Kennet & Avon Canal meanders delightfully through the fertile Vale of Pewsey before heading for the fine walking country of the Avon valley. This route offers constant surprises, both natural and man-made, and only by following the winding towpath can you fully appreciate the ingenuity of this renowned waterway's builders.

Planning

Day 1 is Pewsey Wharf to Devizes.

Day 2 is Devizes to Trowbridge.

Walkers can travel back to Pewsey from Trowbridge by train, changing at Westbury. Due to the flat nature of the terrain and good underfoot conditions, fit walkers may like to attempt the whole 23-mile (36.8-km) route in one day.

The trail could also be undertaken as two separate day walks, as bus services are good.

Start *Pewsey Wharf, SU157610. Situated ½ mile (0.8 km) north of Pewsey on A345 Pewsey to Marlborough road. Owners of cars left in the car park here for more than 12 hours are expected to make a donation to the Kennet & Avon Canal Trust (tel. 01380 721279), operators of Pewsey Wharf. Alternatively, park at Pewsey railway station (daily charge), your return point.*

*To do **Day 1** as a single-day walk (Mon–Fri only) catch Wilts & Dorset bus (7.30 am, 9.12 am, 10.12 am – 20 minutes) from Marlborough to Pewsey; **return** by bus (5.20 pm – Harley Travel) from Devizes to Marlborough.*

*To do **Day 2** as a single day walk, park in Devizes (market square or pay-and-display car parks); **return** via frequent bus service to Devizes. Contact Wiltshire Bus line for further details (tel. 0345 090899).*

Route directions

Day 1 From Pewsey Wharf pass under road bridge and follow towpath in westerly direction through Vale of Pewsey, keeping to south bank of waterway. Cross to north bank at next road bridge and skirt grounds of Stowell Park to next road bridge. Continue to Wilcot Wide Water and keep

going for 1 mile (1.6 km) before crossing to south bank at next bridge. Beyond following bridge at Honeystreet pass Barge Inn and continue to Stanton Bridge and All Cannings bridge beyond. Follow road south to visit village; walk continues along towpath for 2½ miles (4 km) to bridge near Horton. Canal then makes dramatic loop to reach Bridge Inn and route continues towards Devizes town centre via Coate Bridge and Brickham Bridge. Canal swings right by bridge carrying A361 London Road, then in half a mile (0.8 km) towpath crosses to north bank at bridge by old granary building and just before Wharf Theatre. To reach town centre do not cross bridge; instead turn left along Couch Lane.

Day 2 Return to Wharf Theatre and head west along north bank of canal. Make for Kennet Lock and return to south bank at A342 road bridge. Walk under A361 and pass several locks to Queen Elizabeth II Lock; a plaque marks spot where the Queen reopened the restored canal. Descend slope, passing alongside Caen Hill flight of locks. Pass beneath B3101 and shortly cross to north bank and continue to Sells Green and the Three Magpies pub. Continue, passing remains of Wragg's Wharf and Scott's Wharf to next road bridge (Seend Cleeve) and Barge Inn (good lunchtime stop), located on site of Seend Wharf, beyond. Continue for 2¼ miles (3.6 km) to A350 bridge; Semington village and Somerset Arms just south. Back on towpath head for Semington Aqueduct which spans Semington Brook. In 1 mile (1.6 km) reach bridge and lane between Whaddon and Hilperton and continue to bridge over B3105. After ½ mile (0.8 km) reach bridge with sign for Hilperton and Bradford-upon-Avon and follow waterway for few yards to aqueduct, where towpath runs high above route of railway line. Beyond lies second elegant aqueduct carrying canal over River Bliss. Return to bridge, cross canal and follow private road (public footpath only) as it cuts between industrial buildings to main road. Continue straight on, following signs for Trowbridge town centre and railway station, or bus station.

Return To Pewsey Wharf – take regular train service to Westbury, then change on to main Paddington – West Country line for Pewsey. If parked at Pewsey Wharf follow A345 Marlborough road north for ½ mile (0.8 km). To Devizes – see page 68.

To Devizes – see page 68.

• **KENNET & AVON CANAL** is generally acknowledged as one of the great engineering achievements of the 18th and 19thC. Running into the Thames at Reading, the canal is 87 miles (140 km) long and was finally completed in 1810. Along its route are graceful stone bridges, neoclassical aqueducts and five Sites of Special Scientific Interest. At a cost of a million pounds the canal took 16 years to complete, complicated by the need for more than 100 locks between Reading and Bristol, though in places the route follows two river navigations – the Kennet and the Avon. The canal played a key role in the transportation of timber, coal and agricultural products, although the development of the railways inevitably led to a decline in its fortunes. In 1948 the canal was abandoned and quickly fell into disrepair, closing to navigation in 1951. The Kennet & Avon Canal Trust, established soon after its closure, spent 40 years restoring derelict locks, canal beds and pumping stations and in 1990 the Queen officially reopened the canal.

• **WILCOT WIDE WATER** Here the canal assumes a different and unexpected face, albeit briefly, when it becomes a wooded ornamental lake. The

FOOD AND DRINK
Various canal-side inns along the route allow walkers to break their journey and enjoy the hurried scene.
Day 1: Barge Inn at Honeystreet; Bridge Inn at Horton.
Day 2: Barge Inn at Seend; Somerset Arms in Semington (just off canal).

ACCOMMODATION
Devizes has a few hotels, notably the **Bear Hotel** (tel. 01380 722444), a character 16thC inn, and the **Castle** (tel. 01380 729300). B&B – **Pinecroft** (01380 721433) & **Rathlin Guest House** (tel. 01380 721999). Contact Devizes Tourist Information Office (tel. 01380 729408) for more establishments.

design and landscaping were the inspiration of the local landowner who feared the canal would create an unsightly scar.

• **HONEYSTREET** The wharf was owned and operated by canal traders. Many of the vessels which plied the waters of the canal were built at Honeystreet. The Barge Inn, near the towpath, used to be a slaughterhouse, a bakery, and then a brewery.

• **DEVIZES** includes many fine buildings, particularly in and around the Market Place – the Town Hall, the Market Cross, the Bear Hotel and the Corn Exchange among them. The distinctive red-brick, late-19thC façade of the Wadworth Brewery is also notable.

• **DEVIZES WHARF** Here the canalside has been much improved in recent years. Signs of industry have gone and today a stroll along the towpath reveals a pleasant scene, enhanced by the former granary, which now houses a canal museum.

• **CAEN HILL LOCKS** This famous flight of locks is one of the great wonders of the canal era. Completed by John Rennie in 1810, in order to carry the canal to a height of 237 ft (72.2 m), the flight consists of 29 locks in all, extending over 2 miles (3.2 km). The Caen Hill sequence of locks, 16 of them climbing up the hillside, has been described as the giant's vertebrae. In the early days the canal was so busy that gas lighting was installed in order that boats could negotiate the locks day and night. Passage cost an exta shilling (5 pence) after dark. A record for ascending all 29 locks was achieved in 1991 when the crew of a narrow boat came through in 2 hours, 6 minutes and 51 seconds.

• **SEEND CLEEVE** This part of the walk once witnessed plenty of bustling activity, when it was the setting for local ironworks during the second half of the 19thC.

Introduction

The Cotswolds

An intrinsic part of the British landscape and long acknowledged as a major tourist attraction, this enchanting corner of England, much of which lies in Gloucestershire, is perfect for walking. For some, the region is marred by a twee, chocolate-box image of mellow stone cottages, quaint old towns and idyllic pastoral scenery. True, many of the Cotswolds towns and villages pander to the constant throng of international visitors, and few tourists leave their cars and coaches to venture into the hills. If they did, they would discover glorious old beechwoods and breezy limestone uplands where there are a tremendous sense of freedom and views for miles. Here you can truly escape the crowds and queues and savour the authentic Cotswolds. In the words of a recent book on the area: 'Nowhere in all England is there such a lack of stridency. The colours seem softly blended. The landscape is a watercolour.'

Early history

Covering 790 square miles (245 square kilometres) and designated an Area of Outstanding Natural Beauty, the history of this region dates back 180 million years, when the area now defined as the Cotswolds was submerged beneath a shallow sea consisting of clay, sand and shell fragments. This gradually solidified to form the oolitic limestone which characterizes the region today.

The Cotswolds have been shaped by humans over the centuries and everywhere you look there is evidence of their influence. Long before the era of tourism, these hills were the domain of neolithic tribes who cleared and farmed the land. Successive generations which also left their mark here include the people of the Bronze Age and, subsequently, the Iron Age, around 500BC. The Romans came here too and were responsible for two important arterial routes, the Foss Way and Ermin Way, still very much in use as part of Britain's overburdened national road network.

The Domesday Book indicates that large tracts of the region were cultivated by the time it was published in 1086. However, it was the wool trade in the Middle Ages that really gave the Cotswolds their status. The region prospered and the familiar tracks along which sheep drovers once steered their flocks still survive, populated by armies of walkers, cyclists and horse riders and watched over by graceful stone manor houses and solid parish churches serving the wool merchants who built them.

The Enclosures Act brought much change in the countryside, especially in the Cotswolds, where at least 120,000 acres of open land were divided up by a network of hedges and drystone walls – still in evidence in the region today.

> **WEATHER**
> The weather in the Cotswolds can be mixed – just like any other part of Britain. The ridges and scarp edge can be cool at times and bitingly cold in winter. However, the lowland areas are very pleasant in any season.

Looking south to the sleepy Cotswold village of Naunton.

Trekking across the Cotswolds

Walking is undoubtedly the best way to appreciate the rich, unspoilt countryside of the Cotswolds, whose name is thought to originate from the Saxon *cod* and *wold,* meaning forest or wood. With over 3,000 miles of public rights of way, there is certainly plenty of scope to get out and discover the region on foot. The Cotswolds also boast several long distance paths – including the Heart of England Way which begins in the Midlands and cuts across the northern half of the region to reach the delightful town of Chipping Campden, a former wool-trading town famous for its gabled Jacobean market hall and buildings of mellow stone.

Chipping Campden is also the starting point for the better known Cotswold Way which stretches for almost 100 miles (160 kilometres) to Bath along the Cotswold Edge, the scarp slope of a limestone pavement, visiting many pretty villages and historic sites on the way and providing magnificent views over the Severn Vale to the hills of south Wales beyond. Britain's third longest long-distance path also cuts across the region, starting at Oakham in Rutland and finishing at Abbotsbury on the Dorset coast. The 235-mile (378-kilometre) Macmillan Way was officially opened in 1996 and is named after Douglas Macmillan MBE, who founded the organization now known as the Cancer Relief Macmillan Fund.

Don 't overlook the picturesque towns and villages of the Cotswolds – Moreton-in-Marsh, Broadway, Burford, Bibury and Bourton-on-the-Water among them.

The Thames tributaries of the Evenlode, Windrush, Leach and Coln also run through the region, the focus of gently winding river valleys, with lush meadows and lazy streams.

Stow-on-the-Wold

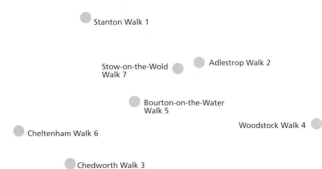

Stanton Walk 1

Stow-on-the-Wold
Walk 7

Adlestrop Walk 2

Bourton-on-the-Water
Walk 5

Cheltenham Walk 6

Woodstock Walk 4

Chedworth Walk 3

They say that all roads lead to Stow-on-the-Wold. Not quite all, perhaps, but at least five routes, including the Roman Foss Way, converge on this charming old town – which, at almost 800 feet (234 m), is the highest in the Cotswolds.

Stow-on-the-Wold, which in old English means 'the meeting-place on the hill', was an important junction before the Roman invasion, but improved access during the Middle Ages helped strengthen its role as a prominent wool town. Daniel Defoe, who wrote *Robinson Crusoe*, paid a visit to Stow's twice yearly sheep fair in the late 17thC, noting that more than 20,000 sheep were sold that day. The sheep fairs later became horse fairs and are held annually in early summer and autumn.

Many of Stow's buildings are constructed of the familiar Cotswold stone and can be seen clustered around the town's striking square. Look out, too, for the carved headstone of the market cross which depicts the receiving of the town's royal charter from William Rufus in the late 11thC.

A short walking tour of Stow's winding streets and narrow alleys, known locally as 'tures', is also strongly recommended, enabling visitors to discover the town's many hidden delights and secret places. Sheep Street and Shepherds Way are obvious reminders of Stow's associations with the wool trade, and the Masonic Hall in Church Street, built of rubble masonry in the late 16thC to accommodate St Edward's Grammar School, is also worth a look, as is St Edward's Hall, the Town Hall,

which includes a figure of St Edward the Confessor over the main entrance.

The parish church of St Edward is Norman and thought to take its name from the Saint Edward who lived a solitary, reclusive existence in this part of the Cotswolds, many years before Stow grew up. The church became a makeshift jail for a time – housing Royalist prisoners during the Civil War. The churchyard includes a fascinating and unusual feature – the graves of several wool merchants topped with wool bales carved in stone.

With its assortment of tearooms, hotels, inns and antique shops, Stow attracts its fair share of tourists, but on a summer's evening, when the day trippers have gone, peace descends and Stow reveals its true face.

ACCOMMODATION AND FOOD

Due to its position in the heart of the Cotswolds, historic Stow-on-the-Wold and its surrounding picturesque villages are well served with a wide variety of places to stay, including several luxurious country-house hotels. We list some of them here, alongside charming stone inns and picturesque Cotswold cottages, all of which offer comfortable accommodation and a warm welcome. Finally, we highlight some of the best eating places around the town – those worth a journey. For more details, especially about self-catering accommodation, contact the Tourist Information Office, Hollis House, The Square, Stow-on-the-Wold, Gloucestershire GL54 1AF; tel. 01451 831082.

SLEEPING AND EATING

HOTELS AND INNS

STOW-ON-THE-WOLD
Wyck Hill House; Burford Road; tel. 01451 831936. Handsome, early-18thC country mansion with views over the Windrush Valley. Luxurious bedrooms, elegant public areas and a splendid restaurant serving first-class meals.

Grapevine Hotel; Sheep Street; tel. 01451 830344; closed 24 Dec–10 Jan. Extended 17thC town-centre hotel noted for its warm welcome. Bedrooms vary in size and style but all feature exposed stone and pine or period furnishings. Conservatory restaurant with magnificent vine and imaginative food.

Royalist Hotel; Digbeth Street; tel. 01451 830670. The oldest building in Stow and reputedly the oldest inn in England, dating from 947. Behind the Jacobean façade lies a wealth of character and charm, especially in the beamed bar and cosy lounge with open fire. Attractive bedrooms are well-equipped; four housed in a cottage to the rear.

Old Farmhouse Hotel; *Lower Swell (1 mile/1.6 km west on B2052); tel. 01451 830232; closed two weeks Jan.* Converted 16thC farmhouse in a quiet hamlet and offering 14 fully equipped bedrooms, a friendly atmosphere and traditional home-cooking.

Kings Head Inn; The Green, Bledington (4 miles/6.4 km south-east); tel. 01608 658365. Facing the green and duck pond, this 15thC Cotswold stone inn retains its old-world charm in the low beamed bar, complete with inglenook fireplace and old settles. Excellent pub food and accommodation in 12 well-appointed bedrooms.

BED-AND-BREAKFAST

STOW-ON-THE-WOLD
Crestow House; tel. 01451 830969; closed Jan. Elegant Victorian manor house with views of the town and surrounding countryside. Bedrooms are decorated and furnished in individual style. Indoor pool and mini gym. Dinner by arrangement.

BLEDINGTON
Cotswold Cottage; Chapel Street; tel. 01608 658996. Delightful period cottage set in a quintessential Cotswold village. Attractively decorated bedrooms include a rear Garden Room with four-poster bed. Good breakfasts.

GUITING POWER
Guiting Guest House; (6 miles/10 km south-east); tel. 01451 850470. Former 16thC Cotswold stone farmhouse located in the pretty village centre. Expect a warm welcome (tea on arrival), and pleasantly furnished bedrooms. Dinner by arrangement.

BROADWELL
College House; Chapel Street, (2m north-west); tel. 01451 832351; closed Christmas. Charming, wisteria-clad 17thC village house, built of Cotswold stone and offering comfortable bedrooms. Warm hospitality and traditional English cooking.

UPPER ODDINGTON
Orchard Cottage; Back Lane, (2 miles / 3 km); tel. 01451 830785; closed Dec-Feb. Pretty 18thC cottage with a delightful garden and two comfortable bedrooms. Cosy sitting room with open fire; dinners cooked on Aga.

HOSTEL

Convenient hostel accommodation at the *Youth Hostel (01451 830497)* in The Square in *Stow-on-the-Wold*.

FOOD

Among the best pubs for above-average food within an easy drive of Stow-on-the-Wold are: *Fox, Lower Oddington* (interesting bistro-style food – *tel. 01451 870888*); *Plough, Ford* (also B&B - *tel. 01386 584215*); *Lamb, Burford* (splendid inn with character, excellent bar and restaurant food and B&B – *tel. 01993 823155*); *Tite Inn, Chadlington* (*tel. 01608 676474*); *Crown Inn, Blockley* (also restaurant and good B&B – tel. *01386 700245*).

Noted restaurants in the area, in addition to the hotels mentioned above, include *Lower Slaughter Manor, Lower Slaughter* (first-class accommodation and gourmet menus – *tel. 01451 820456*) and the equally civilized *Washbourne Court Hotel, Lower Slaughter* (*tel. 01451 822143*), and *Lords of the Manor Hotel, Upper Slaughter* (*tel. 01451 820243*). In *Moreton-in-the-Marsh*, try the popular *Marsh Goose Restaurant* (*tel. 01608 652111*).

Stanton and Stanway

Explore two classic Cotswold villages, Shenbarrow Hill and a peaceful woodland stretch. A section follows the Cotswold Way.

Start Stanton,
*SP067343. Small village
located just off the
B4362 between
Broadway and
Winchcombe on the
western edge of the
Cotswolds. Free car
park by the recreation
ground opposite
Stanton Court.*

Route directions
Leave car park, pass
Stanton Court and old
stone cross (church on left), then walk up
village street and turn right along 'no
through road' opposite Pear Tree Cottage.
Leave village via track (waymarked
Cotswold Way) and in 440 yds (400 m)
take footpath right to pass pumping
station (pond right) to reach stile.
Continue steadily uphill (CW), roughly
following line of stream bed to stone
farmhouse at top. Leave CW, go through gate into yard in
front of house and take middle bridleway
up track over rise (Broadway Tower visible
left). At T-junction of tracks, turn sharp
right through gate, head across fields and
maintain direction along woodland edge,
following green-topped waymarkers. Keep
ahead at crossing of tracks, descend
steeply, passing stone hut (right), and in
880 yds (800 m) continue straight on along
track beside wood. On reaching main road
(B4077), proceed ahead along pavement
for 660 yds (600 m) before turning right
on to Cotswold Way (beyond phone box)
into Stanway. Follow road around Stanway
House, then at village edge bear right and
continue along Cotswold Way across
parkland and fields (well waymarked)
back to Stanton.

• **STANTON'S** unspoilt charm is due to the
fore-sight of Sir Philip
Stott of Stanton Court,
who owned and restored
the estate between 1906
and 1937.

• **STANWAY** is a

Essentials

Moderate 4½ miles (7.2
km); 2½ hours; *map*
undulating. Ordnance
Survey 1:50 000
Landranger Map 150,
Worcester & The
Malverns.
Terrain Stony tracks,
woodland paths (muddy
in places) and short-
cropped turf, with some
road walking.

picturesque collection of
mellow stone cottages that
cluster close to its
magnificent 16thC manor,
Stanway House, which lies
beyond a grand,
elaborately carved gateway.
Owned by the Tracy family
for centuries the manor is
open Tue and Thu
afternoons June–Sep; tel.
01386 584469.

• **SNOWSHILL MANOR** (NT)
Fine stone Tudor manor
house filled to the brim
with Charles Paget Wade's eclectic
collections of craftmanship and design,
including musical instruments, toys,
clocks, bicycles and Japanese armour.
Charming cottage garden; tel. 01386
852410.

• **BROADWAY TOWER AND COUNTRY PARK**
Designed by James Wyatt and built in 1798
for the Countess of Coventry who lived
nearby, the 65-ft (20-metre) tower is set at
1,024 ft (313 m) and houses exhibitions on
three floors, with the observation room
affording panoramic views across 12
counties (open summer only; tel. 01386
852390). Thirty-acre Country Park with
nature trails.

• **BROADWAY** Delightful village known for
its broad greens and fine Elizabethan
houses that line its wide main street.
Formerly on old coaching route from
Worcester to London with the impressive
Lygon Arms Hotel serving travellers'
needs.

• **BRETFORTON** Small village on the edge
of the Cotswolds in fruit-growing country.
Seek out the famous half-timbered Fleece
Inn which dates from the 14thC and is
now owned by the National Trust.
Medieval Grange Farm
once gave shelter to Prince
Rupert in 1645 and the
country's largest collection
of dovecotes survives here,
including some rare old
examples.

FOOD AND DRINK
The Mount (pub) in
Stanton and the Old
Bakehouse Restaurant
at Stanway.

Around Adlestrop

This walk takes in Chastleton House (NT) – surely one of the finest Cotswold houses, with additional architectural interest at Cornwell and in Adlestrop itself. All 'discovered' in the depths of unspoilt countryside on peaceful paths and lanes.

Start: *Adlestrop, SP242273. Picturesque village located off the A436 5 miles (8 km) north-east of Stow-on-the-Wold. Free car park at Adlestrop Village Hall.*

Route directions

From car park and facing bus shelter (Adlestrop railway sign inside), take footpath left to stile. Follow arrowed path left to stile in field corner by large oak, then follow field edge to further stile and maintain direction up field to gate and top of hill beyond. Proceed to next gate, then turn right along edge of wood (Chastleton House visible left) and soon walk through wood to reach road. Turn left, then at bend in 50 yds (45 m) divert left to visit Chastleton House ($^{1}/_{2}$ mile/0.8 km), otherwise, turn right over cattle grid to follow bridleway through gate on right. Head up field, roughly parallel with road (passing right of trees), soon to cross farm drive via gates to enter ancient fort ring. Leave through gate opposite, walk down field edge, cross main road and continue ahead along lane to Cornwell ($^{3}/_{4}$ mile/ 1.2 km). At village edge take footpath left via orchard, then turn right beside wooden rails and cross path beyond Manor House down to church (worth visiting). Retrace steps to road and turn left. Walk through village to main gates of Manor House, then cross stile opposite and bear right along footpath to farm. Join track and walk past farm buildings, continuing up-hill to road. Follow bridle-way opposite, then in 550 yds (500 m) reach stony track near house and bear right to Daylesford Hill Farm. Turn left past Hill Farm Cottage and proceed

Essentials

Easy 6 miles (10 km); 3 hours (not including visit to Chastleton House); gently undulating; **map** Ordnance Survey 1:50 000 Landranger Map 163, Cheltenham & Cirencester.
Terrain Field and woodland on the outward route; returning along metalled lanes and stony tracks.

FOOD AND DRINK
None on route, but after the walk why not seek out the Fox Inn at Lower Oddington (1 mile/1.6 km west off A436 towards Stow) for excellent pub food.

along track (walled grounds of Daylesford House right) for 1 mile (1.6 km) to reach road. Turn right, cross A436 in $^{1}/_{2}$ mile (0.8 km) and pass lodge to follow bridleway across Adlestrop Park, skirting cricket ground to gate. Head up track to church, then follow road left past thatched post office back to car park.

• **ADLESTROP** Separated from the main road by Adlestrop House and park, this Cotswold gem – mellow stone cottages and pretty church – was made famous by a poem written by Edward Thomas – 'Yes, I remember Adlestrop'. The village nameplate at the now demolished railway station captured his imagination when his train halted briefly. The Great Western Railway sign is preserved in the village bus shelter. Jane Austen made frequent visits to Adlestrop House, formerly The Rectory, when her uncle was incumbent.

• **CHASTLETON HOUSE** is a magnificent Jacobean manor house that was built for a wealthy wool merchant in 1603. Topiary Gardens. Open in summer (NT).

• **CHASTLETON BARROW** is an Iron Age settlement.

• **CORNWELL** A little-known, or visited, village surrounding Cornwell Manor, rescued from dilapidation in 1938 when a rich American woman commissioned Clough Williams-Ellis (creator of Portmeirion in North Wales) to restore the manor, cottages and gardens. Sadly, her English husband was killed during the war so the couple never lived in their dream home.

75

Chedworth Valley and Roman Villa

*Ponder what life was like at Chedworth's Roman villa, once at the
heart of a thriving community in this quiet corner of the Cotswolds.
A varied and peaceful rural ramble, which also takes in the quaint
old village of Chedworth and glimpses the Elizabethan mansion in
Stowell Park.*

Start *Chedworth,
SP052122. Village
located off the A429
between Stow-on-the-
Wold and Cirencester, 6
miles (10 km) north-
east of Cirencester.
Limited parking by the
parish church, close to
the Seven Tuns.*

Essentials

Moderate 7 miles (11.6
km); 4 hours; easy
valley walking, gentle
climbs and a couple of
steep ascents; **map**
Ordnance Survey
1:50 000 Landranger
Map 163, Cheltenham &
Cirencester.
Terrain Mainly quiet
footpaths through the
Coln Valley, beside the
River Coln and its
tributaries to the
popular Roman villa,
followed by a steep
woodland climb on to
the plateau and the
disused airfield. Can be
wet and muddy
underfoot in winter;
stout shoes or walking
boots recommended.

Stowell Park.

Route directions

Take footpath to right of Seven Tuns, cross disused railway via stiles, then turn right
along river valley below houses for 550 yds (500 m) to lane. Cross and continue on path
to right of cottage, following bend of valley for 550 yds (500 m) before ascending hill to
road. Bear left uphill, then downhill past phone box (signposted Yarnworth). At bottom
of hill continue straight on over stile and along river bank for 880 yds (800 m) to gates.
Go through higher one, walk along boundary and to rear of houses to A429 at

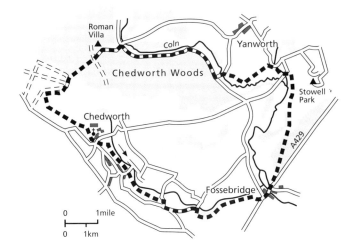

Fossebridge. Turn left, pass inn and cross river, then bear left through gate into Stowell Park. Immediately ascend through bushes on right, bearing slightly away from wall (blue dot on beech tree) to plantation gate. Keep ahead for 50 yds (45 m), then take left fork through trees and along field edge, passing crossing of tracks to join fence on left. Go through gate in field corner, follow boundary on right for 100 yds (90 m), then descend field to gate in wall. Continue downhill (tree belt left) to valley below Stowell House. At bottom proceed through large gate, then pass through next gate left and make for further gate to left of lodge visible ahead. Turn left at road, soon take footpath sharp right (before next house), heading diagonally across field to gate and road. Pass through adjacent gate on left on to track beside wall and follow field edge for 880 yds (800 m) (river left) to road beyond hedge in field corner. Turn left, go 50 yds (45 m), then right along paved bridleway, signposted Roman Villa. On reaching road turn left to reach villa. Where tarmac ends ascend path ahead through woods, passing under old railway bridge and keeping ahead at crossing of tracks. In 330 yds (300 m) at junction of tracks keep ahead up left fork, then at top of steep climb turn left then right on stony track and leave wood. Keep left around perimeter of old airfield,

FOOD AND DRINK
The Seven Tuns in Chedworth, the Fossebridge Inn beside the A429 at Fossebridge, and a picnic area at the Roman Villa.

pass barn left, then in 100 yds (90 m) at footpath marker posts, turn left across field between black and white barns to wall. Cross stile and follow track past small walled plantation to road. Bear left down grassy edge of drive to Manor Farm and cross stone stile to join path down to Chedworth church and your car.

• **CHEDWORTH** Large scattered village attractively situated on the steep hillsides bounding the Coln Valley. Charming 18thC stone cottages nestle below the late Norman church which houses an old font and a wineglass-shaped 15thC pulpit.

• **STOWELL PARK** is situated just north of the Foss Way and contains a fine Elizabethan mansion (private), which was enlarged in 1890 and commands lovely views across the Coln Valley to Chedworth Woods.

• **CHEDWORTH ROMAN VILLA** was developed between the mid 2nd and early 4thC and is one of the best exposed Romano-British villas in Britain. Rediscovered by a gamekeeper in the mid 1900s, the site includes a water shrine, two bath-houses and 4thC mosaics. A museum houses some of the smaller finds and screens an explanatory video. National Trust. Open most of the year; tel. 01242 890256.

Blenheim Park

*With so much of interest to see in Woodstock and at Blenheim Palace
you could easily spend a day here without going any further.
However, this easy ramble takes you through to the open countryside
beyond the park, revealing some extra surprises – a gentle pastoral
scene by the river, a little-known villa site and a delightful small
village with a pub on its green. The views in Blenheim Park are
fittingly splendid and, if the vast Baroque palace is a little daunting,
your pedestrian ticket allows you to rest your legs on a train ride to
the Pleasure Gardens, with a visit to the Butterfly House included.*

Essentials

Easy 9 miles (14.2 km);
4 hours (not including
tour of Blenheim Palace
– 2 hours minimum);
mostly flat; **map**
Ordnance Survey
1:50 000 Landranger
Map 164, Oxford.
Terrain Metalled
drives, stony tracks and
field-edge paths.

*Start Woodstock, SP447168. Historic town situated
on the A44 Oxford to Chipping Norton road, 10
miles (16 kilometres) north-west of Oxford. Park in
the free car park along Hensington Road, east of
A44 adjacent to Library (Tourist Information – tel.
01993 811038) and WCs.*

*Note: there is a charge to enter Blenheim Park
(£1 adults, 50p children, £4.50 cars), but this
includes train ride, Pleasure Gardens and so on.
Check closure times of the Woodstock Gate – 6.30
pm in summer.*

Route directions

Walk along Hensington Road, cross A44, continue along
High Street, then Park Street and pass through gates into Blenheim Park. Turn
immediately right down tarmac drive and alongside lake (Queen Pool) and pass building
at head of lake. Gradually climb valley to reach avenue (660 yds/600 m) in line with
Column of Victory. With Column behind continue along drive for 1,100 yds (1,000 m) to
second cattle grid and turn left on waymarked path across fields. In 710 yds (650 m) keep
ahead at crossing of tracks for further 275 yds (250 m) to belt of trees, then cross park
boundary wall via wooden steps. Maintain direction across fields (signposted Oxfordshire
Way) for 550 yds (500 m), cross lane and continue ahead for 1,310 yds (1,200 m), then
with hedge on right gradually drop to next road. Follow footpath for further 660 yds
(600 m) to stile, then head downhill and turn left across river bridge on to bridleway
(blue arrow) to gate ahead. Ignore path right, instead, follow track over ridge soon to pass
drive to Lower Riding Farm. Continue across railway bridge, then take next left and
shortly reach site of North Leigh Roman Villa. Follow
footpath left of villa complex, cross field, pass under
railway arch and walk along riverbank for 110 yds (100 m)
to cross footbridge. Turn right, follow track uphill to
Lower Westfield Farm, pass in front of farmhouse and
continue along metalled lane, ascending to Combe village.
Pass the green to church and take footpath left through
churchyard to stone 'squeeze' stile. Keep to field boundary
for 50 yds (55 m), go through waymarked gap in hedge and
descend well-worn footpath across field and beside
woodland (left). Bear left uphill at corner of wood (still
following perimeter), then maintain direction across field
to tarmac lane. Turn left, then in 220 yds (200 m) turn
right (no through road) and soon enter Blenheim Park at
Combe Gate Lodge. Bear left along drive for 660 yds (600
m), descending into valley, then leave drive and bear right

FOOD AND DRINK
No shortage of pubs,
tearooms and hotels in
Woodstock, notably the
civilized Feathers Hotel,
the Bear Hotel and the
Linden Tea Rooms.
Along the way there is
the Cockerel Inn at
Combe and both the
Pleasure Gardens and
the Palace at Blenheim
have tearooms/
restaurants.

on grassy swathe to stile before following lakeside path for 1,100 yds (1,000 m). Cross Grand Bridge, turn left at palace and left again at crossroads to return to Woodstock Gate. Walk back to A44 via Market Street (left of Town Hall) and back to car park.

• **WOODSTOCK** Compact, bustling little town with fascinating small shops and galleries to browse in, numerous tearooms and pubs for refreshment and an informative small museum, housed in a 16thC merchant's house (Fletcher's House), displaying an exhibition of the story of Oxfordshire and its people. The fortunes of the town have long been linked to Blenheim Palace, which lies beyond a huge triumphal arch designed by Nicholas Hawksmoor.

• **BLENHEIM PALACE** Built between 1705 and 1722 on the site of an early royal manor for the first Duke of Marlborough, this grand palace covers some 7 acres and features splendid State Rooms, a long

Blenheim.

library, magnificent tapestries and paintings, as well as fine furniture. Capability Brown landscaped the 2,500-acre park, which has beautiful formal Italian and French gardens, a pleasure garden, an adventure playground, nature trail, miniature railway and butterfly house. Sir Winston Churchill was born here in 1874. Open daily mid Mar–Oct; tel. 01993 811091.

• **NORTH LEIGH ROMAN VILLA** was occupied between the 2nd and 4thC and first excavated in 1815. Visitors today can view a 4thC bath, a beautiful mosaic floor and smaller artefacts.

• **COMBE** Unusually for its name, Combe is positioned on top of a hill, after villagers moved uphill from the original settlement and Benedictine monks built St Laurence's Church here in 1395. This contains 15thC wall paintings, a wide unsupported timber roof and a rare stone pulpit.

79

Bourton-on-the-Water and The Slaughters

From the bustling village of Bourton-on-the Water with its many bridges and tourist attractions, this ramble takes in some of the most picturesque small villages of the Cotswolds – Lower and Upper Slaughter along the River Eye and Naunton on the River Windrush – before returning through the quiet Windrush Valley.

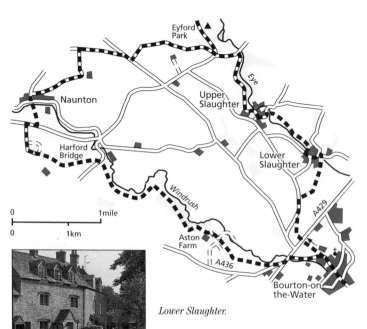

Lower Slaughter.

Start *Bourton-on-the-Water, SP169205. Attractive and popular tourist village situated just off the A429 Stow-on-the-Wold to Cirencester road, 4 miles (6.4 km) south of Stow-on-the-Wold. Choice of pay-and-display car parks. Regular bus service from Stow.*

Essentials

Moderate 9½ miles (15.2 km); 5 hours; gentle hills and river valleys; *map* Ordnance Survey 1:50 000 Landranger Map 163, Cheltenham & Cirencester.
Terrain Mainly well-walked and well-waymarked field and riverside paths.

Route directions Make for the dome of St Lawrence Church from chosen car park and continue along road past church (right) to Mousetrap Inn. After 100 yds (90 m) turn right along alley (arrowed footpath) and follow path over old railway embankment to A429. Cross stile opposite, go up field to stone stile and cross next field to lane. Turn right and continue 270 yds (250 m), then take bridleway right, following edge of trees and hedge to black gate and join tarmac path leading to Lower Slaughter. Turn left by river, walk through village centre to Mill

Museum and turn left just beyond on to 'Warden's Way'. Keep to waymarked path along riverbank and across fields, then turn left over stream for Upper Slaughter. Turn left along road to village square, then right (church left) past phone box and shortly bear left on to stony track. Follow bridleway for ³/₄ mile (1.2 km), passing house and along drive to road, opposite Eyford Park. Turn left along road, continue 440 yds (400 m), then turn right on to track beside cottages (not drive to Eyford Park) and gently ascend arrowed bridleway for 1,350 yds (1,230 m) to barns and soon reach road. Cross, turn right along bridleway (signposted Naunton) and walk parallel with road along field edges and past house, then turn left down stony track. Where track curves left, continue downhill (waymarked) on grassy bridleway, then up narrow path through scrub and cross small plateau before descending into Windrush Valley and Naunton. Walk down to T-junction and (leaving Warden's Way) go straight across (Black Horse left) to cross river on bridleway. Proceed uphill to B-road and turn right. Continue 160 yds (145 m). Take bridleway left alongside golf course, keep ahead where drive bears left and drop into valley. Bear half-left at stile, descend to cross stream via slab bridge and go through gate, then follow path through valley (stream left) for 880 yds (800 m). On approaching hamlet of Harford Bridge, bear right to waymarked gate in top corner of field, then turn left down lane and soon climb stile right, waymarked Windrush Way. Follow river for ³/₄ mile (1.2 km), then bear right uphill through hawthorn trees away from river on well-worn path to field corner. Turn right along woodland edge, then head into wood passing old railway viaduct to reach Aston Farm on field path. Walk past buildings (house left), keep ahead along lane, then ignore bridle-way (track) left and take footpath ahead. Cross field to stile (house left) and continue along field edge, gradually descending towards river. Go through gate, along bank and into plantation to reach main road (A429). Cross to outskirts of Bourton-on-

the-Water and follow Landowne back into village centre.

- **BOURTON-ON-THE-WATER** is probably the most popular village in the Cotswolds and often called the Venice of the Cotswolds, as the River Windrush flows through its centre and is crossed by several bridges. Among the attractions here are the Cotswolds Motor Museum and Toy Collection, the Model Village and the fascinating Village Life Museum housed in the Old Mill.

- **LOWER SLAUGHTER** Idyllically situated on the River Eye which flows peacefully between the rows of charming stone cottages that line its banks. Numerous tiny stone bridges, a 15thC gabled stone dovecote, a fine manor and the fascinating old church complete the rural picture.

- **UPPER SLAUGHTER** remains totally unspoilt: its open square flanked by golden-stone cottages, a 17thC parsonage, an attractive, partly Norman church with a chapel as a memorial to the diarist rector, Francis Witts, and, dominating the village, a splendid three-gabled Elizabethan manor house with 15 tall chimneys.

- **EYFORD PARK** Striking Queen-Anne-style house replaced earlier houses in 1910. Milton wrote *Paradise Lost* here. Beautiful parkland.

- **COTSWOLD FARM PARK** Set on the top of the Cotswold Hills with magnificent views, this is the home of Britain's most comprehensive display of rare-breed farm animals. Farm trail, pets' corner, café, lambing and special events; tel. 01451 850307.

- **BECKBURY CAMP** The stone monument by the old ramparts is known as 'Cromwell's Seat', as this was where Cromwell watched the destruction of Hailes Abbey during the reign of Henry VIII. Views of the picturesque ruins of the 13thC Cistercian abbey and across the Vale of Evesham to the Welsh mountains.

FOOD AND DRINK
Black Horse Inn at Naunton (halfway) and plenty of cafés, pubs and restaurants in Bourton-on-the-Water before and after the walk. For a civilized country-house hotel afternoon tea (or morning coffee en route) return to Lower Slaughter (Washbourne Court, Lower Slaughter Manor) or Upper Slaughter (Lords of the Manor Hotel).

Cotwolds quarries and country churches

*An exhilarating long ramble incorporating a particularly attractive
section of the Cotswold Way, with spectacular scarp and wold views
from Leckhampton Hill, followed by a tour of three charming
Cotswold villages, each with interesting churches to explore. The
Cotswold Way, especially along Charlton Kings Common and by the
Devil's Chimney, is popular in summer and at weekends.*

Start *Seven Springs lay-by on the A436
Bourton-on-the-Water to Gloucester
road; SO966169. Lay-by just west of
junction with A435 Cheltenham to
Cirencester road, 3 miles (4.8 km) south
of Cheltenham.*

*Devil's
chimney.*

signposted
Charlton
Kings. Where
lane curves
sharp left
keep ahead
along
waymarked
Cotswold Way
(CW),
arrowed
Leckhampton
Hill, shortly bearing left to begin ascent.
Follow path near scarp edge for 1¼ miles
(2 km) to top and pass triangulation point
and topograph. In
50 yds (45 m) descend to
lower levels of old quarry
workings to view Devil's
Chimney, then climb back to
main path and continue round
to road. Turn left, climb
steeply and soon take track
right signposted Ullenwood
(CW). Pass Salterley Grange
and golf course to reach
minor road. Turn left (leaving
CW), pass clubhouse and
shortly cross A436 on to
Cowley road. Immediately

Essentials

Strenuous 13 miles (21
km); 8 hours; hilly.
Ordnance Survey
1:50 000 Landranger
Map 163, Cheltenham &
Cirencester.
Terrain Mainly stony
tracks and tarmac lanes
with some field paths.

Route directions

From lay-by walk north-east along main road to crossroads
with A435 and turn left, then left again along minor road

bear right through gates and follow track up South Hill, keeping ahead at junction with track leading to Cuckoopen Barn Farm. At crossing of tracks beyond masts turn left, then where tarmac ends at farm continue ahead on bridleway through field and along field edge to join grassy track leading to lane. Turn right and remain on lane past Stockwell Farm to reach A417. Follow verge left (great care) for 100 yds (90 m), then cross over and pass through gate to right of ruined barn. (For refreshment at Golden Heart pub continue along verge for further 200 yds/180 m. Bear round left, passing behind barn, to gap in hedge and turn right, then with hedge on right descend into valley. Keep hedge right, proceed uphill through gate and follow tree-covered bank on left, soon to bear left on track through gap. On reaching wall take track right to road, keeping ahead through Brimpsfield. Pass Brimpsfield House on left and take bridleway left (tarmac drive) into Brimpsfield Park. Pass farm and house (left), descend into valley on track (woods right), then at fork keep ahead uphill. At next fork bear left steeply uphill to gate, then follow right-hand wall and shortly climb steps and cross A417 (great care) to follow minor road to Elkstone. At crossroads turn left, then right down gravel drive past church and immediately bear left over stile. Cross paddocks, then bear right along drive to Village Hall. Walk up Hillview, then at end of tarmac bear right into field and pass cottage (left) to stone stile. Follow left-hand edge of field, then on nearing line of trees 100 yds (90 m) veer diagonally right across field to lane. Follow footpath opposite, downhill across hummocky grassland looking for markers on trees (can be boggy). Cross small stream, pass through gate on right and proceed through trees to cross footbridge. Follow field edge to lane near Millstream Cottage. Turn left and shortly right to join arrowed footpath by gate to cottage. (For refreshment at the Green Dragon in Cockleford, keep to lane to T-junction and turn right.) Descend to cross stream, enter garden by house and go up drive to A435. Cross over to follow tarmac drive to Westbury Farm and continue uphill on wide track for 1 mile

FOOD AND DRINK

Seven Springs Inn located at the start/finish of the walk plus, via short diversions, the Golden Heart at Nettleton Bottom near Brimpsfield (6 miles/10 km) and the Green Dragon in Cockleford (10½ miles/16.8 km).

(1.6 km) to Upper Coberley. Turn left along lane, then in 50 yds (45 m) bear right down bridleway through trees and across large field to gap in hedge and cross A435. Climb stile, bear half-right across meadow to gateway midway along belt of trees. Beyond gates walk along right-hand side of buildings to road and turn left. (Coberley church is accessed through gate in wall under gargoyle.) Proceed through village, up past phone box, then at end of road continue along bridleway, signposted Seven Springs. Keep ahead at crossing of tracks (hedge right), then climb next stile right and follow right-hand fence back to A436 and lay-by.

• SEVEN SPRINGS The River Churn rises beside the lay-by forming the highest source of the River Thames.

• DEVIL'S CHIMNEY This striking pinnacle of rock rises precariously out of the scarp face of Leckhampton Hill and is a relic of extensive quarrying in this area (stone used for building Georgian Cheltenham). The pinnacle was cut by quarrymen to draw attention to their quality building stone. The quarry thrived until the 1920s. Views from Leckhampton Hill extend across Cheltenham and the Severn Vale to the Malvern Hills and the Welsh mountains beyond.

• BRIMPSFIELD Between the charming parish church and the village lane stands a wide grassy expanse, formerly the site of a 13thC castle built by the Giffard family. It was destroyed in 1322 after John Giffard was executed by Edward II and visible earthworks near the church mark the spot where it stood. Impressive Brimpsfield House dates from the 17thC.

• ELKSTONE'S simple yet interesting church dates from 1160.

• COBERLEY St Giles's Church, originally built as a chantry for the Berkeley family in 1340, is unusual for the fact that it is entered via a barn door and a 'private' garden. See the monument to Joan Berkeley, mother of Richard Whittington (Dick of pantomime fame).

Stow-on-the-Wold to Honeybourne

This ramble ventures into the heart of the Cotswold countryside, incorporating some of the finest valleys, villages and views that the region can offer. Peaceful undulating field paths and tracks link tranquil river valleys (Eye, Windrush) and idyllic villages with picture-postcard stone cottages (The Slaughters, Temple Guiting, Stanton, Stanway, Broadway). Steep ascents along the Cotswold Way are rewarded with breathtaking views across the Severn Vale to the Malvern Hills and the Welsh mountains beyond. Along the way, if time allows, there are historic houses to visit, a farm park and country park to explore; and you could pause at Broadway for its galleries and antique shops.

Start *Stow-on-the-Wold, SP256191. Historic small market town situated on the A429 between Cirencester and Stratford-upon-Avon. Parking available in main square, or, if convenient, begin walk from base accommodation. Stow Tourist Information Office; tel. 01451 831082*

Planning

With limited public transport in this part of the Cotswolds, Walks 7 & 8 can only be undertaken as a two-day walk with overnight accommodation in the picturesque villages of Stanway or Stanton. Return to Stow-on-the-Wold from Honeybourne Station via the regular train service to Moreton-in-Marsh, then by bus back to Stow.

Route directions

Day 1 From south-east corner of main square cut through to A436, turn right to crossroads with A429 and turn left to follow pavement for ½ mile (0.8 km) to junction (traffic lights) with A424. Keep to right-hand side of road and bear half-right along waymarked bridleway (not first right signposted Lower Swell), signed 'Private Drive to Hyde Mill'.

Essentials

Moderate
Day 1 15 or 16 miles (24.4 or 26 km); 8-9 hours. **Day 2** 11.5 miles (18 km); 7 hours. Undulating, with a few steep ascents/descents towards the end of Day 1 and early into Day 2 along the Cotswold Way; flat from Broadway to Honeybourne Station; **map** Ordnance Survey 1:50 000 Landranger Map 163 (Cheltenham & Cirencester) and Map 150, Worcester & The Malverns.
Terrain Pleasant and varied combination of field paths, tracks, bridleways and short sections of metalled lanes. Generally well-waymarked, especially along the Cotswold Way and the Macmillan Way. It can be wet and muddy in winter.

Pass through gate, then beyond avenue of poplars bear right by mill house and turn left over bridge, signposted Lower Slaughter. Cross millpond and follow well-waymarked route (arrowed Lower Slaughter and Heart of England Way) through the Dikler valley, initially close to the River Dikler, then across fields via stiles and gates, eventually reaching sports field on edge of Lower Slaughter. Go through gate behind pavilion, shortly bear right along drive, then left on to road by churchyard. At T-junction (by Washbourne Court Hotel) turn right and walk beside River Eye through village to Mill Museum, bearing left beyond (Warden's Way) to join path along riverbank, then continue across fields, soon to bear left over stream for Upper Slaughter. At road turn left to village square, then right past phone box and shortly bear left on stony track. In ¾ mile (1.2 km) reach road opposite Eyford Park and turn left, then in 330 yds (300 m) turn right along tarmac drive. Pass Eyford House and keep ahead where tarmac ends by lodge, following bridleway for 1 mile (1.6 km) passing Eyford Hill Farm to reach road. Turn left and take arrowed footpath half-right in

110 yds (100 m). Cross stile, follow boundary behind farmhouse left, then cross wall via wooden steps and proceed ahead across field to stile and road. Take track opposite, pass cottage and belt of trees (right) to road and climb stile opposite into Cotswold Farm Park. Follow yellow markers through park (towards picnic area), then through paddocks via gates to reach Bemborough Farm and follow drive to lane. Turn right, then left at T-junction and in 880 yds (800 m), at far end of plantation, turn left along unmarked track. At modern barn (880 yds/ 800 m) bear right steeply down stony track, passing pond to reach lane in Temple Guiting. Turn left through village, passing manor and church to T-junction by school and turn right. In 275 yds (250 m) turn left up fenced path between houses, go through gate and head steeply uphill through small plantation to stile. Keep climbing alongside left-hand boundary to gate, cross saddle of hill and descend, soon following wide track through wood near left-hand edge. At end of track keep ahead on narrow path, following waymarkers over stiles to cross stream to reach track. Bear right uphill, pass farm away to left, then soon cross farm drive to follow field path up valley indentation, becoming narrow and steep to reach lane. Turn left, pass Pinnock Wood Farm and turn right, signposted Farmcote. Immediately take bridleway right up hedged track and in 1 mile (1.6 km), at small walled plantation, look over gate to view ramparts of Beckbury Camp. In 55 yds (50 m) turn left off track, signposted Cotswold Way, and follow field edge round outer ring of earthwork to monument. Take signposted path down

FOOD AND DRINK

Day 1/Walk 7 Morning coffee at the upmaket Lower Slaughter Manor Hotel or the Lords of the Manor Hotel in Upper Slaughter. Tea-room/café at Cotswold Farm Park (in season) Small shops at Lower Slaughter and Temple Guiting.

Day 2/Walk 8 Broadway Tower Country Park (in season), plenty of choice in Broadway, notably Lygon Arms, Collin House Hotel, and the ancient Fleece Inn (NT) at Bretforton for character, excellent ales and bar snacks.

ACCOMMODATION

The **Old Bakehouse** in Stanway (tel. 01386 584204) – open all year, or **The Vine** (B&B) - 17thC farm-house offering three four-poster bedrooms (tel. 01386 73250) and **Shenbarrow Hill Farm** offering four en suite rooms and evening meals (tel. 01386 584468). Evening meals also available at the **Mount** pub in the village.

below ramparts, then turn right (Cotswold Way left), soon to reach stile at corner of woods. Go down beside woodland (on left) via stiles with Wood Stanway soon coming into view. Do not take track towards farm, but keep near trees to cross paddock and enter hamlet via gates. In centre turn right, then shortly left on to waymarked Cotswold Way and cross fields to B4077 at Stanway. Turn left, then right (CW) to enter village (B&B). Follow lane around Stanway House then, at end of village, continue on Cotswold Way across parkland and fields to Stanton (B&B).

Day 2 Walk up village street, turn right along No Through Road opposite Pear Tree Cottage and leave village on stony track, signposted Cotswold Way. After 440 yds (400 m) bear right past water-pumping station (pond right) to stile, then climb steeply (CW), following line of stream bed to reach farmhouse at top. Leave CW, go through gate into yard in front of house and take middle bridleway along track over rise. At T-junction of tracks turn left, then almost immediately take bridleway right, diagonally downhill through two fields to lane. Turn right and continue into Snowshill, then take lane behind church to crossroads. Keep ahead, signposted Broadway Tower, and keep left in 550 yds (500 m) to follow ridge road (views) for 1½ miles (2.4 km) to entrance to Broadway Country Park. Cross stile by entrance gate, continue to tower and follow well-waymarked CW for 1¼ miles (2 km) downhill into Broadway. Turn left down High Street, then where road bears right by green turn right by Swan Inn and shortly left along Walnut Close and Drive beyond to reach

thatched cottage. Bear right, signposted
Willersley, go round to right of cottage,
past factory and through kissing gate on to
track behind houses. Cross footbridge,
follow left-hand field edge to stile and
keep ahead to further stile. Ignore
arrowed diagonal path, but continue
ahead across field soon to join grassy track
into next field. Bear right round field
edge, cross footbridge in corner, continue
with stream right to further footbridge,
then go through gap ahead and on nearing
two houses pass through paddocks to road.
Cross stile opposite, proceed with hedge
left to footbridge near field corner and
turn right. With stream to right continue
across fields via stile, for ¾ mile (1 km) to
farm track. Cross and maintain direction
for 770 yds (700 m), then near tall hedge
(road beyond) go through gap in hedge on
right and cross field corner to stile and
road. Turn left and shortly take driveway
right, then where drive bears right to
house, keep ahead to left of hedge for
220 yds (200 m). Turn right at corner,
passing horse jump over brambles, look for
gap in hedge and cross left to walk along
unhedged bank between fields for 175 yds
(150 m). Keep ahead along grassy track,
cross farm road and follow footpath ahead
along right-hand field boundaries via stiles
for ¾ mile (1.2 km) to lane on edge of
Bretforton. Turn right, then left along
Bridge Lane to church and go left past
church, soon to turn right along School

Broadway.

Lane. Shortly, cross B4035, go through
cemetery gates and follow path beside
glasshouses, then continue through
market gardens along field edge to reach
hedge. Bear right (hedge left) for 175 yds
(150 m) to gap left and cross stone bridge.
Bear half-right across field towards ash
tree near corner, go through gap beyond
on to track and follow it to road. Take
track opposite for 280 yds (250 m),
following it right for further 220 yds
(200 m) to hedge. Turn left for short
distance, cross stile in hedge and cross
paddock to stile in bottom corner. Cross
stream, follow right-hand hedge for
330 yds (300 m) and enter caravan park
via gap in hedge. With gravel circle left,
proceed to stile in top hedge and follow
path through grassy waste ground to
former railway tracks and platforms.
Turn left towards railway bridge with
Honeybourne Station 110 yds (100 m)
on left.

Return to Stow-on-the-Wold
*From Honeybourne Station catch the
regular Thames Train service between
Hereford and London to Moreton-in-
Marsh (11 minutes), then take bus
service B1 from the Town Hall (five-
minute walk from railway station) back
to Stow-on-the-Wold. For timetable
details, tel. 01865 722333.*

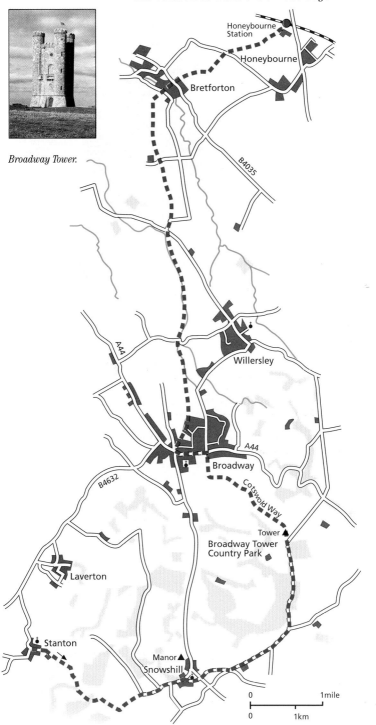

Broadway Tower.

Honeybourne
Station

Honeybourne

Bretforton

B4035

Willersley

A44

A44

Broadway

B4632

Cotswold Way

Tower

Broadway Tower
Country Park

Laverton

Stanton

Manor

Snowshill

0   1mile

0   1km

Suffolk and Essex

I n a changing world, Suffolk, and nearby
parts of Essex covered in this section,
remain a largely 'undiscovered' corner of
East Anglia. Despite being close to London
and the Midlands, it is an area with a
strongly independent air – and that's how its
residents like it. With its extensive tracts of
level countryside, sleepy villages, historic
houses and famous market towns, the region
has much to offer walkers and those seeking refuge from modern life.

The open, flat country facing the European mainland, with easy
access by the rivers, made Suffolk vulnerable in early times to attack
from waves of invaders. In the Middle Ages, however, it prospered under
the wool merchants: it was their wealth that built the great churches
which dominate the landscape.

In recent years great efforts have been made to improve this area's
recreational facilities and in particular to meet the growing demands of
walkers and ramblers. With its many miles of undemanding public
paths and recreational routes, it now stands out as a place worth
visiting just for the walks.

The coast

Suffolk's isolated Heritage Coast is one of the
region's great natural attractions and has a
wonderfully nostalgic feel, as well as a curious,
eerie emptiness. It was here among the salt
marshes and winding river estuaries that
prosperous 18thC smugglers sought refuge from the
dreaded Excise men. Much of the coastal heathland
area is now protected as a designated Area of
Outstanding Natural Beauty and shelters several
rare creatures including the adder, the heath
butterfly and the nightjar.

The only way really to discover this crumbling,
desolate coastline is on foot, following stretches of
the 50-mile (80-kilometre) Suffolk Coast Path
which runs between Felixstowe and Lowestoft.
Near its southerly start, the path passes close to
one of the National Trust's most unusual
acquisitions, Orford Ness. Bought by the Trust from
the Ministry of Defence in 1993, and officially
opened in 1995, this spectacular stretch of
coastline had previously been closed to the public
since 1915 when the Royal Flying Corps chose
Orford Ness as the setting for military research.
Now it is a Grade I Site of Special Scientific
Interest, recognized in particular for its rare

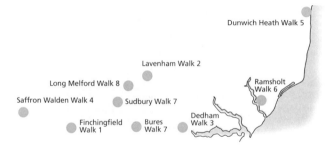

Dunwich Heath Walk 5

Lavenham Walk 2

Long Melford Walk 8

Ramsholt
Walk 6

Saffron Walden Walk 4

Sudbury Walk 7

Finchingfield
Walk 1

Bures
Walk 7

Dedham
Walk 3

shingle habitats. Visitors to Orford Ness cross the River Ore by National Trust Ferry from Orford Quay, then undertake a waymarked walk to the 18thC lighthouse and back, taking in several grazing marshes on the way. The Ness can be wet and cold at times, so dress appropriately.

Beyond Orford, the Suffolk Coast Path parts company briefly with the North Sea and cuts across country to Aldeburgh, a quiet seaside resort which was once an important coastal village. Nearby are Snape Maltings – renowned worldwide as the home of the Aldeburgh Festival.

Further up the coast is the charming little town of Southwold, its distinctive, white-walled lighthouse standing sentinel above it. The final section of the walk is one of the most spectaclar parts of the route, with low, sandy cliffs, several shallow Suffolk broads and the occasional church tower peeping through the trees. If time allows, you can follow the coast path from start to finish, following the route directly beside the sea for more than 30 miles (48 kilometres). Or, for something shorter, you could devise your own circular walk, using the Coast Path as part of the walk.

Inland
However, there is much more to Suffolk than its wild and lonely coastline. Inland there are broad expanses of quiet, undiscovered countryside where you may not meet another soul. Tunstall Forest, south of Saxmundham and Snape, is a haven for those who like peaceful woodland walking. A network of paths leads you between uniform rows of Corsican pines. Beyond the trees you reach the banks of the River Alde at Iken, a fascinating area of heath and creeks and scattered clusters of dwellings buried down sleeping country lanes.

Rivers
The Orwell, Deben and Blyth meander for miles, offering plenty of scope for delightful walking. One of the country's most popular trails is the long-distance Angles Way which follows the boundary between Suffolk and Norfolk for 77 miles (124 kilometres), starting at Great Yarmouth and finishing at Knettishall Heath near Thetford.

WEATHER
The climate is on the whole well suited to walkers, with the lowest annual rainfall in England. Be prepared for breezes, however: the east coast is exposed and even in high summer the strength of the wind may surprise you.

Waymarked walks
For those who like to take things at a gentle pace, there are various waymarked walks all around the area, all easily walked in less than a day. Suffolk and Essex County Councils publishes a directory of trails and rides, as well as information on country parks, picnic sites, nature reserves and woodlands. Many other attractions are listed to provide ideas for endless days out.

Lavenham

Y ou will not find it difficult to understand why we have chosen Lavenham as a base for the walks in this section. It is centrally placed for access to all the routes, and staying here is an experience in its own right, quite apart from walks.

Sometimes described as the finest medieval town in England, Lavenham grew to prosperity in the 14th to 16thC, mainly thanks to sheep: wool made it once the fourteenth richest town in England. A stroll around the town will quickly give you an insight into its wealthy past: the streets are lined with an astonishing collection of beautiful timber-framed medieval and Tudor houses.

One of Lavenham's most impressive buildings is the Church of St Peter and St Paul, dominated by its great square-buttressed flint tower rising to more than 140 feet (40 metres). The church's interior has a fine feeling of space, almost like a cathedral. The sumptuous medieval imagery in the chancel is certainly worth a look. The steeple was endowed by Thomas Spring, a successful Lavenham clothier, and the church bells, famous throughout Suffolk, were rung to mark the death of Queen Mary in 1953.

The Guildhall, with its ancient timbers and crooked lines, is another of Lavenham's notable buildings, constructed soon after the Guild of Corpus Christi was granted its charter in 1529. The Guildhall has a chequered history: after the prosperous wool years, it became a prison and then a workhouse. These days, it houses a musuem devoted to the history of Lavenham, with fascinating displays depicting 500 years of history, farming and industry, including the local railway. Behind it is a delightful walled garden which includes the recently restored 19thC parish lock-up and local mortuary.

The Priory is another of the town's fine buildings. Originally the dwelling of Benedictine monks, it was later acquired by a rich cloth merchant after the Dissolution of the Monasteries in 1536. You can still see the Lavenham wool-mark carved in plaster on the outside wall. Outside is an old couryard and and a herb garden with an unusual design. Round off

Lavenham.

your visit with a cream tea at the Priory's Refectory restaurant.

The Old Grammar School in Barn Street is also worth some of your time (it was attended by John Constable), as is Shilling Grange, the home of Jane Taylor, who wrote 'Twinkle Twinkle Little Star'. And don't miss The Swan Hotel, with its bar counter scored with the signatures of American military personnel based nearby during the Second World War.

The best way to see Lavenham's wealth of historic buildings is to follow the trail described in the illustrated leaflet published by the Suffolk Preservation Society and available at the Tourist Information Centre. There are also various guided tours of Lavenham, and a pleasant walk along the town's disused railway line, extendable to Long Melford and Sudbury.

ACCOMMODATION AND FOOD
The town attracts thousands of visitors, and many of the hotels, inns and other places to stay occupy its historic buildings. Here is a cross-section of accommodation possibilities to suit all budgets. For more information, contact the Tourist Infor-mation Office, Lady Street, Lavenham, Suffolk CO10 9RA; tel. 01787 248207 (summer only), or the Tourist Information Office, 6 Angel Hill, Bury St Edmunds, Suffolk IP33 1UZ; tel. 01284 *757083.*

SLEEPING AND EATING

HOTELS AND INNS

LAVENHAM
Swan; *High Street; tel. 01787 247477.* Magnificent timbered inn dating from the 15thC, featuring examples of Elizabethan woodwork, plenty of beams and a minstrels' gallery in the stunning restaurant. Smart, well-furnished and appointed bedrooms, public areas with great character and good English cooking. Upmarket hotel with room prices to match.

Great House; *Market Place; tel. 0787 24731; restaurant closed Sun evening and all Mon.* Overlooking the Guildhall, this elegant restaurant with a few rooms dates from the 14thC and boasts an imposing Georgian façade. Noted for its creative French cuisine and four charming, bedrooms.

Angel; *Market Place; tel. 01787 247388.* Quaint old inn preserving much of its 15thC character. Welcoming bar with beams and open fire, serving home-cooked bar food and excellent range of real ales. Comfortable bedrooms.

LONG MELFORD
Bull; *Hall Street; tel. 01787 378494.* Originally the great hall of a medieval manor and an inn since 1580, this fine timbered building exudes charm and character, notably well-preserved interior carvings. Comfortably accom-modation. Afternoon teas.

Black Lion; *The Green; tel. 01787 880307.* Family-run coaching inn near the 15thC church with individually decorated bedrooms and

seasonally changing menu featuring sound home-cooking.

BRADFIELD COMBUST
Bradfield House; *Bradfield Combust; tel. 01284 386301; closed one week Christmas; restaurant only Sun evening.* Half-timbered, 17thC country house operating as a restaurant with rooms. Antique furnishings, English and provincial French cooking (dinner only) and four delightful bedrooms.

BED-AND-BREAKFAST

LAVENHAM
Old Rectory; *Nedging, near Hadleigh, 6 miles/10 km E of Lavenham; tel. 01449 740745.* Carefully renovated Georgian house situated in a peaceful hamlet and surrounded by beautiful countryside. Informal atmosphere, comfortable accom-modation and dinner served *en famille.*

Red House; *29 Bolton Street, Lavenham; tel. 01787 248074; no credit cards.* Victorian house with attractive rooms, comfortable sitting room and large sunny garden. Dinner by arrangement.

Street Farm; *Brent Eleigh, 2 miles/3 km SE of Lavenham; tel. 01787 247271; closed Nov–Feb, no credit cards.* High ceilings and beams grace comfortable and spacious bedrooms at this charming farmhouse close to the village centre. Well decorated and furnished.

Brighthouse Farm; *Lawshall, 5 miles/8 km NW of Lavenham; tel. 01284 830385; no credit cards.*

Timbered Georgian farm-house set in 3 acres of gardens. Homely accommodation and winter log fires. Self-catering units.

CAMPING

There are few camping and caravanning sites in the area, the nearest being at **Brighthouse Farm,** *Melford Road, Lawshall, near Bury St Edmunds, tel. 01284 830385.* Flat, grassy 3-acre site; good facilities, electric hook-ups.

FOOD

In addition to the hotels and inns mentioned above, the area offers a reasonable choice of restaurants, including numerous places for afternoon tea. Above-average pub food can be found at the **Peacock Inn,** **Chelsworth,** *tel. 01449 740758;* **Bell Inn, Kersey,** *tel. 01473 823229;* **Beehive, Horringer,** *near Bury St Edmunds, tel. 01284 735260;* **Crown, Bildeston,** *tel. 01449 740510* and the **Brewers Arms, Rattleden,** *near Stowmarket, tel. 01449 736377.*

For a special evening out, try **Scutchers Restaurant,** *tel. 01787 310200* or **Chimneys Restaurant,** *tel. 01787 379806* in **Long Melford**; also **Mabey's Brasserie, Sudbury,** *tel. 01787 374298* and the grand country-house surroundings of **Hintlesham Hall, Hintlesham,** *near Hadleigh, tel. 01473 652334.* Light lunches and afternoon teas can be had at the **Sue Ryder Coffee Room,** *Cavendish, tel. 01787 280252* and **Corn-Craft Tea Room, Monks Eleigh,** *tel. 01449 740456.*

Finchingfield and Great Bardfield

*This relaxing walk, starting from the picturesque village of
Finchingfield and following the banks of the River Pant to the village
of Great Bardfield, shows the Essex countryside at its best. Take the
opportunity to spot the variety of birds which inhabit the trees and
bushes along the river or even catch a fleeting glimpse of a kingfisher
as it disappears around the next bend in the river. The riverbanks are
muddy in wet weather.*

Finchingfield.

Start *The Green,
Finchingfield;
TL685328. Free parking
on the road by the
village green.*

Route directions

From village sign on green,
follow minor road beside
house called Mildmay, then
in 100 yds (90 m), take
waymarked footpath right.
Cross footbridge over river,
immediately left along enclosed footpath,
then keep right through copse and walk
alongside the river. Cross two planked
bridges, then shortly pass through lower
end of garden and continue parallel with
river on waymarked path through paddock
to a track. Cross track, following path to
right of hedge opposite, then ignore stile
left and follow field edge round to iron
bridge. Cross bridge, pass through gate
ahead and just beyond white pargeted mill
house, right between trees and farm
buildings to locate stile in top left-hand
corner. Cross field, through gate then
follow left-hand edge of field to cross stile.
Proceed along right-hand edge of field,
then in 50 yds (45 m), right over planks on
to footpath between houses to a road, and
left into Great Bardfield. Right by village
green, and take signposted footpath right
beside Vine pub. Cross stile at end of car
park and follow waymarker to further stile.
Right down to two stiles
and plank bridge, then
follow worn path across
field to a gate. Keep to good
path to stile, then right

Essentials

Easy 4 miles (6 km);
2½ hours; mostly flat;
map Ordnance Survey
1:50 000 Landranger
Map 167, Chelmsford
and Harlow.
Terrain Footpaths,
riverside walks, grass
tracks; minor road.

along field edge and cross
concrete footbridge on
right, just before farm
buildings. Left alongside
river, cross stile by sluice
and electricity station and
continue to further stile.
Turn right uphill, climb
stile and left along minor
road. Bear right,
signposted Pitley Farm,
then in 50 yds (45 m), right
over waymarked stile and
climb short hill before
bearing left through wide
gap in hedge. Continue
along left-hand edge of
field, cross arrowed
planked bridge, then keep to left-hand side
of next field for 100 yds (92 m) to turn left
through small gap in hedge and cross a
planked bridge. Turn left, follow track
round to right and remain on this now
grassy track for ¾ mile (1.2 km) back into
Finchingfield.

• **FINCHINGFIELD** The quintessential
English village with fine church, restored
windmill, attractive white painted cottages
and period houses nestling around a large
green, complete with white railed pond.
The Church of St John the Baptist has a
Norman tower and a Georgian-style bell-
cote and is worth a visit; a village walk
guide is available from here. Several pubs,
tearooms and restaurants.

• **GREAT BARDFIELD** A bustling village with
plenty of character, thatched cottages,
elegant half-timbered buildings, period
houses and the beautifully
restored Gibraltar
Windmill (a private house),
which dominates the
skyline above the village.

FOOD AND DRINK
Pubs and tearooms in
both villages.

Lavenham and Brent Eleigh

A short, pleasant walk from the delightful village of Lavenham; views over the Suffolk countryside.

Start *Free car park in Church Street, Lavenham, TL 915490.*

Route directions

Right out of car park, then take second right down Water Street. At the bottom, by the common, bear left to join unclassified road and then right along no through road to reach Clayhill Farm. Keep ahead along grass track to join path through the trees (Hill House Farm on left), and stay on path for 1½ miles (2 km) to meet road. Turn right, remaining on road to Brent Eleigh, with short diversion to visit Church of St Mary. Cross river bridge, keep ahead, signposted Hadleigh/ Lavenham, and soon cross A1141 into no through road. Continue over hill and turn right on to waymarked footpath by brick bridge over stream. Follow right-hand edge of field to concrete drive by Hill Farm, and keep ahead to follow arrowed footpath through avenue of trees. Keep alongside ditch and hedge, following markers ahead. Shortly turn right with waymarker, then left towards farm buildings. Right by pond,

Essentials

Easy 5 miles/8 km; 2½ hours; a level walk; *map* Ordnance Survey 1:50 000 Landranger Map 155, Bury St Edmunds and Sudbury. **Terrain** Footpaths, tracks and some minor roads.

Water Street, Lavenham.

just before Bear Lane Farm Cottage, and follow field edge to join farm drive. Turn right, pass Weaners Farm and stay on road to Lavenham. To return to car park, take footpath left after housing estate.

• **LAVENHAM** This attractive medieval village was once one of the richest in the country, its fortune made from the local cloth and wool industries. The village retains many of the fine half-timbered houses from that period, including the 16thC Guildhall, a splendid 15thC hall house – Little Hall – the magnificent Swan Inn and an old priory. See also page 90.

• **BRENT ELEIGH**, a small village, has a mixture of house styles, including some thatched cottages and the interesting period timber and brick farmhouse, Corner Farm. The Church of St Mary dates from 1280 and features 17thC box pews and rare medieval wall paintings behind the altar.

FOOD AND DRINK
A wealth of places in Lavenham; pub at Brent Eleigh.

93

Constable country

You'll be delighted with this route if you enjoy the tranquil scenes expressed in Constable's paintings.

Start *Dedham. Free car park in Mill Lane (B1029), TM 058333.*

Route directions From the car park, enter village via Mill Lane and turn left at the Marlborough Head. Walk along High Street into Brook Street and where it curves right, left into drive of Muniment House. Cross stile on left to a track, signposted Flatford. Beyond another stile, follow track right to further stile (NT sign), then continue through three gates (Dedham Rare Breeds Farm left), before taking worn path across meadow to reach riverbank. Cross sluice, then follow riverbank (waymarkers) for ³/₄ mile (1.2 km) to Flatford. Cross stile next to weighted gate and turn right along track beside river. (To visit NT properties and John Constable Exhibition, cross bridge ahead and turn right.) Keep to riverbank, pass restored Flatford Lock and to the rear of Flatford Mill; then cross concrete water barrier. Turn immediately left by Lower Barn Farm sign, cross two stiles, pass under power lines, and turn right (waymarker) just beyond another stile (Judas Gap Weir on left). Climb a further stile, follow path between bushes, then along track to pass under railway bridge and turn left towards Manningtree Station. Just before the station, opposite car park, turn right up a footpath between iron gates. Gently ascend the winding footpath, enter Lawson churchyard (interesting church to visit). Go through gate opposite main churchyard gates, and cross two stiles in the right-hand corner, signposted Essex Way. Climb further stile, left along track to reach a road, then left and in 100 yds (92 m) right into field. Bear diagonally right with waymarker, pass under power lines, then head for ladder stile in field corner by a line of trees. Keep ahead to a stile and track, turn left and follow the track right. Remain on track, soon to bear right to

Essentials

Easy 6 miles/10 km; 4¹/₂ hours; mainly flat; *map* Ordnance Survey 1:50 000 Landranger Map 168, Colchester. **Terrain** Meadows by the River Stour; footpaths, tracks and a minor road through farmland, pasture and woods.

descend to left of house. Here you have a choice of signposted tracks. Either bear right (Essex Way) – generally very muddy – or, proceed ahead (courtesy route) following track for 50 yds (45 m), then right through woods to footbridge and stile. Continue straight on, cross railway line and keep ahead across stiles to reach a road. Climb stile almost opposite and bear diagonally left across field to stile and lane. Turn right, keeping to road for ³/₄ mile (1.2 km) to join B1029 at Castle House. Turn right, then left down Coopers Lane, soon to turn right along metalled drive between cottages (signposted). Pass through an iron gate and stile behind pink farmhouse, then keep to left-hand side of paddock to cross stile and footbridge into field. Turn right, following field edge to stile and footbridge in far-right hand corner. Keep ahead through two kissing gates, climb stile into playing field, turn right to pass behind pavilion and turn left down The Drift back into Dedham.

• **DEDHAM** Apart from its history and well-preserved houses, this attractive village has connections with two famous painters, John Constable and Sir Alfred Munnings, and the American Civil War hero, General William. T. Sherman. Dedham Mill and Lock can still be seen, although the original mill was replaced by a Victorian one, converted for residential use. Dedham Rare Breeds Farm is adjacent to the car park.

• **FLATFORD** The picturesque Flatford Mill and Willy Lott's cottage of Constable fame are now owned by the National Trust. They can be viewed from the outside but there is no public access to the buildings as they are leased to the Field Studies Council. Also see the John Constable Exhibition in Bridge Cottage, where they serve tea.

FOOD AND DRINK

Café and pubs in Torcross, notably the Start Bay Inn (fresh fish), and the Tower Inn and Queen's Arms in Slapton.

The Saffron Walk – Newport to Great Newport to Great Chesterford

The first part of the walk follows the Harcamlow Way, a designated long-distance footpath. It gives you the chance to explore Saffron Walden before crossing rolling farming countryside to pass through Little Chesterford to Great Chesterford. The prominent church steeples of the towns and villages stand out against the background of the extensive farmland. The fields can be muddy in wet weather.

Start *Newport Railway Station, TL 522335. Station car park (fee) on the west side of the railway and some free parking in the lane on the east side.*

Planning

This is a straight-line route. The return journey from Great Chesterford is by regular trains throughout the day – the route ends at the station.

Route directions

From station car park, cross footbridge over railway and turn left along lane. In 50 yds (45 m), right on to waymarked footpath and cross field. Pass through gap in hedge and proceed left-handed around field edge, soon to turn left along line of fir trees to a road. Turn right, then in about 50 yds (46 m), left along hedged footpath. Follow worn path across field, cross plank bridge and turn right (waymarked) through woodland. Climb stile, turn left uphill, negotiate another stile and proceed to top left-hand corner of field. Turn left by an oak tree, then right to follow waymarkers through two fields to footbridge and bear left beside woodland to reach further footbridge. Keep to well-arrowed route around field edge to reach copse and busy B1052. Follow footpath opposite through woodland. On emerging from trees, bear right over stream and then left along track to road. Cross into drive to Abbey Farm, following it to the pretty village of Audley End. (Refreshments at the post office stores.) Walk through village (Audley End House left), and turn right along road beside

brick wall. After about 500 yds (460 m) left through iron gateway on to footpath across the estate. Exit by another iron gate and follow road ahead into Saffron Walden, via George Street and Hill Street. At the end of Hill Street, turn left (mini-roundabout) on to B1052 to climb Common Hill and Castle Hill. Left by Victory pub down Catons Lane and follow sunken footpath at its end, then walk between fields to reach farm drive (Westley Farm). Turn left, then in 100 yds (92 m) take arrowed path right, signposted Springwell. Follow edge of two fields, turning left with waymarker to pass under power lines, and follow track for 1 mile/1.6 km to Springwell Farm and B184. Turn right, then left on to signposted footpath opposite Springwell Nursery. Keep to edge of field and paddock to kissing gate in lower left-hand corner, then cross further paddock towards church to another kissing gate and road. Turn right through Little Chesterford, soon bearing right on to track beside Orchard Bungalow. Then follow worn path to left of hedge to reach the road in Great Chesterford. Turn left, pass Crown and Thistle pub, then left along B1383 and after crossing river bridge, bear right to railway station for the return journey to Newport.

Essentials

Easy 9 miles/14.5 km; 5½ hours; mostly flat; *maps* Ordnance Survey 1:50 000 Landranger Map 154, Cambridge and Newmarket; also Map 167, Chelmsford and Harlow.

Terrain Footpaths, tracks and some minor road sections but mainly through or by fields; mud after rain.

• **NEWPORT** was mentioned in the Domesday Book of 1086 and it grew up as a market town alongside the old road to Cambridge. When this became a turnpike road in the 18thC, Newport continued to flourish, as it did with the coming of the railway in the 19thC. Then Saffron Walden became the more important centre and Newport was eclipsed, its population reverting more

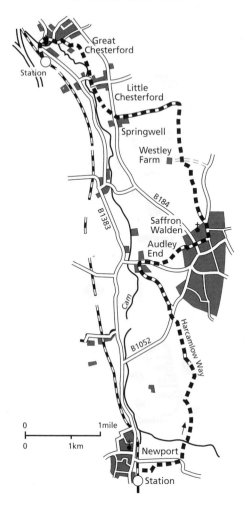

or less entirely to agriculture. However, today Newport is growing once more, due to the reasonable commuting distance to London. The village has many interesting houses from its historic past and St Mary's Church is the oldest building remaining, its size reflecting the importance of the village in earlier times.

• **AUDLEY END** The main attraction here is the large Jacobean house and gardens of Audley End (English Heritage). Both are open to the public.

• **SAFFRON WALDEN** is a medieval town set in the heart of the Essex

countryside and owes its name to its role, until the 18thC, as saffron-producer. The town has some 400 buildings of architectural interest, including the largest church in Essex. The town trail (leaflet available from the Tourist Office) introduces just a few of them.

• **GREAT CHESTERFORD** is a large village which originated in Roman times and once had an important market. Today, many fine old houses remain, adding interest to the final stage of the walk through the village to the railway station.

> **FOOD AND DRINK**
> Good choice in Saffron Walden; teas at Audley End Stores if visiting Audley End House. Pub in Great Chesterford.

Dunwich Heath and Minsmere Levels

The walk starts from the village of Dunwich and crosses heathland. A short walk along the shore is followed by the Minsmere Levels, the famous Royal Society for the Protection of Birds (RSPB) reserve.

Start *Dunwich Beach car park, TM479706, a free car park situated by the beach at the top of St James Street not far from the Ship Inn.*

Planning

The Eel's Foot is an ideal refreshment stop before crossing the dyke and returning to Dunwich.

Route directions

Leave the car park by Beach Road and turn left at the top by the Ship Inn. In a few yds, follow signposted footpath left and climb to the cliffs, noting the remaining tombstones of the graveyard (left) and the Greyfriars ruins (right). Follow Suffolk Coast Path waymarks to join gravel track between houses, then proceed along metalled road. Turn left after Beehive Cottage, signposted Minsmere, on to track, soon to follow path through woods. Cross minor road and continue with coast path signs. Left at crossing of paths and follow coast path to join sandy track. Ignore National Trust markers to left and continue across heathland, bearing left towards white coastguard cottages. Right along the road and through car park (National Trust tearoom, shop, WCs and observatory), then bear right down path to beach, heading towards Sizewell Power Station. Walk beside Minsmere bird reserve, taking the opportunity to use the public hide by the beach path, and turn right through waymarked left-hand gate at a brick sluice. Keep to left of dyke (ruins of old chapel or pillbox on left), for 1½ miles (2.4 km), via five stiles, then go through two gates and climb stile on to worn path leading to Eastbridge. Turn right along road, pass Eel's Foot pub, cross bridge over dyke (look out for otters here) and follow

Essentials

Moderate 8¾ miles/14 km; 4 hours; mostly flat; **map** Ordnance Survey 1:50 000 Landranger Map 156, Saxmundham. **Terrain** Tracks across heathland, farmland and through mixed woodland, plus a stroll beside the sea; mud after rain.

FOOD AND DRINK
Beach Café and Ship Inn at Dunwich; tearoom on Dunwich Heath (NT); Eel's Foot in Eastbridge.

road round to right, signposted Minsmere. At next right-hand bend, continue ahead along bridleway (white sign) through woodland, then continue between fields and across another Minsmere access road back into woodland. Ignore footpath sign right, keeping to bridleway as it becomes a wide sandy track across heathland. The track narrows to a path between bushes to rejoin outward route. Here, turn left to follow circular walk along track, pass through Mount Pleasant Farm and continue ahead to a road. Take footpath opposite, then turn right at bottom of track by Sandy Lane Farm following footpath ahead through some bushes, ignoring arrowed footpath right, soon to join gravel drive to some cottages. At end of drive right along St James Street back to the car park.

• **DUNWICH** It is worth the short walk around the town to view the church and some interesting houses. The museum in St James Street has a model of Minsmere and its port in earlier times, before coastal erosion put it out of business. There are still a few fishing boats; fresh fish available.

Dunwich Heath and coastguard cottages are managed by the National Trust, providing a pleasant area for walks and a licensed tearoom for refreshments.

• **MINSMERE RSPB NATURE RESERVE** was established in 1949 after the discovery of four pairs of breeding avocets in the wet pastures which were flooded during the war as a counter-invasion measure. The site has developed into one of the RSPB's prime reserves, with more than 220 species of birds recorded annually.

97

Ramsholt and the River Deben

This area is known locally as the Peninsula and as such has less traffic and fewer roads than some other parts of Suffolk. The route is an enjoyable ramble over colourful heathland, farmland and along the banks of the River Deben where a variety of sea birds and waders can be seen. There are river views of Woodbridge and the Tide Mill.

Start *Ramsholt; free car park just above the Ramsholt Arms, TM307415.*

Route directions

From car park, descend towards quay and turn right along sandy path below the Ramsholt Arms. After about 50 yds (46 m), take arrowed bridleway right, pass through hedge and follow meandering path uphill towards Ramsholt's church. Continue ahead along sandy track, pass to left of church, then at T-junction of tracks, turn right to reach an unclassified road. Turn left, cross B1083 and take sandy track opposite to Shottisham. Cross the village road and follow lane ahead by the Sorrel Horse pub. Pass church, then at end of lane turn right in front of Tower Cottage and at the garden perimeter, take the footpath left through bushes. Continue ahead uphill, cross stile and field to enter woodland, soon to turn left along sandy track. Continue about 1 mile (1.6 km). Pass Broxtead House, then descend short hill before turning right along another track, eventually reaching end of Ministry of Defence enclosure. Turn left, pass to right of conifer plantation, then go through wooded area (nature trail) and continue ahead over crossing of tracks to reach iron gates. Continue straight ahead over fields to join a lane opposite a house, following it to junction of B1083 at Bromeswell. Follow footpath opposite, signposted River Deben, to reach Anglo-Saxon cemetery at Sutton Hoo. Turn right (signposted footpath), descend to Little Sutton Hoo, then beyond large white house, look for footpath sign at entrance to Dairy Farm Cottage. Follow path to left of the buildings, pass a pumping station, then keep to left-hand side of field to cross wooden footbridge. Turn left along riverbank, eventually climbing steps into a meadow. Left along field edge, then right by a copse and shortly left with bridleway sign. Right at top of field (waymarked), proceed around end of copse and then bear diagonally right along worn path, passing through hedge on to metalled drive. Continue ahead on waymarked footpath, cross another drive and maintain direction to reach Methersgate. Keep right of outbuildings, turn left in front of Methersgate Hall, then just beyond hall right down metalled drive; in ³/₄ mile (1.2 km) turn right on to sandy track 100 yds (90 m) beyond Cliff Farm. (For the pub or village stores at Sutton continue along metalled drive, turning right at end into village.) At T-junction of tracks, go right and then left along field edge, following track left and passing through double iron gates. Turn right, cross stile by gate, then left at T-junction of tracks, soon passing two farm cottages to meet metalled drive by Sutton Hall. Turn right, then at thatched cottages in Sutton Street turn right to follow the drive to Pettistree Hall and Riding School. Bear left on to stony track and turn right on to waymarked footpath to reach River Deben. Bear left along grass track beside river with Shottisham Creek on your left. Climb the bank, pass over Ramsholt sluice, and proceed along riverbank. Keep to well-waymarked and worn path parallel to, or beside river for about 1 mile (1.6 km) back to Ramsholt.

• **RAMSHOLT** is now a popular sailing centre, brimming with modern fibreglass boats. But as recently as the the 1950s barges and sailing smacks were the most numerous craft and before that smugglers were not unknown. A light from the church tower would signal the all-clear to the smugglers to land their contraband.

Essentials

Moderate 13 miles/21 km; 7 hours; mostly flat; *map* Ordnance Survey 1:50 000 Landranger Map 169, Ipswich and the Naze.

Terrain Farm tracks, sandy heath tracks, riverbanks and some metalled drives; riverside paths muddy after rain.

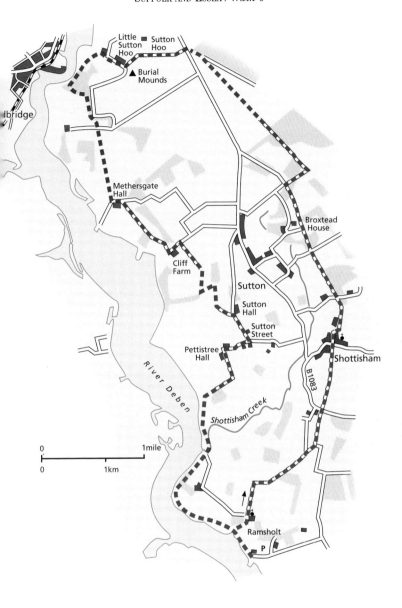

All Saint's Church has an unusual round tower and the line of the original thatched roof can be seen.

• **SUTTON HOO** has a group of ancient burial mounds, where in 1939 an Anglo-Saxon ship containing some magnificent treasure was discovered. The site can be viewed from the footpath and is open from Easter to September on weekend afternoons only.

• **WOODBRIDGE** still retains its charm. It is pleasant to walk around, and has the added interest of the Quay, a marina and two fascinating mills – the six-storey Buttrams Mill (1835) and the carefully restored, 18thC Tide Mill, both open to the public May to September.

99

The Stour Valley

These are pleasant, comfortable day walks along the higher part of the Stour Valley, with beautiful, wide views over rolling farmland. Some sections incorporate the route of a disused railway with the old Victorian iron-and-brick railway bridges still intact: you are taken back to the age of steam, when locomotives seemed to blend into the country scene. Tranquil river meadows and the lazily meandering Stour provide a welcome contrast to the vast arable fields of present-day farming. You also have the chance to explore the market town of Sudbury and some charming and unspoilt villages.

Start in Bures, at the village hall in Nayland Road, or at the railway station (no overnight parking), TL905340. For the shorter version, start at Sudbury: free car park by Somerfield supermarket, TL876409.

Planning

You have a choice of a two-day walk starting at Bures with a stay overnight in Long Melford, returning from Clare by bus and train; or two separate day-long walks, returning to the starting points by bus, train, or both. In addition, Day 1 can be shortened by starting from Sudbury.

Day 1, full length, is from Bures via Sudbury to Long Melford.

Day 2 is Long Melford to Clare, via Cavendish.

Route directions

Day 1 From Bures village hall turn left along Nayland Road into Church Square. Left by church, soon to cross river and turn right on to signposted footpath opposite Swan Inn. From railway station turn left into The Paddocks, then right along Station Hill to junction with B1508 and turn left along the footpath opposite the Swan Inn. Shortly, join and follow track to left and pass between fields, following waymarked Stour Valley Path through woodland. Cross stile, proceed ahead by river (views), keeping left of concrete pillbox to cross railway line via stiles and

Essentials

Moderate Day 1/Walk 7 is 11 miles (18 km), 7 hours, but can be shortened to 4½ miles (7 km), 2½ hours. **Day 2/ Walk 8** is 10 miles (16 km), 6½ hours; fairly flat; *map* Ordnance Survey 1:50 000 Landranger Map 155, Bury St Edmunds and Sudbury.

Terrain Varied combination of footpaths, bridleways, tracks, disused railway routes, river meadows and short distances on minor roads; some sections muddy.

soon reach a road. Bear right through Lamarsh, turning left on to footpath opposite farm buildings, beyond church. Follow waymarked path right at top of field, ignore stile left and continue to a road. Turn left, then in 200 yds (180 m) turn right through iron gate at Valley Farm. Follow waymark, climb stile, descend track to gate and pass farmhouse to cross stile at rear. Walk along left-hand edge of field to wooden bridge and stile in corner and bear right uphill to further stile. Turn left along lower edge of field, cross stile and shortly descend to track by marker. Ignore Stour Valley sign and turn left down field edge; in 50 yds (45 m) bear right across field, following line of pylons to minor road. Take arrowed track opposite, soon following left-hand edge of field. Go through gateway and eventually reach stile into paddock. Walk along grass track, bearing right to take track between barns and farmhouse (Fenn Farm) and join drive to reach the road. Turn left then right, signposted Henny Church. At church, turn left by brick building, rejoining Stour Valley Path and proceed down left-hand side of field to stile, and continue to next stile. Follow footpath sign right, cross footbridge, walk along field edge, keeping to markers uphill and right across open farmland with far-reaching views. Cross stile, follow footpath through trees to playing field by housing estate. Turn right, cross road and walk through Kone Vale,

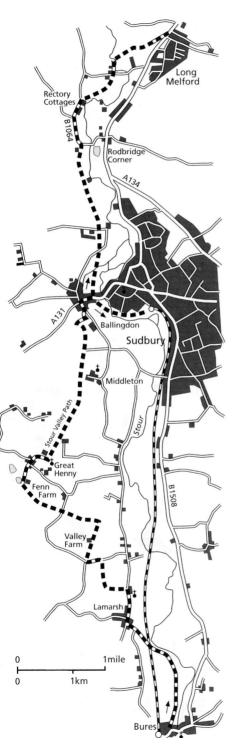

ACCOMMODATION
Several hotels in **Long Melford**, including the timbered **Bull Hotel** (*tel. 01787 378494*) and the **Black Lion** (*tel. 01787 312356*). The noticeboard outside the post office lists numerous bed-and-breakfasts, but in high season it is advisable to contact Sudbury Tourist Information Office (tel. 01787 881320), or Bury St Edmunds Tourist Information Office (tel. 01284 764667) for accommodation lists – and to book ahead.

soon to bear left with marker into Ballingdon Street (A131). Cross over into car park by old railway bridge and climb path on to disused railway track.

You can return to Bures from here by turning left over the bridge and following the railway route for ³/₄ mile (1.2 km) into Sudbury. Locate railway station and use frequent train service back to Bures.

Short version of Day 1
From the free car park in Sudbury, follow the old railway to the bridge in Ballingdon Street (see above); then follow the rest of the route:

Continue along old railway route for 1³/₄ miles (2.8 km), the overgrown banks and adjacent Sudbury Common providing a rich haven for birds, notably goldfinches, flycatchers and kingfishers. Eventually, cross tarmac drive to join footpath leading to B1064 near Rodbridge Corner (picnic area 100 yds / 90 m on right). Turn left and continue for ¹/₂ mile (0.8 km); turn right,

101

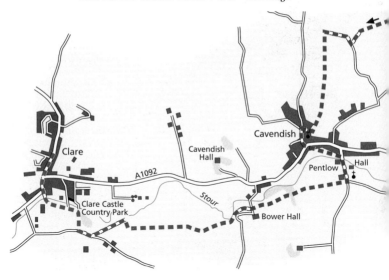

signposted Liston. Pass Rectory Cottages, turn right along footpath, following markers to cross two stiles, then turn right along field edge to further stile and keep ahead to a road (Little Hall). Turn right, then left beyond weatherboard cottage, cross two bridges over weirs and bear left along riverbank. Turn right (waymark) after crossing concrete water barrier and head for waymark by dead tree, soon to pass through kissing gate, then follow track behind industrial buildings. Turn right into lane (Cock and Bell Lane) between cottages and proceed into Long Melford.

To return to Sudbury, use the frequent bus service (several routes).

Day 2

Start In Long Melford at the car park at end of Bull Lane, or along the wide main street, TL864459.

From the green, at the northern end of Long Melford's main street, follow the A134 signposted Kentwell Hall. In 100 yds (92 m) turn left along drive to hall, then just before the main gates follow waymarked path left and pass through gate. Turn right immediately before next gate to cross stile on to a track and keep ahead to reach a crossing of tracks. Turn left by signpost and follow worn path for 1 mile (1.6 km), then descend between farm buildings (Cranmore Green Farm) to a road. Turn right, then in 200 yds (190 m), before reaching Mill Farm, turn left and cross iron bridge. Bear right to cross a

wooden bridge, then turn right and proceed alongside ditch, following waymarkers straight on. Divert slightly to cross brick-and-earth bridge over further ditch, then maintain direction, soon to climb the bank on right (waymarker) to reach a road. Turn left and in 50 yds (45 m), turn left along defined field path leading to Glemsford church. Pass through churchyard to village road, then follow it through the Broadway and climb hill to Tye Green by village sign. Turn right by grass triangle into Cavendish Lane, then just beyond Clockhouse Farm turn right into New Street. Pass by thatched cottage on to farm track, then turn left before New Street Farm along field edge. Enter next field with hedge on left, then at end of hedge maintain direction across large field, keeping right of small copse and pond. Head for Nissen hut and descend to road by paddock and concrete drive by September Cottage. Turn right, then left following waymark before iron gate and barn and keep to right-hand side of field. At next waymark, turn left uphill and follow arrowed path for 1 mile (1.6 km) to Cavendish church. Leave churchyard by main gates, turn left, then left again along A1092 and take arrowed footpath right, opposite The Bull. Follow signs closely through small housing estate and gardens, do not cross new bridge but follow stream left to pass behind fence and cross footbridge. Cross stile, follow markers left to further stile and road. Turn right, pass Pentlow House, then take bridleway right

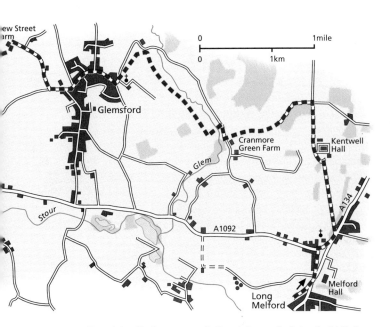

at road junction. Keep right of hedge, descend through woodland, then follow field edge to join a track below Bower Hill Farm. Bear right on to bridleway by converted barn and brick pumping station and remain on path through fields, eventually reaching marker pointing right down to track by river. Turn left, then right on reaching road and in 200 yds (180 m) turn right again along arrowed footpath. Cross steel bridge, head for kissing gate by brick building, but ignore gate and turn left along top of field to cross wooded bridge with stiles. Walk alongside river and shortly turn right over disused railway bridge into Clare Castle and Country Park. Exit by Maltings Lane and turn right along A1092 into centre of Clare.

Return To return to Long Melford or Sudbury use bus service 236 which leaves from the Market Cross in Market Hill. The frequent train service completes the return journey back to Bures.

• **Bures** A pretty little village with fine half-timbered houses and an elegant church dating from the 13th to 15thC. Chapel Barn is an old thatched building that was once attached to the former Earl's Colne Priory.

• **Sudbury** A busy little market town with Saxon origins set in the heart of the Stour Valley. Attractive winding streets of 17th and 18thC houses converge on the Market Square and its imposing 15thC church.

Sudbury is famous for being the birthplace and home of painter Thomas Gainsborough (1727–88). The Georgian town house in which he was born displays more of the artist's work than any other gallery.

• **Long Melford** is one of Suffolk's finest villages, its impressive mile-long main street lined with fine old buildings and dominated by a magnificent 15thC church. It is a delightful place to stroll round – there are more than 30 antique shops, numerous other specialist shops and several timbered inns. Melford Hall (NT), a turreted brick Tudor mansion with 18thC and Regency interiors, is well worth a visit, as is nearby Kentwell Hall, a mellow red-brick and moated Tudor mansion.

• **Cavendish** is the perfect Suffolk village, with the noble Church of St Mary rising above half-timbered thatched cottages clustering around an idyllic village green. The 16thC Old Rectory was used by Sue Ryder as a home for concentration-camp victims and houses an interesting museum, as well as a tearoom serving light lunches.

• **Clare** is a market town with medieval roots. There are the ruins of a Norman castle, built in 1090, surrounded by a country park; extensive remains of the first Augustinian priory in England, founded in 1248; and numerous old timber-framed houses, many of which display intricately decorated plasterwork (pargeting), notably Ancient House in the High Street.

Introduction
North Norfolk Coast

The North Norfolk Coast, designated an Area of Outstanding Natural Beauty, has been described as 'a long way from anywhere' and 'a remote corner of England that has been able to hold on to its traditions and ancient secrets'. It is easy, therefore, to see why the best-selling thriller writer Jack Higgins set his classic adventure yarn *The Eagle Has Landed* on this delightfully undiscovered stretch of coastline.

War relics

The book, about a wartime plot to kidnap and assassinate Winston Churchill while he was spending the weekend at a country house in East Anglia, vividly conveys the feel and atmosphere of the North Norfolk Coast much of which has hardly changed at all since the Second World War. You can stroll beside expansive salt marshes and sand dunes stretching into the distance and still spot relics of war – old pillboxes, tank traps and the crumbling remains of machine-gun posts.

Higgins describes the area as 'a strange, mysterious sort of place, the kind that made the hair lift on the back of the head. Sea creeks and mud flats, the great pale reeds merging with the mist and somewhere out there, the occasional cry of a bird, the invisible beat of wings.' He writes also of 'the little villages that you can find once in the maze of little lanes, and then never find again.'

GETTING THERE

The North Norfolk Coast is one of the least accessible parts of England. There are no motorways in the area, but the region is served by an adequate network of roads, including the A140, A148 and A149. From London it is best reached via the M11 to Cambridge, then the A10 to King's Lynn, or via the A11 to Norwich. Trains from London and elsewhere stop at King's Lynn, Cromer and Norwich and there are various bus and coach services throughout the county.

Seaside walking

Exploring on foot is the best way to capture the flavour of *The Eagle Has Landed*. The 93-mile (150-kilometre) Peddars Way and North Norfolk Coast Path, one of Britain's most popular national trails, offers plenty of scope. Consisting of two paths joined together to form one continuous thread and officially opened by the Prince of Wales in 1986, the route begins near Thetford on the Suffolk/Norfolk border and follows ancient tracks and Roman roads north to meet the sea near Hunstanton, at the point where it sweeps round towards the Wash.

Your first objective on reaching the coast is Holme-next-the-Sea, which may well have been a port at one time. Certainly the Romans used Holme as a convenient base from which to cross the Wash en route to the Lincolnshire coast. Today this pleasant village survives as a popular destination for walkers heading for the sand dunes and day trippers intent on enjoying the sea views. The nearby nature reserve and bird sanctuary tend also to draw visitors in large numbers.

Heritage Coast

From here, Peddars Way heads for Cromer, where it terminates, meandering delightfully between quiet towns, old ports and sleepy villages. The views over Norfolk's Heritage Coast are breathtaking and in places there is ample evidence of how the local communities have battled for survival against the destructive forces of the sea.

Beyond Holme, the trail makes for Wells-next-the-Sea, once the chief port between Yarmouth and King's Lynn. It may no longer be as busy or as prosperous but with its modest fleet of sprat, crab, shrimp and whelk boats and its community of ropemakers and chandlers, Wells still thrives as a sustainable fishing port, retaining the timeless charm of a small coastal town. Visitors and holidaymakers make for the old harbour, stroll along the quay and admire its High Street of striking houses and cottages. The coast's silting process has resulted in many of the old ports now being some way from the sea and not 'next the sea' as they used to be. Sadly, Wells-next-the-Sea is no exception.

> **WEATHER**
> The weather on the North Norfolk Coast is changeable and walkers should be prepared for breezy conditions. An unexpectedly cool wind can easily catch you out — even at the height of summer.

Blakeney

To the east of Wells, the Peddars Way and North Norfolk Coast Path runs alongside a vast, bleak landscape of salt marshes, creeks and mudflats before reaching Blakeney. The medieval parish church of St Nicholas, dedicated to the patron saint of seafarers, is one of the town's great landmarks and can be seen from miles around standing guard over Blakeney, watching the estuary of the River Glaven where it flows towards Blakeney Point, a distinctive elongated shingle spit which protrudes like a gnarled finger into the North Sea. Common seals breed on this stretch of coast and the spit is also the home of the oystercatcher and ringed plover, among many other waders and seabirds. You can walk out to Blakeney Point or use the local ferry service.

Beyond Blakeney, Cley-next-the-Sea – pronounced 'cly' and once a bustling port – is renowned for its vast expanse of salt marshes, a Mecca for ornithologists and naturalists.

Cromer

From here you can follow the path to Cromer, one of East Anglia's most popular resorts and often dubbed the 'gem of the Norfolk coast'. One of Jane Austen's characters in *Emma* describes Cromer as 'the best of all the sea-bathing places'.

At 160 feet (50 metres), the distinctive tower of the town's church is the highest in the county, overlooking Cromer's old fishing village and rows of hotels. The town is also renowned for its Victorian pier and lifeboat.

Away from the coast there are miles of paths and tracks which allow you to explore a peaceful rural world of flint cottages, pretty windmills, historic villages, picturesque towns and stately homes. Holkham Hall (the magnificent Palladian home of the Earls of Leicester), Sandringham (where members of the Royal Family gather for Christmas and New Year), and the National Trust properties of Blickling Hall and Felbrigg Hall, are probably the most famous.

'Very flat, Norfolk' was one of Noel Coward's many witty observations. No one would dispute that, but within its boundaries is a host of things to see and do. However, the long and invigorating walk alongside Norfolk's desolate and marshy coastline, described as probably the finest of its kind in Europe, provides the greatest thrill of this section.

WALKING BASE

Burnham Market & the Burnhams

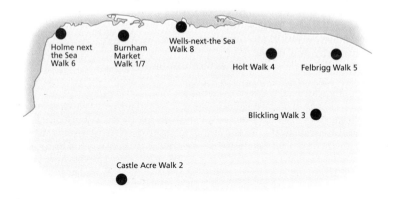

Holme next
the Sea
Walk 6

Burnham
Market
Walk 1/7

Wells-next-the Sea
Walk 8

Holt Walk 4

Felbrigg Walk 5

Blickling Walk 3

Castle Acre Walk 2

Between Hunstanton and Wells-next-the-Sea are a handful of peaceful villages all with the prefix 'Burnham'. Early records suggest they once formed part of a bustling port on Norfolk's wild and treacherous coast. However, the dawning of the railway age signalled the port's death knell and now all that remains of this once thriving community are a few quaint streets and clusters of picturesque cottages.

At the heart of the Burnhams lies Burnham Market, a handsome and civilized small market town with a tiny green and a variety of fine Georgian houses, pretty cottages and upmarket specialist shops lining its wide main street. Enjoying a splendid position overlooking the main street from the top of the green is St Mary's Church. Its tower dates from 1310 and the distinctive battlements (added in 1500) are decorated with sculptures representing Biblical scenes.

Burnham Thorpe is where Horatio Nelson was born in 1758 – his father was rector of the parish between 1755 and 1802. A plaque denotes the site of the rectory. The 13thC Church of All Saints contains several mementoes of him, including a crucifix and a lectern made from timbers taken from HMS *Victory*, There is also a bust of Nelson, and the pubs in the area are a reminder of Britain's greatest seafaring hero – The Lord Nelson, The Victory and The Trafalgar among them.

Burnham Overy Town is also a delight, with its prominent Norman church and a

watermill (1737) over the River Burn, with its three-storey brick-built miller's house. A mile to the north is Burnham Overy Staithe which was built as a port in the early 19thC after navigation upstream to Burnham Overy Town became impossible because of silting and the receding sea. The village boasts a striking watermill, whose wheel remains intact, a little harbour that attracts small-boat sailors, a row of brick-and-flint cottages overlooking the village millpond, and a beautifully restored windmill (1814), all of which are under the care of the National Trust.

Burnham Norton and Burnham Deepdale are renowned in these parts for their churches with splendid Norman fonts and unusual round Anglo-Saxon towers. Near here is a memorable view of the Burnham Deepdale and Norton Marshes stretching towards Scolt Head Island Nature Reserve and the sea beyond.

The Burnhams, and notably Burnham Market, make an ideal base from which to explore the North Norfolk Coast.

ACCOMMODATION AND FOOD
Burnham Market is small in comparison with other walking bases in this guide, but a very popular destination, especially during summer and on winter weekends. Consequently, accommodation and eating options are surprisingly varied. We list here our favourite choices; more comprehensive lists can be obtained from the Tourist Information Office, Staithe Street, Wells-next-the-Sea, Norfolk NR23 1AN; tel. 01328 710885.

SLEEPING AND EATING

HOTELS AND INNS

BURNHAM MARKET
Hoste Arms; The Green; tel. 01328 738257. Handsome 17thC inn overlooking the green and parish church. Charming bedrooms (four with four-posters) are individually decorated with designer fabrics. Characterful bar, comfortable conservatory and smart dining areas.

MORSTON
Morston Hall; near Blakeney; tel. 01263 741041. Substantial 17thC flint house set in secluded gardens in a small coastal village. A warm welcome, fresh flowers, comfortable bedrooms and accomplished cooking.

TITCHWELL
Titchwell Manor; near Brancaster; tel. 01485 210221. Welcoming, family-run hotel with glorious views of the sea and salt marshes (RSPB reserve). Comfortable bedrooms and an attractive restaurant, specializing in local fish and seafood.

THORNHAM
Lifeboat Inn; near Hunstanton; tel. 01485 512236. 16thC smugglers' inn overlooking unspoilt meadows and Thornham harbour. Beamed bars, open fires and oil lamps. Comfortable pine-furnished bedrooms with views. Bar and restaurant meals.

WELLS-NEXT-THE-SEA
Crown Hotel; tel. 01328 710209. A part-Tudor inn on the village green offering modestly furnished accommodation and generous bar meals.

BED-AND-BREAKFAST

BURNHAM MARKET
Millwood; Herrings Lane; tel. 01328 730152; closed Christmas. Small country house within walking distance of the village green; splendid salt marsh and coastal views.

DOCKING
Holland House; Chequers Street; tel. 01485 518295. Former dower house to Docking Hall featuring spacious, antique-furnished bedrooms and a warm family welcome. Dinner by arrangement.

HEACHAM
Malthouse Farmhouse; Cheney Hill; tel. 01485 670513. Beautifully renovated 17thC farmhouse with walled garden and comfortable rooms. Close to Norfolk Lavender.

WELLS-NEXT-THE-SEA
Ilex House; Bases Road; tel. 01328 710556. Listed Georgian property set in its own grounds close to the centre of Wells.

TITCHWELL
Briarfield Hotel; Main Street, near Brancaster; tel. 01485 210742. Delightful small hotel created from several traditional Norfolk barns and set in landscaped gardens. Restaurant.

CAMPING, and SELF-CATERING HOSTELS

Many of the coastal sites between King's Lynn and Wells-next-the-Sea are large and impersonal and dominated by permanently parked caravans. Smaller, quieter sites in the area include the award-winning *Old Brick Kilns* (also B&B) at *Barney*, near Fakenham *(tel. 01328 878305)*; the peaceful little site within the old walled gardens of *Syderstone Hall*, near *Great Bircham* and *Rickels* campsite in *Stanhoe*, 5 miles/8 km north of Burnham Market *(tel. 01485 518671)*. *Deepdale Farm* at *Burnham Deepdale* has a small site (August only) and cheap bunkhouse accommodation (showers, kitchen) in a converted granary *(tel. 01485 210256)*. Coastal villages offer a wealth of self-catering properties – contact *English Country Cottages* at *Fakenham (tel. 01328 851155)*, *Norfolk Country Cottages (tel. 01225 791199)*, or the tourist office.

FOOD

Worth seeking out: *Three Horseshoes, Warham All Saints (tel. 01328 710547 –* also B&B); *Hare Arms, Docking (tel. 01485 518402)*; *Red Lion, Stiffkey (tel. 01328 830552)*; *Lord Nelson, Burnham Thorpe (tel. 01328 738241)* and the *White Horse, Blakeney (tel. 01263 740574 –* also B&B). The *Windmill Tea Room* in *Great Bircham Windmill* offers delicious teas and lunchtime snacks; *Byfords, Holt* has a civilized atmosphere, good cakes and light meals. For evening dining try *Fishes, Burnham Market (tel. 01328 738588)* and *The Moorings, Wells-next-the-Sea (tel. 01328 710949)*. For fresh local fish and seafood, try *The Old Bakehouse, Little Walsingham (tel. 01328 820454)*.

Around the Burnhams

A delightful short stroll starting from charming Burnham Market and incorporating the tiny hamlets of Burnham Norton and Burnham Overy Town. It is varied and interesting, with the opportunity to extend the walk out along the Peddars Way/Coast Path to explore the breezy salt marsh and its rich birdlife. Along the way you will pass a restored windmill, two historic churches and the remains of a friary, before enjoying a leisurely amble around Burnham Market.

Start *Burnham Market, TF833422. Picturesque village located on the B1155 and B1355, 1 mile (1.6 km) off the A149 coast road between Wells-next-the-Sea and Brancaster. Adequate parking space along the main village street.*

Essentials

Easy 4 miles/6.4 km; 2 hours; mostly flat; **map** Ordnance Survey 1 : 50 000 Landranger Map 132, North West Norfolk.
Terrain Field paths, defined tracks, village streets and country lanes.

Route directions

Walk down main village street taking 'No entry' side of one-way system. Shortly, turn right along Town's Lane, then at Higher Greystones Farm cross stile and follow footpath along field edge, via two more stiles. On reaching open meadows descend steeply, maintaining direction through two gates to partly hidden stone stile leading to hedged track. Follow stony track downhill to lane and cross bridge over River Avon. Follow peaceful lane beside river for ¼ mile (0.4 km), then just beyond junction take waymarked footpath left over stile. Bear right around boggy ground, cross small wooden footbridge visible 100 yds/90 m ahead, then continue along riverbank path for ¼ mile (0.4 km) to reach road bridge. Cross road (not river bridge) and continue beside river to road at New Mill. Along road for ¾ mile (2 km), passing under old railway bridge to reach Loddiswell Station (private residence). Take footpath alongside former railway yard, then in 200 yds (180 m) join old railway track (private path open to public, except first Monday in January). After ¾ mile (1.2 km) pass through small cutting, then cross river via stone railway bridge and immediately take path left to double back along river-

bank. Ignore footpath right and follow river downstream past weir, then through woods and alongside old leat for ¼ mile (0.4 km) to reach open grassy area. Turn right, away from river, follow path uphill beside stream, soon to pass Read's Farm and join farm road, which steeply ascends for ¼ mile (0.4 km) back into Loddiswell.

• **LODDISWELL** Referred to as 'Lodeswilla' in the Domesday Book, the name probably originates from 'Our Lady's Well', one of the many natural springs and wells in the village. The Church of St Michael and All Angels dates from the 13th and 16thC.

Nearby are the Blackdown Rings which form a large earthwork with a motte and inner and outer baileys.

• **RIVER AVON** At Hatch Bridge you can take a short detour right down a cul-de-sac footpath along the riverbank. In spring and early summer the riverside here is a riot of colour from celandines, wild daffodils and garlic – a great spot for a picnic.

• **PRIMROSE RAILWAY LINE** Single-track branch line of the Great Western Railway which ran from South Brent on the edge of Dartmoor to Kingsbridge, via Loddiswell. The picturesque line opened in 1893 and closed 70 years later in 1963, but evidence of the fine Victorian engineering can be still be seen at some of the remaining railway bridges and at Sorley Tunnel, a 660-yd (600-m) tunnel constructed between 1891 and 1893.

FOOD AND DRINK

None along the route. Return to the welcoming Hoste Arms (open all day) for excellent bar meals, afternoon teas, real ale and wines.

Castle Acre and the Nar Valley

The Nar Valley has often been described as 'Norfolk's Holy Land' due to the presence of numerous monastic remains, including the striking ruins of Castle Acre and West Acre priories. The gently rolling landscape and picturesque Nar Valley make this delightfully relaxing walk a real pleasure. Incorporates a section of the Peddars Way.

Start Castle Acre, TF816152. Village located 1 mile (1.6 km) off the A1065 Swaffham to Fakenham road, 4 miles (6.4 km) north of Swaffham. Park in the village centre by the green, or at the Priory, if intending to visit the ruins.

Route directions From the village green walk eastwards passing the parish church. At sharp right-hand bend turn left to visit the impressive ruins of Castle Acre Priory. Return to lane, following it to next sharp right bend by End House and veer off left along wide track. On reaching reed-fringed River Nar, bear left through metal gate to follow waymarked Nar Valley Way. Remain on defined path (can be wet and muddy) parallel with river for 1 mile (1.6 km), passing through belt of trees and crossing rough meadow to footbridge. Continue along fenced path (renovated Mill House left), cross footbridge over River Nar and shortly cross metalled track, remaining on Nar Valley Way. Keep right on merging with wide track, then just before large coniferous trees bear left into broad field (not waymarked) and follow right-hand edge to road. (To visit West Acre – pub, priory remains and church – keep to main track (NVW) and cross River Nar and soon turn left along village lane.) Cross road, go up gently ascending sandy track, signposted 'public path', to barn, then in field corner turn left (blue arrow) along field edge. Soon cross field boundary right and maintain direction at crossing of tracks. At next junction turn left (Petticoat Drove) towards isolated cottage

Essentials

Moderate 6 miles (10 km); 3½ hours. Gently undulating; *map* Ordnance Survey 1:50 000 Landranger Map 132, North West Norfolk. **Terrain** Pleasant mix of wide tracks, waymarked footpaths and quiet country lanes. Paths close to the River Nar can be wet and muddy in winter.

(Fingerhill Cottage) and gradually descend back into valley, eventually reaching lane near South Acre Hall. Turn right, pass church and manor, then bear off left at 'ford' sign to follow narrow lane to footbridge over River Nar, with excellent views of Castle Acre Priory ruins left. Shortly, cross stile right and proceed along riverbank to further stile and main village access road. Turn left into village, passing ruins on right, then bear left beyond arch back to green.

• **CASTLE ACRE** Pretty village of brick and flint cottages set on a hill overlooking the Nar Valley and dominated by the earthworks of the castle (formerly a manor house) of William de Warenne, son-in-law of William the Conqueror. In the village centre is a 13thC gateway which was part of the original outer bailey. Impressive St James's Church dates from the 15thC and features a fine screen and 15thC pulpit.

• **CASTLE ACRE PRIORY** was founded in 1090, is the oldest Cluniac priory in England and probably the finest monastic remains in East Anglia. Decorated 12thC west front, 16thC gatehouse and prior's lodgings (English Heritage – 01760 755394).

• **WEST ACRE PRIORY** was founded in 1100 for Augustinian canons and despite the few remains was larger than its near neighbour.

• **SOUTH ACRE CHURCH** See the north chapel which contains a decorated monument to Sir Edward Barkham who was Lord Mayor of London in the 17thC.

FOOD AND DRINK
Two pubs (notably the Ostrich) and two tea-rooms in Castle Acre. The Stag (traditional village local) in West Acre.

Blickling Hall and the Bure Valley

*This gentle ramble explores the splendid parkland (access all year)
that surrounds Blickling Hall, and some of the lush meadows in the
peaceful Bure Valley. If you plan to see Blickling this walk makes an
ideal morning outing, before an afternoon tour of the hall and
gardens (open Apr–Oct only).*

Start *Blickling,
TG176285. Village
situated on the B1354 2
miles (3.2 km) north-
west of Aylsham and 11
miles (17.8 km) south of
Cromer. Park in the
National Trust car park
near Hall.*

Route directions:

If beginning walk from car
park, cross grassy area to
information post, drop
down to lane and turn left. (From Hall
entrance take 'no through road' lane right
past Garden Centre and Buckinghamshire
Arms). Enter Blickling Park via gate and
take left fork of two wide tracks, signed
Weavers' Way. Follow track for ¾ mile (1.4
km) to edge of Great Wood (Tower visible
left) and turn right with red arrow along
woodland fringe to view Mausoleum. Return
to main track. Descend through wood, go
through parking area beyond gate and bear
left along metalled lane by cottage. At
hamlet of Itteringham Common (½ mile/0.8
km), just before junction, take waymarked
path right across footbridge and, in winter,
quite boggy pasture to footbridge across
River Bure. Shortly, turn right over further
bridge, then bear half-left towards stile and
cross two dykes. Disregard stile, keeping
right along field edge and footbridge
(river right), then keep left through river
meadow, following field edge left on defined
path gently uphill via stile
towards White House Farm.
Go through arrowed gate
between barn and
farmhouse and turn right
along farm track (Wolterton
Hall visible left) which soon
becomes metalled. Pass
waymarked bridleway left,
signposted Saracen's Head
(1 mile/1.6- km track passing
Wolterton Park to excellent
inn), and brick cottage, then

Essentials

Easy 6 miles (10km);
3 hours; almost level;
map Ordnance Survey
(1:50 000) Landranger
No 133 North East
Norfolk.
Terrain Parkland paths
and drives, good tracks
and field paths and a
short stretch of
metalled road.

where lane curves bear
right with Weavers' Way
along grass-centred track.
Leave track following WW
sign along right-hand edge
of field. Ignore first stile,
cross second stile and keep
left, soon to cross footbridge
over River Bure. Keep to
WW via boardwalk to stile
and lane. Turn right, then
left in front of cottages and
keep to field edge to enter
Blickling Park. At arrowed
post by bench and
woodland, leave WW and turn left along
grassy track (blue arrow) with good views of
lake and hall. From here, follow blue-
arrowed estate walk round lake, then left in
front of hall and on good path skirting
gardens via gates, eventually reaching
metalled access drive to hall. Bear left
towards church, cross gravel path in front of
hall and follow footpath back to car park.

- **BLICKLING HALL** dates from the early
17th century and is one of the finest
Jacobean houses remaining in England.
The Dutch-gabled hall stands inside a
moat and houses collections of fine
furniture, pictures and tapestries. Of
particular note is the 127-ft (40-m) gallery
with its spectacular plaster moulded
ceiling of the 1620s. Tel. 01263 733084.

- **MAUSOLEUM** Built of Portland stone in
1796-97 by Joseph Bonomi, this pyramid
shaped structure houses
the tomb of the 2nd Earl of
Buckinghamshire.

- **TOWER** Castellated brick
grandstand built in 1773 to
overlook the 'Raceground'.

- **ST ANDREW'S CHURCH**
dates from the 13thC and
features interesting
monuments.

FOOD AND DRINK:
The Buckinghamshire
Arms outside the gates
to Blickling Hall offers
food, accommodation
and a summer garden
(tel. 01263 732133).
Lunches and teas in the
National Trust
restaurant adjacent to
the hall.

Holt Country Park and Baconsthorpe Castle

Beginning at Holt Country Park with its delightful woodland trails and wealth of wildlife, this pleasant and varied ramble crosses gently rolling Norfolk countryside to the fascinating ruins of Baconsthorpe Castle and the attractive village of Hempstead. Combine the walk with a relaxing stroll around the charming Georgian town of Holt with its shops and tearooms.

Start *Holt Country Park, TG082378. Free parking, WCs, visitor centre and woodland picnic area located on the B1149 ½ mile (0.8 km) south of Holt.*

Route directions

Walk back towards country park entrance and take wide path left beyond wooded barrier (coloured arrows). At crossing of paths turn right (blue and red), then shortly follow green 'circular walk' marker right. Continue parallel with B-road, climb stile, keep ahead at crossing of paths and climb stile right in few yds. Follow meandering path to stile close to road on woodland fringe and cross field on worn path to stile. Follow markers

Essentials

Easy ¾ mile (12.6 km); 3½ hours; gently undulating. Ordnance Survey 1:50,000 Landranger Map 133 (North East Norfolk).
Terrain Well-waymarked forest trails, farmland tracks, field paths and quiet country lanes.

downhill into coniferous woodland, keeping left at fork to stile on edge of trees. Soon cross stream, bear left through rough grassland, then turn right uphill through trees and keep ahead at top along wide farm track towards barn. Bear left round barn, then right along field path (arrowed post) and cross stile in perimeter hedge. Head straight across field, join grass track between properties to road junction and proceed ahead along Marlpit Lane. Lane curves right round Pine Farm, then in few yds turn left along track and climb steps right to follow defined path across vast field (views) to meet lane by junction with further track. Turn left, following it to water tower and turn right into

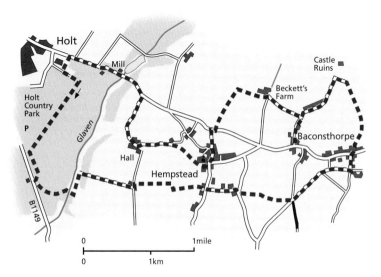

Baconsthorpe. At T-junction by shop turn right, then left along waymarked footpath to stile (keep to lane for refreshment at Margaret's). Follow well-arrowed path around field edges and across footbridges to concrete farm road and turn left to reach ruins of Baconsthorpe Castle – an ideal picnic spot. At gate to barns and junction of tracks, turn left along grass-centred track at field edge. Beyond gate keep to well-defined track, bearing right with arrowed 'circular route' at junction of routes, eventually reaching Beckett's Farm. Cross drive and stile opposite, follow field edge to stile and keep ahead, soon to reach open field and fork of paths. Bear diagonally left across large field (can be ploughed) to lane. Turn right, then left at footpath fingerpost along field edge to lane in Hempstead. Turn left, pass village hall, then at Chapel Lane take arrowed (Holt Country Park) path right along edge of playing field and field beyond beside churchyard. Shortly, walk beside dyke to footbridge and bear left along metalled drive to Hempstead Hall. Keep right between pond and house, cross waymarked stiles beside gates, then stream and follow

Holt Country Park.

grassy path by pond to further stile (circular-walk marker). Follow markers uphill along field edge, joining track leading to road. Turn left, pass old mill and pond, then ascend to cross stile left (concessionary path). Follow green circular-walk arrows back through wooded country park to car park.

• HOLT Small attractive country town nestling in undulating countryside. Main street is lined by Georgian buildings built after the fire in 1708, many housing interesting galleries and specialist shops. Among former pupils of Gresham's School, founded in 1555 by Sir John Gresham a former Lord Mayor of London, are poet W. H. Auden and composer Benjamin Britten.

• BACONSTHORPE CASTLE was a fortified manor house built by Sir Henry Heydon in 1486. The remains include the well-preserved inner and outer gatehouse, the curtain walls and a 17thC dwelling.

Felbrigg Hall

*Incorporating the beautiful parkland that surrounds Felbrigg Hall,
a handsome 17thC house built on the site of an existing medieval
hall, this rural ramble explores some of the peaceful paths, lanes
and ancient byways that criss-cross the gently undulating and
little- visited countryside inland from the busy resorts of Sheringham
and Cromer.*

Start *Felbrigg Hall,
TG193394. This
National Trust property
is reached from the
B1436 and signposted
off the A148 Cromer to
Holt road, 2 miles (3.2
km) south-west of
Cromer. Free car park
close to hall. Parkland
and woodland walks
open daily all year,
dawn to dusk.*

Essentials

Moderate 8¹/₂ miles
(13.6 km); 4¹/₂ hours;
undulating; *map*
Ordnance Survey 1:50
000 Landranger Map 33,
North East Norfolk.
Terrain Parkland paths,
established tracks, field
and woodland (wet and
muddy after rain)
footpaths and sections
along quiet country
lanes.

Route directions

Just before cattle grid and
information board turn left to wooden
gate. Follow defined path across parkland
to Felbrigg church and walk beside
churchyard wall to enter cultivated field.
Bear diagonally right (or round field edge
if in crop) towards trees and stile in
corner. Head towards lake by flint wall,
cross further stile by gate and soon reach
Felbrigg Pond. Ignore gate ahead marked
'private', turn left through gate and bear
half-right across meadow towards
converging trees (Common Plantation),
looking out for gate and stile on woodland
fringe. Follow meandering path through
wood, passing lodge on right to stile and
road. Turn right, then where woodland
ends on left take green lane left. Track
soon narrows (can be boggy), eventually
reaching pond and farm drive leading to
narrow lane. Turn left, the lane curving
right and crossing stream, then turn right
along Hellgate Lane (first right). Shortly,
at distinct right bend, go
through gap in hedge left
and walk along field edge,
following perimeter left
before crossing dry ditch
and hedge on right into
field beyond. Keep left-
handed along field edge to
lane. Turn right, soon
noting tree-covered

FOOD AND DRINK

Excellent tearoom and
restaurant in Stable
Block by Felbrigg Hall
for light lunches and
afternoon teas.
Chequers pub in
Gresham.

enclosure on left in field
(remains of Gresham
Castle – not accessible).
Bear left at fork by
Chequers pub, then at T-
junction with Church Lane
turn left into Gresham
village. Pass post office,
then take arrowed
bridleway right between
properties and uphill as it
curves right, then left up
Anguish Hill. At junction of
paths, keep ahead along
right-hand edge of fields to
reach lane. Turn right into
East Beckham and turn
right at T-junction along unmade byway
(Mill Lane). Climb steeply to junction of
tracks and turn left along tree-lined byway
(Bennington's Lane). In about 1 mile
(1.6 km) cross A148 on to waymarked
bridleway between hedge and fence. Skirt
woodland on left, then bear left to follow
path (can be boggy) through wood
(Beeston Regis Heath/Stone Hill) to
junction of routes. Turn right, then left
keeping to main track as it descends
steeply into valley. Just before thatched
cottage, path curves right along base of hill
to reach established track. Turn right
(Calves Well Lane) and soon fork right at
National Trust sign and start climbing
along Peddars Way. At top, by open area
and crossing of ways (NT pillar), turn left
along wide track through wood, then
straight across field to A148 left of
Woodlands Guest House. Turn right (take
great care), soon to cross road and
waymarked stile into
meadow. Keep right to
stile, bear slightly left
across field to gap in
hedge, then half-left over
next field to gap by second
telegraph pole from left.
From here, aim for
Aylmerton church across
large field to reach white

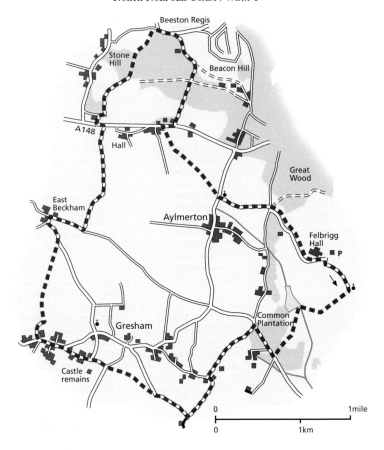

gate and road opposite church. Turn right, then left along track beside church, passing farm buildings to road opposite lodge to Felbrigg Park. Go through gates and follow metalled drive back to hall and car park.

• **FELBRIGG HALL** Splendid 17thC house set in 1,700 acres of woods and parkland and containing a fine collection of 18thC furniture, paintings and an outstanding library. Walled garden, orangery and restored octagonal 18thC dovecote built for 2,000 birds. Open Apr–Oct, tel. 01263 837444.

• **FELBRIGG CHURCH** Rebuilt by Sir Simon Felbrigg around 1400, the church is the private chapel of the Felbriggs and contains some magnificent brasses and monuments to the Felbrigg and Windham families, notably one to William Windham the First by Grinling Gibbons.

• **GRESHAM CASTLE** was a fortified manor house built around 1319 for Sir Edmund Bacon. With four bastion towers (bases preserved) it was 150 ft (45 m) square and moated. In 1429 it was bought by the Paston family but razed to the ground in 1450 by the Molyn family during the War of the Roses. Gresham village was the ancestral home of Sir Thomas Gresham, who founded the Royal Exchange in 1566.

• **BEESTON REGIS HEATH** comprises 30 acres of heathland and woodland, as well as ancient iron workings, and affords good views of Sheringham and the coast. Adjoining land, known as the Roman Camp and also owned by the National Trust, is the highest point in the county.

• **AYLMERTON'S CHURCH** is mainly 15thC and boasts a well-preserved Norman tower and a beautifully carved sedilia (decorated stone seats) and piscina (stone basin).

114

Holme Dunes and Ringstead Downs

From vast beaches and a fascinating duneland nature reserve to a unique wooded valley and charming brick-and-flint villages, this ramble captures the real atmosphere of the North Norfolk Coast.

Start Holme-next-the-Sea, TF698439. *Coastal village just north of A149, 3 miles (5 km) north-east of Hunstanton. Follow signs to beach car park. Bus service to and from Burnham Market to Holme on certain days in summer only – tel. 0345 626116 for information.*

Essentials

Moderate 11 miles (17.8 km); 6 hours; level along coast path; gently undulating inland around Ringstead; *map* Ordnance Survey 1:50 000 Landranger Map 132 North West Norfolk. **Terrain** Boardwalk through nature reserve (or along beach if tide out), wide tracks and quiet metalled lanes.

Route directions

Leave car park and turn left. Take coast path arrowed right alongside River Hun (caravan park right) and follow markers along left-hand side of golf course for 1 mile (1.6 km) to road near clubhouse and Links Way Hotel. Turn left uphill to crossroads with A149 and go straight over into Church Road. Shortly, bear left past pond to visit St Mary's Church in Old Hunstanton. Return to junction and turn left. In ¹/₂ mile (0.8 km) where lane bears right (bench) take hedged track left. In ¹/₂ mile (0.8 km) curve round Lodge Farm to T-junction and turn left along gravel track. Keep right by pond (Hunstanton Park -private access left), continue on track with ruined church right, then just before barn (Downs Farm) keep left to follow excellent grassy track through Ringstead Downs, a delightful wooded valley. In 1 mile (1.6 km) reach road and turn left into Ringstead. Turn left again into High Street, passing Gin Trap pub, gallery and church. Proceed along Holme Road (pavement), then Peddars Way North, passing sail-less tower windmill, then ignore footpath left (Peddars Way) and take track right which affords extensive views of coastline. In 1 mile (1.6 km) merge with metalled lane, pass triangulation point, then turn left at T-junction and

descend into Thornham. Turn right along A149 into village centre and turn left by King's Head into Church Street. For Lifeboat Inn take first left turn, otherwise, keep ahead to take arrowed coast path left to cross plank bridge. Follow narrow path to further bridge and road, Turn right to creek and bear left with coast path sign on to raised bank and enter Holme Dunes Nature Reserve. Head towards sea, then either follow boardwalk through dunes skirting bird observatory or, if tide and conditions allow, walk along beach to rejoin board dune path later. Continue on path between dunes and golf course back to car park.

• **Holme-next-the-Sea** is where the Peddars Way, an old Roman road from Ixworth in Suffolk, terminates. As it peters out on the beach, it is assumed a ferry once crossed the Wash from here to Lincolnshire. Members of the Nelson family are buried at St Mary's Church.

• **Hunstanton's church** Charmingly situated opposite a duckpond and close to entrance to Hunstanton Hall and Park, St Mary's features an unusual white stone and alabaster pulpit and splendid memorials to the le Strange family who were lords of the manor for centuries.

• **Ringstead** Attractive village with an interesting church and gallery. Ringstead Downs, a pleasant wooded valley, is a haven for numerous wild birds and flower species.

• **Holme Dunes Nature Reserve** covers over 395 acres and a wide range of habitats from foreshore and sand dunes to salt and freshwater marsh.

FOOD AND DRINK

Tea room and the Gin Trap pub in Ringstead; King's Head, the atmospheric Lifeboat Inn (open all day) and a baker's in Thornham; the White Horse (closed Mon lunchtime) at Holme-next-the-Sea.

115

Burnham Market to Cley-next-the-Sea

Although reasonably short, Day 1 (Walk 7) has much for those who enjoy a leisurely pace and who like to explore along the way. En route to Wells one can visit Burnham Thorpe church with its many memorials to Nelson, stroll around Holkham estate and deer park, or tour Holkham Hall, one of Britain's most majestic stately homes, and, finally, relax on the vast expanse of sandy beach (very popular close to car park in summer) that stretches for miles along Holkham Bay to Wells. Tidal creeks and the eerie call of the curlew across windswept salt marsh characterize Day 2. Appealing to keen birdwatchers and those who savour the peace and quiet of wild open spaces, the walk takes in several nature reserves, as well as the bustling fishing village of Blakeney and the delightful flint village of Cley-next-the-Sea with its well-preserved windmill. Route-finding on Day 2 is particularly straightforward.

Start Day 1 *Burnham Market, TF916438. Park in main street.*
Day 2 *Wells-next-the-Sea Town Quay, located off A149, the Hunstanton to Cromer road. Park in pay-and-display car parks near Quay.*

Route directions
Day 1 From green/ church walk along main street, keep left at triangle and head out of village passing The Stables. Turn right up Joan Short's Lane, then at junction with lane bear immediately left along concrete track (route of disused railway) to reach sewage farm. Continue ahead along worn path through trees on top of old embankment and look out for waymarked stile on right. Follow path across pasture, via footbridges, towards Burnham Thorpe church, reaching stile by gate and continue to lane on edge of village. Turn right to visit Nelson church. Turn left uphill on wide track beside copse. Cross lane and follow straight track, passing left of barn on to path leading to T-junction of paths beside perimeter wall of Holkham

Essentials

Easy Day 1/Walk 7 – 9½ miles (15.2km); 5 hours (longer if visiting Holkham Hall).
Day 2/Walk 8 – 10 miles (16 km) 5–6 hours; mainly flat; **map** Ordnance Survey 1:50 000 Landranger Map 132 (North West Norfolk) and Map 133 (North East Norfolk).
Terrain Day 1 (Walk 7) sees a varied combination of field paths, bridleways, parkland drives and sandy tracks (or beach if tide out!). Day 2 (Walk 8) follows the well-waymarked North Norfolk Coast Path/ Peddars Way (muddy in winter) beside extensive salt marsh.

estate. Turn left (course of Roman road), then at lodge and estate road turn right to enter Holkham Park via small gate. Walk along metalled drive, pass Garden Centre, then beyond cattle grid bear left with drive passing between lake and mansion. (All parkland and drives open to pedestrians.) Leave park at estate village and reach A149 by Victoria Hotel (tearoom, pottery, shop right). Cross straight over and follow drive (Lady Ann's Road) to gate and enter nature reserve. Walk along duckboard path over dunes through coniferous woodland to Holkham beach. If tide is high bear right with Peddars Way/Coast Path waymarker to follow sandy path to lee of trees for 1½ miles (2.4 km) to metalled road beyond caravan site by creek and lifeboat station.

If tide is out, walk east along vast expanse of sand, eventually passing beach huts to slipway near creek/river entrance. Join raised metalled path beside road and head inland to Wells, parallel with river and enjoy extensive views of salt marsh.

Return to Burnham Market, May to September, use bus service from Buttlands in Wells (Tue, Wed, Thu last bus around 7 pm; Sun and bank holidays; 4 pm; Nov) Norfolk Bus Information tel. 0345 626116. Few buses run at other times so use local taxi – details in yellow pages and at tourist information office (business cards in window out of season when office closed).

ACCOMMODATION
Good selection of B&B establishments in Wells, notably **Ilex House** (tel. 01328 710556), **Mill House** (tel. 01328 710739) and **The Crown Hotel** (tel. 01328 710209). For reliable food try the **Moorings Restaurant** (tel. 01328 710949) near The Quay. Tourist Information Office (tel. 01328 710885 summer only).

---

among many other resident or migrant species.

• **WELLS-NEXT-THE-SEA** Small resort and port with narrow streets lined with flint cottages and a picturesque quay and harbour, where fishing boats unload their catches of whelks, crabs and sprats.

Day 2 From Wells Town Quay walk east, keeping left by chandlery along road by water's edge. Pass between sheds, then at end of tarmac bear left on to waymarked path (coast path) along embankment, with salt marshes again dominating view. Follow path round inlet and through undergrowth, soon to emerge beside Warham Marshes. Continue on grassy coast path for 2 miles (3.2 km) to car park by inland track, then, if you want to explore Stiffkey (refreshments), take next green lane (Hollow Lane) inland ($^1/_2$ mile/0.8 km). Beyond, Stiffkey Marshes (NT – public hide) flank the established path, which soon skirts Freshes Creek en route to Morston Quay beside Morston Greens (NT), affording views to Blakeney Point. At Morston join lane, then climb steps and cross car park (information/ observation gallery, summer ferry to Blakeney Point). To visit village (hotel, church) follow track inland. Follow winding embankment path alongside Agar Creek for 1 mile (1.6 km) to Blakeney, now visible ahead. Walk along quay (ferry trips to see seals and birds), pass Blakeney Hotel and turn right up High Street to explore village (refreshments). At far end of Quay climb sea bank to begin exhilarating $2^3/_4$ mile (4.4 km) walk along bank to Blakeney Eye (13thC chapel ruins), then inland beside River Glaven. Open and isolated, this stretch affords stunning views across open marsh to Cley and its distinctive windmill. On reaching A149 turn left into village (smokery, café, pubs).

• **DISUSED RAILWAY** This used to be the small branch line between Heacham and Wells. Sections were washed away during disastrous floods in 1953 and never replaced.

• **BURNHAM THORPE** is famous as being the birthplace of Lord Nelson. His father was rector of the parish and the family lived at the old vicarage (now demolished). A plaque in the wall ($^1/_2$ mile/0.8 km from church) commemorates this and the church is filled with Nelson memorabilia.

• **HOLKHAM HALL** is a classic 18thC Palladian-style mansion situated in a 3,000-acre deer park. Home of the earls of Leicester, it has a splendid marble hall and sumptuously decorated state rooms containing fine furniture and a collection of paintings by Rubens, Van Dyck and Gainsborough. Also of interest are the pottery, the Bygones Museum (housed in a 19thC stable block and featuring more than 5,000 exhibits), and a History of Farming exhibition. Near the lake is a 17thC thatched ice house. Tel. 01328 710227 for opening times.

• **HOLKHAM NATURE RESERVE** comprises marshland, sand dunes, larch woods and mudflats which provide a haven for wintering geese, curlews, shelducks, bearded tits, marsh harriers, natterjack toads and sea astors,

---

FOOD AND DRINK
Day /Walk 7/ – Tea-room, picnic area and the Victoria Hotel (bar snacks) on Holkham estate. Plenty of cafés in Wells.
Day 2/Walk 8/ – Short diversions to reach Red Lion at Stiffkey (11 am–3 pm) and Morston Hall Hotel (civilized afternoon teas). Tearooms and pubs in Blakeney, especially the White Horse and Kings Arms (open all day). Whalebone Tea Room in Cley-next-the-Sea.

Return to Wells or Burnham Market catch bus (Tue, Wed, Thu approx 6.45 pm, Fri approx 5 pm Wells only, Sun & BH 3.30 pm) during summer months only (Bus Information tel. 0345 626116), or by taxi – Peter Wordingham, Blakeney (tel. 01263 741015), Link Taxis, Holt (tel. 01263 713068).

• **WARHAM MARSHES** One of the best examples of salt marsh in western Europe, supporting a number of rare plants – matted sea lavender, sea heath – and a valuable feeding area for brent geese and shelducks.

• **STIFFKEY** is a pretty village noted for its flint-and-brick cottages, the 16thC Stiffkey Hall with its odd external towers, and for its cockles, known locally as 'Stewkey Blues'. Stiffkey Greens comprises 487 acres of undisturbed salt marsh, winter feeding grounds for large numbers of geese and duck.

• **BLAKENEY** An important port in medieval times, and which sent three ships to fight the Spanish Armada, this attractive, upmarket fishing village has narrow, cottage-lined cobbled streets leading down to the quay, a 15thC church and a 14thC Guildhall with a brick-vaulted undercroft (open). Blakeney Point, an elongated shingle and sand spit supporting a wealth of birdlife and salt marsh flora (NT Nature Reserve), shelters Blakeney and its harbour, now over a mile away due to the silting up over the centuries.

Shelduck.

• **CLEY-NEXT-THE-SEA** Pronounced 'Cly', this lovely flint village now lies a mile from the sea after land reclamation in the 17thC. Although it has a small quay, an 18thC Custom House, a fine windmill (B&B accomodation; open at certain times), a 14thC church and an excellent smokery, Cley is most famous for its marshland and its birdlife, notably rare birds, migrating waders and thousands of wintering geese and wildfowl.

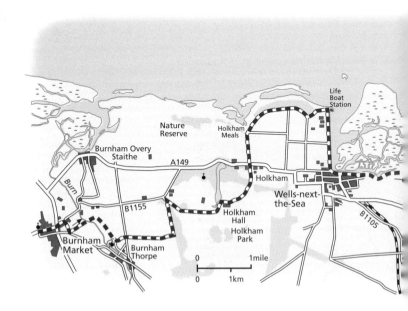

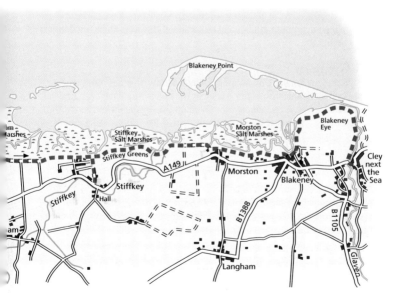

Above: the Windmill at Cley.

119

Introduction
The Welsh Borders

T he remote border country of England and Wales is not as well known as other British beauty spots – the Cotswolds or the Lake District for example – but within the boundaries of this extensive rural district lies a varied range of landscapes where mountains, river valleys and forest together offer a perfect area for those who enjoy country walking in restful, out-of-the-way surroundings.

The Forest of Dean

This offers many attractions, including miles of footpaths, and is a popular retreat for local townsfolk and a Mecca for outdoor enthusiasts. Squeezed between the River Severn and the Wye Gorge, the forest, populated largely by the English oak, was once a royal hunting ground. Later, it provided timber for ships. Today, it survives as one of the oldest forests in the country, but it is not just a place of woodland trails and secret glades – the Forest of Dean is renowned for its local customs, legends and historic traditions. The late-17thC Speech House, between Coleford and Cinderford, was built as an administrative centre for the forest and the famous Court of Verderers, first appointed by King Canute in 1016, still meets here. The Queen and Prince Philip planted trees in the vicinity of the Speech House during a visit here in the late 1950s. Dean, as it is more commonly known in these parts, was also the setting for iron-ore mining and remnants of this long-abandoned industry still remain.

The Wye Valley

Designated an Area of Outstanding Natural Beauty, this has often been described as the most romantic valley in Wales. Visitors have been drawn to the area for over 200 years, among them William Wordsworth who was captivated by its beauty – in fact it inspired him to write 'Lines Composed a Few Miles Above Tintern Abbey' in 1798. The river is noted for its salmon and trout, while the valley's woodland walks are probably best appreciated in autumn when the trees are turning.

Symonds Yat is is one of the valley's most-visited spots, with the climb to Symonds Rock rewarding you with a classic view down over the valley below – probably one of the most famous views in the country and reproduced in thousands of pictures and postcards. Yat, the name given to this part of the valley, is understood to mean gate or pass.

From Symonds Rock, on a clear day, you can spot the steeple of St Mary's Church at Ross-on-Wye. This charming town, on a sandstone cliff at the northern end of the Forest of Dean, is a popular base for visitors touring the Wye Valley. Anyone visiting Ross should make their way to The Prospect, a patch of elevated ground and walled public garden area close to the church, famous for its setting directly overlooking a loop of the river: magnificent views over the Wye and surrounding countryside. Ross is a starting point for a variety of walks and the nearby Penyard Woods are a delight in any season.

The Marches

To the west of the Malvern Hills, renowned for their walking potential and still remembered as the inspiration of Edward Elgar, lies Ledbury where John Masefield, Poet Laureate from 1930 to 1967, was born. The town is worth exploring, as is historic Hereford through which flows the 130-mile (210-kilometre) Wye on its way from Plynlimmon in Wales, where it rises, to the mouth of the Severn.

South-west of Hereford are numerous opportunities for adventurous hiking. The Black Mountains, stretching towards the Brecon Beacons, are more suited to the hardened walker. Here you can unwind by escaping into a world of rolling hills, fertile valleys and ancient ridge tracks. Pony-trekking is particularly popular here.

Those who enjoy walking at a gentle pace will find much to their liking in an area of the Welsh Marches bounded by the historic border towns of Ludlow and Knighton to the north, and Kington and Leominster to the south. Touring here on foot offers insights into some of the loveliest and least crowded landscapes in Britain. Only by walking can you fully appreciate how the level farmland and gentle hills of England give way to the more mountainous landscapes of Wales. This is rural Britain at its best, largely undiscovered, with winding lanes, sleepy villages and timber-framed cottages lurking behind thick hedgerows. In this part of the Welsh Marches you can climb high into border territory, exploring tracts of broadleaved woodland and timeless limestone edges.

Return of the otter

With pollution greatly diminished, the Teme, Lugg and Arrow rivers have become a recognized wildlife habitat and are considered an ideal home for that most elusive of creatures – the otter. Driven away over the years by the use of organochlorine pesticides, among other pollutants, otters are slowly making a comeback to these waterways, witness to a cleaner, healthier environment.

Battleground

This part of the borders is also littered with the remains of Iron Age hill-forts and Norman strongholds, evidence of the power struggles between English and indigenous Welsh for control of the Wild West. The Dark Ages witnessed the worst of the fighting, but in Roman times this was a bloody battleground, too, as the invaders sought to subdue tribal factions.

Long-distance paths

Several long-distance paths cut through the Welsh Borders, including the delightful Wye Valley Walk, which follows the course of the river for over 50 miles (80 kilometres), and the more famous Offa's Dyke Path – a spectacular route of more than 160 miles (260 kilometres) following an ancient earthwork which takes its name from the 8thC Mercian King Offa who declared that a frontier should be defined between Mercia and the Welsh kingdoms. The path keeps to Offa's Dyke for much of the route and is yet another way of discovering the Welsh Borders on foot.

GETTING THERE
The most direct route to the Welsh Borders by car is from the east via the M5, turning off at Gloucester or Worcester. The region can be reached by train, with services stopping at Ledbury, Hereford, Leominster and Ludlow.

WEATHER
The weather in this part of the country does not, on the whole, present any major problems. However, the border hilltops and the summits of the Black Mountains and the Brecon Beacons can be bitterly cold in winter. It is not unusual for a cool breeze to blow here on warm summer days.

WALKING BASE:

Hay-on-Wye

Each year thousands of book-lovers descend on Hay to visit its new and antiquarian bookshops: it is famous for it claim to be the 'book capital' of the British Isles.

There is, however, more to Hay than books. Situated at the northern tip of the Brecon Beacons National Park, this delightful old market town, on a hill overlooking the Wye, is a perfect base for exploring the Welsh Borders and the Black Mountains.

Its network of narrow streets is worth close investigation. Many of the old buildings huddle around a 17thC mansion known as the Castle, which occupies the site of an earlier 13thC stronghold. Attacked by King John and also beseiged by Owain Glyndwr, the 15thC Welsh warrior statesman, only the gateway and tower remain, forming part of the newer

building. The Castle was, in more recent times, bought by Richard Booth who subsequently opened Hay's first second-hand bookshop.

Hay's parish church of St Mary provides spectacular views of the river and close to it is The Bailey Walk, a pleasant riverside path which is especially popular with visitors and locals. Nearby is St John's Chapel, famous in the town for its somewhat chequered history. Founded more than 700 years ago, in its time the chapel has been a prison, fire station, school and college. John Wesley preached here in the 1770s.

To the south of Hay lies the little community of Cusop, where the Dulas Brook winds through a wooded valley beyond which several roads lead to Hay Bluff, one of the highest summits in the Black Mountain range.

SLEEPING AND EATING

HOTELS AND INNS

LLYSWEN
Llangoed Hall; tel. 01874 754525. Owned by Sir Bernard Ashley, husband of designer Laura Ashley, this magnificent Edwardian retreat on the banks of the Wye, is surrounded by lush parkland and wooded hills. Elegant public rooms are filled with antiques and paintings; luxurious bedrooms.

Griffin Inn; tel. 01874 754241. Charming 15thC fishing inn. An ideal walking base. Cottagey bedrooms, characterful bars and imaginative home-cooked food.

HAY-ON-WYE
The Swan-at-Hay; Church Street; tel. 01497 820841. Former coaching inn built in 1821 on the edge of the town, offering a relaxed atmosphere, well-equipped

accommodation, an elegant sitting room and modern British cooking.

Old Black Lion; 26 Lion Street; tel. 01497 820841. Old coaching inn dating back to the 13thC, with creaking, sloping floors and old beams in the inviting bedrooms. Welcoming, cosy bars and and imaginative food.

THREE COCKS
Three Cocks Hotel; (6 miles/ 10 km SW); tel. 01497 847215; closed Dec and Jan. Ivy-clad, 15thC hotel set in beautiful countryside. Formerly an inn, this atmospheric building with its uneven floors, heavy beams and cobbled courtyard offers comfortable accommodation with period furnishings and interesting food.

WHITNEY-ON-WYE
Rhydspence Inn; tel. 01497 831262. With splendid views over the Wye Valley and Black Mountains, this old half-timbered inn has five attractively decorated bedrooms with beams and sloping floors. Home-cooked food in the timbered bars.

BED-AND-BREAKFAST

WINFORTON
Winforton Court; tel. 01544 328498. Historic, black and white timbered manor dating from 1520. Well-equipped and comfortably furnished bedrooms, including a four-poster room. Hearty breakfasts.

NEWCHURCH
Dolbedwyn; tel. 01497 851202; closed Christmas and New Year. Fine Tudor farmhouse set in unspoilt

Ludlow Walk 7 ●

● Aymestrey Walk 8

● Llynheilyn Walk 1

Hay-on-Wye.

● Dorstone Walk 3

● Llyswen Walk 4

Fownhope Walk 2 ●

● Llanthony Walk 5

● Skirrid Walk 6

ACCOMMODATION AND FOOD

A cross-section of places to stay in the town and surrounding area exist to satisfy the considerable demand for accomodation, especially at festival time. Here we highlight a few of the best places. For more detailed information, contact the Tourist Information Office, Oxford Road, Herefordshire HR3 5DG; tel. 01497 820144.

countryside on the Herefordshire/Powys border. Comfortably restored, featuring oak panelling, beams and a splendid Jacobean staircase. Imaginative menus highlight home-grown produce.

CUSOP

York House; Hardwick Road; tel. 01497 820705. Large, late-Victorian house within walking distance of the town centre. Friendly and welcoming atmosphere, well-appointed bedrooms. Evening meals available.

TALGARTH

Upper Trewalkin Farm; Pengenffordd; tel. 01874 711349. Typical stone and slate Welsh hill farm with views of the Black Mountains. Expect a warm welcome, cosy bedrooms and wholesome, home-cooked meals.

LLANIGON

Old Post Office; tel. 01497 820008; closed Jan. 17thC whitewashed cottage located close to Offa's Dyke Path. Period furnishings, thick stone walls and heavy beams characterize the cosy interior. Comfortable cottagey bedrooms. Breakfast only.

CAMPING AND HOSTELS

Hay-on-Wye and its immediate area is well served with camping facilities, notably *Radnors End Campsite* (tel. 01497 820780) overlooking the Wye and town; *Holly Bush Inn* (tel. 01497 847371 – 2 miles/3.3 km south); *Forest Park, Clyro* (tel. 01497 820156 – 2 miles/3.2 km north-west); *Riverside International, Talgarth* (tel. 01874 711320 – 6 miles/10 km south-west).

The nearest **youth hostels** are located close to the Offa's Dyke path north (*Glascwm*, near Llandrindod Wells – *01982 570415*) and south (*Capel-y-Ffin* – *01873 890560*) of Hay-on-Wye.

FOOD

Apart from the hotels and inns already mentioned, the following are worth considering for good food: the award-winning *Sun, Winforton* (**tel. 01544 327677**); *Kilverts, Hay-on-Wye* (tel. 01497 821042 – also B&B); *Oscars Bistro, Hay-on-Wye* (tel. 01497 821193); *Pandy Inn, Dorstone* (tel. 01981 550273); *Radnor Arms, Llowes* (tel. 01497 847460); *Old Salutation Inn, Weobley* (tel. 01544 318443 – also B&B); *Ancient Camp Inn, Ruckhall* (tel. 01981 250449 – also B&B).

123

Llynheilyn and Summergill Valley

This walk encircles 'Mynd' (1,568 ft/478 m) and gives a taste of the Welsh mountains without making too many physical demands. The route starts at a peaceful lake – perfect for birdwatching and picnics – and, the highlight is the delightfully named Water-break-its-neck Waterfall, pictured below. The return leg aound the Summergill Valley offers views towards the impressive hills of Radnor Forest. You are unlikely to meet another soul, other than crossing the main road, but there are plenty of sheep and cattle grazing the open hillsides.

Start *Small car park (free) beside Llynheilin Lake on the A481, 9 miles (15.2 km) north-east of Builth Wells and ¼ mile (0.4 km) from the junction of A481 and A44 Kington to Llandrindod Wells road, SO166582.*

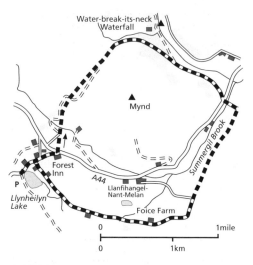

Route directions

From car park follow A481 towards Kington to junction with A44 (440 yds/400 m) and Forest Inn. Cross main road, look for small gate in fence (just up from junction), then walk down field towards farm. Go through gate in bottom corner and turn left in front of farm to pass through white gates on stony track. In 100 yds (90 m)

Essentials

Moderate 5½ miles (8.8 km); 3 hours; undulating; **map** Ordnance Survey 1:50 000 Landranger Map 148, Presteigne & Hay-on-Wye.
Terrain Hill paths and tracks with some open-pasture paths. Generally easy level walking on stony and tarmac roads, plus a short 'riverbed' section – could be wet.

Radnor Forest from Summergill Valley.

turn right uphill on further stony track, continuing for 600 yds (550 m) to metal gate by trees. Continue ahead to small plantation, follow left-hand side, then before reaching end of tree belt and 'no entry' gate bear half-left up to gate in corner of fence (100 yds/90 m). Shortly, pass gate on right, bear slightly right and go downhill on path for short distance to further gate leading to stony track near modern barn. Cross track on to grassy bank and descend to cross stream via two gates, then follow path uphill with craggy gorge opening out to your right. Continue across edge of small field soon to join well-worn track running parallel with gorge. Pass stable, then in 50 yds (45 m) – in line with house on left – go through small gate on right. Turn right down narrow path to cross bridge, then climb other side (gorge left), soon to follow path along top edge of gorge, eventually merging with forest track. Head downhill on grassy trail to reach stony forest track. Here, take a short detour left to see Water-break-its-neck Waterfall, by going down track for 600 yds (550 m) to where streams meet, then bear left up stream bed (if not in full spate) for 220 yds (200 m) to waterfall. Retrace steps along stony track, following to the main road. Cross and proceed down track, passing cottage and crossing stream, then in

Left: Water-break-its-neck-Waterfall.

100 yds (90 m) where track bears left, turn right on to grassy path. Follow wire fence for 440 yds (400 m), join more defined track and maintain direction. By farm gate keep ahead on small path and climb to metal gate. Continue steeply uphill (fence right) to reach gate and convergence of tracks. Beyond gate continue up track (fence now left) for 440 yds (400 m) to reach further gate at top. Turn right along track via gates to pass Foice Farm and go along tarmac lane for nearly a mile (1.6 km) to the lake. At pink cottage go through second gate on left towards lake and follow round to car park.

• **WATER-BREAK-ITS-NECK WATERFALL** is the focus of this short walk (best appreciated after heavy rain) and can be viewed from above and below. From the latter, it is approached along a narrow, winding ravine which has a brooding atmosphere and is worth exploring even if the fall is not in spate. Retreating from the waterfall there are views back across the green cloak of Warren Plantation to Nyth-Grug, where the water supplying the falls-stream rises. Further north, above Fron Hill, soar the peaks of Radnor Forest, Whimble, Bach Hill and Black Mixen; bare, rounded domes above the trees.

FOOD AND DRINK
Forest Inn (close to car park at junction of A481 and A44) and the Red Lion Inn at Llanfihangel-Nant-Melan (good bar food – closed Tuesdays) – on A44 1½ miles (2 km) east of Llynhellin.

125

Fownhope – The River Wye and Common Hill

Fownhope, with its attractive half-timbered cottages, makes an interesting start to this exploration of the surrounding hills, which give good views across the Wye Valley and down to the 'Little Cathedral', as Townhope's parish church is often called. Descending towards the Wye, the scene is dominated by the dark tree-clad hillside of Capler Wood, topped by its ancient 'camp'. The route finishes with an easy circuit around a lazy meander of the great river.

Start *Fownhope, SO580342. Small village located on the B4224 between Hereford and Ross-on-Wye. Free parking by the sports field, located down a track just past the church on minor road south of B4224.*

Route directions

Walk back past church, cross B-road and proceed along lane opposite, taking first left through housing estate. At Nover Wood Drive bear right up arrowed footpath, then where path starts to dip down, go over stile on left and head diagonally across small field to further stile. Follow path uphill through woods to reach crossing of tracks. Turn right (past half-timbered cottage) and continue uphill for 100 yds (90 m), then take left fork (Wye Valley Walk) and gently climb along ridge of Common Hill. Descend from ridge, initially on path then track and pass white house on left to reach junction of tracks. Take middle path (blue arrow) uphill, fork left in 220 yds (200 m), leaving WVW to follow bridleway, then track to metalled lane. Turn right, then opposite Common Hill Farm, cross stile on left (WVW) and head downhill through meadow (wire fence left), round to stile leading into wood. Climb

Essentials

Moderate 6¼ miles (10.4 km); 4 hours; generally undulating with one steep climb at start and level walking beside the Wye; *map* Ordnance Survey 1:50 000 Landranger Map 149, Hereford & Leominster.
Terrain Mainly open short-cropped grass walking with wooded footpaths and bridleways, sometimes following the waymarked Wye Valley Walk (WVW). It can be boggy underfoot after heavy rain and in winter (walking boots recommended). The last ¼ mile (0.4 km) of wooded riverbank is overgrown, steep and unstable, so if difficult to negotiate take heed of suggested alternative route.

through wood for 440 yds (400 m) to crossing of paths, keep ahead down to gate on woodland fringe. Maintain direction through rough pasture, past pond and through gate, then downhill beside hedge for 220 yds (200 m) to gate and bear right on to stony track. Pass farm buildings (right), keep straight on through gate (mast in sight) and along track for 220 yds (200 m) to where track curves left. Here, bear right past small pond towards Birds Farm Cottage and enter garden via gate. Pass in front of cottage, turn sharp right along its side, go through metal gate and walk along shady track for 150 yds (135 m) to gate leading into rough pasture. Shortly, climb concealed stile in hedge on right and follow left side of field for 440 yds (400 m) to crossing of paths. Turn left (WVW), cross stream and head for stile in top of field (left of farmhouse) by walking left around edge. Cross stile, turn right along hedge, join stony track to reach main B-road. Turn left for 100 yds (90 m) then right down road to Capler Farm. Head towards farmhouse, then bear right through gated stockyard (farm left, barn right) and continue into meadow. Continue ahead through two more fields, pass through gate into next field, head straight across and down towards farm. Cross wooden fence,

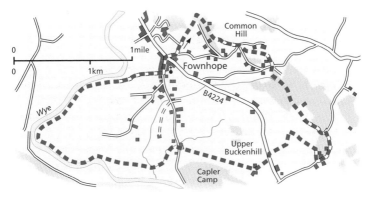

Fownhope and church.

continue to gate between barns to road and cross into field opposite. Head for right-hand boundary, following it round (stream right) to cross stile and bear right to field corner. Clamber down bank, over stream and up other side (awkward), then turn right along field edge; continue 100 yds (90 m), then bear left and strike out across this and next large field, route marked by three oak trees, to reach cottage on banks of River Wye. Cross stiles to left of cottage and walk along riverbank for approximately 1¼ miles (2 km), eventually reaching stile on edge of wood. Next section has suffered severe landslip and may be impassable. If conditions allow, follow it to reach house; otherwise do not cross stile but turn right along side of wood to top, then left through gate and along top edge of wood to rejoin path. Continue ahead over stile (house left), along field edge to stony track. Turn right, following it back to sports ground and church.

• **FOWNHOPE** is a picturesque Wye-side village with many old black-and-

white timbered buildings and is one of a triangle of villages in the area whose names end in 'hope' – meaning a settlement beneath a hillside. The parish church of St Mary (one of the largest in the county) has an octagonal spire clad in oak shingles, a beautiful Norman tympanum on the west wall and a huge hollowed-out oak tree-trunk, fashioned into a lidded chest in the early 14thC. Note also the portable Carolean font on display, which on its slender stem has the appearance of great antiquity, and a Tudor font, whose design looks rather modern. The wooded ridge above the village is an ideal habitat for scores of speckled wood butterflies which flutter among the trees in late summer.

• **CAPLER CAMP** crowns the hill which dominates the scene halfway round the walk. It is steep-sided and thickly covered by broadleaved woodland to the north and where it faces the river. With its command of the Wye, it is not surprising that it was chosen as the site for an Iron Age hill fort.

• **RIVER WYE** is wide at this point, with a backdrop of wooded hillside to the south across the river, and open meadows of short-cropped turf along the riverside walk, making it easy to see the water and any interesting plants, fish or birds. On this stretch of the walk watch for lapwings rising from the fields as you approach, or for herons flapping lazily away in the distance.

FOOD AND DRINK
Green Man in Fownhope – 15thC inn offering reliable food and good accommod-ation – tel. 01432 860243.

Kilvert country and the Golden Valley

Climbing from Dorstone to the summit of Merbach Hill there are wonderful views across the mountains and the mighty River Wye, glistening in the valley below. Beyond, Bredwardine is a 'must' for all fans of the 19thC diarist, (Robert) Francis Kilvert. He lived in the village for the last two years of his life and walked extensively in the surrounding countryside, often heading for Arthur's Stone. Consisting of a group of stones, this ancient monument is superbly positioned close to the edge of steep hillside, with the Golden Valley stretching into the distance.

Start *Dorstone, SO313417. Historic village located just off the B4348, 7 miles (11.6 km) east of Hay-on-Wye. A reasonable bus service (route 39) links Hay with Dorstone. Small free car park behind the Village Hall on the edge of Market Square (green), just south of the B4348 in the village centre.*

Essentials

Strenuous 7 miles/ 11.6 km; 4½ hours; two long steep ascents on the outward and return legs, alternating with steep descents and some flat, comfortable walking along hilltop and valley bottom; *map* Ordnance Survey 1: 50 000 Landranger Map 148, Presteigne & Hay-on-Wye.
Terrain Field paths and tracks (one short hedged section near the start tending to be overgrown), short-cropped turf; brief road sections and some woodland paths. Fields could be muddy after rain and in winter – good stout shoes or walking boots advisable.

Route directions

From the green take path along left side of church, cross B-road, go through kissing gate and continue through playing fields to stile. Bear slightly left, soon cross stream on metal bridge and cross stile. Turn left along track (old railway line), then shortly take footpath right along field edge to stile in corner. Beyond, turn left along rough track (can be overgrown) for 100 yds (90 m) then, after stile, bear right uphill by row of trees to farm road. Turn left and soon bear right over stile to follow path uphill via stile to bypass farm. Keep to top side of barn, rejoin track to reach metalled lane. Turn right, soon to go left over stile to head uphill through meadow (fence right) to cross further stile. Bear right along track for 25 yds (23 m), then cross stile right and keep by hedge on right through two fields to reach

road (house right). Turn left along road for 440 yds (400 m), then by house (Caemwar) on bend, continue straight ahead on to open hillside, keeping above trees left. Go through old quarry area to reach summit of Merbach Hill. From triangulation point turn right (east) through bracken on path towards wooded hill. Join bridleway, head downhill on grassy path between bracken for 440 yds (400 m) and keep ahead at crossing of paths to pass through gate. Continue across clearing, past wood on left (two gates) along track, then at gate by barn bear half-right to ash tree to follow stony track steeply downhill towards farmhouse. Turn right through gate on right just before farm, walk through woods and soon rejoin farm track. After 440 yds (400 m) cross cattle grid, then bear slightly left (leaving track) to cross open grassland between trees (woods left, farm right) and soon descend for 440 yds (400 m). In second field drop more steeply to gate below hawthorn hedge and continue to further gate, turning right on to track. On reaching road turn left, descending steeply into Bredwardine. Cross main road, soon to bear right along avenue towards church. Take footpath to right of church, pass through gate and turn right into dip between trees. Shortly, go through gate (river left), pass pond via boardwalk and continue to cross stream, then take path right past huge oak to follow right boundary to stile and grassy track leading uphill to B-road. Turn right, go 300 yds (275 m), then bear left along minor road. After 100 yds (90 m) take bridleway right and follow blue arrows via gates, zig-zagging uphill and steeply across meadow, keeping right further up to reach metal gate (not wooden gate left). At farm turn left along track to corner by stone cottage, then cross stile opposite to follow footpath very steeply uphill via stiles. At top proceed across field (farm left) to minor road and Arthur's Stone. Walk round monument, continue on footpath over rough pasture to stile, then head steeply downhill to pass modern house on right to join track out to B-road. Continue down road into village and cut through churchyard back to car park.

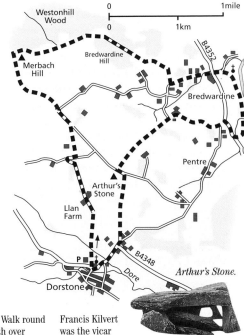

Arthur's Stone.

- **DORSTONE** is a pretty little village nestling at the head of the Golden Valley and boasts a triangular green with an unusual sundial mounted on the tall stem of an old stone cross. The Pandy Inn also overlooks the green and is said to have housed the workmen who constructed the first church here in 1185. This was founded by Thomas de Brito, one of the four knights who murdered Thomas à Becket in Canterbury Cathedral.

- **MERBACH HILL** Stony outcrops near the triangulation point on the summit of the Merbach Hill indicate the site of a long-abandoned quarry, parts of which were probably worked some 2,000 years ago. The views are magnificent and far-reaching – 11 counties are said to be visible on a clear day.

- **BREDWARDINE** Rev.

Francis Kilvert was the vicar here from 1877 until his untimely death in 1879 at the age of 38. *Kilvert's Diary*, published around 1940, covers the period 1870–79, when Kilvert was vicar first at Clyro near Hay, then at Bredwardine where he lived at the Old Vicarage. It is a fascinating record of Victorian country life. The 17thC Red Lion is where Kilvert's churchwarden meetings were held and local magistrates met in the Court Room. Kilvert is buried at St Andrew's Church, which has Norman origins, with later additions and restorations, and contains two life-size effigies, one being Sir Roger Vaughan who was killed at Agincourt.

- **ARTHUR'S STONE** dates back some 4,000 years, pre-dating any legends associated with King Arthur, though the name may be a corruption of Thor's Stone. Once a burial chamber, with upright stones supporting a huge ceiling of rock, the site would have been covered in earth and turf but over the millennia the covering has eroded away, leaving the stones which form a small chamber.

FOOD AND DRINK
Head for the old Pandy Inn (the county's oldest pub) for good food and garden (closed lunchtime Mon and all Tue in winter – tel. 01981 550273). Along the way is the Red Lion at Bredwardine.

129

Wye Valley Ramble from Llyswen

A peaceful ramble through contrasting Wye Valley scenery, from a sheltered and shady section along the tree-fringed River Wye, to an open and invigorating stretch around the slopes of Mynydd Forest to Brechfa Pool, where you get outstanding views towards the Black Mountains and the Brecon Beacons.

Start Llwysen, SO133380. Small village located at the junction of the A479 and A470, 12 miles (19.2 km) south of Builth Wells and approximately 7 miles (11.6 km) west of Hay-on-Wye via B4350. There are a few parking spaces off the main road just before the church, and one or two behind it.

Route directions

From church turn right along A470 for 440 yds (400 m) to reach Bridge End Inn. Turn right, then just before river bridge (Boughrood Bridge) bear left along metalled lane beside River Wye. When tarmac ends continue ahead on riverside path for 1½ miles (2.4 km), eventually reaching main

Essentials

Moderate 7 miles (11.6 km); 3 hours; flat for almost half the way followed by a gradual climb for 2 miles (3.2 km), then downhill or flat with a steep downhill finish; **map** Ordnance Survey 1:50 000 Landranger Map 161, Abergavenny & The Black Mountains. **Terrain** Easy walking on paved or well-defined riverside paths. Some narrow woodland paths (can be muddy), plus open hillside walking on wide stony tracks or grassy swathes with few stiles or gates. Short, steep rocky descent to finish which tends to be slippery and very wet. Good stout shoes or walking boots recommended.

Wye country.

road (A470) at Trericket Mill. Cross and after, turn right along road 100 yds (90 m) and go left up metalled farm road, soon to become stony track. Climb past first farm, then at next farm bear left around barn and, shortly (50 yds/45 m), turn left down path by wall, bearing left down to river. Go over footbridge and up bank opposite, then turn left past house on right. After 100 yds (90 m) go through five-bar gate to road, turning right (back past house) and proceed uphill for 1,000 yds (900 m) to a fork. Keep left, then after 220 yds (200 m), where lane bends right, take grassy path left which runs almost parallel with lane to reach rusty gate and boundary wall. Follow wall along and round left to further gate ahead, then continue up track (wall still left) which, after 220 yds (200 m), bears right away from wall up on to open moor. After 880 yds (800 m) track divides into three, take middle path on to green swathe and follow round so that boundary wall, still visible on left, gradually gets nearer. The swathe leads down towards minor road, where turn right and follow down to Brechfa Pool and small chapel. Go round pool clockwise to point opposite chapel, then turn left along wide grassy swathe to metalled lane. Cross cattle grid, then, where lane bends right, continue ahead down steep, stony and narrow bridleway (slippery) to reach main road. Turn left back into Llyswen.

• LLYSWEN means 'white court' and denotes the edict of Prince Rhodri-mawr in the 9thC that such a place be built in the vicinity where it served as a meeting place for his three sons who, between them, controlled most of Wales. A church was also erected around this time, perhaps a former religious site, and was named after St Gwendoline, a local saint buried at nearby Talgarth. Rebuilt in Norman times, the church was restored in 1862; however the Norman font survives intact from the old church, with all its period simplicity.

• BOUGHROOD BRIDGE was opened in 1842 as the 'little ford' was very prone to flooding, necessitating a long detour. It has four main and two flood arches and tolls were collected at the little lodge at one end until 1934.

• LLANGOED HALL Visible from the tranquil riverside path that passes through the estate, Llangoed Hall, formerly known as Llangoed Castle, has had a chequered history, having once changed hands in a gambling bout. In the early 20thC it was redesigned by Clough Williams-Ellis (architect of Portmeirion), who concluded that a house had been on the site since 560AD and last rebuilt in 1632. He retained the Jacobean panelled library and constructed a building which incorporated the tall chimneyed outlines of the old house. It is now an elegant country-house hotel, owned by Sir Bernard Ashley (see page 123).

The Wye.

• TRERICKET MILL is an unusual, early-18thC brick-and-stone watermill that went out of use in the 1930s. Now charmingly restored, it offers B&B. A tearoom is situated alongside the old workings, or one can sit in the streamside garden.

• BRECHFA POOL enjoys a magnificent position with the Black Mountains as a backdrop. It was a favourite haunt of 19thC rector Francis Kilvert, whose diary of rural life in this area has become a minor classic. Wild white ponies and sheep graze at the water's edge in summer and the little white chapel was Welsh Calvanist until it was taken over by the Presbyterian Church of Wales in 1904.

FOOD AND DRINK
Good food and B&B at the Griffin Inn in Llyswen (tel. 01874 754241) – the perfect place to head for at the end of the walk. Also in Llyswen is the Copper Kettle coffee shop. At the halfway point is Trericket Mill for tea, coffee and light lunches. Llangoed Hall (01874 754525) – one of the best hotels in Wales – serves after-noon tea in elegant surroundings.

Llanthony Priory and the Vale of Ewyas

Dramatically situated in the heart of the Black Mountains, the romantic ruins of Llanthony Priory are the focal point of interest on this ramble. The unique church at Cwmyoy is also worth exploring and the steep climb for the return journey is rewarded by exhilarating mountain walking with far-reaching views.

Start, Llanthony, SO288277. *Village and abbey, located on minor road between Hay-on-Wye and Llanfihangel Crucorney, 11 miles (17.6 km) south of Hay-on-Wye. No public transport. Free car park at Llanthony Priory.*

Route directions

Return to entrance drive past St David's church (left) and turn left (signposted pony trekking) through farmyard. Follow waymarkers through pasture on to footpath via gates, gradually climbing to reach small wood in 550 yds (500 m). Go through wood via stiles, continue uphill for further 550 yds (500 m) and pass in front of ruined barn (stream on left). Cross stream by second barn, climb stile and follow wire fence for 100 yds (90 m) to field gate and maintain direction on bridleway. Follow hill contour for 1,350 yds (1,250 m) (Maes-y-Beran farm below), keeping ahead beyond ruins, then gradually descend for 260 yds (250 m) to reach boulder-strewn stream. Bear right and pick your way steeply down to ruined farm. Pass between ruins, locate footpath sign and bear left across field, passing large oak tree to distant stile. Continue over two more stiles, then descend on grassy path to river near footbridge. Cross stile (not bridge) and climb track through woods and along grassy trail to Darren

Essentials

Moderate 8 miles (13.2 km); 4½ hours; generally level outward section through the Vale of Ewyas followed by a steep climb, then a more gradual one on to high ground; steep descent back into Llanthony; **map** Ordnance Survey 1:50 000 Landranger Map 161 Abergavenny & Black Mountains or 1:25 000 Outdoor Leisure Map 13, Brecon Beacons – Eastern Area.

Terrain Fields and meadow paths (can be muddy in places – possibly through Darren Farm) and comfortable mountain walking through bracken and heather on rocky tracks; care needed on steep descent by ravine near the finish.

Farm. Go through yard in front of farmhouse, then behind cottage and gently climb to reach grass track. Climb to where track veers sharp left, then bear right to stile to left of buildings and follow path, soon to pass wooden chalet before forking right down to Cwmyoy church. Pass through churchyard and kissing gate to road, continuing down to river bridge and T-junction. Turn left, then right over stile and climb meadow to track. Turn right uphill through wood to stile (ignore bridleway left), then after 220 yds (200 m) cross wide forest track and continue to climb steeply. Shortly, follow track left, cross minor track and proceed up past house (right) to reach open hilltop, then turn right along ridge track for 1 mile (1.6 km). Once on open moor start to climb more steeply and take most defined path to cairn ahead (260 yds/200 m). Keep to ascending path for ½ mile (0.8 km) over next rise (Bal-bach), then descend for 550 yds (500 m) into dip. Do not climb next summit, instead, turn right by pile of stones to follow path towards valley. Soon cross stream bed and bear right into steep valley (ravine right) and drop steeply, soon to pick up signs for Llanthony beyond farm. Go through pasture, cross footbridge over stream and follow waymarkers to cross river bridge leading out to road and Priory car park.

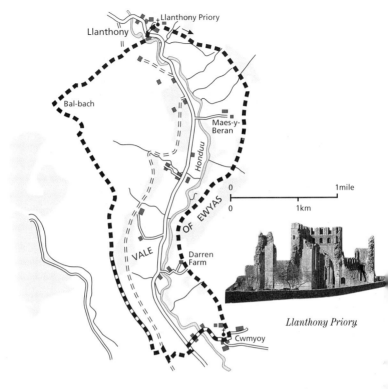

Llanthony Priory

• **LLANTHONY PRIORY** An Augustinian house founded in the 12thC. It flourished until the 15thC when the monks, tired of the harsh existence in the valley, built a new establishment in Gloucester. In 1807, the poet Walter Savage Landor bought the ruin with dreams of creating a grand estate, but his plan failed to succeed due to local opposition. The adjacent Abbey Hotel is built into what was once the prior's lodging and part of the Abbey church. The evocative ruins of the Priory, over 60 ft (18 m) high in places, are well worth exploring (free).

• **VALE OF EWYAS** still retains an air of remoteness despite having a road running through it. In early days the valley was closed off at the southern end by thick woodland and bogs, the only entrance being via the high pass from Hay-on-Wye, known as the Gospel Pass, a name that probably derived from a preaching tour in 1188 to raise funds

for the Third Crusade.

• **CWMYOY** means 'valley of the yoke', which refers to the shape of the indentation in the hillside where the village sits. This may have been caused by a landslip, which is certainly the reason for the strange appearance of St Martin's Church. No wall is at right angles, the tower leans dangerously and from the south the roof looks completely bowed. It is very old and contains a medieval cross, thought to have been one of the crosses on the Pilgrim's Way to St David's.

FOOD AND DRINK
Abbey Hotel in Llanthony and Half Moon Inn just north of village. Detour halfway round on back lane from Cwmyoy (1 mile/ 1.6 km) to visit Queens Head by river. Grassy banks beside the River Honddu provide delightful picnic spots.

• **GARN-WEN CAIRN** is a tall, beautifully symmetrical structure (almost 10 ft/3 m high) made by craftsmen. From this point on the walk there are striking views towards Skirrid and Sugar Loaf mountain in the middle-distance and right across the Bristol Channel as far as Exmoor.

133

Skirrid

*This walk makes a complete tour of Skirrid Fawr, so that you view it
from every angle before finally climbing to the summit. Parts of the
route use the very popular Offa's Dyke long-distance path, so expect
not to be alone on these sections. Plenty of interest along the way,
including Llanfihangel Court (not open), Skirrid Inn (reputedly the
oldest pub in Wales) and far-reaching views along the Monnow Valley
into Herefordshire from the summit of Skirrid Fawr.*

Start *Free car park,
SO328164, at the foot of
Skirrid Fawr on the
B4521 near Llandewi
Skirrid, 1¹/₂ miles (2.4
km) north-east of
Abergavenny.*

Llangattock Lingoed's church.

Route directions

Go through gates to join wide Skirrid Trail,
then after 50 yds (45 m) where it curves
right, cross stile ahead and bear
diagonally right across field to stile in top
left corner. Keep ahead via stiles to reach
stile on right by farm
buildings, then cross next
field (hedge left) to stile
by gate and pass to right of
house through overgrown
orchard and over stream.
Continue ahead with hedge
left (ignore stile left) to
field corner, then field gate
ahead. Turn left along stony
track and in
50 yds (45 m), turn right
through gate, keeping right
of farm and slightly right
uphill to stile in hedge.
Cross stream ahead to gate,
follow hedgerow on right,
then cross stile and small
bridge before bearing left
down towards white house.
Head for stile at end of
fence, cross garden and
drive and proceed along
lane to T-junction. Turn
right, walk up lane for
1,350 yds (1,250 m), then,
opposite stone bridge to
farm on right, go through
gate and follow hedge (on
right) down and right to
further gate. Head
diagonally downhill to next
gate and turn left down

track to junction.
Bear right along
stony track, pass
modern barn, then
old cottage and
houses to reach lay-
by. Walk to far end,
climb stile on right
into parkland and
bear half-left down to ditch, following it to
bridge. Cross and continue to stile, then
cross overgrown plantation to drive of
Llanfihangel Court. Turn left, go straight
across main road to partly ruined church,
then along road to Skirrid
Inn. Immediately beyond
inn turn left down lane,
then at bottom of hill turn
right on to riverside path.
After 880 yds (800 m) path
bears away slightly from
river, passing caravan site,
then after stile head across
meadow to gate opposite,
go over bridge and shortly
reach stile and main road.
Turn left, then in 50 yds
(45 m) cross road to Offa's
Dyke footpath sign (ODP)
and turn right past house
to follow long-distance
path (well waymarked) for
2¹/₂ miles (4 km) to
Llangattock Lingoed. Walk
through churchyard, across
meadow to track by house
and leave ODP by turning
right along farm track for
100 yds (90 m) to go
through second gate on
left. Proceed up field to
stile in right-hand corner
and continue steeply uphill
to stile left of tree belt on
skyline. Pass through gate
ahead, head for farm
visible in distance and two

Essentials

Moderate 10 miles
(16 km); 5 hours;
undulating, with an
extremely steep climb
to the summit of Skirrid
Fawr; *map* Ordnance
Survey 1:50 000
Landranger Map 161,
Abergavenny & The
Black Mountains.
Terrain Mostly through
or along the edge of
grassy fields and
generally well-
waymarked, particularly
on the Offa's Dyke,
where parts of the walk
can be muddy in wet
weather. A few
stretches of stony track
and metalled road, and
a couple of short but
very over-grown
sections, through an
orchard near the start
and at Llan-vihangel
Court, where a stick
might be useful to beat
back the nettles.

134

Skirrid from Offa's Dyke.

trees, crossing stile in hedge, then bear diagonally down to field corner to cross stream by footbridge. Maintain direction up to stile in hedge, cross field to gate and head steeply up to barn. Pass through gate on right (between barns), follow concrete drive past farm and bear right to follow clump of trees to left (concrete path) to gate. Cross field to right-hand corner and keep ahead along metalled road for 100 yds (90 m) to bend. Take footpath ahead over stile and climb by hedge to stile in corner, then continue up to stile above house. Turn right (90 degrees), head up towards Skirrid, go over farm gate and stile ahead on to bracken-covered slopes of Skirrid Fawr. Climb very steeply (with care) to summit, then walk along ridge and descend on well-worn path through trees, over stone wall and down track back to car park.

• **LLANFIHANGEL COURT** A fine Tudor mansion (not open) that is said to have been visited by Queen Elizabeth I. A short detour right along its drive gives a glimpse of the gardens and the gables of the house through heavy, studded, latticed wooden gates.

• **SKIRRID INN** An old stone inn that served as a courthouse. Between 1110 and the 17thC nearly 200 people were hanged here. The scorch marks of the rope are still visible on the beam above the foot of the stairs which served as the scaffold. Medieval windows and heavy oak beams remain but much of the building is Tudor.

• **ST CADOC'S CHURCH, LLANGATTOCK LINGOED,** with its massive stone roof-tiles, chunky window tracery and solid buttresses, is worth stepping into to appreciate a simple and unspoilt interior. Unusual old features include box pews and a beam between the chancel and nave bears traces of intricate carving, the only evidence of a delicate screen it must have once supported.

• **SKIRRID FAWR** is also known as the Holy Mountain. Legend has it that on the day of the crucifixion a bolt of thunder hit the mountain and rent it in two parts – a possible explanation for the rocky mass below the north-west edge of the mountain. At the summit, little remains of the chapel built so that persecuted Catholics could worship in peace – it is just a round indentation where wall brown butterflies bask. Magnificent views in all directions can be savoured, from the Black Mountains in the north-west and Exmoor in the south to the Malverns and Cannock Chase in the north.

FOOD AND DRINK
Skirrid Inn at Llanfihangel Crucorney (reliable bar food & B&B – 01874 665276). Hunters Moon at Llangattock Lingoed and, near the start at Llandewi Skirrid (on B4521), the Walnut Tree for some of the best cooking (Italian) in Wales – 01873 852797.

The Mortimer Trail

*One of the region's loveliest upland walks, officially opened in 1996,
The Mortimer Trail takes you to the heart of the Welsh Marches, a
once bitterly contested land of lush pastures, wooded valleys and
rolling hills. The well waymarked trail takes its name from the
autocratic Mortimer family whose seat was at Wigmore. They ruled
this country with awesome authority in medieval times. The route
climbs a series of spectacular ridges, with magnificent views of the
Black Mountains and the Clee Hills. From these breezy tops the trail
runs down to the banks of the Rivers Lugg and Arrow where you
might spot a kingfisher or perhaps a heron. The Mortimer Trail has
plenty of tree cover, welcome shade on a hot day.*

Planning

A two-day walk beginning at
Ludlow and concluding at
Kington. As public transport
is limited, several hoteliers
and bed- and-breakfast
proprietors offer a flexible
transport service for those
who might want to complete
only part of the trail. Those
who plan to undertake the
whole walk could leave a car
at Kington, then travel by
bus or train to Ludlow via
Leominster.

Day 1 Ludlow to
Aymestrey

Day 2 Aymestrey to
Kington.

The official guide to the
Mortimer Trail also lists
various loop walks which
enable walkers to leave the
main route for refreshment
or accommodation.

Start *Leave your car in
Kington and take the bus
(9.30/10.30 am – does not
run on Sunday) to Hereford
to link up with the half-hour
train service to Ludlow – total journey
time approx 1¹/₂ hours. For travel
information: County Bus, tel. 01345
125436, Shropshire Traveline, tel. 01345
056785. This should allow plenty of time to
complete the 12-mile (19-km) first-day
walk. The route itself starts at the main
entrance to Ludlow Castle in the town
centre. Ludlow's British Rail station is off
Corve Street, about five minutes from the
start of the walk.*

Essentials

Moderate fairly tough
for inexperienced
walkers;
Day 1/Walk 7 13 miles/
(20 km); 6 hours; a few
meandering climbs,
quite strenuous in one
or two places.
Day 2/Walk 8 17
miles/(27 km); 8 hours;
several steep climbs but
essentially quite level;
map Ordnance Survey
1: 50 000 Landranger
Map 137, Ludlow and
Wenlock Edge and Map
148, Presteigne and Hay-
on-Wye.
Terrain Paths and
tracks, some stretches
of road. Second stage
can be overgrown and
rather rough underfoot
in places during the
summer months. Some
sections wet and muddy
after rain.

Route directions

Day 1 Facing Ludlow
Castle turn right and follow
path down below its walls.
Bear right at fork and drop
down to road. Turn left to
Dinham Bridge, then right
across River Teme. Look for
steps on far bank and bear
right at top. Follow path as
it bends left, pass over
cross- track and keep going
to road. Turn right and walk
down to hairpin bend.
Follow no through road for
several steps, then veer left.
When path forks, take lower
route and climb gradually
through the trees of
Mortimer Forest. Keep
going, turning left at
junction to reach road
almost immediately. Take
track opposite, pass Forest
Enterprise buildings and
visitor car park and follow
drive deeper into forest.
Views of the Mary Knoll
Valley open up further on.
Keep going on track,
following it down to hairpin
bend. At the next bend join path running
down to stream. Cross it, bear left, then
almost immediately right to climb path
between trees. Turn right at junction of
tracks and follow sunken path over forest
track and across Climbing Jack Common.
When main track swings left, continue
ahead and soon reach fork. Keep left here
and make for the 1,200-ft/(370-m) summit
of High Vinnals. The views across to the
Welsh mountains are tremendous. Drop

down to junction of tracks; turn left, then immediately right to follow woodland path. Pass through gate and keep to right edge of field. Pass farm road on right and continue to gate leading on to track between banks and hedges. Follow bridleway through woodland to road at hamlet known as The Goggin. Bear left, then right at fork and go up slope. Turn left at next junction and walk along Stockin Lane, dropping down slope to next junction. Bear right to junction with Waterloo Lane. Keep left here for about 110 yds (100 m), then swing right to join track. Pass Spout House and continue on thin path running to left of farm outbuildings. Turn right at road and keep left at next junction, passing several houses. Bear right at stile into field and cross three boundaries with hedge close by on right. Follow old dirt track towards Lodge Farm, keeping to right of farmhouse. Do not turn right, but continue ahead along green lane through bracken, still with hedge on right. Turn left at top corner of field, cross stile to gate leading on to Bircher Common, a peaceful place ringed by trees. Turn right about 30 paces beyond gate and cross common to enter Croft Wood via stile. Follow woodland track, eventually dropping to junction in clearing. Turn right, up bank to gate on Yatton Common and veer left to follow path alongside perimeter fence of Croft Ambrey hill fort. Avoid turnings off and head for spectacular viewpoint at western extremity of site. Swing left at bench and follow path down to junction with track. Turn left, keeping right in front of gate, and, with views on right, follow path into woodland. Come up to junction with forest track and turn right. Descend to School Wood, pass barn to reach gate and lane. Head down the road, bearing right after 330 yds (300 m) to join track running into field. Turn

---

ACCOMMODATION
The Riverside Inn at **Aymestrey** (tel. 01568 708440) offers bed-and-breakfast throughout the year and is directly on the route of the Mortimer Trail, close to the halfway point of the walk; **The Stagg Inn** at **Titley**, nearer to Kington, has rooms available in the summer months (tel. 01544 230221). There are other inns and guest houses on or near the trail and in Ludlow and Kington. *The Mortimer Trail Walker's Guide* and full details of accommod-ation and public transport are available from the tourist information centres – Ludlow (tel. 01584 875053), Kington (tel. 01544 230778) and Leominster (tel. 01568 616460).

FOOD AND DRINK
Few opportunities along the route so it is advisable to take your own food and drink, especially on Day 1. Within easy reach from the trail on Day 2 are Batemans Arms, Shobdon, Herbs Tea Room (Garden Centre) at Horseway Head, Stag Inn, Titley – see map.

---

right to twin stiles in boundary, head obliquely left across pasture to next stile, then make for coniferous Pokeshouse Wood ahead. Descend steeply between trees, pass over crossing track and keep following path through woodland. Take care as the ground here can be slippery at times. Emerge from wood and ahead is the River Lugg. Veer a little to the right, cross stile and look for gateway slightly left. Follow raised track to lodge and gate beyond which is the road at Aymestrey. The Riverside Inn can be seen on the left.

Day 2 From the inn bear left and take first left turning for Lye and Lingen. Follow lane through gloriously wooded valley, sweeping left, then right to reach house with attached greenhouse. Turn left opposite (signposted Kington), cross field to stile. Follow green track running along edge of Sned Wood for more than 1 mile (1.6 km) and turn left at road junction to cross River Lugg. This is the trail's halfway point. Follow lane to left bend; cross stile here, then go straight ahead up hillside path to woodland edge. Turn left at track and follow it for some time. Draw level with some sheds and turn right here at junction of tracks. Go straight on when track bends left and climb steeply through trees. Keep left at fork, curve left at hilltop and follow track between bracken and oak trees. Pass turning to Shobdon and continue along avenue of trees. When it swings left, veer off to right and follow path along woodland edge. Bear left at sign 'caution – steep descent' and take path over stile, out across Byton Common. Path is rough and uneven underfoot in places and can get overgrown with bracken and wild grass in summer. Eventually it descends to path junction. Turn right

137

and go down to gate. Just beyond it track curves left by stone cottage. Go up steps in right bank, cross pasture to gate and join lane. Turn right and follow it to next junction in centre of Byton. Opposite are several farms. Bear left here to next junction (B4362), turn right, then left for Wapley hill fort. Look for steps in right bank after 35 yds (30 m) and follow path up hillside with fence on left. Drop down slope, cross stile, turn right and make for next stile. Head slightly right for top right corner of field, join path along woodland edge and go deeper into trees and undergrowth. Turn left at next junction, follow wide grassy track for almost 100 yds (90 m) to next junction. Bear right and follow track between trees. At next signposted junction veer half-right and soon you emerge from trees by ramparts of Wapley Hill. Turn left down slope and merge with track. Swing sharp left by house and after 70 yds (65 m), turn right to join path which soon veers left to pleasant forest track. Descend hillside, pass over cross-track, enter field and aim slightly right towards house. Make for stile in field boundary, turn left across

railway bridge before lane narrows to become rough green track. Cross stile and head slightly right up field slope; maintain same direction in next field and make for far corner. Go out to road, turn right and walk along to Mowley Farm. Cross stile on left just beyond it and turn right to stile in far hedgerow. Follow path ahead alongside hedge, pass several houses and then bear left at stile for road. Turn right along to junction at Titley. Bear left and then turn right immediately before Titley church, following track along field perimeter. Keep to field edge, pass through gap into next field and continue along boundary. When field opens out to right, go straight on to stile in boundary hedge. Aim slightly right in next field, making for barred gate. Head down

towards farm, cross several stiles and then turn left through barred gate. Bear right and follow green lane through gate to ruins of an isolated farm. Cross stile, swing right and follow field edge to corner, passing several stiles in right boundary. Cross stile and enter wood. Cross another stile, break cover from trees and follow field edge to next stile leading into wood. Path cuts through bracken, undergrowth and between trees; eventually you reach stile. Go straight on through conifer plantation, descend steps to junction and turn left along grassy swathe. Turn left by beech trees and follow path up slope to gate. Go straight ahead alongside

old orchard to stile by road. Bear right and walk along to T-junction in Stansbatch. Turn right, then left after about 70 yds (65 m) and follow narrow lane. Pass Slate House, then a Baptist chapel and the remains of an old boundary fence and up slope to stile. Follow track between gorse bushes and out across Rushock Hill Common. The earthworks ahead are part of Offa's Dyke. When the track peters out, aim for

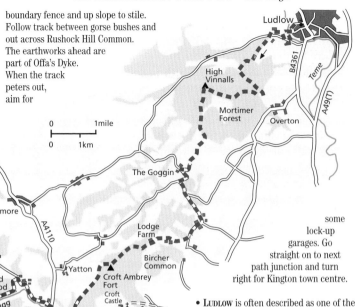

right edge of gorse patch. Look for waymark here and drop down to stile. Go diagonally across field, making for right of farmhouse. Cross stile and follow lane, dropping down steeply to junction. Turn right, then left over stile and up green lane beside boundary to next stile. Cross it and follow track down towards farm. Go through gate, veer left and up bank to stile in trees. Bear right along field edge, cross over farm track and keep to right of solid oak tree. Make for three gates in bottom corner of field. Go through middle gate and straight on following field perimeter round corner to next stile, exiting to road. Cross and take track for Mill Farm. Cross ford, take next stile on right, then cross footbridge to stile in next boundary. Go straight on through fence gap; the River Arrow lies to the left. Cross stile and follow hedge to next stile by bungalows. After a few steps, you reach road. Turn left, walk to junction with A44, cross over to Old Foundry. Pass entrance and follow lane between stone walls. After about 60 yds (55 m) bear left opposite a low building with slate roof. Follow alleyway running along backs of houses, cross road, veer right to join tarmac path. Continue ahead to junction with path by

some lock-up garages. Go straight on to next path junction and turn right for Kington town centre.

• **LUDLOW** is often described as one of the loveliest towns in the country. The focal point of Ludlow is Castle Square, guarded by an awesomely sturdy 11thC fortification built to keep out the Welsh, though a stroll around the town and a study of its medieval street pattern reveal a multitude of picturesque and historic listed buildings – almost 500 in all. Ludlow is also famous for its annual arts festival.

• **CROFT AMBREY** This spectacularly sited Iron Age hill fort dates from about 390BC and was occupied until about AD50. The camp originally covered 24 acres and is now in the care of the National Trust.

• **AYMESTREY** Its lovely wooded river valley setting makes this village a popular base for walkers and visitors. Aymestrey, which also includes a number of period houses and cottages, once boasted a charming tradition. One of the church bells was tolled every evening to help guide travellers who might be lost in nearby Pokeshouse Wood.

• **KINGTON** Situated on the banks of the River Arrow, Kington is often associated with Offa's Dyke Path, which runs through it. The town has a traditional market place and a historic Norman church. Tales of a ghostly dog on nearby Hergest Ridge inspired Conan Doyle's *The Hound of the Baskervilles*.

139

Introduction
Snowdonia

George Borrow, the 19thC writer and traveller, wrote of Snowdonia 'perhaps in all the world there is no region more picturesquely beautiful.' Certainly, nowhere in England and Wales offers the same grandeur and sense of isolation. Known in North Wales as the ' Eagles Nesting Place', Snowdonia is a land of towering summits, craggy, mist-covered peaks and breath-taking passes with more than 150 lakes, 25 miles (40 kilometres) of coastline and the highest range of mountains in England and Wales. It is not just this spectacular scenery that draws more than a million visitors each year. The area is steeped in ancient myths and legends and there is a real sense of history, especially in the castles which Edward I built in order to establish a united Britain.

History

Wherever you walk in this wild country you can see how the past has influenced the landscape. There was a strong Celtic presence, evidenced by the hill forts. The Romans built roads and excavated copper, gold and manganese. In more recent years the area played host to extensive and exhaustive slate mining, now an integral part of Snowdonia's fascinating industrial heritage.

Snowdonia has long been a Mecca for the climbers, and Edmund Hillary and his team practised here for the first successful assault on Everest in 1953. The mountains have a timeless, mystical quality, though the age of leisure and recreation has encouraged a new breed of adventurer to take to the hills and with so many visitors there is now little chance of having it completely to yourself.

Mount Snowdon

The Welsh for Snowdon is Yr Wydffa, meaning the tumulus, a reference to the final resting place of Rhita Fawr, a giant slain by King Arthur. Rising to 3,560 feet (1,085 metres) and the highest mountain south of the Scottish Highlands, Snowdon lies at the heart of the 827-square-mile (2,142-square-kilometre) National Park – the very centre of the historic struggle for Welsh independence. Six paths climb to the rocky summit – the Miners' Track, Beddgelert Path and Snowdon Ranger Track among them – and from the top the views are breathtaking. Mountain peaks and ridges crowd in

> **GETTING THERE**
> Snowdonia is best approached via the M54 or M56 which link with the M1, M5 and M6. The A5 and the A55 then provide direct routes into the park.
>
> You can travel to Snowdonia by train via Llandudno, Prestatyn and the North Wales holiday coast. There are stations along the Conwy Valley to Blaenau Ffestiniog and the railways make ideal starting and finishing points for some enjoyable walks. The region is also well served by a network of famous narrow-gauge railways at Bala, Llanberis, Tywyn and Ffestiniog. There is also the spectacular Snowdon Mountain Railway for those who don't want to make the climb.

Llynnau Mymbyr.

Roewen Walk 2

Nant Peris Walk 3

Pen-y-Gwryd
Walk 7/8

Betws-y-Coed
Walk 6

Beddgelert Walk 1/4

WEATHER
Always check
conditions before
venturing into the hills.
Guidance on when to
walk is given by the
National Park Office at
Penrhyndeudraeth (tel.
01776 770274). You can
also ring Mountain Call
service on 0891 505285
to get a detailed
weather forecast for the
Snowdonia National
Park.

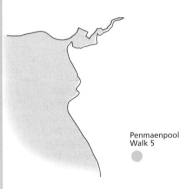

Penmaenpool
Walk 5

tightly in every direction and to the west the smooth expanse of Caernarfon
Bay glistens on the far horizon beyond Snowdonia's spectacular coastline of
glorious beaches, mudflats and estuaries. To the east of Snowdon the River
Conwy runs north towards the Irish Sea, passing through the lush pastoral
Vale of Conwy.

Lowland walking
But Snowdonia is not just about mountain peaks. There are plenty of gentler
alternatives, including an extensive network of lowland routes, forest trails and
numerous waymarked walks. Below Snowdon lies the historic village of
Llanberis, one of the region's most popular attractions and conveniently placed
for touring Snowdonia. Betws-y-Coed is another mountain resort with a range
of delightful walks exploring unspoilt river scenery and pretty pastoral uplands.
The nearby Gwydyr Forest is a haven for walkers. Ffestiniog, to the south-west,
offers riverside rambles, and Porthmadog with its pretty harbour setting,
gateway to the renowned Lleyn Peninsula, is also an obvious destination for
many visitors to Snowdonia.

Beddgelert

Snowdonia backdrop.

However, the original building was eventually dismantled by Henry VIII during the first half of the 16thC during the Dissolution of the Monasteries, though, thankfully, the chapel survived and was restored in 1830. You can see the two remaining 12thC arches, the doorway to the vestry, believed also to have provided access to the prior's cell, and the east wall with its superb triple lancet window.

Beddgelert offers the visitor an excellent choice of waymarked trails and forest walks. A stroll along the banks of the Glaslyn, to the south of the village, brings you to a stone monument supposedly marking the site of Gelert's Grave. This is said to be the grave of Prince Llywelyn's dog, which he'd left to guard his baby son. On his return he found the cradle overturned and the dog's jaws stained with blood. In a rage he slew the hound. He then heard his baby crying under the cradle and found the body of a wolf nearby. Full of remorse, Llywelyn buried Gelert at this spot and marked the spot with a cairn. Many have disputed the legend over the years and some even suggest that a local publican dreamt up this version of events at the beginning of the 19thC in an effort to boost tourism. Visitors can also take a short walk to the Sygun Copper Mine which is just outside Beddgelert and open to the public.

F ew would dispute Beddgelert's tag as Snowdonia's loveliest mountain village. Its picturesque, unspoilt position at the confluence of the rivers Glaslyn and Colwyn makes it an ideal holiday base. Just a few miles to the south of Snowdon, Beddgelert is surrounded by some of the grandest and most beautiful country in Britain. Close by is the spectacular Aberglaslyn Pass. Not surprisingly, thousands of people head for the village every year to go walking, fishing, sailing and pony-trekking – among other outdoor activities.

Beddgelert has long been a popular haunt of visitors to North Wales and many literary figures have been captivated by its charms over the years, among them the poet William Wordsworth who came here and climbed Snowdon from the village in search of inspiration.

The parish church of St Mary's is chiefly associated with a Celtic Christian community established on this site in the 6thC and claimed to be the oldest religious foundation in Wales after Bardsey. During the 13thC it became an Augustinian priory chapel and by the Middle Ages had prospered greatly under the influence of wealthy nobles and princes. The priory was destroyed by fire late in the 13thC but later restored by Edward I.

ACCOMMODATION AND FOOD

The Beddgelert area is well served with a varied selection of places to stay, from friendly farmhouses to stylish country-house hotels. For further details on these and the wide range of self-catering properties in Snowdonia, contact Beddgelert Tourism Association, The Post Office, Beddgelert, Gwynedd LL55 4UY (tel. 01766 890201), or Snowdonia Tourism Association, Beddgelert LL55 4NE (tel. 01766 510100).

SLEEPING AND EATING

HOTELS AND INNS

BEDDGELERT
Royal Goat Hotel; *tel. 01766 890224.* Modernized, 200-year-old hotel set in mature woodland. Comfortably furnished public areas and spacious, attractively decorated bedrooms (some with four-posters).

Tanronnen Inn; *tel. 01766 890258.* Situated at the head of the Glaslyn Pass, this welcoming small hotel is a popular walking base. Cosy bars, residents' lounge and high standard of accommodation in seven well-appointed bedrooms.

Sygun Fawr Country House; *tel. 01766 890210; closed Nov–Jan.* Surrounded by mountains with magnificent views of the Gwynant valley, this peaceful, 17thC Welsh manor house (exposed timber and stone) offers small, comfortable and well-decorated bedrooms, and several sitting rooms.

PORTMEIRION
Hotel Portmeirion; *(10 miles/16 km S); tel.: 01766 770228; closed Jan.* Fairytale, Italianate village created by Sir Clough Williams-Ellis in the 1920s, this sumptuously decorated hotel has individually furnished bedrooms and elegant sitting rooms, most with stunning sea views. Warm hospitality and good food.

CAPEL GARMON
Tan-y-Foel Country House; *Betws-y-Coed; tel. 01690 710507.* Stylishly refurbished 16thC farmhouse enjoying a splendid hillside location with views

across the Conwy valley. Thoughtfully-equipped and well-furnished bedrooms feature four-poster or brass beds. Cosy sitting rooms and imaginative home-cooking.

MAENTWROG
Grapes Hotel; *(12 miles /19.2 km SE); tel. 01766 590365.* Popular coaching inn, supposedly haunted, serving home-cooked food in the three characterful bars and dining room (spit-roasts over open fire). Comfortable accommodation.

BED-AND-BREAKFAST

GELLIYDAN
Tyddyn Du; *Ffestiniog (12 miles/19.2 km SE); tel. 01766 59028; closed Christmas.* 400-year-old working farm in spectacular scenery, offering a relaxed atmosphere and character accommodation in comfortable main house bedrooms and cottage suite in converted outbuildings. Hearty farmhouse cooking. Four bedrooms.

PENTREFELIN
Tyddyn Iolyn; *Criccieth (8 miles/12.8 km S); tel. 01766 522509.* Secluded 16thC farmhouse in peaceful setting with fine views of Snowdonia and the coast. Three bedrooms (one four-poster) and traditional home-cooking.

LLANFROTHEN
Y Wern; *Penrhyndeudraeth (7 m/11.2 km S); tel: 01766 770556.* Creeper-clad, stone-built farmhouse dating from the 17thC. Five large and comfortable bedrooms enjoy splendid views and the relaxing

sitting room has a working inglenook fireplace. Sun terrace, trout stream and traditional farmhouse food.

CAMPING AND HOSTELS

Beddgelert Forest Campsite *(tel. 01766 890288)* is a well-run site set in mountainous wooded country just north of the town. Further north on the A4085 is the excellent ***Bryn Gloch Caravan and Camping Park, Betws Garmon*** *(tel. 01286 650216)*, a picturesque, well-equipped site beside the River Gwyrfai. Youth Hostel accommodation includes ***Beddgelert*** *(at* ***Nant Gwynant*** *– tel. 01766 890251)*, ***Rhyd Ddu*** *(Snowdon Ranger – tel. 01286 650391)* and ***Llanberis*** *(Llwyn Celyn – tel. 01286 870280)*.

FOOD

Restaurants worth investigating, in addition to ***Hotel Portmeirion and Tan-y-Foel***, both mentioned above, include ***Y Bistro, Llanberis*** *(tel. 01286 871278)*; ***Ty'n Rhos, Llanddeiniolen*** *(near Caernarfon – tel. 01248 670489)* and, especially, ***Maes-y-Neuadd, Talsarnau*** *(tel. 01766 780200 – also upmarket, country-house hotel accommodation)*. Good home-cooked pub food, in addition to ***Grapes Hotel*** above, is served at the ***Cwellyn Arms, Rhyd-Ddu*** *(tel. 01766 890321)*; ***Bryn Tyrch Hotel, Capel Curig*** *(tel. 01690 720223 – also B&B)*, and the ***Groes Inn, Ty'n-y-Groes*** *(near Conwy – tel. 01492 650545 – also B&B)*.

Gelert's Grave and Sygun Copper Mines

An interesting and easily followed 'family' ramble that takes in the Aberglaslyn Pass, a noted beauty spot, where the River Glaslyn has eroded a gorge through the rolling hills, before climbing Cwm Bychan, its hillsides strewn with old copper mine workings. On the way you will go through a 350-yard (320-metre) rock tunnel.

Start Beddgelert, SH588481, at junction of A408 from Capel Curig and A4085 from Caernarfon. Park in main public car park (near Royal Goat Hotel).

Route directions

From car park turn left along main road through village, then just before bridge over river take small road right, signposted Gelert's Grave. Before footbridge follow arrowed path right to visit Gelert's Grave (¼ mile/ 0.4 km). Return and cross footbridge to take well-worn footpath right alongside River Glaslyn. Shortly, path joins course of old railway, following trackbed through spectacular wooded gorge towards Aberglaslyn Pass. Go through small tunnel, then a long and quite dark tunnel (350 yds/320 m) – surface even underfoot – to reach stone waymarker by grassy picnic area. Turn left, signposted Cwm Bychan, and ascend beautiful small valley alongside stream to gate near little waterfall. Continue to climb, pass disused mine workings and soon follow line of old pylons ahead up wide grassy path towards col (depression) between rocky outcrops. Cross stile at top, bear left on path through heather to waymarked junction of tracks. Turn right towards Llyn Dinas, keeping to good path steeply downhill to lakeside. Turn left across stile and soon follow left-hand side of river, passing Dinas Emrys (ruins of castle keep) on opposite bank to reach Sygun Copper Mine (well worth closer inspection). Beyond, path soon becomes

Essentials

Easy 4½ miles (7 km); 2–3½ hours (if visiting Sygun Mines); generally level with one steady climb and a steep descent; **map** Ordnance Survey 1:50 000 Landranger Map 115, Snowdon or 1:25 000 Outdoor Leisure Map 17, Snowdon & Conwy Valley.
Terrain Good riverside paths and grassy hillside tracks; middle section of walk can be wet after heavy rain. Stout walking shoes recommended.

FOOD AND DRINK
Full range of facilities in Beddgelert; café in visitors centre at Sygun Copper Mine.

metalled, then at bridge cross stile in wall left and keep to left side of river. Go through gate, cross road and in 150 yds (135 m) re-enter Beddgelert by footbridge crossed at start.

• **BEDDGELERT** See p. 142.

• **DISUSED RAILWAY** The old trackbed once formed part of the Welsh Highland Railway, the longest narrow-gauge railway in Wales, which ran for 22 miles (35 km) from Porthmadog to Dinas Junction near Caernarfon. It served local mines before finally closing in 1973. Part of the route has been reopened from Porthmadog to Blaenau Ffestiniog and there are plans to extend the working line to Beddgelert.

• **CWM BYCHAN** is a beautiful little valley filled with sweet chestnut, oak, birch and mountain ash trees.

• **DINAS EMRYS** Set on a wooded hill overlooking Llyn Dinas, this castle mound with ruined walls of a 12thC keep was built on the site of an Iron Age hill fort. It served, like many castles in the area, to defend Snowdonia from the English.

• **SYGUN COPPER MINE** With the aid of an informative audio-visual tour and an expert guide, visitors can explore the old workings of this 19thC copper mine set deep in the Gwynant Valley and gain an insight into the underground world of the Victorian miner. Stalactites and stalagmites.

Celtic sites and sea views

From the charming village of Rowen and the lush Conwy Valley this peaceful walk climbs steadily to 2,000 feet (610 metres) to the summit of Tal y Fan, where glorious mountain, valley and sea views can be enjoyed. In an area rich in history the walk incorporates a visit to a remote 14thC church, passes neolithic standing stones and a burial chamber, and follows the route of an old Roman road.

Start *Rowen, SH759720. Picturesque village situated 2 miles (3.2 km) off B5106 Conway to Llanwrst road, 2.5 miles (4 km) south of Conwy. Parking is possible opposite the Ty Gwyn Hotel or near the shop.*

Route directions

With hotel on right, walk through village and take first road right, signposted Youth Hostel. Continue uphill and turn right into narrow lane just beyond cottage called Bod Adwen. Pass Cold Mawr Hall, continue 300 yds (270 m) to lane left and climb steeply to stile on right-hand bend before farm. Follow stream and wall to join well-defined track. Turning right, continue climbing through broadleaved woodland with views over Conwy Valley, right. At fork keep right (yellow arrow on tree) to stile and stream, then follow path ahead, bearing left through trees on open land and derelict cottage. Pass between cottage and shed and bear left by ash tree, following path uphill to ladder stile on skyline. Bear left alongside wall to stile and walled track by Llangelynin church. Take time to visit this simple, isolated church, then follow green lane uphill through gates on to open hillside. In 200 yds (180 m) fork right at junction, cross stream and pass between two walls, then follow left track uphill across open ground. Pass old quarry, left, and shortly reach Maen

Essentials

Moderate 6½ miles (10.8 km); 4 hours; long gradual uphill climb; steep descent in places back to Rowen; **map** Ordnance Survey 1:50 000 Landranger Map 115, Snowdon or 1:25 000 Outdoor Leisure Map 17, Snowdon & Conwy Valley.
Terrain Lofty tracks and grassy paths across open hillside; sections of metalled road; paths can be very wet (not muddy) after rain. Walking boots recommended.

Penddu (standing stone) near junction of tracks. Turn left, then where track bears left into old slate quarry, follow path right, rising round shoulder of hillside. Keep hill and crags left, climbing on ill-defined sheep tracks to wall along summit ridge. Turn right, eventually reaching triangulation point on top of Tal y Fan. Follow wall to ladder stile and turn left downhill on waymarked path, leading downhill across stiles to road. Turn left, soon to fork left on well-defined track (Maen-y-Bardd burial chamber left) that descends steeply in places back to Rowen.

- **LLANGELYNIN CHURCH** Built of stone and slate, this simple building has seen over 500 years of worship and continues to be used every third Sunday at 3 pm between May and September.

- **MAEN-Y-BARDD** Well-preserved neolithic burial chamber consisting of a capstone and four upright stones. Numerous dolmens and standing stones litter the hillsides indicating that neolithic man actively used this area about 4,000 years ago.

FOOD AND DRINK
None along the route. Ty Gwyn Hotel and The Willows (seasonal tearoom) in Rowen. Good food and views at the Groes Inn (open all day) at Ty'n y Groes nearby.

- **ROMAN ROAD** The track follows the course of a Roman road linking Chester and Caernarfon. It was later used by cattle drovers and local farmers.

145

Llyn Y Cwm and the
Top of Y Garn

*A tough walk from the base of the Llanberis Pass up Cwm Cneif to
Llyn y Cwm, a peaceful spot for a welcome rest – because you then
have a steep zigzagging path to overcome, leading to the summit of
Y Garn. Stunning mountain views, including all the Welsh peaks
higher than 3,000 feet (915 metres), greet your arrival on a clear day.
Next, a lofty ridge walk before descending a valley back to Nant Peris.*

Llanberis.

Start Nant Peris,
SH607583. *Small village
located on the A4086
Caernarfon to Capel
Curig road, at the base of
the Llanberis Pass. Park
in the National Park car
park. Regular bus service
(Snowdon Sherpa 96 –
additional buses
June–October) links
Beddgelert to Nant Peris.*

Essentials

Strenuous 7 miles (11.8
km); 5–6 hours; hilly;
one steep, strength-
sapping climb; *map*
Ordnance Survey
1:50 000 Landranger
Map 115 Snowdon or
1:25 000 Outdoor
Leisure Map 17,
Snowdonia & Conwy
Valley.
Terrain Steep grassy
paths; rock steps; some
scrambling up scree
and a section of
metalled road. It can be
wet and slippery
underfoot in winter;
walking boots and warm
clothing essential.

summit of Foel-Goch. The
ridge ends abruptly, so
take great care in poor
visibility. Cross stile close
by, descend stony path and
pass stile right, then in 150
yds (145 m) look for
initially indistinct path left
heading down valley. (If
time and energy allows,
follow path beside fence,
then bear left, keeping to
path round and up hillside
to col. From here you can
ascend Elidir Fawr or
Mynydd Perfedd (or both)
before returning to valley
path). Continue downhill,
path soon becoming more
distinct, then bear right at
fork of paths to reach
fence and stile. Keep
straight on, downhill
towards stream. Now head

Route directions

From car park turn right along main road
¹⁄₂ mile (0.8 km) until, just after passing
track on right, take footpath left through
gate, signposted Tay y Gadlas. Head
steeply up hillside on stony path via stiles,
alongside Afon Las. Leave stream to climb
rock step and continue, soon to rejoin
stream, following it to Llyn y Cwm and a
welcome rest. A short distance north-east
is the Devil's Kitchen (well worth the
detour). From Llyn y Cwm follow clear
path north towards Y Garn and climb
steadily over grass then
scree to crags of Castell y
Geifre. Keep to path (close
to edge in places) up to
summit. Follow main ridge
path downhill to fence and
then right for 200 yds (180
m) to cross stile. Maintain
direction (fence left) to

down valley on ill-defined path, then with
joining of walls and fences left, climb two
stiles and follow wall. Cross two further
stiles, then pass stile right, keeping to
path to gateway. Beyond, bear left
downhill across field to gate and road
(phone box right). Continue ahead to the
main road in Nant Peris, turning left back
to car park.

• **DEVILS' KITCHEN** Also known as Twll Du
(the black hole), this dark chasm cuts
deeply into the crags and displays all the
characteristics of being a
hellish place. The stream
from Llyn y Cwm flows to,
and cascades down, the
Devil's Kitchen. A short
diversion to Twll Du
affords views down to Llyn
Idwal and the Ogwen
Valley.

FOOD AND DRINK
Enjoy a picnic on the
summit of Y Garn, or
head for the Vaynol
Arms in Nant Peris for
a well earned drink on
completing the walk.

Beddgelert Forest and Cwm Pennant Valley

An adventurous ramble in the foothills of Snowdon exploring part of Beddgelert Forest before crossing into the upper reaches of Cwm Pennant. A short return bus journey is necessary at the end.

Start *Beddgelert, SH588481, at junction of A408 and A4085 in the heart of the National Park. Park in main public car park.*

Return *regular buses depart from Rhyd-Ddu car park for Beddgelert every two hours from noon to 6 pm, at 9 minutes past the hour.*

Wooded gorge, Beddgelert area.

Route directions From car park turn left into village. Cross river bridge, turn left along A4085 and in ¹/₂ mile (0.8 km) look for waymarked footpath through gate left (opposite road sign – 'Croeso Beddgelert Welcome'). Bear half-right downhill across field to wooden bridge over stream, then ascend through field, passing to right of stone outbuilding to gate and track. Turn left, then in 20 yds (18 m) climb stone steps and go through broken kissing gate. Head uphill across deforested area on ill-defined path. Cross track and continue climbing (wall right) towards woods. Join forest track, turn right and follow it left to cross bridge over stream. In 100 yds (90 m) turn left at junction of tracks. Turn left again at next junction and shortly cross two more concrete bridges. Take arrowed path right and for ¹/₂ mile (0.8 km) follow indistinct route (occasional footpath markers) uphill through dense forest, crossing three forest tracks.

Essentials

Moderate 9 miles (14.4 km); 6 hours; undulating; one steep climb; *map* Ordnance Survey 1:50 000 Landranger Map 115, Snowdon or 1:25 000 Outdoor Leisure Map 17, Snowdon & Conwy Valley.

Terrain Hill tracks through open mountain country; defined forest tracks. Very wet underfoot in middle section after heavy rain, otherwise generally dry. Strong waterproof boots are essential.

FOOD AND DRINK
None along the route. Cwellyn Arms (open all day) at the finish in Rhyd-Ddu.

Exit forest at fence stile immediately below crags of Moel yr Ogof. Cross old wall ahead and follow rough path left, uphill to junction of wall immediately below Ogof Owain Glyndwr (views south-east of Moel Hebog and down Cwm Llefrith). Cross wall stile and descend grassy path, passing old mine workings on left. Keep stream left and continue down Cwm Llefrith to stile and gate beyond. In 300 yds (270 m) turn right along excellent grassy path in front of wall. Follow route of Gorseddau Railway for 2 miles (3.2 km), contouring high above Cwm Pennant, towards old mine workings. Negotiate several stiles and gates, keeping to 'permissive' path to old quarry buildings. Climb grassy ramps beside tiered slate workings, then bear right to reach Bwlch-y-ddwr-elor (pass of two biers) and pause for wonderful mountain views. Keep to good path down through

147

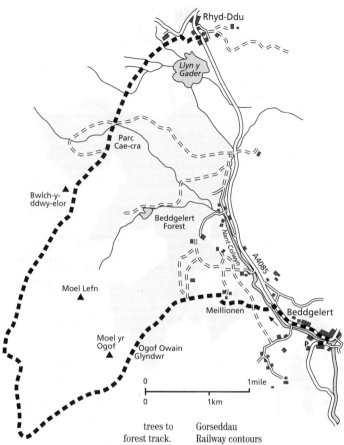

trees to forest track. Turn right then almost immediately left, then at junction by bridge, proceed ahead along path through trees towards open hillside. Pass through gap in wall and descend defined path (arrows on rocks) towards Rhyd-Ddu (Llyn-y-Gadair right). Just before road turn right along waymarked track. Cross stile and footbridge over stream, then follow slate-flagged footpath to A4085 opposite Rhyd-Ddu car park (bus stop). Cwellyn Arms ¹/₄ mile (0.4 km) left.

• **BEDDGELERT FOREST** has a thriving population of siskins, small, yellowy-green finches that feed on pine cones and are constantly on the move.

• **OGOF OWAIN GLYNDWR** Cave high in the cliffs, legendary hideout of the Welsh 14thC leader Owain Glyndwr.

• **CWM PENNANT** Peaceful valley where

Gorseddau Railway contours high above floor. This was part of the narrow-gauge system built to carry slate from the Prince of Wales slate quarry down to Porthmadog.

• **LLYN-Y-GADAIR** Low-lying ground with views of Snowdon and Yr Aran. Llyn-y-Gadair provides a marvellous foreground to the backdrop of mountains. In the Ice Age, this whole area was under about 2,000 ft (610 m) of ice. The huge glaciers altered the whole landscape and when they began to retreat, Snowdonia appeared as the jagged mountains we see today.

• **RHYD-DDU** The car park lies on the old track of the Welsh Highland Railway, which ran from Porthmadog to Caernarfon, through the Aberglaslyn Pass to Beddgelert. The narrow-gauge railway had a limited life, from 1922 to 1937, and was an offshoot of the Ffestiniog Railway.

148

Cader Idris and the Mawddach Estuary

A varied and not-too-demanding ramble through the foothills of Cader Idris, the second most popular peak in Wales, to Cregennen Lakes, two beautiful lakes sheltering beneath the mountain's northern escarpment. A short climb up Bryn Bryth gives magnificent views north across the Mawddach estuary towards the Rhinogs and Snowdonia beyond. The final easy few miles along the old railway line beside the estuary will interest birdwatchers (take binoculars). Visit the Wildlife Information Centre before starting the walk.

Start *Penmaenpool, SH 696185. Small village located on A493, 1 mile (1.6 km) west of A470 and Dolgellau. Use car park at Penmaenpool Bird Sanctuary and Information Centre, adjacent to Toll Bridge.*

Route directions

From car park turn right along A493. In 200 yds (180 m) take waymarked footpath left and gently climb through trees. After 600 yds (540 m), opposite pond on left, turn right along arrowed path and head uphill through woodland to stile. Proceed ahead to farm track and turn right, then just before cottage bear right on to Tir Cymen 'permissive' path. Pass stone barn right, cross two stiles and pass through gate to Penmaenucha Farm. Turn right to gate, then turn left and head gently uphill across field. Climb two further stiles and head towards ridge. Cross wall stile, turn right along track to old mine workings left, then follow wall right down to road. Turn left past Tyr Ysgol and in 150 yds (135 m) turn left through gate. Keep to track through trees to gap in wall beside gate and follow waymarker across field to gate. Turn right, then immediately right again through further arrowed gate into field.

Essentials

Moderate 11¾ miles (18.8 km); 7 hours. Gradual ascents; level alongside estuary; **map** Ordnance Survey 1:50 000 Landranger Map 124, Dolgellau or 1:25 000 Outdoor Leisure Map 23, Snowdonia – Cader Idris Area.
Terrain Grassy footpaths; firm open hillside paths; 4½ miles (6.4 km); follows well-surfaced Morfa Mawddach Cycleway alongside estuary.

FOOD AND DRINK

George III Hotel (open all day) at start point, offering home-cooked food, cream teas, accommodation and lovely estuary views from terrace.

Follow markers, bearing left through old farm buildings to gate. Proceed along track as it bears left, then climbs beside wall on right. Go through gap in wall and walk across field to exit in top corner. Beyond two gates join farm road opposite farmhouse and turn right downhill, passing youth hostel left (pleasant picnic spot by stream). At T-junction turn left uphill along road and in 100 yds (90 m) take footpath left through gate. Head uphill through trees to rejoin road opposite derelict church. Turn left, then where road bears left over stream, follow track ahead through gate. Head towards cottage and barn, aiming uphill of them to go through two gaps in field walls, then bear left to gate. Follow footpath left and remain on excellent grassy route to Cregennen Lakes (tranquil place to rest). (Climb Bryn Bryth on waymarked path for spectacular views.) Cross stile and keep ahead to road. Turn right steeply downhill, pass Gefnir Farm and in 250 yds (225 m), where road bends right, follow arrowed path ahead uphill. Cross fields and stile to walled track. Turn left, then after 100 yds (90 m) bear right alongside wall right to pass derelict building. Beyond gate, cross footbridge over stream and turn immediately right down opposite side. Keep to

149

distinct footpath steeply downhill beside
stream to gate and road (A493) opposite
church in Arthog. Turn left, then right at
end of churchyard to join waymarked path
through field. In 150 yds (135 m) turn left
on to dyke beside stream. Cross two stiles
and turn right along small road to old
railway bridge. Turn right along gravel
track bed (Penmaenpool to Mawddach
Walk/Cycleway) and follow it beside
estuary back to Information Centre and
car park.

• **PENMAENPOOL** is a reminder of the days
when shipping was important on the
Mawddach and ships were built in coves
along the estuary. More than 100 square-
riggers were constructed here between
1750 and 1827 and used in the export of
oak bark and woollen cloth. From 1830 the
trade became coastal with cargo
consisting mainly of pit props, coal flour
and limestone.

• **FORMER RAILWAY** This must have been
one of the most attractive of rail routes in
Britain: it ran the length of the Mawddach
estuary and offered passengers splendid
views of the Rhinog Mountains. A signal
box, now a Wildlife Information Centre,

On Cader Idris.

part of a platform and the line of the
trackbed (now a popular walk/cycleway)
are now all that remain. The railway
closed in 1965 when part of the line was
demolished by flooding near Dolgellau.
Wordsworth described the sweeping views
of the estuary as 'sublime'.

• **CREGENNEN LAKES** These two lovely
lakes nestle in a shallow depression at a
height of 1,000 ft (300 metres), beneath
the towering northern escarpment of
Cader Idris. The mountain is named,
according to legend, after the giant Idris
and means the Chair of Idris. Myth has it
that whoever spends a night on Cader
Idris is said to wake either blind, mad
or a poet.

• **WILDLIFE** In May and June rhododendrons provide a colourful display and the
hillsides are covered with heather. Look
out for otters, curlews, snipe,
oystercatchers, shelducks and lapwings,
among other interesting waders and duck,
that thrive in this rich estuary
environment.

Betws-y-Coed, Gwydir Forest and Swallow Falls

*Although long, this is a moderately easy ramble. The scenery is very
varied, featuring rough upland pasture with views of Tryfan, the
Glyders and Snowdon; sheltered tracks through Gwydir Forest, with its
lead-mining relics and scattering of small lakes; and delightful paths
beside picturesque reservoirs and the River Llugwy, the latter offering a
free view of Swallow Falls. Most of the paths are well defined and
route-finding is generally easy.*

Start *Betws-y-Coed,
SH791567. Popular
tourist village situated at
the junction of A5 and
B5106, 16 miles (26 km)
north-east of Beddgelert.
Public car park off B5106
(the Trefriw road), just
beyond bridge over River
Llugwy. More pay-and-
display car parks in
village.*

Route directions From
car park turn right along
minor road (river to left). In
150 yds (135 m) turn right
uphill by Summerhill guest
house, to reach junction of
tracks and bear right,
signposted Llyn Parc. In 500 yds (450 m),
at brow of hill (coloured waymarker post),
follow small path that angles left uphill
through trees. Path soon contours high
above Aberllyn gorge, then steepens and
passes old mine workings to reach track at
southern end of Llyn Parc. Turn left and at
junction in 300 yds (270 m), bear right for
250 yds (225 m) before taking arrowed
footpath left. Shortly reach forest track and
turn left. Pass track merging from left, then
at next junction follow track left downhill
towards cottage. In 150 yds (135 m) cross
stile over wall right and keep to signposted
footpath right, alongside wall to track. Walk
alongside wall on left to
gateway and climb stile on
right. Cross further stile and
continue straight ahead to
road. Turn right, go a short
distance, taking forest track
left, sign-posted Llyn
Glangors. At junction in 50

Essentials

Moderate 14 miles (22.4
km); undulating; few
demanding climbs; *map*
Ordnance Survey 1:50
000 Landranger Map
115, Snowdon or 1:25
000 Outdoor Leisure
Map 17, Snowdon &
Conwy Valley.
Terrain Firm forest
tracks; open rough
pasture; wooded
riverside paths; short
sections of metalled
road. Some soft ground
which can be wet in
winter; walking boots
essential.

FOOD AND DRINK
Plenty of choice in
Betws-y-Coed; lakeside
café at Llyn Crafnant;
good picnic spots along
the way.

yds (45 m) turn left, then
continue ahead at next
junction past cottage. Over
hill, with Llyn Glangors in
view, look for path left to
lake. Keep to path across
open ground to stile, then
climb further stile and
proceed to track by disused
mine workings. Turn left, go
through gate by farm
buildings and shortly reach
road. Turn right and follow
road to Llyn Geirionydd.
Turn left across southern
end of lake and cross stile
right by cottage to follow
lakeside path (a pleasant
spot in which to rest). At
end of lake cross stile and
bear left up to monument.
Take path directly ahead (to
left of knoll), and descend stony path, soon
to bear left over wall stile. Follow path
right, bear left after 50 yds (45 m) and
keep to distinct path as it bears left around
hillside, passing mine workings to stile and
track. Follow lower track down to car park
(WCs) and take arrowed path to Llyn
Crafnant. At head of lake cross bridge
(keep to east side of lake for café ½
mile/0.8 km) and go through gate to follow
track along west side of lake. Keep to track
beyond lake, then take waymarked path
left, downhill to stile and continue to gate
and track in front of cottage (Hendre).
Turn left through gate and follow track to
end of road by gate. Turn
sharply right on track, pass
farmhouse left and head
steeply uphill on defined
path to ridge. Gradually
descend small valley
(remains of building right),
crossing two stiles to reach

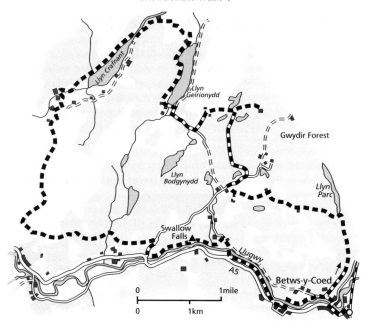

stone footbridge. Turn left along grassy path (can be very wet in places), soon to cross stile and join forest track. In ¹/₂ mile (0.8 km), as track bears left, take footpath right through trees leading to forest track. Turn right and follow uphill track for 100 yds (90 m), then follow footpath right beside wall. Cross stream and stile (cottage right), then in 100 yds (90 m) cross further stream and fence. Proceed on path alongside wall, join larger path, then forest track leading to road. Head steeply downhill for 400 yds (360 m) and take waymarked path beside River Llugwy, by postbox near main road. Path soon narrows to climb along gorge above Swallow Falls (take great care if you leave path to view falls). Soon join rutted track and reach road. Turn right, then in 150 yds (135 m) take narrow path right. Remain on path between road and river to Miners Bridge, then follow pleasant riverside path back into Betws-y-Coed and car park.

• **BETWS-Y-COED** Almost surrounded by forest at the junction of three valleys, pretty Betws-y-Coed was once an important staging post on the Holyhead road. Since Victorian times it has been a popular resort, unashamedly dedicated to tourism in recent decades. It boasts the graceful, iron Waterloo Bridge, built across the River Conwy by Telford in 1815 and the Conwy

Valley Railway Museum (working models, 15 in gauge railway). Its spectacular setting amid Snowdonia's magnificent peaks makes it an excellent walking and climbing base.

• **GWYDIR FOREST** Developed since 1920 by the Forestry Commission on the old Gwydir estate of the Wynn family, the area holds much wildlife, notably pine martens, polecats and interesting birds such as goldcrests, redpolls, siskins and crossbills.

• **MINING** Gwydir Forest is strewn with remains of copper and lead mines which flourished here in the 18th and 19thC. Information boards at some of the sites interpret what is to be seen and give some background history. Great care must be taken when walking through the area as it is riddled with old shafts and tunnels.

• **SWALLOW FALLS** One of the most popular attractions in Wales, these picturesque tumbling cascades are well worth viewing, especially after rainfall. 'Swallow' is a mistranslation of 'Ewynnol' meaning foaming.

• **MINERS BRIDGE** is a curious, steeply angled wooden structure that spans the River Llugwy. Originally a rough step-ladder, it used to be a miners' route to the now defunct lead mines.

Snowdon and surrounding peaks

Keen ramblers choosing Snowdonia as an area to explore are, in general, intent on climbing Snowdon, or its surrounding summits, in order to take in the magnificent panoramas across most of Snowdonia. Here you are offered a choice of walks, from easy to strenuous, depending on personal fitness, experience in mountain walking and weather conditions on the day. All of them capture Snowdonia's splendour and ruggedness. Either stay the night at the Pen-y-Gwryd Hotel, the famous climbing inn set in the heart of the mountains, or do them as separate day walks, making use of the bus service from Beddgelert.

Planning

Day 1 Ascent of Snowdon via the Pyg Track, **or** valley walk around Llyn Gwynant.

Day 2 The Glyders, Ogwen Valley and Capel Curig (alternative routes with varying lengths).

Whether you are a fit, experienced and fully equipped mountain rambler or just a keen walker used to long Sunday strolls, these carefully researched walks will help you explore and appreciate the magnificent landscape around Snowdon.

Day 1 From Pen-y-pass, the adventurous and energetic will want to do the infamous and gruelling Snowdon Horseshoe, while the less fit, or those lacking a head for heights, can enjoy a lower-level ramble around Llyn Gwynant with the Snowdon range towering above them. In summer, though, paths in the area close to Pen-y-pass car park and the summit of Snowdon can be unbearably crowded. **Day 2** offers a choice of walks in the Glyder range of mountains, each varying in length for differing abilities and staminas. After the strenuous walk up to the ridge, peak-baggers can climb Glyder Fach and

Essentials

Day 1/Walk 7
Strenuous Approx 7½ miles (12.6 km); 6 hours; hilly, or **Easy** 7¾ miles (13 km); 4 hours; mainly level.

Day 2/Walk 8
Moderate-strenuous 6 miles (10 km) – 15½ miles (19.8 km); hilly;

map Ordnance Survey 1:50 000 Landranger Map 115, Snowdon, or 1:25 000 Outdoor Leisure Map 17, Snowdon & Conwy Valley.

Terrain Snowdon and Glyders ascents – arduous, rocky mountainsides; well defined and steep zigzagging paths across scree; exposed ridge paths; rough tracks. Llyn Gwynant walk – valley and wooded lakeside paths; metalled lanes. Sections can be wet and boggy on Day 2, especially near start and through Ogwen Valley. Walking boots, waterproof and windproof clothing, detailed map and compass essential on mountain routes.

Glyder Fawr, followed by Tryfan, before descending into the Ogwen Valley for a level walk to Capel Curig and the return bus journey. Or, if time and energy allow, returning along the high ridge back to the hotel. The less able or willing can savour the breathtaking views across the Snowdon and Carnedd ranges before descending the ridge into Capel Curig.

Warning: do not attempt these walks in foggy, icy or stormy weather. Check weather and rock conditions before setting out and be properly equipped.

Start Day 1 *Pen-y-pass (or Pen-y-Gwryd Hotel), SH647556. Highest point of Llanberis Pass on A4086 between Llanberis and Capel Curig, 5 miles (8 km) south-east of Llanberis and 8 miles (12.8 km) north-east of Beddgelert. Car park opposite café (or at hotel).*
Day 2 *Pen-y-Gwryd Hotel (if not staying ask permission to park car and patronise hotel before or after walk), SH660559. Frequent bus service (Snowdon Sherpa 95) between Beddgelert and Pen-y-pass (additional services June–October),*

calling at Pen-y-Gwryd Hotel.

Note: In high season it may be impossible to park at Pen-y-pass, so use free car park at Nant Peris (down Llanberis Pass) and catch park-and-ride Sherpa bus (every half hour – hourly in winter) to Pen-y-pass or Pen-y-Gwryd.

Route directions

Day 1 If staying at hotel either drive or catch bus (best option in summer) to Pen-y-pass (it is possible to walk along A4086 but adds 2 miles (3.2 km) to total distance of walk, and it is busy in summer). Follow well-worn footpath, signposted Pyg Track, from north-west corner of car park and climb gradually for ½ mile (0.8 km). The going gets tougher soon as path crosses rocky steps and steepens. After approximately 30 minutes, disregard smaller footpath right which ascends knife-edge ridge of Crib Goch (dangerous for the inexperienced and not to be tackled on a windy day). Keep to Pyg Track as it zigzags uphill and along hillside below Crib Goch, eventually reaching col between Crib-y-ddysgl and summit of Snowdon. Turn left and walk parallel with railway to summit. Pause for the breathtaking all-round views and (in summer) escape the crowds by following Rhyd-Ddu path in south- south-west direction for 200 yds (180 m), then swing left and zigzag downhill to join good ridge path heading south-east to summit of Y Lliwedd. Remain on ridge path which soon swings north and descend steeply (with care) on defined path to shores of Llyn Llydaw. Walk alongside lake to join Miner's Track beyond shed. Turn right and shortly pass Llyn Teryn and gently descend well-defined track back to Pen-y-pass car park and bus stop (bus back to hotel, Nant Peris or Beddgelert).

Day 1 Easy alternative walk – Gwynant Valley
From car park take waymarked footpath downhill through shallow

valley beside stream (River Trawsnant) towards Gwynant Valley. Pass power station and follow path beside River Glaslyn to reach Llyn Gwynant. Keep to path along hillside through trees above lake, then at far south-west end cross footbridge over river to A498. Turn left along footpath beside road and continue 1 mile (1.6 km), then turn left at north-east end of lake along metalled lane leading to Hafod Rhisgl. Remain on lane, passing settlement of Gwastadannas, then climb steadily up valley (stunning views of Snowdon) to A498, near junction with A4086 and Pen-y-Gwryd Hotel ahead. Walk up A4086 back to Pen-y-pass (or catch bus), if car in car park; or catch bus back to Nant Peris or Beddgelert from hotel.

Day 2 From the hotel turn left along A4086 towards Capel Curig. In 250 yds (235 m) cross stile on left and follow footpath uphill through field (can be wet) to cross metal footbridge over stream. Climb further stile and head directly uphill, ignoring stile left, following grassy path steeply uphill with wall to left. Pass another stile over wall left, then where wall turns east, cross stile on to open hillside. Ascend steeply ahead over rocky terrain, cross stream and climb less steep and often wet ground. Eventually, climb sharply to crossing of tracks on ridge (total 1½ miles/2 km of climbing). **Now you have a choice of routes**:

Either Turn right along the good ridge path for an exhilarating 3½ mile (5.6 km) walk across Y Foel Goch and Cefn y Capel, gradually descending to track opposite River Llugwy. Turn right into Capel Curig and catch bus (Snowdon Sherpa 96) back to Pen-y-Gwryd Hotel from post office (total: 6 miles/10 km).

Or Those who want to climb more peaks can turn left along very rocky ridge path, gradually ascending to rock-strewn summits of Glyder Fach (3,262 ft/994 m) and Glyder Fawr (3,279ft/ 999

Snowdon.

- **PEN-Y-GWRYD HOTEL** Opened in 1847, this celebrated hotel stands isolated high in the mountains. It was used as the training base for the first successful team to conquer Mount Everest in 1953; their faded signatures adorn the ceiling of the rugged slate-floored climbers' bar.

- **PYG TRACK** is one of six established routes to the summit of Snowdon. Originally called the Pig Track because it goes through Bwlch Moch – the pass of the pigs.

m). Splendid views across Snowdon Horseshoe, down to Nantfrancon Valley and Llyn Ogwen – in fact some of the finest in Snowdonia. Retrace steps to Glyder Fach to take path left for the steep scramble up neighbouring Tryfan (3,010 ft/917 m) with its two massive pillars (Adam and Eve) on summit. Return to Glyder Fach and follow ridge back to junction of ridge paths. You can now return to Capel Curig (see above) (total: 9½ miles/15.2 km).

Or Turn left (straight ahead from junction if omitting ascents), then shortly right to follow defined path steeply downhill through Cwm Tryfan into Ogwen Valley, path eventually entering Gwern Gof Uchaf (campsite). Take footpath right along valley bottom, soon merging with track to Gwern Gof Isaf farm (campsite). Keep to old track for 3 miles (4.8 km) parallel with Afon Llugwy, into Capel Curig and bus back to Pen-y-Gwryd (total: 10½ miles /16.8 km or 7 miles/ 11.2 km omitting ascents of Glyders and Tryfan).

Or On merging with lane just before settlement (Gelli) and reaching Capel Curig, turn right on to defined path that climbs steeply along the Glyder ridge – more stunning views. Continue 3½ miles (5.6 km) to the crossing of tracks and turn left to retrace steps downhill back to the hotel (total: 15½ miles/24.8 km or 12 miles/19.2 km omitting ascents of Glyders and Tryfan).

- **SNOWDON LLYN LLYDAW** Llyn Llydaw is by tradition the lake into which Excalibur was hurled. The Snowdon Horseshoe, a wall-like line of knife-edge ridges around the rim of a cwm (combe), is regarded as one of Britain's best high-level walking routes.

- **MOUNTAIN RAILWAY** Britain's only rack-and-pinion steam railway has been transporting armchair climbers up Snowdon since 1896. It climbs over 3,000 ft (915 m) in just 4½ miles (7.2 km) and takes an hour each way.

- **NANT GWYNANT AND LLYN GWYNANT** One of the finest mountain valleys in Snowdonia with the jewel-like lake (Llyn Gwynant) nestling beneath the vast, craggy and waterfall-threaded slopes of Gallt-y-Wenallt.

- **THE GLYDERS** The wild, rock-strewn summits of Glyder Fach and Glyder Fawr are less than a mile apart and feature huge slabs and boulders shattered and shaped into weird forms, notably Castell y Gwynt (Castle of the Wind) – a jagged rock affording splendid views of Snowdon.

- **CAPEL CURIG** remains, thankfully, a popular climbing centre with several hotels, climbing shops and the National Mountain Centre (Plas y Brenin), rather than a bustling tourist resort.

155

Introduction
The Yorkshire Dales

T he Yorkshire Dales have been attracting
visitors for more than 250 years but it
was the writings of one man that in recent
times put them so firmly on the map. James
Herriot, who became a best-selling author in
middle age, had no inkling when he began
writing in the 1970s that his simple prose
and honest portrait of life as a Dales vet
around the time of the Second World War
would capture the imaginations of so many.

The television series based on the books helped Herriot to reach a
massive audience, and even towards the end of his life devotees
regularly beat a path to his door, anxious to meet the man who had
brought alive for them the atmosphere and the beauty of this corner of
England.

Path network
The Yorkshire Dales, third largest of Britain's eleven national parks, offer
almost endless opportunities for outdoor recreation, but walking, not
surprisingly, is one of the most popular. An extensive and complex 1,250-mile
(2,000-kilometre) network of public rights of way exists within the 680-square-
mile (1,760-square-kilometre) national park and here countless paths and
tracks, once used by packhorses and sheep drovers, lead you well away from
roads and other intrusive reminders of civilization into some of the finest
scenery in the country. About eight million people a year visit the Dales, with
almost half of them taking at least one walk.

Long-distance paths
One of the best ways of exploring on foot is to walk sections of the region's
long-distance. The Dales Way, running for 80 miles (130 kilometres) between
Ilkley and Windermere; and Wainwright's 190-mile (300-kilometre) Coast to
Coast route, which crosses the northern half of the park and extends the width
of Northern England, are both famous enough but the 250-mile (400-kilometre)
Pennine Way, running south to north through the heart of the Dales and the
first designated route of its kind, is now legendary.

The Yorkshire Dales are characterized by their rivers – the Wharfe, Ribble,
Ure, Nidd and Swale among others – and here the walker can stroll along
peaceful paths beneath towering fells and crags.

Many of the region's most famous landmarks are to be found in the north of
the national park. Swaledale, renowned for its sheep and long-abandoned lead
mining industry, is particularly beautiful during the spring and summer months
when the hay meadows and woodlands conspire to create a dazzling carpet of
wild flowers. At the eastern entrance to Swaledale is the picturesque hilltop
town of Richmond, dominated by the keep of its famous Norman castle.

Wensleydale and Wharfedale
Wensleydale, the largest and perhaps the finest of all the Yorkshire Dales, is a
sweeping patchwork of fields, pastures and broadleaved trees. From various

On the Pennine Way near Keld.

vantage points you can spot the outline of Bolton Castle, where Mary, Queen of Scots was imprisoned in 1568.

The village of Hardraw is famous for its slender waterfall, almost 100 feet (30 metres) high, and the spectacular Aysgarth Falls, which rush headlong over the River Ure for about half a mile (0.8 km), are best appreciated after a spell of heavy rain. Much of Wensleydale, including the delightful village of Askrigg, was put on the map by the BBC who used a variety of locations there for the filming of James Herriot's *All Creatures Great and Small.*

Away to the south lies Wharfedale, one of the most accessible of the Yorkshire Dales – particular from Leeds, Harrogate and the south – one of the most popular areas for walking. The village of Kettlewell is a good base for exploring Wharfedale. From here you can follow delightful riverside paths and tracks, including a stretch of the Dales Way, south to the remains of historic Bolton Abbey. The scenery in Wharfedale is dominated by the Great Scar Limestone and virtually wherever you look, the valley slopes and dramatic escarpments are flecked with white scars of rock. Kilnsey Crag, north of Grassington, is one of the most spectacular overhanging limestone faces in this part of the Dales. Soaring 170 feet (52 metres) above the road, this famous landmark is especially popular with rock-climbers.

Adventure country

To the west of Wharfedale lies real limestone country. This is the land of the Three Peaks – Ingleborough, Whernside and Pen-y-ghent – a place of endless views and wild summits and a favourite haunt of those with a sense of adventure. The western Dales are the setting for the famous Three Peaks Challenge, a strenuous 22-mile (35-kilometre) hike over the highest summits in the area, including Whernside which, at 2,415 feet (736 metres), is Yorkshire's tallest mountain. Competitors have to complete the challenge within 12 hours to qualify for membership of The Three Peaks of Yorkshire Club. This part of the Dales is popular with potholers, too, who test their ability by descending into a dank, subterranean world of passages, caves and waterlogged caverns.

GRASSINGTON

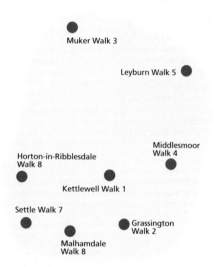

Muker Walk 3

Leyburn Walk 5

Middlesmoor
Walk 4

Horton-in-Ribblesdale
Walk 8

Kettlewell Walk 1

Settle Walk 7

Grassington
Walk 2

Malhamdale
Walk 8

a conservation area and a short but comprehensive walking tour of the village is thoroughly recommended as part of any visit to the Yorkshire Dales. Begin at the bottom of the cobbled Market Square and then head for 18thC Grassington House, the Black Horse Inn and the Upper Wharfedale Folk Museum; also see the Victorian town hall, Theatre Cottage, and the early-19thC Congregational Church.

From the village there are numerous paths running off in different directions. A short stroll along the Dales Way brings you to the site of several medieval villages and an area of extensive woodland. Grass Wood, which comprises 200 acres of woodland and was once part of the Duke of Devonshire's estate, is now in the care of the Yorkshire Wildlife Trust.

Further to the north is Lea Green, renowned as the setting for a Bronze and Iron Age settlement, and to the south of Grassington, just across the Wharfe, lies the 12thC St Michael's Church. Linton Falls, where the river plunges over the North Craven fault, and the nearby stepping stones spanning the Wharfe, help to make this a delightful spot.

W ith a population of about 1,200, Grassington, part of the old district of West Riding, is more of a small town than a village. A stop here is usually on the itinerary of most first-time visitors to the Yorkshire Dales and Grassington's quaint old streets are often packed with people during the summer months; it is generally acknowledged as one of the region's main tourist centres.

Towards the end of the 13thC, the village was granted a weekly market and an annual fair. In later years the lead-mining industry brought a certain amount of prosperity to Grassington, with the local population rising to more than 3,000. Some of the old miners' cottages in the village have been converted into holiday accommodation and include beehive ovens and inglenook fireplaces.

Towards the end of the 18thC the local textile industry expanded significantly with the acquisition of several water-powered former corn mills which closed when water power was superseded by steam. However, it was the coming of the Yorkshire Dales Railway in 1901 that really gave Grassington a new lease of life, many of the new residents finding work in nearby limestone quarries.

The centre of Grassington forms part of

ACCOMMODATION AND FOOD

Within easy reach of Malham and its famous cove, and the delights of Lower and Upper Wharfedale, and just a leisurely drive from Wensleydale and 'Herriot' country, the picturesque, often bustling village of Grassington is an ideal base from which to explore the Yorkshire Dales. There are plenty of useful choices of accommodation, but book ahead in summer and for winter weekends. For more detailed information contact the National Park Centre, Grassington, Skipton, North Yorkshire BD23 5LB; tel. 01756 752774.

SLEEPING AND EATING

HOTELS AND INNS

BOLTON ABBEY
Devonshire Arms Hotel; *(8 miles/13.2 km SE); tel. 01756 710441.* Much-extended 18thC coaching inn located on the edge of the Abbey estate and owned by the Duke and Duchess of Devonshire since 1753. Offers every comfort.

BUCKDEN
Buck Inn; tel. 01756 760228. Attractive, creeper-clad Georgian coaching inn standing in beautiful Dales country-side. Characterful bars with open fires and stone floors, pretty bedrooms with smart en suite bathrooms.

BURNSALL
Red Lion; (3 miles/4.8 km SE); tel. 01756 720292. Standing beside the River Wharfe, this former ferryman's inn dates from the 16thC and is full of old-fashioned charm. Comfortable bedrooms; good food.

ARNCLIFFE
Amerdale House; (6 miles/10 km N); tel. 01756 770250; closed mid Nov–mid Mar. Peaceful, family-owned manor house situated in peaceful landscaped grounds, surrounded by unspoilt Dales scenery. Well-furnished bedrooms, excellent dinners and friendly service.

GRASSINGTON
Grassington House Hotel; 5 The Square; tel. 01756 752406. Attractively furnished small hotel overlooking the cobbled square.

BED-AND-BREAKFAST

GRASSINGTON
Ashfield House; tel. 01756 752584; closed Jan. 17thC cottage tucked away off the main street and surrounded by pleasant gardens. Freshly decorated bedrooms are comfortable and value for money.

HANLITH
Coachman's Cottage; near Malham; tel. 01729 830538; closed Christmas & New Year. Pretty, 300-year-old whitewashed cottage nestling in a quiet hamlet on the Pennine Way. Oak beams, thick stone walls and antique furniture characterize the welcoming bedrooms.

KIRKBY MALHAM
Holgate Head; near Malham; tel. 01729 830376; closed mid Oct–Feb. Fine old house set in 3 acres of beautiful gardens. Well-appointed sitting rooms with 17thC oak panelling and open fires, and upmarket bedrooms. Dinner on request.

KETTLEWELL
Langcliffe Country House; (4 miles/7.2 km N); tel. 01756 760242. Small private hotel offering well-equipped bedrooms. Conservatory dining room with delightful outlook. A warm welcome, family atmosphere.

STARBOTTON
Hilltop Country House; (6 miles/10 km N); tel. 01756 760321; closed mid Nov-mid Mar. Former 17thC farmhouse tucked away in Wharfedale village, with attractive gardens, an elegant sitting-room and comfortable bedrooms. Dinner available.

CAMPING AND HOSTELS

Cheap hostel rooms can be found at *Malham* (*tel. 01729 830321*), *Linton* (*tel. 01756 752400*) and *Kettlewell* (*tel. 01756 760232*). Good-value bedrooms of various sizes for individuals, families or groups are available at *Malham Hill Top Farm Bunk Barn, Malham* (*tel. 01729 830320*). The area is well served with camp-sites, notably the *Wood Nook Caravan Park, Grassington* (*tel. 01756 752412*), and *Howarth Farm Caravan Park, Appletreewick* (4 miles/5.6 km SE – *tel. 01756 720226*).

FOOD

For the best pub and restaurant food in the area head for the *Angel Inn, Hetton* (3 miles/4.8 km SW – *tel. 01756 730263*). Other choices, apart from the hotels and inns mentioned above, include the *Fox and Hounds, Starbotton* (*tel. 01756 760269* – also B&B); the *Old Hall Inn, Threshfield* (*tel. 01756 752441*); the **Fountaine Inn, Linton** (01756 752210); the unspoilt and rustic *George Inn, Hubberholme* (*tel. 01756 760223* – also B&B); the discerning *Sportsman's Arms, Wath-in-Nidderdale* (near Pateley Bridge – *tel. 01423 711306* – also B&B). For lunches, afternoon teas and cakes try *The Dales Kitchen Tearooms & Brasserie, Grassington* (*tel. 01756 753208* – also dinner) and *The Garden Room, Kilnsey* (*tel. 01756 752150*).

Wharfedale

A magnificent patchwork of pastures, woods and soaring green fells.

Start Kettlewell, SD967723. Free car park close to the river bridge at the western end of the village on the B6160 between Grassington and Buckden.

Route directions

From car park turn right across road bridge over River Wharfe and bear right on to Dales Way, noting NT sign for Upper Wharfedale. Beyond it, swing right (signposted Buckden and Starbotton) and descend slope to follow riverbank. Through kissing gate and continue in same direction with river right. In field corner go through gate and follow concrete path parallel to river. Through gate on to track, walled at intervals, as it traverses numerous field boundaries to reach ladder stile. Leave wall at this point, follow waymarker across pasture towards trees, then keep to path alongside wall to stile and continue along riverbank. Climb stile (NT sign), continue beside river, cross footbridge and keep right of wall. Make for several more stiles and footbridge; Starbotton now visible ahead. Cross gated stile, bear diagonally across field towards line of trees and rejoin riverbank. Cross stile, bear immediately left at gap in wall, cross next boundary and turn right at foot-bridge. Follow walled track up into Starbotton, turning left at road to reach Fox and Hounds. Pass phone box, take second left and after a few steps bear right and look for gate on left (dogs on lead sign). Follow path as it curves left, then veer right towards boundary wall. Beyond next wall turn left and head up slope

Essentials

Easy 4 mile (6.4 km); 2 hours; mostly flat; **map** Ordnance Survey 1:50 000 Landranger Map 98, Wensleydale & Upper Wharfedale or 1:25 000 Outdoor Leisure Map 10, Yorkshire Dales Southern Area.
Terrain Riverside, field and packhorse paths, tracks and short stretches of road.

The Wharfedale village of Linton.

FOOD AND DRINK
Good food and Theakston ales at the Fox and Hounds, Starbotton (closed Mon in winter and Jan–mid Feb). Pubs and tearooms in Kettlewell.

to gated stile, then bear right, heading south along lower slopes of Wharfedale, following contours of valley. Climb next wall, maintain direction across several crumbling boundary walls. Pass beneath trees, path soon bending left then right to ladder stile. Continue along slopes, cross further ladder stile and pass under power lines to next stile. Keep to path, heading towards stile with buildings of Kettlewell coming into view. Negotiate two more ladder stiles, then descend slope diagonally, passing under more power lines and head towards village. Climb stile, follow wall on right, path soon curving right down to gated stile. Continue into Kettlewell, joining track between houses to road on bend. Keep ahead to main junction and turn left back to car park.

• **KETTLEWELL** Once a bustling and prosperous market centre when three abbeys – Fountains, Bolton and Coverham – had property here. In the late 18th and early 19thC the village thrived on the local lead mining. Its name means a bubbling spring.

• **Starbotton** An attractive and compact limestone village in Upper Wharfedale, very popular with walkers and trippers. The quaint old 17thC cottages and nearby packhorse routes make it an obvious choice for a holiday or day out. The Methodist chapel became a holiday home a few years ago. Starbotton acheived a degree of fame in 1686, when a terrible flood swept away many of the houses.

Grassington, Dales Way and Linton

A varied and peaceful route featuring one of Wharfedale's most attractive villages, with packhorse bridge, 18thC almshouses, and a lovely riverside section of the Dales Way.

Start Grassington, SE002640. Limited parking in main square; best to park at National Park Centre car park on the B6265 220 yds (200 m) east of the square.

Route directions

Follow Threshfield road out of Grassington, then just before river bridge turn left over stile and follow path to next footbridge. Cross, admiring Linton Falls, then bear right; at T-junction note packhorse bridge right and turn left, then at road go left to visit medieval Linton church, otherwise turn right to continue the walk. At next T-junction turn right over bridge and just before Threshfield School go through gate on left and along track with wall left. Where wall bears left, keep forward on track. Cross bridge over old Grassington railway line, then bear slightly left on track leading down to gate and road. Go right for few yds then through gap-stile on left (signposted Linton), following path down through wood, then straight ahead over field to stile and clapper bridge. Bear slightly left, pass under power lines and old railway line and bear right to gate. Keep forward across next field, then on nearing far side bear very slightly left to gate in wall ahead. Follow walled lane to Linton, emerging on to road by bridge. Turn left over bridge, then right passing youth hostel on left and delightful packhorse bridge on right. Follow road, then at last farm turn left between farmhouse (left) and farm buildings (right) to pass through gate and continue forward along walled lane to another gate, the track continuing with wall on left. Ignore track right (signposted Cracoe) and ladder-stile in wall on left, and track forking left through gate. Follow your

---

Essentials

Moderate 5½ miles (9 km); 2½–3 hours.; gently undulating with level return leg; **map** Ordnance Survey 1:50 000 Landranger Map 98, Wensleydale & Upper Wharfedale; 1:25 000 Outdoor Leisure Map 10, Yorkshire Dales Southern area.
Terrain Easy walking on clear tracks and well waymarked footpaths.

---

track until it passes through gateway and peters out, but still keep forward along wall on left to ladder-stile ahead. Climb ahead on gently rising path (noticing old cultivation terraces) to pass left-hand end of narrow strip of woodland, then follow wall on right to step-stile just to left of ruined building. Turn left along minor road, then at more major road turn right into hamlet of Thorpe. At foot of hill fork left and climb out of village; shortly descend to B6160. Cross over to gate opposite and follow wall on right, go over stile and down next long field to small gate in wall ahead. Pass to left of telegraph pole (Hebden half-left across river) and follow marker posts down slope to footpath sign, then diagonally down to gate to right of suspension bridge. Cross River Wharfe and immediately turn left through stile to follow defined riverside path. Go through kissing gate into large pasture (Grassington visible ahead), bear slightly right away from river, over wooden footbridge and forward to stile. Follow lane past old mill and trout farm and continue to gap-stile on right-hand bend (signposted Grassington Bridge). Keep to path (Linton's church across river), crossing three stiles to walled lane. Turn right to return to Grassington.

• **LINTON** is one of the most picturesque villages in the Dales. It is divided by a beck with a variety of crossing points – a clapper bridge, a packhorse bridge and some stepping stones among them. The village green is overlooked by lines of 17th and 18thC houses.

• **LINTON CHURCH** Known as the 'cathedral of Upper Wharfedale', this 12thC building shows Norman features but was largely rebuilt in the 15thC.

FOOD AND DRINK
The Fountaine Inn at Linton (interesting bar food and idyllic position. Cafés and pubs in Grassington.

161

Muker and Upper Swaledale

*Fine river-valley scenery, a gorge and several waterfalls; return along
the Pennine Way with superb views across upland moorland.*

Start *Muker, NY910978.
Remote Swaledale
village located 20 miles
(32 km) east of
Richmond on the
B6270. Park in the
National Park pay-and-
display car park.*

Route directions

Leave car park and turn
left across bridge over
Straw Beck. Turn left again
into village, but after
100 yds (90 m) fork right
up No Through Road by
Literary Institute. Fork
right again by post office,
then left by signpost to
Gunnerside & Keld. Where
tarmac bears left, go right
to stile by gate and follow
track over field to further
stile. Head for barn, pass to
its right, then turn left and
cross five fields before path
turns right to follow wall
and fence to footbridge.
Cross, climb steps and turn
left along path, soon
joining track. Follow this about 1³/₄ miles
(3 km), at first in valley, then climbing
slightly before descending to cross side
valley of Swinner Gill and climbing again
to pass below ruined Crackpot Hall; with
deep limestone gorge on left. Hamlet of
Keld soon comes into view. Pass through
gate, begin to descend, then go through
another gate and fork left, joining the
Pennine Way. The path drops down past
waterfall – a fine picnic spot. Cross bridge
over River Swale and climb steeply right to
T-junction. To visit Keld turn right; walk
route follows Pennine Way,
left. Pass through gate and
descend, ignoring path
signposted left to Kisdon
Upper Force, then climb
again to reach fork, where
keep to Pennine Way right.
Soon follow narrow,
contouring path (at times
stony) skirting Kisdon Hill,

Essentials

Moderate 5¹/₂ miles
(9.2 km); 3 hours;
undulating – a few
modest ascents and
descents; ***map***
Ordnance Survey 1:50
000 Land-ranger Map
92, Barnard Castle &
Richmond or 1:25 000
Outdoor Leisure Map
30, Yorkshire Dales
North-ern & Central
areas.
Terrain Well-defined
tracks and paths.

*Muker and Upper
Swaledale.*

high above valley, with
wide views opening up over
Upper Swaledale. After 1³/₄
miles (2.8 km) cross
wooden ladder-stile and
walk down field edge
beside wall on left. Cross
wooden step-stile on to
track, following it down to
barn. Leave barn to left
and reach a crossing track.
Here leave Pennine Way
(right) and keep ahead
down walled lane. Join
access road to Kisdon Farm
and follow it down to
Muker.

• **Muker** is the largest of
a trio of pretty villages
near the head of
Swaledale. Relics of the
prosperous lead-mining
days (shafts, ruined
buildings, spoil heaps)
litter the hillsides around
the village. Pioneer
botanists Cherry and
Richard Kearton (first to
use photographs to
illustrate botanical books)
went to school in the village and are
commemorated in the chapel.

• **Crackpot Hall** A ruined farm set on
the hillside above Swaledale and named
after the Norse for 'hole of the crows'. In
the 1950s a cave (Fairy Hole) was
discovered nearby, explaining its unusual
name.

• **Pennine Way** Where this long-distance
path comes into Muker from Kisdon Hill it
follows the old 'Corpse Way', a route used
by coffin-bearers from
Muker to the church at
Grinton, before St Mary's
Church in Muker was built.

• **Kisdon Force** The short
detour off the Pennine Way
will bring you to this
attractive waterfall located
in a dramatic rocky gorge.

FOOD AND DRINK
None along the route
but the unpretentious
Farmers Arms in Muker
offers substantial bar
snacks; also the
Theakston Café in
Muker.

Middlesmoor and Upper Nidderdale

A delightful exploration of Upper Nidderdale, commencing with an invigorating ramble across high moorland to Scar House Reservoir, with splendid views towards Great Whernside and Dead Man's Hill. Much of the return route follows the Nidderdale Way through unspoilt Nidderdale beside the River Nidd.

Start *Middlesmoor, SE092743. Remote village in Upper Nidderdale located on minor road 7 miles (11.2 km) north-west of Pateley Bridge. Park in village car park (free), near the top end of the hamlet, shortly before the tarmac ends. No public transport.*

Route directions

Turn right out of car park, follow the tarmac lane which soon gives way to stony track and ignore track forking right short distance. Where walled lane ends in 1¼ miles (2 km), continue along track over moor with magnificent views, following it to Scar House Reservoir. Turn right along tarmac road, then soon bear left over reservoir dam. At far side bear half-left up stony track, then in 100 yds (90 m) turn sharp right at Nidderdale Way sign on to grassy bridleway and, shortly, cross track coming up from house down on right. Pass through gateway (wall on right), keep to deteriorating track, then where wall ends continue ahead over footbridge. After passing small wood, track descends into ravine, crosses Woo Gill via bridge, then climbs steeply before fording another beck and continuing to climb. About 150 yds (140 m) before flat-roofed shooting-house, fork right on to track by white-topped marker post and follow line of posts downhill to gate in wall on right. Track bears right downhill, soon turning sharp left to gate in fence, and another in wall to reach Nidderdale Way sign (points back along route). Keep to track beside wall on left, pass

Essentials

Moderate 7¼ miles (11.6 km); 3–4 hours; mostly level through Nidderdale with a steady climb and descent on to and off high moorland; **map** Ordnance Survey 1:50 000 Landranger Map 99, Northallerton & Ripon or 1:25 000 Outdoor Leisure Map 30, Yorkshire Dales Northern & Central Areas.
Terrain High-level moorland tracks and paths close to River Nidd.

FOOD AND DRINK

Café and the Crown Inn in Middlesmoor; otherwise, take a picnic lunch (picnic site beside Scar House Reservoir).

through another gate, keep left (main track) at faint fork by solitary hawthorn and pass under telegraph wires to wall corner and Nidderdale Way sign. Turn sharp right downhill on track, soon with beck on left and, shortly, bear left to pass through gate. Bear slightly right across next field to reach wall (on left) and follow it to further gate. Keep wall left and River Nidd right until reaching access road at New Houses (river bridge right). Walk forward along track to gate, then bear right to follow riverbank. Cross stile, pass through gate, then halfway along next field cross stile in fence on right and footbridge. Turn left along field edge to gap-stile in wall at far end and keep ahead to stile into next field. Continue along bottom of slope on right, passing solitary hawthorn. (The stile high in fence on right gives access from road above to Manchester Pot, which is down on your left, reached by another stile.) Reach track and follow it with fence left, the track soon picking up fence on right to pass through gate, but where clear track ends, keep forward along fence on left, passing stile providing access to Goyden Pot. Continue beside dry river bed until forced right by side beck, then in few yds bear left to ford it and keep forward (wall on right) to gate at Limley Farm. Keep bearing right through farmyard (noisy chained dogs), pass through another gate on right and continue to further gate, then cross over centre of field to gap-stile on to road. Cross over (gap-stile), continue up field, then bear half-left across next field to enter

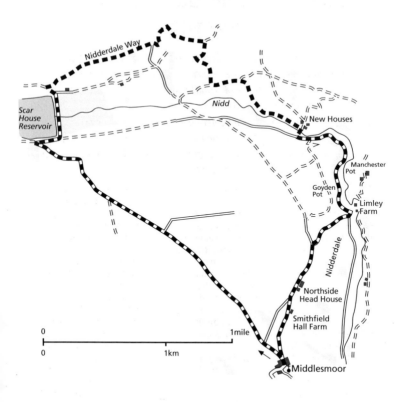

following field. Bear right round field edge to step-stile (few yards left of corner), then slightly left to next stile just to left of tree. Now bear half-left to ford beck and head steeply up to stile by gate in top corner of field (edge of wood). Beyond stile turn immediately left through gate – views open up left down Nidderdale to Gouthwaite Reservoir. Follow track past Northside Head House, then 40 yds (37 m) before wood on right ends, cross gap-stile in wall on left and bear half-right to the next stile, continuing ahead to further stile. Proceed ahead on clear path, passing to right of Smithfield Hall Farm and crossing access track to next gap-stile in wall ahead. Keep on towards right-hand end of wood ahead, pass round it, through two more stiles, then with wall on right to another stile. Walk across next field, passing two wall corners on right to gap-stile by building ahead. Turn right to road and right again to car park.

• **MIDDLESMOOR** At the head of Upper Nidderdale this is regarded as one of the most spectacularly situated villages in the Yorkshire Dales. It stands on a breezy 900-ft (272-m) hilltop, a delightful collection of stone cottages and winding streets, and from many vantage points – particularly in the vicinity of the church, rebuilt in the 1860s – there are superb views of the dale stretching towards Gouthwaite Reservoir.

• **NIDDERDALE** Dominating Upper Nidderdale are three large reservoirs (Scar House, Angram, Gouthwaite), built between 1901 and 1936 and providing water for Bradford. Before they appeared, Nidderdale was one of the most industrialized dales, with the manufacture of linen and hemp and the mining and smelting of lead-ore. Much of the Upper Dale, however, has always been very rural with farming the main activity.

Leyburn, Bolton Hall and Lower Wensleydale

Although relatively long, this is a gentle ramble through typical Wensleydale countryside, a relaxing landscape of lush green pastures, generous stretches of woodland and isolated farmsteads. Starting from the attractive old market town of Leyburn, you explore charming stone villages of Redmire and Wensley, the grounds of a stately home (Bolton Hall) and peaceful woodland beside the River Ure. Glorious views of Lower Wensleydale, especially from Leyburn Shawl.

Start *Leyburn, SE110905. Market town located at junction of A684 and A6108 between Richmond and Ripon. Park in the Market Place or various car parks in the town.*

Route directions

From top end of Market Place cross main road and take No Through Road in far right-hand corner, signposted Way to the Shawl. At top of lane bear left and in few yards turn right through kissing gate along paved path – glorious views up Wensleydale and to the fells at head of Coverdale. Walk along edge of escarpment towards wood and follow ridge on well-defined path to top edge of the wood, with ever-changing views into dale on left. Path curves left and drops slightly to stile in fence at end of escarpment. Cross stile, bear half-left across corner of field to wall-stile on left (just behind a tree), and head straight down field to stile at bottom (aim some way to right of barn). Bear half-right across next field to stile by gate, then keep forward towards wood, soon following wall on left, to far corner of field to crossing of tracks. Turn left through gateway, but immediately fork right into wood on narrow path which at first keeps parallel to track but then bears right away from it. For short distance, until leaving wood, pay close attention to route-finding.

Essentials
Easy 9½ miles (15.2 km); 5 hours; gently undulating or level close to the River Ure; *map* Ordnance Survey 1:50 000 Landranger Map 99, Northallerton & Ripon or 1:25 000 Outdoor Leisure Map 30, Yorkshire Dales Northern & Central Areas. **Terrain** Easy field paths and tracks.

FOOD AND DRINK
Kings Arms in Redmire (at halfway with good views from garden). Pub in Wensley and the Sandpiper or Golden Pheasant in Leyburn (both B&B).

Down on right is a beck. On reaching obvious crossing track turn right, descend to cross beck and turn left. Next short section can be wet and muddy. Just before reaching next beck to be crossed, fork left off track along narrow path to slab bridge over this beck. Immediately path forks; keep right to rejoin track. When route is barred by another beck, ford it via large stones and, shortly, negotiate one final beck (tricky after rain) to reach gap-stile in wall ahead and leave wood. Bear slightly right to meet wall on left. Pass a corner in wall and keep forward to gate in far left-hand corner of field. Join track from barns on right, following it to metalled road and bear right to reach Preston-under-Scar. Continue ahead at first junction then, at next fork, keep right along No Through Road past phone box. Leave village along tarmac lane straight ahead (footpath sign). Shortly, keep left at fork where tarmac ends, then by first barn on right (sign to Laurel Tree Farm), cross stile on left and bear slightly left across field to stile by two power-line poles. Cross track and stile opposite, bear half-left to gap-stile in wall (footpath sign) and road. Turn right (Castle Bolton visible ahead, views up Bishopdale left), then just before the road bends right (300 yds/285 m) cross stile (footpath sign) in wall on left. Bear slightly more than half-right to

165

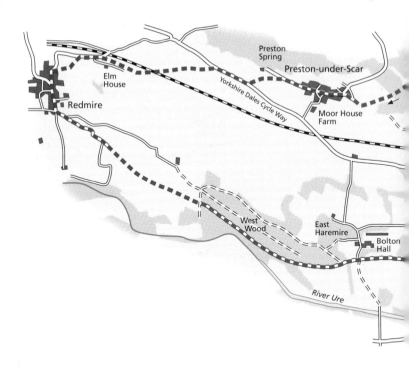

gap-stile, then keep roughly same line to next stile and continue along edge of low escarpment for 100 yds (90 m) before dropping sharp left to gap-stile in wall below. Bear half-right across field to stile (20 yds left of gate), then maintain direction across next field, passing to left of large tree to ladder-stile across railway line. Follow railway for few yds right, then cross ladder-stile and bear half-right across field to thin line of trees on far side. Keep right along fence to stile and walk along lane. Pass Elm Lodge, go out through gateway of Elm House and fork left to reach road on bend with Redmire ahead. Beyond village name-stone descend steps on left to stile, then follow beck (wall left), but halfway down field, at gap in wall and ford over beck, bear half-right across field, ignoring gate-stile in wall to pass through gateway in wall ahead. Follow wall on left to stile and ginnel between houses to reach Redmire village green. Turn left through village, keeping left at fork, and where main road bears right at foot of village, keep ahead along No Through Road, immediately forking left, following sign to St Mary's Church. In

100 yds (90 m) turn right along stony track (waymarked), cross beck by slab bridge, then ignore track forking right and shortly, cross another beck. Track bears right and left (Norman St Mary's Church visible left), then at next right-hand bend keep straight ahead through stile by gate and follow boundary on left to gap-stile at far end of field. Bear slightly right across next field to stile in wall and traverse four fields via visible stiles to reach iron kissing gate on edge of Bolton Hall Estate. At crossing of tracks keep ahead for few yards to T-junction and bear right. Remain on track through gounds of Bolton Hall for 2 miles (3.2 km). The track becomes concrete by Bolton Hall and leads into village of Wensley. Fork right to main road, go right for short distance, then take minor road left before church (well worth visiting). Cross beck and immediately take tarmac lane on left which climbs and bears right, then where it bears left again, go through left-hand of two gates on right (yellow waymark) to follow well-defined path slightly left to stile. Bear slightly right along boundary on right, eventually passing under the power lines to stile in

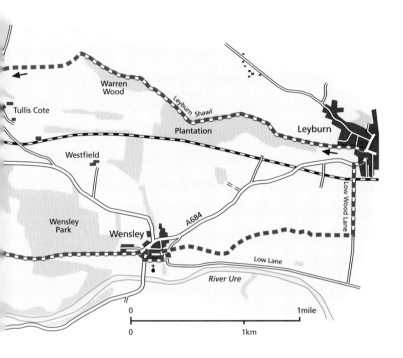

field corner. Keep ahead (fence right) and in far corner of field turn sharp left uphill to stile on right at top corner of wood. Continue with fence on right, cross wall-stile and bear left (wall now left). Cross stile in field corner and walk straight across several fields to large gate. Bear slightly left to gap-stile between two trees and follow fence left over another stile to next corner and two stiles. Ignore one on left, cross stile ahead and continue across fields and stiles to stile left of barn. Descend cautiously into lane and turn left to return to Leyburn.

• **LEYBURN** developed as the main market, commercial and trading centre for the dale, receiving its charter in 1684. The focal point of this delightful little town is the sloping market place with its 18thC houses, the Bolton Arms, and Regency-style Market Hall (1856).

• **LEYBURN SHAWL** is a tree-clad limestone ridge providing fine views across Wensleydale. Mary, Queen of Scots was recaptured here two hours after her

escape from nearby Bolton Castle in 1568. According to some sources, she dropped her shawl here while fleeing.

• **REDMIRE** was predominantly an industrial village of lead-miners, coal-miners and craftsmen in the 18th and 19thC. The post office was originally built as a drill-hall for Volunteers in 1862.

• **BOLTON HALL** was built by the Marquis of Winchester who married one of the daughters of the last Lord Scrope of nearby Bolton Castle. After the castle was beseiged by Parliamentary forces in 1645, Bolton Hall bacame the new family home, though the house was substantially rebuilt after a major fire in 1902.

• **WENSLEY** had the only market in the dale from 1202 to the 16thC when the plague struck the village. Its church is one of the finest in the Dales: dating from 1300, it features a richly adorned interior, notably 17thC box pews, a fine rood-screen, a two-decker pulpit and traces of a 14thC wall painting.

167

Malhamdale

Some of the finest limestone scenery of the dales, including spectacular Malham Cove, a monastic road, a moorland bridleway (which can be very wet after rain), glorious views and one of the most beautiful stretches of the River Aire, shared by the Pennine Way and the Airedale Way. Sections of the route can be very busy, especially in summer. Walking boots essential.

Start Malham, SD900626. Popular village located 11 miles (17.6 km) north of Skipton, signposted off A65. Park in the National Park Centre car park.

Route Directions

Turn left out of car park and left again through village. Keep left where road forks, then by phone kiosk turn right and immediately left through small gate to follow path through wood. Emerge to gate, cross road on to bridleway opposite and follow walled lane up to T-junction. Turn left, continue for 30 yds (27 m), then keep right at fork. The track climbs and bears right to next fork, just past Water Treatment Works. Keep right (views to Malham Cove over wall right), then at end of walled lane go through gate and keep forward on track to gate on far side of field to road. Turn right and in 200 yds (180 m) cross stile on left signposted Dean Moor. Walk across field to stile in wall opposite, then head straight up next field on faint grassy path. Beyond first group of windswept trees bear half-left to track and keep forward to ladder-stile. Cross corner of field to wooden step-stile, then follow clear path across two fields via stiles and enter National Trust land (Ewe Moor). Keep forward, pass through broken wall, join track and proceed ahead, but when you see next ladder-stile half-right

Essentials

Moderate 12 miles (19.2 km); 5½ hours; one steady climb from Malham village up to the tarn, otherwise not difficult; **map** Ordnance Survey 1:50 000 Landranger Map 98, Wensleydale & Upper Wharfedale and No 103, Blackburn & Burnley, or 1:25 000 Outdoor Leisure Map 10 Yorkshire Dales South. **Terrain** Well-established open moorland tracks and paths, some field paths beside River Aire and one short stretch of metalled road.

FOOD AND DRINK

Pubs and cafés in Malham, but none along the route; may well be a refreshment van at Malham Tarn or Gordale Scar (slight diversion) in summer and at weekends. Best to take a picnic.

ahead, bear right off track and pass between two limestone pavements, then turn right down by wall to stile. Keep forward on faint path, drop to ladder-stile and turn left (signposted Water Sinks and Malham Tarn) up slope of Dean Moor Hill. At clear crossing of tracks turn right, then after crossing brow, with Malham Tarn in view left, bear half-right off track to Water Sinks, where beck which flows from tarn goes underground to emerge as River Aire at Aire Head. Follow beck, soon to bear half-left away from it on clear path leading to footpath sign and rejoin track. Turn right to kissing gate on to road. Turn right, cross beck, go through gate and on reaching footpath signs on each side of road, turn left through parking area and follow broad grassy track on other side (*not* path heading off further right through tree stumps). Track leads to Malham Tarn, the source of the River Aire. Continue with Tarn to left and soon reach clear path bearing right away from tarn towards wood. Keep right of wood, then make for right-hand edge of another small wood on far side of access road (not gate some way to left of it). Walk along right-hand edge of wood, then keep forward to wall and continue with wall left (Great Close Scar and Hill left). Shortly after passing another small wood (Great Close Plantation), turn right along farm road to next junction, Street Gate. Turn left through gate (signposted Grassington) along Mastiles Lane. Descend and cross Gordale Beck via clapper bridge, climb and follow track to gate in wall. Immediately beyond, go through gate on right and follow wall on right (Cracoe Pinnacle on Barden Moor comes into view) to gate in next wall on to Smearbottoms Lane, with Lee Gate Farm left. Turn right, ignore first walled lane left, but take second (signposted Calton). With fine views behind over Malhamdale to Kirkby Fell, climb to gate at top of lane (Weets Top triangulation point left – superb views). Shortly, take right fork (signposted Calton) and follow track downhill (parallel to wall right) to where wall turns right, then keep forward along track. Soon drop steeply, pass through two gates into wooded area, then on reaching Calton, keep

• *Classic Dales prospect.*

forward along road to junction on far side of hamlet. Continue downhill to Airton and follow road down to river. Cross bridge, turn left down track, cross stile into field and walk parallel to river. Follow well-established Pennine Way across fields, stile and footbridges close to River Aire to road by bridge on edge of Hanlith. Leave Pennine Way, turn left over bridge, then immediately right along access road to Scalegill Mill. Go through kissing gate to left of entrance and pass to left of buildings. Follow old mill leat, pass the mill reservoir, and soon Malham Cove comes into view. Cross stile, follow wall on right and soon pass spring on right (Aire Head, official source of the River Aire). Cross stile, follow cairns across field to ladder-stile and keep forward to footbridge and ladder-stile, with Malham Beck right. Cross next field to further ladder-stile on to road in Malham. National Park Centre and car park on left.

• **MALHAM** With its pretty stone cottages and humpback bridge, Malham is one of the most popular villages in the Yorkshire Dales – a honeypot for walkers and tourists. Close by is Malham Cove, a

natural amphitheatre consisting of a sheer limestone cliff rising to 250 ft (76 m) and topped by a pavement of fissured limestone slabs. It was formed by the combined erosion of ice and water on the weak Craven Fault. The Pennine Way, Britain's first long-distance path, was officially opened at nearby Malham Tarn House in 1965.

• MALHAM TARN is a unique natural lake created around 12,000 years ago, and has been protected over the years as a nature reserve. It is a haven for lime-loving plants and wintering duck.

Together with much of the neighbouring farmland, renowned for its outstanding nature conservation value and exceptional wild-flower meadows, it is owned by the National Trust.

• MASTILES LANE An ancient green lane (Strete Gate) probably pre-Roman in origin. Used by monks of Fountains Abbey during the Middle Ages to reach their lands around Malham and further afield in the Lake District.

169

Through Ribblesdale to Dentdale

Magnificent two-day ramble through some of the finest scenery in the Yorkshire Dales, from the impressive limestone landscape on the flanks of Ingleborough Hill to the rugged and wild upland country of Upper Ribblesdale and Dentdale, between the lofty summits of Pen-y-ghent and Whernside. Spectacular views across Ribblesdale at every turn, especially on Day 2 from the Pennine Way and the Dales Way. Some sections can be very wet, so walking boots are essential, as is warm, waterproof clothing.

Pen-y-ghent from the Pennine Way.

Planning

You have a choice: either a two-day walk starting in Settle with overnight accommodation in Horton-in-Ribblesdale and returning from Dentdale via the famous Settle to Carlisle railway; or two separate day-walks, again using the railway to return to the respective starting points.

Day 1 Settle to Horton-in-Ribblesdale.
Day 2 Horton-in-Ribblesdale to Dentdale.

Start Day 1 *Settle, SD820635. Market town on the A65, 16 miles (25.6 km) north-west of Skipton. Pay-and-display car parks, railway station and Market Place (check if parking overnight allowed).* **Day 2** *Horton-in-Ribblesdale, SD808727, on the B6479 north of Settle. Pay-and-display car park and station car park in village.*

Route directions

Day 1 Leave Market Place past National Westminster Bank and climb Constitution Hill (1 in 7, No Through Road). About 110 yds (100 m) after road curves left, fork right up stony track, then where double-walled lane ends, keep alongside wall on left. Pass through gate into another section of walled lane. When it ends, follow wall on left for 275 yds (250 m), cross ladder-stile and follow another wall on left, but soon bear slightly right away to gate at top corner of wood. Walk along top edge of wood, then follow wall on left down to road at Langcliffe. Head for village, but in 87 yds (80 m) at end of car park turn right along waymarked track. Keep right at fork along walled lane out of village. At its end 770 yds (700 m), keep ahead beside wall on right to gate, then keep straight up facing slope (clear path) to pass through broken wall to reach gate in top corner of large field. Carry on through hawthorns, pass between two wall

Ling Gill Bridge.

corners and follow wall on left to stile. Bear half-right over field, passing to left of power-line pole to stile on far side and turn left down track to Lower Winskill Farm. Pass between farmhouse and barns to ladder-stile, then turn half-right and follow marker posts to stile. All Three Peaks are visible: Ingleborough, Whernside and Pen-y-ghent. Turn half-left, descending towards Stainforth, keep along edge of steep drop to stile and follow clear path down through wood, then alongside fence, from where marker posts lead down to track and through gate. Bear slightly left down next field, ignoring gate opposite, and follow track down to stile, from where it turns left down to lane in Stainforth. Turn right then immediately left and soon turn right over bridge, then take next road on left (passes car park – W.C.'s) to reach B6479. Turn right and in 220 yds (200 m), take first minor road left, which leads over railway and down to cross River Ribble, (17thC packhorse bridge, a favourite picnic spot). Continue up road to Little Stainforth, passing Hall and Edward VII postbox.

Essentials

Moderate-strenuous Day 1/Walk 7 12 miles (19.2 km); 6–7 hours; several quite stiff climbs. **Day 2/Walk 8** 12½ miles (20 km); 5–6 hours; undulating with some steady climbs; *map* Ordnance Survey 1:50 000 Landranger Map 98, Wensleydale & Upper Wharfedale or 1:25 000 Outdoor Leisure Map 10, Yorkshire Dales South Area and Map 2, Yorkshire Dales Western Area.

Terrain Historic tracks and well-used foot-paths, with much of Day 2 following designated long-distance footpaths, also a section of metalled road through Dentdale.

Keep straight on at crossroads, go through gate and up track, soon to cross ladder-stile at fork, then rejoin track further uphill. Where track ends, keep forward along smooth grassy path through hummocky terrain. After crossing stile and breasting rise, the triangulation point on Smearsett Scar and the line of Pot Scar come into view, and half-left on skyline is Celtic Wall, thought to be more than 2,000 years old. Follow path parallel to scars on right, and on descent to Feizor. After crossing stile follow wall on left down into remains of walled lane, then cross farm track and go through small gate to follow path down to stile and road in Feizor. Turn left, cross ford, and after road curves right take first track on right, leading into another walled lane. After ¾ mile (1 km), by barn, merge with walled lane from left, pass Wood House and reach crossing of tracks. For detour to Austwick (refreshments!), adding 1¼ miles (2 km) to walk, take track straight ahead. Main route turns sharp right (still in walled

171

lane), keep left at fork, then at Wood End Farm turn left along farm road. Turn right at road, then in 165 yds (150 m) turn left at next minor road by barn to reach hamlet of Wharfe. Follow track forward between two houses, turn left and shortly fork right up stony bridleway. In ³/₄ mile (1 km) keep left at fork, cross Austwick Beck by clapper bridge (picnic spot), then at T-junction turn right but when track swings right towards wood, with Crummack Farm beyond, keep forward through two gates and follow right-hand wall up field. About 87 yds (80 m) before ladder-stile at far end, follow arrowed bridleway left up slope. Track curves gently left, following edge of gulley, before becoming more defined. When slope eases, do not take track forking off left, but keep straight up. The track soon bears right (views). At top (Ingleborough half-left), soon reach cross-track (old route from Clapham), turn right and keep immediately right at fork towards cairn. After almost 0.8 mile (1 km) follow wall on right, cross ladder-stile by gate (Sulber Gate) and keep forward along track for further 330 yds (300 m) to meet clear cross-track at wooden signpost. Turn right, follow path (Three Peaks Walk) all the way (1¹/₂ miles/2.6 km) to railway station at Horton-in-Ribblesdale, with village beyond.

Return *Either catch the train (Settle to Carlisle Line) back to Settle (timetable information tel. 01228 44711), or use the very frequent bus service from the village centre.*

Day 2 From bridge over River Ribble in Horton, walk past front of Crown Hotel and into walled lane (Pennine Way – old packhorse route from Settle to Langstrothdale in Upper Wharfedale). After about 1 mile (1.6 km) track curves left to gate and crosses stream bed by natural bridge. Here are Sell Gill Holes, two well known potholes into which Sell Gill Beck disappears. Almost 1¹/₄ miles (2 km) further on, track is crossed by clear path (Three Peaks Walk), and in further ¹/₄ mile (0.5 km) ford stream, go through gate, then immediately after gate in next crossing wall fork left off track up well-trodden path. Follow it (wet in places) to ladder-stile by gate and near stone shed, then follow wall on left to well-made track and bear left along it. Cross stile with Old Ing Farm left and follow track forward,

but when it goes through gate ahead, turn right along another track leading into walled lane (old packhorse route from Settle to Hawes). At end of walled lane look over wall on right to see Calf Holes, another well-known pothole, then continue along track with wall on left. In 1 mile (1.6 km) reach spectacular limestone gorge of Ling Gill. Cross stream by 16thC packhorse bridge, then after further mile (1.6 km) track reaches Roman Road on Cam Fell. Turn left, leaving Pennine Way for Dales Way. Superb views: the Three Peaks, Pen-y-ghent, Ingleborough and Whernside, also Pendle Hill away down Ribblesdale and famous Ribblehead Viaduct on Settle-Carlisle line. Follow track to next road (1 mile/1.6 km), crossing infant Ribble just before reaching it. Bear left along road for 220 yds (200 m) to farm access road on right (signposted Dent Head – Ribble Way). Follow road to Winshaw Farm, pass to left of buildings and head uphill with wall to right. When wall turns sharp right follow it, and after ¹/₂ mile (0.8 km), when wall turns sharp right again, keep straight on to join track coming up from right. Follow this track (wet in places) to next road (1¹/₄ miles/2 km). Remainder of route is on tarmac. Turn left along road, pass under Settle-Carlisle line at Dent Head Viaduct ¹/₂ mile (0.8 km), then after 1¹/₄ miles (2 km) reach Sportsman's Inn. Shortly, recross River Dee at Lea Yeat and take road on right (signposted Dent Station), for a stiff ascent of about ³/₄ mile (1.2 km) to catch train back to Settle.

Return *to Horton-in-Ribblesdale or Settle by train. Regular train services between Settle and Carlisle (timetable information – tel. 01228 44711).*

• **SETTLE** is a classic little town in the western Dales, boasting a fine collection of buildings and a market charter dating back to 1249. Famous market square. Standing guard over the town is Castleberg Crag which soars to 200 ft (70 m). In Victoria Street there is an interesting museum of North Craven life.

• **SETTLE TO CARLISLE RAILWAY** Probably the most famous stretch of regional railway line (72 miles/115 km long) in Britain and a classic example of triumph over adversity. During the late 1980s the railway seemed doomed to closure, but after a desperate rescue plan by

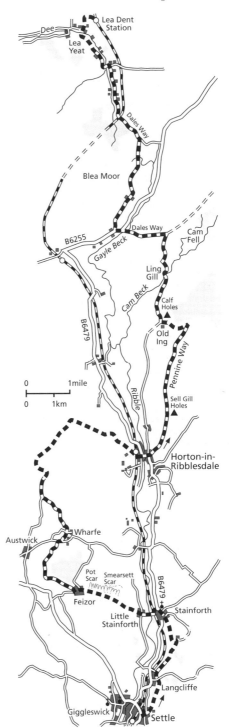

FOOD AND DRINK
Day 1 Full range in Settle and Horton-in-Ribblesdale, notably *the* walkers' café (Pen-y-ghent Café) in Horton, plus Craven Heifer in Stainforth and the Game Cock in Austwick (short diversion). None along the route on **Day 2** except the Sportsman Inn near Dent Station at the end of the walk. Take food and drink with you.

ACCOMMODATION
Being a popular walking village on the Pennine Way, Horton-in-Ribblesdale is well serviced with a campsite, B&Bs and inns. The 17thC **Crown Inn** (tel. 01729 860209) has nine bedrooms (two en suite) and offers home-cooked food. Contact the tourist information office in Horton (Pen-y-ghent Café; tel. 01729 860333) for a list of B&Bs.

enthusiasts in 1989, it remained open. Passengers are treated to a backdrop of wild and breathtaking Pennine scenery.

• **STAINFORTH** takes its name from the 'stony ford' that linked two settlements across the Ribble; it is now crossed by a fine 17thC packhorse bridge (NT) near Stainforth Force, where the river falls over limestone ledges into a deep pool. The village comprises an interesting collection of 17th to 19thC cottages.

173

Introduction

The Lake District

The only way truly to discover the beauty and grandeur of the Lakes is to explore it on foot. Despite traffic congestion and increasing numbers of tourists, this magical corner of England retains a special place in the hearts of all those with a passing affection for England's countryside. Even at the height of summer you can escape the cars and the crowds by following remote paths and tracks well away from the roads.

The Lake District covers a small and compact area, but within its 866-square-mile (2,240-square-kilometre) National Park, there is more than enough to attract visitors over a lifetime.

Keswick and Derwentwater

At the heart of Lakeland's northern region lies the little town of Keswick, sheltering below Skiddaw and Saddleback and famous for the manufacture of lead pencils – a local industry dating back to the 16thC. If time allows, a stroll through Keswick's maze of narrow streets and a look at it 18thC Moot Hall in the Market Place are recommended. Note the hall tower with its quaint, one- handed clock. Sometimes referred to as the Jewel of Lakeland, this market town is a popular base for tourists, climbers and fell walkers throughout the year.

Several walks take you from Keswick to the edge of Derwentwater – the 'Queen of the English Lakes'. The widest of all the lakes and, without question, one of the finest, Shelley described Derwentwater as 'smooth and dark as a plain of polished jet'. At its northern end there is a cluster of small wooded islands which are visible from almost every vantage point. One of them, St Herbert's Island, includes what could be the remains of the home of St Herbert, a disciple of Saint Cuthbert of Lindisfarne in the 7thC. Curiously, Saint Herbert died on the same day as his close friend Saint Cuthbert – March 20, AD687. The inspiration for Beatrix Potter's Owl Island in *The Tale of Squirrel Nutkin* came from here, and red squirrels are known to inhabit the woods overlooking Derwentwater.

South of Derwentwater is Seathwaite, a small collection of cottages and old stone farm buildings at the southern end of Borrowdale, one of the loveliest of the Lakeland valleys. Despite its surroundings, Seathwaite is a lonely place, with the distinction of being the wettest spot in England. Rainfall here can be four times the London average.

For those who prefer something a little more challenging, there is a path running north of Keswick to the 3,054-foot (930-metre) summit of Skiddaw where, weather permitting, there are breathtaking views over the whole region.

GETTING THERE
By car, the easiest access to the Lake District is via the M6. Leave the motorway at junction 40 for the A66 to Ullswater and the Cumbrian coast. Kendal and Windermere can be reached from junctions 36 and 37. Trains on the west coast line call at Lancaster, Kendal, Windermere, Penrith and Carlisle.

174

Northern lakes

West of Skiddaw, you can stroll along the shores of Bassenthwaite Lake, the most northerly of all the lakes and less crowded than some other parts of the region. 'Thwaite' comes from the Norse word meaning cleared or open land. The lake's close proximity to the wildfowl breeding grounds of Morecambe Bay and the Solway Firth draws a variety of migrating birds to its shores.

Lakeland fell and peak.

To the south lie Buttermere, Wast Water, Crummock Water and Ennerdale Water, which, like Bassenthwaite, are among the region's lesser-known, more remote lakes. Buttermere is at the heart of some of the wildest and most spectacular scenery in the Lake District. Here, the fells and peaks of High Stile, High Crag and Haystacks invite the more intrepid walker into another world.

Popular centres

It is possible to tour the whole area during one visit to the Lake District. But those with a sense of adventure will, sooner or later, make for the towering summits of Helvellyn, Scafell, Scafell Pike and Great Gable, the highest peaks in England. These famous landmarks, located roughly at the heart of the lakes, are perennial favourites with fell walkers and climbers.

Windermere, in the south, is the largest of all the lakes and very much a tourist base. The town rose in status after the opening of the local railway in 1847 and today remains of the few places in the Lake District which can be reached by train. Not surprisingly, Windermere is a renowned venue for watersports but if you want to escape all the bustle and activity, there are pleasant, undemanding walks along the thickly wooded shores of the lake and between Windermere and Hawkshead. The adjacent Grizedale Forest will also appeal to those who enjoy woodland strolls.

Ambleside is another popular centre for visitors to the Lake District. The town, part of a conservation area, has many literary associations and William Wordsworth and his siter used to make a regular journey on foot from nearby Grasmere to collect their post. Among the town's many historic buildings is the famous Bridge House, which perches literally over the Stock Ghyll. Many first-time visitors to Ambleside are known to peer increduously at this charming, unique building. The house is now in the care of the National Trust.

Several long-distance paths allow walkers to explore large tracts of the Lake District, absorbing something of the spirit of the area along the way. The most famous route is surely the Cumbria Way, a 70-mile (112-kilometre) walk which tends to keep to the valley floors rather than the mountain tops. Running south to north through the heart of Lakeland, the route begins at Morecambe Bay and concludes at Carlisle.

WEATHER

The weather in the Lake District can be notoriously fickle and unpleasantly deceptive. The sun can be shining in a clear blue sky one moment and then the hills and mountains shrouded in mist and rain the next. It is essential for those wishing to explore the region on foot to be fully prepared for such conditions. May, June and September are the driest months and it is during the spring and autumn that the Lakeland colours are best appreciated.

The Lake District
Walking Base:

ULLSWATER

Keswick Walk 7

Legburthwaite
Walk 4

Braithwaite
Walk 1

Patterdale Walk 5

Grasmere Walk 6

Great Langdale Walk 8

Boot Walk 3

Coniston Walk 2

Ullswater is often described as the most beautiful of the great English lakes. Some 0.8 miles (13 km) long and ½ mile (1 kilometre) at its widest point, it is the second largest of all the lakes in the region, with the Goldrill Beck acting as its main source of water.

Ullswater is also famous in the area for its steamer service, enabling visitors to explore and enjoy the lake and its scenery at a gentle, leisurely pace. Many other kinds of boating activity also take place on Ullswater.

Beside the lake, towards its southern end, is the village of Glenridding overlooked by Glenridding Common, where more than 2,000 acres of fell land extend from the village towards the summit of Helvellyn. There is a delightful drive north from Glenridding along the lakeshore, offering unspoilt views over classic Lakeland scenery. The road leads on to Gowbarrow Park, renowned for its dazzling array of spring daffodils, immortalized by Wordsworth.

At the northern end of Ullswater lies the village of Pooley Bridge, a popular spot. The church, with its striking Norman central tower, is worth a visit and the village is a useful base for those who want to go fishing, cycling or trekking. From Pooley Bridge you can travel by steamer to Howtown and Glenridding.

To the south of Ullswater sits the unexpectedly named High Street – one of Lakeland's highest peaks and well worth exploring. Indeed, the whole area offers numerous opportunities for those who want to walk and relax amid beautiful surroundings.

ACCOMMODATION AND FOOD

Demand for accommodation in the Lake District is strong at most times of the year, especially in the popular areas. Ullswater, tucked away in the north-east corner of the Lake District, is far enough away from main tourist centres to be a peaceful, unspoilt area in which to base yourself, yet within an easy drive of all the walks and attractions. It also offers some of the best country-house hotel accommodation in the Lakes, alongside quiet hill farms, rural inns and peaceful camping grounds. Here we list a small selection to suit a range of tastes and budgets. For more detailed information on where to stay contact Keswick Tourist Information Centre, Moot Hall, Market Square, Keswick CA12 5JR (tel. 017687 72645) or Penrith Tourist Information Centre, Penrith Museum, Middlegate, Penrith CA11 7PT (tel. 01768 867466). Summer offices at Pooley Bridge (tel. 017684 86530) and Glenridding (tel. 017684 82414).

176

SLEEPING AND EATING

HOTELS AND INNS

HOWTOWN
Sharrow Bay Country House; *Ullswater; tel. 017684 863301; closed late Nov–late Feb.* Bordered on three sides by 12 acres of gardens on the very edge of Ullswater, this enchanting building was Britain's first true country-house hotel, opened in 1949. Sumptuously decorated public rooms, beautifully furnished bedrooms, and memorable cooking – all at a price.

WATERMILLOCK
Old Church Hotel; *Ullswater; tel. 017684 8636; closed Nov–Mar.* Stylish, 18thC country house set on the shores of Ullswater, offering splendid views, individually decorated bedrooms and a relaxing atmosphere. Charming service and enterprising British cooking.

GLENRIDDING
Glenridding Hotel; *Ullswater; tel. 017684 82228.* Friendly, family-run hotel in the village centre enjoying views of the lake. Comfortable accommodation, relaxing public areas, including several sitting rooms and a lively bar; home-cooked food.

Ullswater Hotel; *Ullswater; tel. 017684 82444.* Large, Victorian village-centre hotel set in 20 acres on Ullswater. Lakeland views from well-equipped bedrooms.

MUNGRISDALE
The Mill; *(5 miles /8 km N); tel. 01768 779659; closed Dec and Jan.* Beside a stream in a peaceful village, this former mill cottage dates from 1651 and is full of character, with low ceilings and antique furniture.
   Those seeking luxury and good food may also find ***Leeming House Hotel*** *(tel. 017684 86622)* or ***Rampsbeck Country House Hotel*** *(tel. 017684 86442)*, both in ***Water-millock***, to their liking.

BED-AND-BREAKFAST

WATERMILLOCK
Waterside House; *Ullswater; tel. 017684 86038.* Fine 18thC house set in a secluded position and glorious gardens on the edge of the lake. A peaceful base with comfortable bedrooms (most with lake views).

Land Ends Country Lodge; *Ullswater; tel. 017684 86438.* Converted farmhouse/barn set in 7 acres of gardens and woodland. Comfort-able bedrooms and home-cooked food.

MATTERDALE END
Bank House Farm; *Ullswater; tel. 017684 82040.* Splendid period house set above a tiny hamlet with glorious views. Well-equipped, pine-furnished bedrooms and hearty breakfasts.

TROUTBECK
Netherdene Guest House; *(off A66 N of Ullswater); tel. 017684 83475.* Traditional Lakeland country house. Cosy bed-rooms, warm service.
Lane Head Farm; *(off A66 north of Ullswater); tel.. 017687 79220; closed early Jan-mid Mar.* Former 18thC farmhouse with panoramic views. Now a comfortable guest house offering a friendly atmos-phere, log fires and cosy bedrooms. Dinners.

CAMPING AND HOSTELS

The area is well served with camping grounds, notably the award-winning ***Cove Caravan & Camping Park*** *(tel. 017684 86549)*, ***Ullswater Caravan & Camping Site*** *(tel. 017684 86666)* and ***The Quiet Site*** *(tel. 017684 86337)* at ***Watermillock; Hillcroft Caravan & Camping Park, Pooley Bridge*** *(tel. 017684 86363)* and the unspoilt ***Troutbeck Head Caravan Park, Troutbeck*** *(tel. 017684 83521)*. Hostel accommodation is available at ***Patterdale Youth Hostel*** *(tel. 017684 82394)* and the remote ***Helvellyn Youth Hostel***, near ***Glenridding*** *(tel. 017684 82269)*. For self-catering and camping barn accommodation in the Ullswater area, contact the tourist information office.

FOOD

The best restaurant food in the area is served at the country-house hotels listed above, especially at Sharrow Bay Country House and Rampsbeck Country House Hotel. For good pub food head for the ***White Horse, Scales*** *(tel. 01768 779241 – on the A66)*; ***The Gate, Yanwath*** *(tel. 01768 862386*; ***Queens Head, Tirril*** *(tel. 01768 863219 – also B&B – both on B5320 NE of Ullswater)*; ***Royal, Dockray*** *(tel. 017684 82356 – also B&B)*, and the ***Punchbowl Inn, Askham*** *(tel. 01931 712443)*.

Cat Bells

Cat Bells, south-west of Keswick, is a very popular walking area because of the bird's eye views it gives of Derwent Water and its cluster of islands. Views also extend to Keswick, Bassenthwaite Lake and across folds of Lakeland fells in every direction. The majority stroll up Cat Bells from the car park before taking a road and lower fell route back to their cars. For the more adventurous, this short circuit incorporates a climb to Cat Bells Ridge, with a delightful footpath (Cumbria Way) which hugs the wooded west shore of Derwent Water and gives the walk extra variety. You could combine the walk with a sightseeing cruise around the lake: catch the regular (March–November) launch from Hawes End jetty (for timetable tel. 017687 72263).

Start Free car park (signposted) on minor lane near Skelgill, 3 miles (4.8 km) south-west of Keswick, NY247212. Take B5289 from Keswick, join A66 then turn left through Portinscale, following signs for Grange. Cross cattle grid and fork right signed Skelgill to reach car park.

Route directions

Facing the car park, take gravel footpath in left-hand corner and immediately climb through bracken, passing footpath on left and NT sign – Cat Bells Ridge. Zigzag uphill past erosion fences and shortly pause to savour first views of Derwent Water to your left. Negotiate a ridge of rocks via well-worn path and pass stone memorial plaque, then follow wider path to reach grassy saddle with the route ahead and the southern end of Derwent Water clearly visible. Cross a second ridge (ideal picnic spot), then descend to another saddle immediately below Bull Crag (1900 ft/576 m). In this hollow, dotted with cairns, take the footpath which branches left, clearly identified by erosion fences. These veer sharp right then left and are useful to hold on to as you negotiate further outcrops of rock which may be slippery when wet.

Essentials

Moderate 5½ miles (8.8 km); 3½ hours; first half of walk uphill; **map** Ordnance Survey 1:25 000 Outdoor Leisure Map 4, North-Western Area or 1:50 000 Landranger Map 89, West Cumbria.
Terrain Stony paths, a little scrambling on rock outcrops, grassy paths and wooden walkways over boggy areas. Boots or strong shoes recommended.

FOOD AND DRINK

None in the immediate vicinity of the walk.

Continue downhill on curving path, the Lodore Swiss Hotel getting nearer on your left, and skirt a wood to where a footpath converges from the left by NT sign (Cat Bells). Turn right to gate and stile, ignore permitted path to Hollows Farm, and keep ahead to the road. Turn right, pass Manesty Holiday Cottages and Yewdale Knott, then in 75 yds (70 m) take footpath left signposted Lodore. Pass through two kissing gates and head for southern end of lake at Great Bay, making use of the wooden walkways as it can be boggy underfoot. Keep left at the lake shore, enter woodland and shortly reach a cottage called The Warren. Turn right towards Brandlehow and another cottage, the footpath passing between the house and garage before heading back towards the lake to a private landing stage. Here, one path continues through woodland, whilst another skirts round a small, scree-like headland. They merge by another jetty, then continue along the shore before bearing off left over a stile and to the right to the rear of Hawes End Outdoor Centre. Cross stile to right of Centre's metal gate, pass another jetty, then climb up through woodland to join road near Hawes End. Turn right, then in ½ m (0.8 km) at road junction, turn left uphill to a parking area.

Derwentwater – the view from Catbells.

Continue over cattle grid back to car park.

• CAT BELLS fells and nearby Newlands Valley were rich with veins of copper and lead and even a little gold around the time of the reign of Queen Elizabeth I. Although the ravages of mining have long since gone, grassy spoil heaps and mossy adits can still be seen.

• BRANDLEHOW WOOD was the first area of land in the Lake District purchased by the National Trust (1902), in order to guarantee public access to the shores of Derwent Water.

• DERWENT WATER The lake was once an important highway. Boats transported ore from mines along the lake shore and adjacent valleys for smelting in Keswick. It is 3$^1/_2$ miles (5.6 km) long from north to south and has several wooded islands dotted around its northern end. On St Herbert's Island are the remains of the cell inhabited in the 7thC by the saint of the same name.

179

Coniston Old Man

*Although not the most attractive of mountains– because of the scars
left by copper mining and slate quarrying – the old Man of Coniston
is perhaps the most imposing of Cumbria's southern fells. It is also
one of the most popular for walkers because of the panoramic views it
gives of Blackpool, Morecambe, Heysham and Ulverston to the south;
the Isle of Man to the west and in other directions most of the
Lakeland's major peaks. On a clear day the views are well worth the
effort of the final stretch to the top. Having scaled the heights, this
varied ramble returns to Coniston via a pleasant lakeside path beside
Coniston Water.*

Start *Coniston,
SD302976. Attractive
village on the A593
between Ambleside and
Broughton-in-Furness.
Pay-and-display car
park in village centre.*

Route directions

Leave car park, take road
on right opposite petrol
station, signposted Old
Man. Shortly, fork right
down to Sun Inn and turn
left, waymarked Old Man
and Levers Water 2½ miles
(4 km). Pass High Dixon
Ground Farm and an
arrowed route to youth hostel. Gradually
climb alongside Church Beck to reach
attractive waterfalls, then at stone bridge
(do not cross), take narrow path left
through bracken on the shoulder of the
hill with wide open basin and youth hostel
to your right and Old Man straight ahead.
Keep to path as it veers left away from
valley, soon to merge with another path
from left. Coniston Water soon comes into
view. From this point the path becomes
steeper and stonier, but you are rewarded
with views over Coniston to Windermere
and the East Cumbria fells.
After an hour's walking,
reach former slate quarry
– well worth a short break
to study this fascinating
site. Continue to climb,
take almost a U-turn to
right, just before opening
to mine shaft (Levers
Water visible right), and

Essentials

Strenuous 9 miles/14.4
km; 5 hours; steep and
stony for much of the
first two hours; ***map***
Ordnance Survey
1:25 000 Outdoor
Leisure Map 6, South-
Western Area or
1: 50 000 Landranger
Map 97, Kendal and
Morecambe.
Terrain Steep stone-
and scree-strewn paths,
open fells, woodland
and lakeside trails.

FOOD AND DRINK
Tearooms (Bridge
House Café) and pubs,
notably The Sun in
Coniston and The
Church House and
Wilson Arm's pubs in
Torver.

within minutes path opens
up to Low Water which
nestles directly below
Coniston Old Man. Final
climb to top involves
scrambling across scree
faces, via any one of
several narrow tracks
taken by previous walkers,
eventually reaching the
summit cairn on Coniston
Old Man after approx-
imately two hours' walking,
with brief stops to savour
ever-changing views. Walk
along ridge with cairn
behind, then where path
forks, drop downhill to left
with Goats Water, below
sheer face of Dow Crag, now in view. Turn
left again to follow short and stony track
down to tarn, then soon after passing end
of Goats Water, the terrain becomes
gentler, opening up on to wide fells with
coastline and sea views. Your path ahead
is clearly visible along left-hand shoulder
of fell, eventually crossing old Coniston-
Walna Scar road by large cairn. Keep
straight ahead, now following broad grassy
track through bracken, which gradually
curves left downhill. With small rivers on
both sides, take obvious right fork towards
old quarry workings and
then skirt left round
flooded quarry, complete
with plunging waterfall.
Pass through corridor
formed by slate heaps, and
follow route right,
signposted Scarr Head and
Torver. Go through three
gates, cross stone bridge

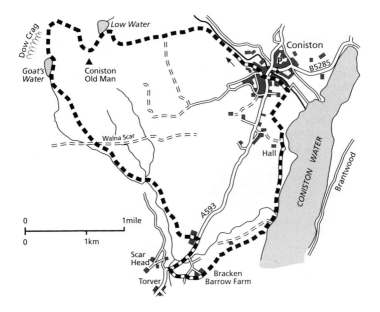

and continue ahead between stone walls, track eventually becoming metalled as it winds down to A593. Turn left, then in 100 yds (90 m) turn right beside guest house on to waymarked path (hidden sign) and cut diagonally across field (boggy in places) to gate in top left-hand corner and road. Cross on to arrowed footpath, pass behind Brackenbarrow Farm and continue through woodland down to Coniston Water. Turn left along shoreline, pass Birmingham University's Water Sports Centre before veering slightly away from lake, through camping area, to Coniston Old Hall. Views of Brantwood, the home of John Ruskin, on the opposite side of the lake. Pass through farm, with Coniston Sailing Club on right, and where road swings left uphill, take wide gravel path right through two fields. Where it turns sharp right, before curving uphill to main road, turn immediately right again into another field, and follow left-hand edge to road linking Coniston to landing stage on Coniston Water. Turn left back into the village.

• **CONISTON** Attractive village of whitewashed cottages nestling at the tip of beautiful Coniston Water and below the mighty peak of the Old Man of Coniston (2,635 ft/823 m). Notable features of this former mining settlement include Coniston Old Hall, built in 1250 but much altered and extended, and recently restored by the National Trust. Its massive stone chimneys are particularly striking and are one of the lake's landmarks. John Ruskin, the 19thC writer and artist is buried in the churchyard and the Ruskin Museum traces his life, as well as recalling the death of Donald Campbell, who died trying to break his water-speed record in the boat *Bluebird* in 1967.

• **BRANTWOOD** Set on the shores of Coniston Water, this fine house was Ruskin's home from 1872 to 1900 and contains many items associated with the writer and artist. Gardens, restaurant and nature trail. A pleasant way to reach Brantwood is via the Coniston Launch (Easter–October) across the lake .

• **STEAM YACHT GONDOLA (NT)** Built in 1859 and beautifully restored by the National Trust in 1980, this historic vessel plys the length and breadth of Coniston Water during the summer months – stopping at Brantwood.

• **WALNA SCAR ROAD** Ancient route that links Coniston with Seathwaite in Dunnerdale. It is listed as a county road.

181

Eskdale

The early part of the walk, from Boot to Burnmoor Tarn, is across wild, open moorland, but the views of the mountain ranges after 2 miles (3 kilometres), dominated by England's highest peak, Scafell Pike (3,210 feett/977 metres) are well worth waiting for. Later, the scenery from Illgill Head overlooking Wast Water and its 1,760-foot (550-metre) high screes are as dramatic as any in the Lake District. The short ride on the Ravenglass and Eskdale narrow gauge railway at the end of the walk rounds off the day perfectly.

Start Eskdale, NY172007. *This valley on the south- west side of the Lakes is at the base of the Hard Knott Pass between the Langdale Valley and the A595 Whitehaven to Millom road. Park at Dalegarth Railway Station pay-and-display car park near Boot.*

Return *to Dalegarth Station from either Irton Road or Eskdale Green stations. Trains run throughout the year, with limited services during the winter months and more trains and later running times during the summer, at Easter and on bank holidays. For timetable tel. 01229 717171.*

Essentials

Moderate 11 miles/17.6 km; 5½ hours; *map* Ordnance Survey 1:25 000 Outdoor Leisure Map 6, South-Western Area or 1:50 000 Landranger Map 89, West Cumbria.
Terrain Stony paths, grassy tracks and boggy ground both on the fells and through Miterdale Forest. Boots or strong shoes essential.

Route directions

From car park turn left along road and in 400 yds (360 m) turn left again into Boot. Continue past working corn mill, cross river to gate at bottom of fells and bear right up wide, cobbled track. In 100 yds (90 m) keep right at fork, go through gate and follow stony path beside steep gulley on right before it gradually swings away to left. Pass through three gates in high stone walls, the last where wall ends by lone tree, your path becoming more grassy and in places quite wet. At this point Scafell Pike can be

FOOD AND DRINK
Tearoom at Dalegarth Station and the Burnmoor Inn, Woolpack Inn and Brookhouse Hotel at Boot.

seen ahead and Eel Tarn behind. The fell now opens out on to a broad plain with hills on both sides and a river to your right. On reaching Burnmoor Tarn, cross wooden bridge at top end and follow shoreline dotted with small cairns, your path ahead clearly visible as it cuts a swathe through bracken along low ridge. The recognized path then veers right to meet path leading to Illgill Head from Wasdale Head. Successive walkers have, however, cut off a big corner here and a narrow track diagonally left cuts across the lower slopes of the fell to meet up with main route to the top. This saves time and energy as the climb up to Illgill Head is steep and therefore slow – and you don't miss the views towards Wasdale Head and Great Gable. The path negotiates a couple of stony ridges on its way up, but the effort is well rewarded with views of Eskdale, the coast at Ravenglass, and on clear days the Isle of Man. From the summit, the way ahead is clearly visible as it stretches out to Whin Rigg (1,712 ft/535 m), but several short detours right to peer over Wasdale Screes to Wast Water below are a must. Towards the lake's end, you start to descend and the path passes Greathall Gill on right. Negotiate a gate, field and stile before the wall turns sharply left and then right again along edge of Miterdale Forest. Again, a track made by walkers heads diagonally left to gate into wood by sign: Forestry Commission

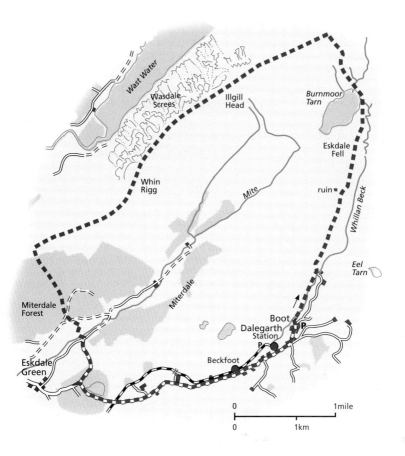

Miterdale. Descend through trees, then at second Forestry Commission road, which loops from left to right, follow it round bend for about 200 yds (180 m) before rejoining path through woods. Eventually, cross bridge over small river, then minor road on to wide path between high stone walls. Continue between farmland and woodland to main road, where you either turn left to Eskdale Green Station or right to Irton Road Station, (both 750 yds/675 m away), for the miniature train back to Dalegarth.

• **BOOT** Terminus of the Ravenglass and Eskdale Railway which opened in 1875 to carry iron ore from mines in the area to the Furness coast. It started taking passengers a year later and when the iron ore trade dwindled, it was bought by a model maker and converted into a 15-inch

(38-cm) narrow gauge railway.

Eskdale corn mill was built in 1578 and was used for milling corn until the 1920s. Restored in 1975 to working order, it is open to the public and houses an exhibition about milling; also about the agricultural techniques used in the area.

• **WASDALE HEAD** This small parish at the head of Wast Water is said to contain England's highest mountain (Scafell Pike), deepest lake (Wast Water at 250 ft/75 m), smallest church (St Olaf at 35 ft by 14ft 2 in/10.6 m by 4.3 m) and biggest liar (Will Ritson, 1808–1890).

• **HARDKNOTT ROMAN FORT** Located 3 miles (4.8 km) up the valley from Boot are the remains of this Roman fort, built around AD100 and once housing about 500 men.

183

St John's-in-the-Vale

Although bounded on three sides by quite busy roads, this is a surprisingly peaceful, lonely walk – and a less taxing option than most others in the section.

Start *Legburthwaite car park (North-West Water & Lake District National Park) on B5322 Threlkeld road, ¹/₂ mile (0.6 km) north of junction with A591, NY318190.*

Route directions

Go through gate at rear of car park and turn left into narrow lane leading to A591 in 300 yds (270 m). Turn right alongside main road and in 100 yds (90 m) climb stile on right and follow yellow arrow pointing uphill. At fork, keep right beneath trees to join narrow path with land on your right shelving steeply away to river (care to be taken). Across valley Helvellyn (3,118 ft/949 m) can be seen. The track eventually descends to river, then climbs away again with open fields on right. Look for sign Path to Church which takes you behind and slightly above farm. In view now are Skiddaw (3054 ft/930 m), ahead, and Blencathra (2847 ft/868 m), right. Your path is quite clear, passing through trees and hugging wall before climbing and curving left round shoulder of fell, eventually reaching narrow lane by St John's Church (well worth visiting). Benches in attractive churchyard make it an ideal picnic spot, while for the more energetic there is a rewarding scramble up the hill behind church for splendid views of Thirlmere and beyond to the south and Bassenthwaite Lake to the north-west. Continue past church and small school and descend towards Naddle valley. At Sykes Farm turn left, pass properties called Shaw Bank and Ku-Hus, then ignore turning right and carry on to end of road. Keep ahead through bracken to join bridleway which skirts round shoulder of fell. Aim for small copse on edge of A591 and soon cross road

Essentials

Easy/moderate 6 miles/10 km; 3¹/₂ hours; almost level; *map* Ordnance Survey 1: 50 000 Landranger Map 90, Penrith, Keswick & Ambleside or 1: 25,000 Outdoor Leisure Map 4, North-Western Area. **Terrain** Grassy paths, roads and tracks. Option of a strenuous 15-minute scramble to the top of the fell.

(footpath and Caravan Club sign), keeping ahead into Shoulthwaite Farm. Turn left by stone barn, cross bridge (caravans right) and take path through woodland. Ignore tracks left and right along this pleasant wooded stretch, remaining on main path to minor road. Turn right, then almost immediately left across field, keeping left of derelict barn to pass two further barns. Cross river via stepping stones or wooden bridge (right), turn left, then right uphill through field towards farm. Climb stile at top, turn left and shortly cross A591 to follow narrow lane back to car park.

- **St John's-in-the-Vale** The name given to a scattered farming community which occupies the valley on both sides of St John's Beck between Threlkeld and Thirlmere.

- **St John's Church** Isolated church enjoying a romantic position on a hill between the St John's and Naddle valleys. Present church dates from 1845 but a church is thought to have been on the site as long ago as the 13thC. However, earliest evidence of a chapel here is 1554; the main reason for its remote existence is that the road was an important link from Matterdale to the road leading to Keswick.

- **Castlerigg Stone Circle** (2¹/₂ miles/4 km north-west) Famous megalithic collection of 60 rough-hewn stones, the tallest 7 ft (2 m), standing in a circle on a hill east of Keswick.

FOOD AND DRINK
King's Head Inn (1 mile/1.6 km south of the car park on the A591).

Patterdale

You have the choice of a long circular walk or a shorter walk with a half-hour motor-boat crossing of Ullswater. In places and at certain times, this route can be very popular, yet in complete contrast, other places along the way are remote and peaceful. Whichever option is taken, Ullswater is never far away and the views along and across its waters are among Lakeland's best.

Start *For full walk or shorter ramble to Howtown returning by boat start at Patterdale on the A592; car park opposite Patterdale Hotel, NY398157. For boat trip first and return walk start at Glenridding; car park in village, NY385170.* **Boat** *Eight regular services (extra late service July and August) Easter, May Day bank holiday weekend and mid May to September. Four services Easter, mid April to mid May and end September to early November. For timetable tel. 01539 721626 or 017684 82229.*

Essentials

Moderate 12 miles/19.2 km; 6½ hours, **or** 6 miles/10 km and a boat trip on Ullswater; 3 hours; undulating fell walk; **map** Ordnance Survey 1: 50,000 Landranger Map 90, Penrith, Keswick & Ambleside or 1: 25 000 Outdoor Leisure Map 5, North-Eastern Area. **Terrain** Stony paths, farm roads and grassy paths by Ullswater. Boots or strong shoes recommended.

Route directions

From car park at Patterdale turn left along road, pass White Lion Hotel and in about 200 yds (180 m) turn left towards cluster of cottages. Ignore first turning right by wooden signpost, keeping ahead towards Side Farm and Boredale Hause. At Side Farm the path curves right and gradually climbs diagonally up lower slopes of Place Fell (2,102 ft/ 657 m) with spectacular views unfolding in every direction – Helvellyn, Striding Edge, Brothers Water and Kirkstone Pass. Tracks radiate off in several directions on reaching cairn on first ridge, with one clearly leading to summit of Place Fell. Follow track slightly to right of this, which soon veers sharp right and then almost immediately left

into narrow gulley looking down into broad Boredale Valley. Descend into valley which is sheltered by fells on all sides, the stony path becoming a wide grassy ledge and Hallin Fell (1,124 ft/388 m) with its 12-ft (3.7-m) obelisk visible straight ahead. Head downhill to farmhouse at Boredale Head, then with option of passing to its rear to avoid muddy yard, soon join the well-made and quiet farm access road. Follow valley bottom lane for 1 mile (1.6 km), crossing Boredale Beck to reach another farm. Turn right between farmhouse and barn, following arrowed path to Martindale. Climb quickly to ridge giving views of Boredale and Martindale (left) valleys. Turn sharp left along ridge to cairn and keep ahead, downhill to high stone wall. Turn right alongside wall, then left at bottom and bear sharp right to cross bridge at confluence of two becks. Walk up road ahead to reach St Peter's Church in Martindale. A pleasant and rewarding diversion (other than visiting the delightful church) is to take the waymarked and well-used path up to viewpoint and obelisk on Hallin Fell – a round trip of about an hour to enjoy magnificent views of major Cumbrian Fells. 100 yds (90 m) along road from church, by a natural lay-by overlooking Ullswater, take footpath left which leads around shoulder of fell. Howtown Motor Yacht Pier is now visible and those wishing to take the boat should go through gate in the wall to reach lakeside

FOOD AND DRINK

Glenridding: Moss Crag and Fairlight cafés, Traveller's Rest, Ratchers Tavern and Glenridding Hotel. Patterdale: White Lion Inn, Patterdale Hotel. Howtown: Howtown Hotel.

Ullswater shore: Old Church Hotel, Watermillock – see page 177.

road and pier. Those who take boat first from Glenridding will join walk here (short walk option); a very popular section, especially weekends and bank holidays. An undulating path, stony in places, hugs tree-lined shore, but frequently opens up by bays to give clear views of lake. At one stage it veers away from the water and passes through fields to hamlet of Sandwick. Here, turn left on to road and at end of row of cottages take footpath right along stone wall. The path returns to a lovely stretch of Ullswater's shore, then having rounded Silver Point the path soon reaches Side Farm where signpost points right to pick up road (A592), back to Glenridding (for those who started the walk with the boat there). Otherwise, keep straight ahead, waymarked Angle Tarn and Boredale Hause, to pick up outward path across meadows back to Patterdale.

• **ULLSWATER** Ullswater is Cumbria's second largest lake (7 miles/11 km long), and is surrounded by beautiful Lakeland scenery, notably the 60-ft (18-m) Aira Force waterfall and some 8,000 acres of National Trust land. Two 19thC steamers, now converted to oil, cruise the lake – the *Lady of the Lake* and *Raven*. Combining a walk with a boat trip is probably the best way to enjoy the varied and spectacular scenery around Ullswater.

• **PATTERDALE** is named after St Patrick who is said to have walked to the area in AD540 after being shipwrecked on Duddon Sands. Now a popular tourist village, it is noted as the best starting point to climb Helvellyn; for its sheepdog trials and for its tiny parish church which displays fine tapestries by Ann Macbeth, an exceptional embroiderer who lived in the area between 1921 and 1948.

• **GLENRIDDING** is the southernmost settlement on the lake and the base for the passenger boats that ply its waters. Glenridding Common extends to the summit of Helvellyn and is an important area for nature conservation and industrial archaeology. Near the junction of the A592 and A5091 (north of village) are numerous fields covered with daffodils in spring and thought to have inspired Wordsworth to write his poem, 'Daffodils'.

• **MARTINDALE** is almost the smallest independent parish in the Church of England yet, surprisingly, is possesses two delightful churches. Nestling in a peaceful and timeless valley, the old Church of St Martin dates from the 16thC, although a church has existed on the site since the 13thC. It fell into disrepair in 1880 and St Peter's Church was built half a mile away – it boasts some interesting stained-glass windows. St Martin's has been repaired and is a charming place to visit.

186

Grasmere to Ambleside via Rydal Mount

Grasmere and Rydal abound with reminders of the Romantic poet William Wordsworth, and much of this ramble around these attractive and popular villages follows his footsteps – in fact it incorporates the path that Wordsworth and his sister Dorothy took into Ambleside to collect their post. Fine views throughout of Grasmere and Rydal Water and the chance to visit Rydal Mount, Wordsworth's home between 1813 and 1850.

Start Grasmere, NY336074. Busy tourist village situated just off the A591 between Ambleside and Keswick, 3½ miles (5.6 km) north of Ambleside. Park in the pay-and-display car park alongside Grasmere Garden Centre in Red Bank Road, opposite the parish church.

Return Catch the hourly bus service (Stagecoach 555 or 556) from Kelsick Road in Ambleside back to the centre of Grasmere.

Essentials

Moderate 6 miles/10 km; 3 hours; mainly on the lower slopes of the fells; **map** Ordnance Survey 1: 25 000 Outdoor Leisure Map 7, South-Eastern Area or 1: 50 000 Landranger Map 90, Penrith, Keswick & Ambleside. **Terrain** Stony, grassy and, in places, boggy. Boots or strong shoes recommended.

Route directions

Turn left out of car park and follow road to end of lake, then turn right opposite boathouse on to waymarked and well-used footpath, initially bounded by high stone walls. Gently climb for some distance through gates (yellow arrows), with Siver Howe ahead and Grasmere and Rydal Water soon visible over wall on left. Where wall curves sharp left there is a junction of footpaths. Follow central track which bears gently uphill towards Spedding Crag. Before top, take footpath left which soon becomes fine ridge walk above Dow Bank and Huntingstile Crag, then on reaching final ridge (cairned summit), pause for the views: Grasmere and Rydal Water left, Loughrigg Tarn and

FOOD AND DRINK

Wealth of pubs and tearooms in the tourist settlements of Grasmere and Ambleside. Good café/restaurants at Dove Cottage and Rydal Mount (on route).

Windermere ahead and Elterwater and quarry workings right. Your path is now clear, heading downhill in general direction of Windermere. Descend into dip with paths visible on opposite slope, then take path right to reach minor road. Turn left, pass youth hostel and NT properties at High Close and in 300 yds (270 m) cross Coniston-Skelwith Bridge road into Deer Bolts Wood. Follow wide track through wood, ignoring left fork by double gate and continue ahead through kissing gate on to Loughrigg Terrace. Take lower of two footpaths towards weir at end of Grasmere. This popular part of the walk has views along Grasmere to Helm Cragg (1229 ft/398 m), better known as The Lion and The Lamb. Descend towards Rydal Water, continue through Rydal Woods then cross wooden bridge to reach Ambleside road. Turn right, then in 100 yds (90 m) cross road at signpost to Rydal Mount, Hall and church. In another 100 yds (90 m) turn right, signposted Tea Shop, then turn left in front of tea shop. Cross bridge, follow waymarker for Ambleside, passing campsite on right. The path widens and passes through pleasant farmland to join main road again by stone lodge. Turn left and walk into Ambleside to take the bus back to Grasmere.

• **GRASMERE** Parts of St Oswald's Church date from the 13thC and its impressive interior is

thought to be
unique.
Wordsworth and
his wife, who
worshipped at the
church, are buried
beneath one of the
eight yew trees
planted in the
churchyard. Also
buried here are
Hartley Coleridge, the
Lake artist William Green
and Sir John Richardson,
the Arctic explorer.

• **DOVE COTTAGE**
Wordsworth's home from
1799 to 1808, it was here
that he wrote 'Michael',
'Resolution' and
'Independence', 'Ode:
Imitations of Immortality'.
The poet's life and work
are illustrated with
portraits, memorabilia and
manuscripts in the
adjacent converted barn.

• **RYDAL MOUNT** Home to
the Wordsworths from 1813
until the poet's death in
1850, it contains personal
possessions and first
editions, and the 3½ acre
landscaped garden,
complete with
terraces, rock pools
and magnificent
views, is a delight
to explore.

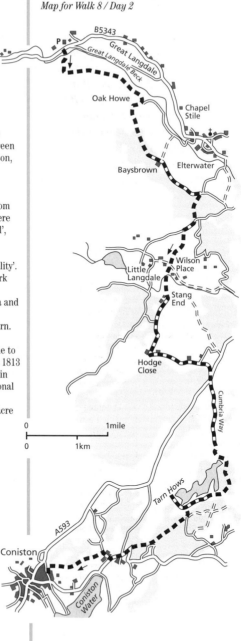

Map for Walk 8 / Day 2

Keswick to Coniston

The stunning scenery in this area attracts many visitors, especially during the high season. Nonetheless, the Borrowdale Valley, where the route starts, never quite loses its serenity. South of Keswick the valley is noted for its broadleaved woodlands which stand on the lower slopes of the peaks. These, together with the pretty villages of Grange and Rosthwaite, and the challenge of the climb over to Great Langdale, are the highlights of Day 1. Day 2 starts below the Langdale Pikes and continues to Tarn Hows, one of the region's most famous and, surprisingly, relatively unspoilt beauty spots. It winds up in the village of Coniston, in the shadow the the Old Man (2,631 ft/802 m), on the west shore of Coniston Water.

Planning

Choice of *either* a two-day walk of 26 miles (41 km) from Keswick with overnight accommodation in the Langdale Valley, then returning to Keswick from Coniston at the end of the second day by bus; **or** two separate day-walks, returning to starting points by bus.

Day 1 Keswick to Great Langdale via Derwentwater, Borrowdale and Stake Pass.

Day 2 Great Langdale to Coniston via Little Langdale and Tarn Hows.

Note: An early start is essential if the walk is to be done in a day. The last 'Langdale Rambler' bus (Stagecoach Cumberland, tel. 01946 63222) leaves Old Dungeon Ghyll Hotel at approximately 4.30 pm to connect with the frequent bus service (555 Lakeslink) at Ambleside back to Keswick. An early start is also needed for Day 2.

Start Day 1 Keswick. Long-stay car parks suitable for overnight parking, NY263237.
Day 2 National Trust Car Park on the B5343 by the New Dungeon Ghyll Hotel, NY294065.

Essentials

Moderate/strenuous; **Day 1/Walk 7** 15 miles (24 km); 8 hours; mainly level through Borrowdale with short, stiff climb up and over Stake Pass, then steep descent into Langdale Valley. *Map* Ordnance Survey 1:25 000 Outdoor Leisure 4 and 6, North-Western and South-Western Areas or 1:50 000 Landranger Map 90, (Penrith, Keswick & Ambleside). **Day 2/Walk 8** 11 miles (17.6 km); 5 hours; mainly level ground with a few gentle inclines; *map* Ordnance Survey 1:25 000 Outdoor Leisure Maps 6 and 7, South-Western and South-Eastern Areas or 1:50 000 Landranger Map 90, Penrith, Keswick & Ambleside and Map 97, Kendal & Morecambe. **Terrain** Stony tracks, grassy farmland paths and short stretches of metalled road are all experienced on this walk, which faithfully traces much of the Cumbria Way.

Route directions

Day 1 From main shopping street walk in westerly direction away from town, then in 440 yds (390 m) cross river by Cumbria Pencil Factory and take footpath left to Portinscale. Pass between road and sports field, cross single-span bridge and pass Derwentwater Hotel, then shortly turn left at road junction, signposted Grange and Longholm Gardens. In ½ mile (0.8 km) at a sharp right bend take footpath in corner up in to woodland – a delightful stretch. At gates to Lingholm Gardens take footpath on right, waymarked Catbells. Eventually leave woodland, pass in front of Hawes End Centre and follow footpath down to lakeside. Follow the shoreline passing jetties and series of small bays, then at stone cottage (The Warren) by entrance to Manesty Woods turn left towards Lodore. Near the end of lake cross series of plank bridges, then at end of third, with Lodore Swiss Hotel ahead, turn right along avenue of tall trees to reach road at Manesty (views down Borrowdale). Turn left and after 10/15 minutes walking enter

189

Grange. Opposite church turn right on to bridleway arrowed Honister, then at triangle of land (Hollows Farm ahead) turn left towards woodland, the path soon reaching banks of River Derwent. Here, just above bend in river, follow yellow arrows left, waymarked Rosthwaite, the bridleway veering right away from river before sweeping back to it, soon to cross bridge towards Rosthwaite. At Yew Tree Farm turn right, then right again through village and at house called Stonecroft turn right, almost immediately taking arrowed footpath to Longthwaite YHA. Keep to yellow arrows, then after wall-stile turn left along road. At crossroads keep ahead to Stonethwaite where road ends for cars.

Here, by phone box, follow path signposted Stake Pass, then where track bends right by hotel, keep ahead along path parallel to Stonethwaite Beck through campsite. Path veers right to place called Johnny House and junction of paths; one straight ahead and footbridge left to join Cumbria Way. Take the latter, a stony path that follows Langstrath Valley bottom. Pass footbridge on right, then cross further footbridge over Stake Beck, just above confluence of Stake Beck and Langstrath, then turn sharp left and begin zigzag climb up fellside to Stake Pass (25 minutes). At tarn (partially hidden by hillock), path veers right with Bowfell (2,960 ft/902 m) and Crinkle Crags (2,816 ft/858 m) towering ahead. Shortly, path descends steeply down rocky Stake Gill into Langdale Valley. In half an hour on the flat you are at Old Dungeon Ghyll Hotel.

Return *See under* **Planning.**

Day 2 From car park cross road to join footpath directly opposite, following sign by barn. Climb gently up shoulder of hill (yellow arrows) away from valley and look for large tree by stone barn at Oak How,

---

ACCOMMODATION

As the Great Langdale Valley comprises scattered farms and houses, so accommodation possibilities are limited. However, the walk does end at the **Old Dungeon Ghyll Hotel** (tel. 015394 37272), a slate-and-stone building offering comfortable rooms, good food and a friendly walker's bar serving real ale. Just along the road (and equally close to the start of Day 2) is the **New Dungeon Ghyll Hotel** (tel. 015394 37213); also B&B at Long House (tel. 015394 37222), a 17thC cottage with superb views.

---

then continue into Baysbrown Wood, through Baysbrown Farm and on to bridleway. Keep ahead at stone cottage, follow main path and, shortly, pass bridleway sign, then take stony path right, waymarked Little Langdale. Leave wooded area (Weatherlam, 2,502 ft/763 m, clearly in view), climb and cross wider track, eventually reaching track on edge of forest. Turn right through gate, then at second field bear off left through gate and follow obvious path across fields to Wilsons Place (Little Langdale). On reaching road (Three Shires Inn right) turn left, then in 100 yds (90 m) take footpath right, crossing fields and footbridge to reach large farmhouse at Stang End.

Follow sign for Hodge Close, pass through a wooded area and keep left of large house (Wythe Howe), then keep left at fork, uphill towards end of quarry. Turn left again through large gate to pass through a farm to reach road and soon take right fork leading to main Coniston-Skelwith Bridge road (A593). Cross over to minor road to High Arnside Farm and, shortly, keep right signposted Tarn Hows. At NT notice 'The Tarns', by a stile and gate, head into woodland, then at end of lake take footpath on left to walk round east side of tarn. On reaching grassy slopes and numerous tracks at other end of lake, keep left to join road near disabled car park. Opposite, by stone wall, take footpath that descends into woodland, then at junction with further path turn sharp right and in 200 yds (180 m) veer sharp left, cross a stream and minor road by NT sign to Coniston. The path runs parallel to road, ending 50 yds (45 m) from row of cottages. Pass in front of these and turn right through NT wood yard. Shortly, cross stile by gate, follow diagonal path across field, gently climbing to

---

FOOD AND DRINK

The Grange Café and Grange Bridge Cottage Tea Shop (and pubs) in Grange; Riverside Inn (Scafell Hotel) at Rosthwaite; the Langthwaite Hotel in Stonethwaite. The Three Shires Inn, Little Langdale.

Guards Woods with views of Coniston ahead. Keep to track, heading south across Hay Meadow (NT) to reach football ground, then either turn left or right into Coniston village centre.

Return *For those doing this as a one-day walk: Service 506 leaving Coniston at 3.15 pm is the last bus to connect with the 516 (4 pm/3.50 pm Sat) from Ambleside back to Langdale.*

If completing the two-day walk arrive in Coniston by 3.55 pm to take service 505 for Ambleside, then join service 555 (5.18 pm) for Keswick. Check times with Stagecoach Cumberland (tel. 01946 63222) before setting out.

• **Lingholm Gardens** Formal and woodland gardens best seen in spring.

• **Grange-in-Borrowdale** Once the site of a granary of the monks of Furness Abbey, this is now one of the prettiest villages in the area. A mile (1.6 km) north are the famous Lodore Falls, reached from a path near the Lodore Swiss Hotel, while ³/₄ mile (1.2 km) south is the Bowder Stone. At 62 ft (18.6 m) long and 36 ft (10.8 m) high it is the largest boulder in the Lake District and dates back to the Ice Age.

Wastwater: see Walk 3.

• **Cumbria Way** is one of England's most glorious long-distance treks, traversing the heart of the Lake District from Carlisle in the north to Ulverston in the south, a total of 70 miles (112 km).

• **Great Langdale** A dramatic Lakeland valley overshadowed by lofty fells, notably the Langdale Pikes (Harrison Stickle, Pike O'Stickle), and featuring secluded green dales and peaceful little tarns. The spectacular roaring waters of Dungeon Ghyll Force, reached via a footpath from the New Hotel, are worth visiting.

• **Little Langdale** Although not as dramatic as Great Langdale, Little Langdale is blessed with some equally beautiful scenery. Numerous farmsteads are strung out along the valley, notably Fell Foot Farm where the smuggler Lanty Slee kept his distilleries and spirit storeroom. Tales of smuggling are common throughout the valley.

• **Tarn Hows** Collection of beautiful tarns interspersed with peaceful woodland and enjoying stunning views of the Langdale Pikes.

191

Northumberland

Northumberland, England's most
northerly county, is a wilderness of
outstanding and dramatic natural beauty: a
lonely and unspoilt corner of country that is
hard to equal. It is one of the few regions in
Britain where you can still experience a
tremendous sense of space and distance,
walk for miles without meeting another soul
and really feel at one with the landscape.

National Park

Extending from Hadrian's Wall to the Scottish Border, the 398-square-mile
(1,030-square-kilometre) Northumberland National Park offers many
attractions. The Cheviot Hills, a chain of low, grassy domes stretching to the
horizon like a rumpled green tablecloth, are among Northumberland's more
famous landmarks. These hills, which cover 300 square miles (780 square
kilometres) either side of the Scottish Border, are an obvious choice for those
who enjoy more strenuous walks. Hedgehope and the Cheviot are the two
highest summits, but there are other equally demanding hills to climb among
the range.

Britain's biggest forest

Coquetdale and the forests of Harwood and Rothbury are more easily
accessible by car, offering a variety of woodland walks and waymarked trails.
However, sooner or later, most visitors to Northumberland head for the huge
Border Forest, covering 200 square miles (320 square kilometres) and
comprising a handful of man-made plantations which collectively make up the
largest forest area in Britain.

Kielder Water, the largest man-made lake in Western Europe, lies at the
heart of the forest. The 250-mile (400-kilometre)
Pennine Way, Britain's first long-distance path, cuts
through Kielder and across the Cheviots before
terminating at Kirk Yetholm on the Scottish border.
A network of woodland trails of every type and
description draw people from far and wide to the
Border Forest.

Hadrian's Wall

Many sites in the county illustrate
Northumberland's long and bloody history –
certainly none more comprehensively and
accurately than Hadrian's Wall, once the northern
boundary of the Roman Empire. It was Emperor
Hadrian who, after visiting Britain in AD122, ruled
that a line of defence was needed to protect these
vulnerable and exposed tracts of country,
particularly from the unconquered north. The idea
of a wall was kindled, essentially to act as a line of
defence against Pictish invaders but also to help

WEATHER
Parts of
Northumberland are
climatically deceptive -
particularly the
Cheviots. With their
smooth, rounded
shapes, these hills often
look soft and inviting.
But when the weather
changes abruptly for
the worse, they can be
deadly and inhosp-
itable. Walkers should
only attempt to tackle
them in appropriate
conditions and even
then to take the
necessary precautions
mentioned on page 9 .

Dunstanburgh Castle.

control the flow of people and trade. Completed by about AD138, the wall originally ran for 73 miles (117 kilometres) between the west and east coasts and is still regarded as a masterpiece of skill and ingenuity. Hadrian's Wall has been designated a World Heritage Site and there are plans for a new national trail to follow its course.

The coast, and other attractions

Northumberland's coastline is outstanding. Here you can stroll along empty, unspoilt sandy beaches protected by a chain of historic fortresses and stately castles. A popular walk follows the coast between Bamburgh Castle and Amble-upon-Sea. Holy Island, better known as Lindisfarne, and the Farne Islands, a national nature reserve inhabited by puffins, guillemots and kittiwakes, are among the more famous landmarks in this area.

But there is so much more to Northumberland than its obvious attractions. One of the county's lesser-known gems is the delightful village of Blanchland, between Hexham and Stanhope, which has a timeless air and boasts many charming stone-built cottages. Embraced by glorious wooded hills, the village includes a famous and historic inn – The Lord Crewe Arms – which is reputedly haunted by the ghost of the sister of Tom Forster whose family acquired the inn in 1623. Forster was a Jacobite commander in the uprising of 1715 and The Lord Crewe includes a priest's hole where he escaped capture.

Close by is Allendale, a bustling village perched 1,400 feet (430 metres) above sea level and the setting for an ancient annual tradition, thought to have pagan origins. Every New Year's Eve the people of Allendale parade through the streets carrying blazing barrels of tar above their heads. The climax takes place at midnight when the barrels are tossed into the flames of a spectacular bonfire in the market place. The distinctive beauty and character of this area inspired the writer Catherine Cookson to use it as the setting for her trilogy *The Mallens*.

Some of the county's loveliest scenery forms the backdrop for a new annual event – The Roof of England Walks – launched in the North Pennines in 1996. Hundreds of people from far and wide take part in the hikes which are of varying lengths, the longest being less than 20 miles (32 kilometres), and designed to suit all participants. The county is also ideally suited to something more ambitious, with plenty of weekend walking excursions taking you to the heart of this spectacular hill country.

GETTING THERE
By road from the south, the best way to approach this area is by following the M1, M18, A1 and A1 (M) north to Newcastle-upon-Tyne. There is a regular, fast train service from London to Newcastle and Berwick.

WALKING BASE:

Hexham

Craster Walk 5

Alwinton Walk 6

Bellingham Walk 3

Haltwhistle Walk 8

Haydon Bridge Walk 7

Dipton Mill Walk 2

Ridley Walk 4

Blanchland Walk 1

canons to get from their dormitory down to the nave in time for Matins. The south transept contains the grave of Flavinus, a young Roman standard-bearer, decorated with a carving depicting an ancient Briton locked in combat with a Roman soldier armed with a dagger.

In the 13thC choir is a stone seat or throne, known as St Wilfrid's Chair, or the Frith Stool, upon which the kings of Northumbria may have been crowned. In medieval times, it was a seat of sanctuary, where a law-breaker could seek the protection of the church. Close to the abbey is a pleasant park with a stone memorial and a row of 18thC buildings used as public offices.

This famous market town, the administrative centre for Tynedale, has a delightful setting and grew up around the monastery and abbey at a crossing of the Tyne. Renowned as a focal point for local farmers, and for its sheep and cattle sales, the town is also a popular and convenient base for visitors to Hadrian's Wall, a short drive to the north, as well as the spectacular upland country of Northumberland and the North Pennines.

It was Wilfrid, the 7thC bishop and saint, who really put Hexham on the map. The son of a local nobleman, and bishop by the time he was 35, he was spiritual adviser to and close associate of Northumbria's King Egfrith and Queen Etheldreda, though he later fell out of favour with them when he persuaded Etheldreda to leave her husband and become a nun. After a period of imprisonment, Wilfrid spent many years in exile before living out his last years in the town.

The church he built here was described at the time as the finest and largest church north of the Alps. Sadly, it did not survive as a lasting monument to Wilfrid – 150 years after his death, the church was largely destroyed by the Danes.

The present abbey was built during the 12th and 13thC above the crypt of the old church and includes the famous, well-worn Midnight Stair, used by Augustinian

Hexham is a town of great charm and character. A leisurely walking tour is recommended, as its streets are lined with quaint Georgian buildings and mellow stone houses. The late 14thC Moot Hall is worth a look, as is the Manor Office in Hallgate, which dates from the same period. Originally a prison and now housing the local tourist information centre, this building was constructed with stones from Roman ruins. The market place is where, allegedly, the Duke of Somerset was beheaded after the Battle of Hexham in 1464, during the Wars of the Roses. The river bridge's setting is renowned for its impressive views of Hexham.

ACCOMMODATION AND FOOD

Accommodation ranges from traditional working hill farms and homely village inns to welcoming town guest houses and well-appointed country hotels. There are a number of budget youth hostels, as well as campsites and plenty of self-catering properties. In addition to the establish-ments listed here, detailed information can be obtained from Hexham Tourist Information Office, Manor Office, Hallgate, Hexham NE46 1XD; tel. 01434 605225.

SLEEPING AND EATING

HOTELS AND INNS

HEXHAM
Beaumont Hotel;
Beaumont Street; tel. 01434 602331; closed Christmas and New Year.
Overlooking the abbey and park in the town centre, this popular business and tourist hotel offers bright bedrooms, a comfortable foyer/sitting area and imaginative cooking.

LANGLEY-ON-TYNE
Langley Castle Hotel;
Haydon Bridge; tel. 01434 688888. Resplendent 14thC castle set in a 10-acre wooded estate. Full of architectural interest with 4-ft (1.2 m) thick walls, spiral staircases and preserved garde-robes. Five 'feature' bedrooms (four-poster or half-tester beds) and eight Castle View bedrooms housed in converted outhouses. Characterful drawing room.

BLANCHLAND
The Lord Crewe Arms;
near Consett; tel. 01434 675337. Historic inn containing the relics of the 12thC Blanchland Abbey lodge and set in a cloister garden within an attractive and unspoilt conservation village, 3 miles (4.8 km) south of Derwentwater. Individually-styled bedrooms are split between the main building and former estate buildings across the road.

CORBRIDGE
Angel Inn; Main Street; tel.
01434 632119. Creeper-clad, 17thC inn overlooking the river bridge in this Saxon village. Neatly refurbished bedrooms; well-equipped pine furnishings and satellite TV.

CHOLLERFORD
George Hotel; *tel. 01434 681611.* Extended riverside hotel with delightful gardens, comfortably furnished bedrooms (most with river views) and excellent leisure facilities. Close to Hadrian's Wall.

BED-AND-BREAKFAST

JUNIPER
Dene House; *Hexham (4 miles S); tel. 01434 602030.* Converted stone farmhouse set in 9 acres with open fires and exposed beams in the welcoming sitting room and dining room, and three pine-furnished bedrooms. Evening meals.

Peth Head Cottage;
Hexham; tel. 01434 673286. Pretty, stone, creeper-clad cottage in a quiet hamlet south of Hexham. Beamed sitting room with log fire, and welcoming bedrooms.

HENCOTES
Middlemarch; *Hexham; tel. 01434 605003.* Former farmhouse and chapel, now an elegant listed Georgian house over-looking the abbey. Spacious, well-appointed bedrooms (one four-poster), and hearty, Aga-cooked breakfasts.

MOUNT PLEASANT
The Courtyard; *Sandhoe, Corbridge; tel. 01434 606850.* Elegantly restored former farm buildings enjoying a beautiful country setting above the Tyne valley. Beams and flagged floors characterize the large sitting room and the comfortable bedrooms are attractively furnished. Evening meals available.

SLALEY
Rye Hill Farm; *Hexham (4 miles/5.6 km S); tel. 01434 673413.* Three-hundred-year-old stone farmhouse set in 30 acres. Old byres set around the courtyard provide comfortable accommodation. Home-cooked food.

CAMPING AND HOSTELS

Due to the close proximity of Hadrian's Wall, the area is well served with youth hostels, namely **Acomb** (just outside **Hexham** – *tel. 01434 602864*); **Once Brewed** (*near Bardon Mill* – *tel. 01434 344360*) and **Ninebanks** (*Allendale* – *tel. 01434 345288*). Camping grounds with full facilities near Hexham include **Fallowfield Dene Caravan and Camping Site, Acomb** (*tel. 01434 603553*); **Caravan Club Site, Hexham Racecourse** (*tel. 01434 606847*); **Causey Hill Caravan Park, Hexham** (*tel. 01434 602834*); **Riverside Leisure, Hexham** (*tel. 01434 604705*).

FOOD

Pubs offering reliable, home-cooked food within easy reach of Hexham include the **Dipton Mill Inn, Dipton Mill** (*tel. 01434 606577* – also Hexhamshire Brewery tap); **General Havelock Inn, Haydon Bridge** (*tel. 01434 684376*); **Queens Head, Great Whittington** (*tel. 01434 672267*) and, in particular, the **Manor House Inn, Carterway Heads** (*tel. 01207 255268* – also B&B). Try also **Black House, Hexham** (S on Dipton Mill road – *tel. 01434 604744*).

Blanchland and the Beldon Burn

Taking advantage of some of Northumberland's loveliest moorland and woodland scenery, this walk begins in Blanchland, one of the most visited villages in the north of England. It follows the pretty Beldon Burn before climbing into unspoilt moorland.

Start *Blanchland, NY965505, is on the B6306 midway between Stanhope and Hexham. On summer weekends and bank holidays, the village can become very congested with traffic. On those occasions it is probably easier to use the car park at Baybridge and begin the walk there. Otherwise, park in the village centre.*

Essentials

Easy 3½ miles (5.6 km); 2 hours; flat apart from one lengthy climb; **map** Ordnance Survey 1: 50 000 Landranger Map 87, Hexham & Haltwhistle.
Terrain Riverside, moorland paths and tracks, stretch of quiet lane.

Route directions

With your back to Lord Crewe Arms, turn left and walk down towards road bridge over Beldon Burn. Turn right just before bridge (signposted Baybridge). Follow pleasant riverside walk with steeply rising wooded banks on opposite side. Cross ladder-stile and at road turn right for Baybridge (car park left). As road to Blanchland bends right, go straight on along No Through Road. The lane begins to rise quite steeply. Pass pine plantation and turning to Birkside Farm. Beyond trees pass through gate and continue on No Through Road. Approach gate to an installation and veer half-right on clear track running across heather moorland. The track runs alongside wall on right. Cross stile and head towards farm buildings at Pennypie. Follow track as it bends right, pass through gate and walk straight on down track. Pass various farm buildings and byres and head towards an old smelt-mill chimney on right. Ignore path to Blanchland Moor and keep going to next main junction. Veer left here and return to village centre.

FOOD AND DRINK
Lord Crewe Arms and a café in Blanchland.

• **BLANCHLAND** has a timeless quality and when the visitors have gone, it is possible to imagine how this tenanted model village might have looked when, in the early part of the 18thC, the trustees of the Crewe estate built the grey stone cottages around the central square to accommodate local lead miners. The abbey was founded in 1165. Following the Dissolution of the Monasteries, the monks fled, but the abbey church continued to be used for worship. Don't miss the medieval gatehouse which guards the road to Hexham.

• **THE LORD CREWE ARMS** was built in the early part of the 13thC as a guest house for adjacent Blanchland Abbey. This solid old building, which became an inn around the mid 1700s, is supposedly haunted by the ghost of the wife of Lord Crewe, asking anyone she sees to send a message to her Jacobite brother in France, where he fled after the rebellion of 1715, telling him that it is safe for him to return to England (see page 195).

• **PENNYPIE HOUSE** acquired its name from the pies the owner baked and sold for a penny to the miners or drovers who used the track.

• **SHILDON** From medieval times to the late 19thC this quiet hamlet was a thriving lead-mining centre. Evidence of such industrial activity can still be seen in the area – spoil heaps, old engine house, disused shafts and the old smelt mill chimney.

Dipton Mill and Hexham Racecourse

This area, just south of Hexham, offers quiet woodland paths and bridleways. The outward leg of the walk meanders through the trees beside Dipton Burn. Leaving the burn, you climb to the higher ground towards Hexham racecourse. On race days there is plenty of colourful activity here.

Start *Dipton Mill. On the B6306 Whitley Chapel road, 2 miles (3.2 km) south of Hexham, NY929610. There is usually room to park opposite the Dipton Mill Inn. Not on bus route, but Dipton Mill can easily be reached on foot from Hexham.*

Essentials

Easy 4 miles (6.4 km); 2 hours; mostly flat; **map** Ordnance Survey 1:50 000 Landranger Map 87, Hexham & Haltwhistle.
Terrain Riverside and woodland paths, bridleways, country lanes and field paths.

right, signposted Hole House and Dipton Mill. Cross stile in field corner. Look for sign – Newbiggin 1 mile – turn right, then immediately left by dilapidated building and follow left-hand edge of field towards Hole House. Cross several stiles towards woodland and go through gate into trees. Walk past Hole House, cross stile on

Route directions

From inn turn left, cross road bridge over Dipton Burn and, almost immediately, bear left along woodland path, waymarked West Dipton Wood. Continue with burn left, cross stile and continue through woods, path rarely straying far from Dipton Burn. Keep water parallel on left, then where trees thin on right, revealing glimpses of tree-lined meadow, follow path alongside fence. In corner, keep ahead under beech-tree canopy and shortly follow rock-strewn path beside burn again. Pass footbridge, then in 50 yds (45 m) veer half-right, following zigzagging bridleway up bank, then along sunken path to gate on woodland edge. Head straight across field (fence left), with striking views over wood behind; shortly, Hexham racecourse comes into view. Pass through several gates, draw level with grandstand, then beyond further gate head towards wood. Join drive leading to Black Hill (house) and pass beneath trees to junction. Turn right along lane, pass entrance to racecourse and path to Dipton Burn, then at main junction cross over to pass several houses. Follow road uphill, take next path

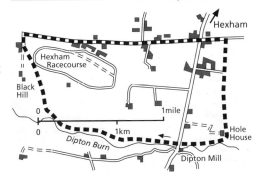

right and follow grassy ride beside paddocks to stile. Proceed to gate in next boundary, follow track beside Dipton Burn and turn left at road back to Dipton Mill.

• **DIPTON MILL** is one of Northumberland's most famous inns. Rural and totally unspoilt, it is a reminder of how traditional country pubs used to be. Formerly a farmhouse, and an inn since the 1800s, it features a cosy bar with low beamed ceilings, leaded windows and good real ales from the local Hexhamshire Brewery. In the rear garden one can view the restored mill stream.

FOOD AND DRINK
Dipton Mill Inn (excellent ales, good value bar food).

• **HEXHAM RACECOURSE** plays host under National Hunt rules to several annual steeplechase meetings.

Bellingham and Hareshaw Linn

*Starting from the small market town of Bellingham, a useful base
from which to explore the beautiful North Tyne countryside, this easy
route follows the North Tyne Walk before traversing upland pasture
with views back to Bellingham. The highlight is the delightful stroll
up a secluded wooded gorge, noted for its wild flowers and birdlife, to
an impressive cascading waterfall in a rock amphitheatre. The
atmosphere and acoustics of the waterfall, and the charm of
Hareshaw Dene, make the short woodland section very popular
in summer.*

Start Bellingham,
NY840834. Small
market town situated
on the B6320 between
Otterburn and
Hexham. Park in the
main street or National
Park car park off West
Woodburn Road.

Route directions

Walk down main street
towards church, bear left
in front of snack bar along
road to rear of houses and
soon turn left, signed No Through Road to
motor vehicles. Cross bridge over
Hareshaw Burn and take grassy track
right, arrowed North Tyne Walk, behind
house to stile and private garden. Climb
further stile and follow path beside North
Tyne river for ³/₄ mile (1.2 km) to Boat
Farm. At gate, turn right along drive, pass
in front of farmhouse, then bear right of
gateway (permissive path). Follow fence
with river right across two fields, then at
clump of ash trees in third field veer up
left to gate and road opposite Redeswood
Farm. Turn right (great care), pass under
old railway bridge and bear off
immediately left along rough track
(Border Trail). Pass through two gates,
then go through first field gate left and
bear half-left across field towards single
tree on horizon. Pass
through gate, keep well to
right of pylons and cross
burn en route to stone stile
to right of solitary tree.
Head diagonally down to
stile (gate) on edge of
hawthorn hedge and
continue downhill to gate
in field corner. Continue

Essentials

Easy 6 miles (10 km);
3 hours; level along
river, otherwise gently
undulating.; **map**
Ordnance Survey
1:50 000 Landranger
Map 80, Cheviot Hills &
Kielder Forest.
Terrain Riverside paths
and the Hareshaw Burn
(can be muddy after
rain), also field paths.

along edge of next field to
gate and follow road with
several houses. Turn left at
end back into Bellingham.
Turn right opposite garage,
signposted Hareshaw Linn.
Pass car park and follow
defined and well-
waymarked path past
Foundry Farm, then via
wooden walkways and
footbridges up quiet
wooded valley beside
Hareshaw Burn to
waterfall, or linn, at its top
end. Retrace steps back to
car park, or main street.

• **BELLINGHAM** was once the centre for a
busy ironstone and coal mining area in the
1840s. Foundry Farm and overgrown spoil
heaps along Hareshaw Dene are evidence
of its bustling industrial past. St
Cuthbert's Church, named after the saint
whose body is supposed to have rested
here on the way to Durham, dates from
the 13thC and has an unusual early stone-
ribbed roof of 22 arches. Nearby, the water
in St Cuthbert's Well (Cuddy's Well) was
thought to have healing properties and is
still used for baptisms.

• **HARESHAW LINN** The secluded wooded
dell leading to the 30 ft- (9-m-) high
waterfall is noted for its wild flowers, –
namely primroses, marsh
marigolds, harebells,
foxgloves and many
interesting mosses, ferns
and fungi. Expect to see
dippers and grey wagtails
along the burn and
woodpeckers, wood
warblers and deer in the
woodland.

198

Allen Banks to Plankey Mill

A glorious walk through Allen Banks, 200 acres of National Trust hillside and woodland. You will stroll along the steep banks of the River Allen and visit Briarwood Nature Reserve and Plankey Mill, a popular picnic and bathing spot. The return is on upland field paths and tracks across farmland and a splendid woodland path beside the River Allen. An optional (and much recommended) extension is to explore Morralee Wood and its secluded tarn. Abundant wild flowers in late spring and early summer; also look out for herons, dippers, woodpeckers, and, if you are lucky, the red squirrel. Paths in the immediate vicinity of the car park are popular in the summer and at weekends.

Start *Allen Banks, NY796641. National Trust car park and picnic site close to Ridley College, signed ¹/₂ mile (0.8 km) off the A69 between Haydon Bridge and Haltwhistle, 1¹/₂ miles (2.4 km) east of Bardon Mill.*

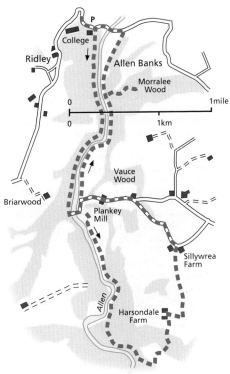

Essentials

Moderate 6 miles (10 km); 2¹/₂ hours; undulating riverside paths; some steep climbs; *map* Ordnance Survey 1:50 000 Landranger Map 87, Hexham & Haltwhistle. **Terrain** Riverside and woodland paths, field paths and a short section of tarmac road.

Route directions

Take well-waymarked path at end of car park into woodland and follow path beside River Allen. In ¹/₂ mile, just before footbridge, climb stone steps right and climb steep path up valley side. On reaching stile into Ridley Park (do not cross), turn left along park fence and through beech and oak woodland. At deep ravine, near Bone-floor Viewpoint, follow steep, winding path beside stream downhill (great care) to riverside path and turn right. Continue through pine woods (Briarwood Bank Nature Reserve), cross footbridge over stream and shortly cross suspension bridge over River Allen to Plankey Mill. Turn right, climb stile and follow riverbank path, initially with lush meadows left, then through woodland. Climb wooden steps left and bear right through woods along well-worn track. Cross small bridge over stream and continue on main woodland path with

199

widening river right. Cross wall with gateposts either side, keep ahead at two arrowed posts, ignore small track right and climb steeply through trees to further waymarker post. Turn left uphill to stile and keep straight ahead across tussocky field to gate into woods. Follow yellow arrow right, descend sharply on worn path (may be slippery), then climb steeply to arrowed stile and field.

Dipper, right and below, seen on the River Allen.

Continue to corner of hedge, follow wall to stile and head for Harsondale Farm. Cross stile, turn right along gravel drive and climb stile on left before wood. In field cross wall steps left and walk beneath beech trees (wall left). Continue downhill, pass ruin left and traverse two fields via gaps (first is open gateway) in walls to gate by old shed at Sillywrea Farm. Turn left along tarmac drive; shortly turn left into long, narrow field. Go through gate at end and keep fence on right across two fields, heading

Great spotted woodpecker, right and below, resident of Allen Banks woods.

downhill to house. Climb stile, turn left downhill along road and take arrowed footpath right. Descend to River Allen. Follow worn riverside path along field edges and into gorge. Enter woodland, keep to lower zigzagging path (care) close to river,

eventually reaching suspension bridge. To explore Morralee Wood and hidden tarn, climb steps right and follow white-topped posts and paths to reach tarn. Retrace steps (beware: area has maze of paths) back to bridge and River Allen. Continue along eastern bank of river through meadows to road bridge. Turn left over bridge back to car park.

- **ALLEN BANKS** Close to Ridley Hall, an 18thC mock castle (now a college), Allen Banks comprises 200 acres of National Trust woodland and hillside flanking a precipitous gorge created by the River Allen. A maze of zig-zagging paths criss-cross the area which comprises splendid mixed woodland, notably some fine beech and oak trees, and much wildlife, from dippers, herons and leaping salmon to beautiful flower-filled meadows. It is also one of the last places in England to see a red squirrel.

- **PLANKEY MILL** is a secluded beauty spot which was bequeathed to the National Trust by Francis Bowes-Lyon, an uncle of the Queen Mother. A mile (1.6 km) south of the mill stands ruined Staward Pele, once one of the strongest defensive sites in Northumberland.

FOOD AND DRINK
None along the route, so pack a picnic and seek out one of the many quiet spots by the river. Picnic site at start.

Craster, Howick Hall and Dunstanburgh Castle

A memorable figure-of-eight route, which can be done either as a single walk, or two short walks, exploring the celebrated and unspoilt Northumbrian coastline. From the tiny fishing village of Craster, you head south along low cliffs before heading inland, where there is the opportunity to visit Howick Hall Gardens. After returning to Craster (ideal place for lunch), the second loop follows the well-trodden coast path (busy in summer) north to the magnificent ruins of Dunstanburgh Castle, returning to Craster along farmland tracks and field paths. On wild winter days the sea can be spectacular and the walk especially exhilarating.

Start *Craster, NU259198. Fishing village signposted off B1339 between Alnmouth and Embleton, north-east of Alnwick. Park in National Trust car park (charge) in old quarry; WCs and tourist information centre – tel. 01665 576007, seasonal.*

Essentials

Easy 9 miles (13.2 km), figure-of-eight – two 4¹/₂ mile (5.6 km) loops; 4.5–5 hours (longer if visiting sites along way); generally level; *map* Ordnance Survey 1:50 000 Landranger Map 75, Berwick-upon-Tweed and Map 81, Alnwick & Morpeth. **Terrain** Well-worn coastal path, field and woodland paths and quiet metalled lanes.

Route directions

From car park take footpath parallel with road down to harbour and bear right to pass Robson & Sons smokehouse. Shortly, at end of road, bear slightly right, then follow Heugh Road and turn left on to coast path. At junction of paths beyond school, bear left towards sea and keep to cliff path around Cullernose Point. Walk between road and sea through gorse, then follow cliff path to old stone house on cliff edge. Good picnic spot in little sandy cove (Rumbling Kern) a short stroll beyond. Turn right through gate, signposted Howick Burn Mouth, and head inland passing Sea Houses Farm (left). At gate and road, keep ahead for ¹/₂ mile (0.8 km) to entrance to Howick Hall. Turn right through car park, signposted Craster, track soon petering out to footpath alongside woods

towards Hips Heugh Crag. Beyond gate at end of woods, ignore arrowed stile left and walk across meadow to stile. Bear left alongside wall to ladder-stile and junction of paths. Bear left to follow right-hand edge of two fields to Craster South Farm. Turn right down drive to road and take footpath opposite (kissing gate) across field to gate. Continue on delightful woodland path (Arnold Nature Reserve) back to car park and harbour. Turn left along seafront, pass through gate and follow well-signposted coast path to Dunstanburgh Castle. Bear left at keep (fork right to visit castle), walk inland around castle and follow defined path around golf course and along beach (interesting stones). Leave coast path along track to Dunstan Steads Farm. Turn left through farmyard, signposted Dunstan Square, and follow concrete farm road for 1 mile (1.6 km). At farm, turn left through gate opposite barn, signposted Craster, and walk along field edge towards crags (The Heughs). Beyond gate, turn right through further gate and follow path beneath crags back to car park.

FOOD AND DRINK

Jolly Fisherman (delicious crab sandwiches), Bark Pot Tea Room and seasonal cafés in Craster. You could picnic on one of the several beaches.

• **CRASTER** is a popular little fishing village with

smokehouses that produce its famous kippers. Sadly, the herring fleet has gone, the fish being brought in from larger ports, but a few boats, usually the high-prowed coble, still fish for crab and lobster. The harbour, built in 1906 as a memorial to Captain Craster who was killed in Tibet in 1904, has a concrete hopper, a reminder of the whinstone that was quarried here until the 1930s and used for kerbstones in Britain's major cities.

- **HOUSE ON CLIFF** Former bathing house belonging to the Grey family who owned Howick Hall. Its sandstone was weathered into fascinating shapes.

- **HOWICK HALL GARDENS** surround a late-18thC house (private) built on the site of a 15thC tower. Formerly the home of the second Earl Grey, who was Prime Minister at the time of the Reform Bill, and who gave his name to Earl Grey tea. The gardens, best visited in spring and early summer, feature beautiful rhododendrons, formal terraces and woodland walks. Open daily Oct–Apr.

- **DUNSTANBURGH CASTLE** Largest of Northumbria's castles, Dunstanburgh was begun in 1313 by Thomas, Earl of Lancaster (and much altered in 1380–84 by John of Gaunt) for use as an outpost on the Lancastrian side of the Wars of the Roses. Turner included the castle in three of his paintings, and it is a magnificent spectacle, standing high above the sea on outcrops of the Whin Sill, the rock system that carries Hadrian's Wall. Open daily Apr–Oct; certain days Nov—Mar.

- **COASTAL WILDLIFE** This area is well known for its sea birds, namely fulmars, kittiwakes, cormorants and eider duck. Purple thyme grows on the thin limey soils of whinstone grassland, thrift and white scurvy-grass enjoy the salty air of the low cliffs. The 3-acre Arnold Nature Reserve is noted for woodland flowers (bluebells, primroses, foxgloves and marsh orchids), and often attracts rare migrant birds.

Upper Coquet Dale

An exhilarating expedition into the wild and dramatic scenery of the Cheviot Hills for the energetic and adventurous. From the peaceful and isolated stone hamlet of Alwinton, this long and lonely ramble follows an ancient track (Clennell Street) north towards the Scottish border into beautiful hill country, with spectacular views. Much of the route follows exposed, windy ridges and, other than sheep, you are not likely to meet another soul, especially out of season, so set out prepared with weatherproof (and waterproof) gear.

Start *Alwinton, NT919063. Hamlet on minor road off B6341 north-west of Rothbury. Park in the National Park car park.*

Route directions

From car park turn left to village green. Cross footbridge over Housedon Beck across green and turn left along road (Clennell Street), signposted Border Ridge. Tarmac gives way to defined stone track in ¼ mile (0.4 km). Gradually climb to gate, reach open moorland and keep to rough track uphill to pass hill fort left (views). Disregard branch right to shepherd's cottage, but near top of hill keep left at fork (marker post) through gate, remaining on old drove road. After short downhill section continue to climb to watershed (wild views left), then follow exposed windy ridge with magnificent views to Coom Fell beyond Kidland Forest, left. Follow line of forest away to right, cross stile (plantation left) and keep ahead at junction of tracks. Track becomes grassy (less obvious), but maintain direction soon to follow fence left and pass stone circle right. Beyond stile, path winds right, becoming less defined to reach gate

NORTHUMBERLAND / *Walk 6*

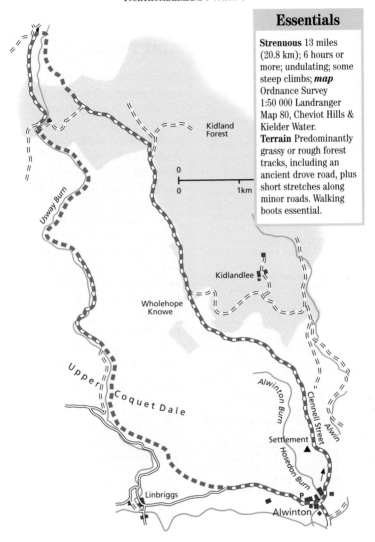

Kidland
Forest

0

0   1km

Kidlandlee

Wholehope
Knowe

U p p e r

C o q u e t   D a l e

Usway Burn

Alwinton Burn

Clennell Street

Alwin

Hosedon Burn

Settlement

Linbriggs

P

Alwinton

Essentials

Strenuous 13 miles
(20.8 km); 6 hours or
more; undulating; some
steep climbs; *map*
Ordnance Survey
1:50 000 Landranger
Map 80, Cheviot Hills &
Kielder Water.
Terrain Predominantly
grassy or rough forest
tracks, including an
ancient drove road, plus
short stretches along
minor roads. Walking
boots essential.

by ruined building close to Wholehope
Knowe (1,453 ft/443 m). Continue ahead
to gate, enter forest on well-defined path,
then keep left on merging with forest
track. Leave forest by gate in ¼ mile (0.4
km), remain on hard track, ignoring
arrowed path left and
forest path right. Gentle
walking for 1 mile (1.6
km), then keep left at fork
(blue arrow), leaving main
track on path leading to
gate and forest. Shortly,
follow defined path sharp

FOOD AND DRINK
None along the route,
so take adequate
provisions. Rose and
Thistle pub on your
return to Alwinton.

left, then in ¾ mile (1.2 km) at clearing
ignore path left, keeping straight ahead on
narrower path, soon to leave forest
(splendid valley views). Follow ill-defined
path across hillside (criss-crossed by
sheep tracks) towards sound of waterfall.
(If you lose path, head
down to stream, following
it upstream.) Eventually
reach grassy knoll above
waterfall (picnic spot) and
cross wooden bridge 50 yds
(45 m) upstream. Turn
right, cross stile into field

203

and follow path to top and turn left on to track along ridge. Climb stile into forest, follow path to top of hill, then in glade veer left downhill to junction of paths by stream. Cross bridge, turn right and pass derelict cottage to track. Walk uphill for 55 yds (50 m), take small path right following fence beside stream. Keep to well-defined path beneath overhanging trees for ³/₄ mile (1.2 km), soon to leave forest. Cross burn (marshy land) and follow it for 1 mile (1.6 km) to farm. Go round farm, proceed downstream on track through narrow winding valley, cross bridge over stream, then in 200 yds (180 m) cross stream again. Do not cross next bridge but follow narrow stony path ahead (awkward landslip to negotiate). Join farm track (bearing left) for short distance, then veer right at stone wall with sign – Alwinton 3 miles. Stream is now the river below. Keep to path, ignore path merging left and follow wall on right. Gently climb, cross track and pass small cairn. Cross brook to stile, path then curves steeply uphill, becoming ill-defined on top, but keep straight ahead to two cairns (blue arrows). Eventually join track (Alwinton visible), following it downhill to join metalled road, passing Barrow House back into village (1 mile/1.6 km) and car park.

• CLENNELL STREET One of the many ancient roads that crossed the highlands of northern England to Scotland, developed by Cistercian monks in medieval times.

• SETTLEMENT Small knoll to left of Clennell Street was formerly an Iron Age hillfort defended by wooded barricades. In the valley to the right of the ancient drove road lies Clennell Hall, once inhabited by an ancient family of the same name.

• RUINED BUILDING Formerly Wholehope Youth Hostel and reputedly haunted.

• BARROW HOUSE is a farm with a fortified tower, or peel tower, where livestock were kept safe during attacks, such as those by the Scots in the 16thC.

• WILDLIFE Lookout for heron dipper, curlew (nest in summer on moors), goosander, hooded crow and the occasional deer.

Walks 7 & 8 – 2 days

Hadrian's Wall and Pennine Way

Two exciting and dramatic day-walks, or a tough two-day expedition. For the fit and energetic. Follows some of the best-preserved sections of the Hadrian's Wall, the largest Roman monument in Britain, and a stretch of the Pennine Way. Allow time to explore some of the fascinating Roman forts, excavated settlements and museums along the way. The Wall, especially close to the more famous sites, will be busy in summer and at weekends. The route also uses a section of the Pennine Way, passing Featherstone Castle and following the South Tyne Valley into Haltwhistle.

Planning

During the summer it is possible to tackle this long ramble as two separate day-walks, returning to Hexham via bus and train, rather than a two-day outing with an overnight stop.

Day 1 Haydon Bridge to Cawfields Picnic Site (near Chesters Fort – 2 miles/3.2 km north of Haltwhistle). Seasonal (Easter–Sep) bus service (or walk) to Haltwhistle, then train (Tyne Valley Line) back to Haydon Bridge (car) or Hexham.

Day 2 Cawfields Picnic Site (Chesters Fort) to Haltwhistle via Thirlwall Castle, Pennine Way and South Tyne Valley. Tyne Valley Line back to Haydon Bridge (car) or Hexham. Two-mile (3.2 km) walk up Haltwhistle Burn (or bus) back to car park.

Start Day 1 Haydon Bridge, NY841645. Small town on A69 6 miles (10 km) west of Hexham. Use regular train service from Hexham, or park in main car park (charge).

Day 2 Cawfields Picnic Site & Car Park (near Great Chesters Fort), 2 miles (3.2 km) north of Haltwhistle, NY713666. If taking train to Haltwhistle, or using Cawfields car park, be prepared for extra half hour walk to Wall (start and end of walk respectively), if doing single day walk.

Route directions

Day 1 From Haydon Bridge railway station head uphill, signposted Grindon/Roman Wall with High School left. At top of steep hill, bear right and pass left turn to Chesterford to reach arrowed footpath, left. Cross several fields via stiles towards farm, then climb ladder-stile on to farm road. Turn right and soon take waymarked footpath left between cottages (yellow arrow on garage). Proceed along narrow passage to gate into field with oak tree. Cross stile in corner, continue with large trees right and descend into dip. Walk along fence line (path ill-defined), cross stile into dip with little bridge. Keep fence on right, walk through wood to stile and head downhill to stile and road. Turn right over bridge, then bear right, signed Whinnetley & Prior House, and climb hill, ignoring signposted left. In ½ mile (0.8 km), at dead-end sign, turn right along rough road and pass beneath pylons to T-junction of tracks. Turn right and shortly take arrowed path left through gate into field (Hadrians Wall 3, Sandyford ¾). Follow clear track across marshy field, go through gate and on to open moorland. Pass through farmyard (Seldom Seen Farm) and follow track to road. Turn left past house, taking path through gate on right, signposted Moss

Essentials

Day 1/Walk 7
Strenuous 12 miles (19.2 km); 6–7 hours.;hilly; some steep climbs.
Day 2/Walk 8
Moderate 12 miles (19.2 km); 6–7 hours; undulating; **map** Ordnance Survey 1:50 000 Landranger Map 87, Hexham & Haltwhistle and Map 86 Haltwhistle, Bewcastle & Alston.
Note possible extra 2 miles (3.2 km) walking (if no bus) at end of both walks/days.
Terrain Tracks; field, woodland and open moorland paths; sections along wide Hadrian's Wall and metalled lanes. Wet and boggy in places. Walking boots, windproof and waterproof clothing essential.

Kennels & Hadrian's Wall. Walk down wall to telegraph pole and continue ahead on ill-defined path (farmhouse left). Cross stile ahead near old kiln (crooked wall), then leave quarry on right and cross field to locate small arrowed post in middle. Follow directions carefully from here. Continue ahead to stile and gate (strange section of wall right, wavy hills in view left), enter field and head towards dark-painted barn. At barn take left-hand track leading to B6318 near Moss Kennels. Turn right, then left across stile, signposted Hadrians Wall & Kings Wicket, on to muddy track. Climb stile onto Vallum, then steep grassy hill (good views) on to Hadrian's Wall. Turn left and follow wall to Housesteads (Roman Fort/National Trust) – well worth exploring. Keep to well-trodden path through woods along wide section of Wall, signposted Hotbank, with stunning views ahead towards lake and crags. Head downhill, pass Hotbank Farmhouse right and cross arrowed stiles to gravel track. Turn right across cattle grid, then left over stile on to path into woods, with lake (Crag Lough) through trees right. Climb stile with wall left. Shortly, cross wall, climb very steep steps ahead and follow rolling path to tarmac road. Turn left to visit Once Brewed Visitor Centre (½ mile /0.8 km), Twice Brewed Inn and waymarked ½ mile (0.8 km) walk to visit Vindolanda (Roman Garrison & Museum). Retrace steps back to wall, taking path through gate signposted Pennine Way/Shiel on the Wall. Continue beside or along wall following obvious path, via gates and step-stiles, with spectacular views for 1½ miles (2 km) to metalled road. Cross straight over, signposted Milecastle 42 & Cawfields Quarry, and follow Pennine Way along Wall through Milecastle Fort to reach Cawfields picnic site and car park. Turn left down road, cross B6318 by Milecastle Inn to reach

205

Auld White Craig Farm (B&B). For accommodation in Haltwhistle catch bus (Easter–Sep) or turn right along B6318 at Milecastle Inn, then follow path left beside Haltwhistle Burn to town.

Return Between Easter and September, catch regular bus (check times tel. 01434 605225 – Hexham Information Office) to Haltwhistle. At other times follow walking directions above to town. Then take train back to Haydon Bridge or Hexham.

Day 2 From Cawfield car park, cross right over cattle grid, then left and right again over little bridge. Cross stile left (signposted Greenhead, Great Chesters) and walk along right-hand edge of fields to Great Chesters Farm (Roman Fort & Museum). Follow pathway through site, then through fields via stiles to cottage and cross stile into woodland behind. Leave wood, follow fairly rugged path through bracken to stile. Wall soon ends but path is obvious ahead along edge of cliff (Walltown Crags). After some very steep drops and climbs, pass Wall Town Fort (Turret 44b), then dip and rise steeply again following ridge to next turret (45a). Turn left down to small car park and right along road to Roman Army Museum (Carvoran). At road, opposite museum entrance, turn right and shortly take footpath left along the Vallum. Cross two stiles and descend steeply, bearing left then right to cross footbridge over Tipalt Burn at Holmhead. With cottage (refreshments) and Thirwall Castle right, turn left along Pennine Way alongside burn. Pass beneath railway, cross B6318 and follow the Vallum beside golf course, soon to bear left with Pennine Way at junction of paths. Cross A69 (care) on to tarmac path and follow well-waymarked Pennine Way sign (acorn), via gates and

FOOD AND DRINK
Day 1 Café at Housesteads Visitor Centre; National Park Visitor Centre at Once Brewed; Twice Brewed Inn; also at Vindolanda (detour).
Day 2 Café at Roman Army Museum (visitors only) at Carvoran; Tea room at Holmhead opposite Thirwall Castle; pub and café in Greenhead (detour). Picnic sites at most major sites/car parks.

ACCOMMODATION
Ald White Craig Farm (just south of B6318, 1 mile from Chesters Fort). Modernized 17thC croft offering comfortable B&B (tel. 01434 320565). Good food at nearby **Milecastle Inn** (³/₄ mile /1.2 km). Alternatively, take bus (summer) or walk 2 miles (3.2 km) to Haltwhistle for choice of hotels and guest houses – Tourist Information tel. 01434 322002.

stiles, eventually joining track leading uphill on to open moorland towards triangulation point (can be boggy). Cross stile over wall, bear right through gate, cross wooden platform over marshy ground to stile and continue along fence line to small bridge with arrowed post. Keep to Pennine Way towards High Side Farm (roof visible), then bear right 100 yds (90 m) before farm across field towards fence and house. Climb stile in corner, go through farmhouse garden to gate and road. Turn left uphill (leaving Pennine Way), then left again at T-junction, signposted Haltwhistle. At next T-junction turn right. On reaching white cottage (right), go through gate opposite and follow gravel track to pass stone house in middle of field. Keep ahead towards thick wood, descend slippery steps in bank and go through gate into woods. Descend to bridge over South Tyne River leading to Featherstone Castle (private), turn left before it and follow old woodland path beside river to tarmac road. Bear right, then immediately left by bridge through gates (arrow), signposted Wydon Eals. Head towards farm along drive. Follow track up beside wall to gate (beech tree right). Continue uphill through trees into field above, then head diagonally (45 degrees) across field (no evident path) to arrowed gate and stile. Turn right to further waymarked gate to follow defined track ahead. Go through right-hand gate (Haltwhistle visible ahead), walk down left-hand side of field to gate and follow track through farmyard (Wydon). Follow tarmac road, cross white painted bridge and continue to A69. Turn right and follow pavement for ¹/₂ mile (0.8 km) into Haltwhistle and railway station.

Opposite: Hadrian's Wall.

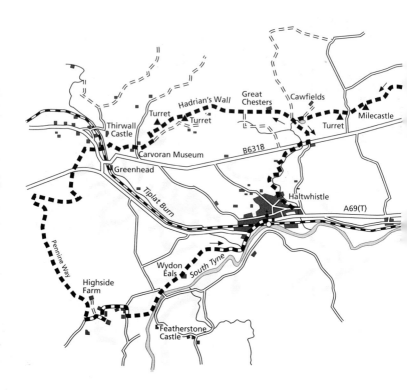

Return By train or bus to Hexham. Those parked at Cawfields car park at Hadrian's Wall can catch the bus (Easter–Sep), take a taxi, or locate and walk up Haltwhistle Burn (north-east of town centre) to B6318, turning left, then right by Milecastle Inn back to car park.

• **HADRIAN'S WALL** The Romans built this great wall between AD122 and 126 as a fortification, a raised military patrol route and as a base for raids against the barbarians to the north. Stretching 73 miles (117 km) from the Tyne to the Solway in Cumbria, it originally stood 20 ft (6 m) high, with milecastles (patrol points) every 1,620 yds (1,481 m), smaller turrets every 540 yds (494 m), plus a defence ditch to the north and a stockade (Vallum) to the south.

• **HOUSESTEADS** is the best-preserved and most impressive of the Roman forts, including barracks, granaries, a hospital, a mess-room with baths and a latrine. Small museum. Open daily all year.

• **NATIONAL PARK VISITOR CENTRE, ONCE BREWED** has various exhibitions, a video theatre and a shop for more information about Hadrian's Wall (tel. 01434 344396).

• **VINDOLANDA** was a garrison for 500 soldiers and a frontier town, with remains dating back to the 3rd and 4thC. Well-preserved headquarters building with full-scale reconstructions of a stone turret and wooden gate-tower. Excavations have revealed houses, taverns, workshops, baths and temples. Museum and gardens. Open daily Feb-Nov.

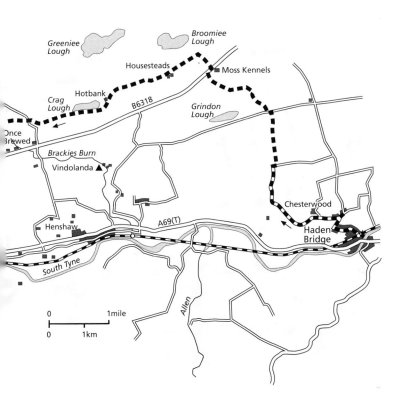

- **WINSHIELDS CRAG** is the highest point on the wall at 1,200 ft (365 m) above sea level.

- **GREAT CHESTERS FORT AND MUSEUM** Located in the park of an 18thC mansion the fort was built for 500 cavalrymen and covered nearly 6 acres. Remains include five gateways, barrack blocks, commandant's house and the finest military bathhouse in Britain. Museum of artefacts. Open daily all year.

- **ROMAN ARMY MUSEUM, CARVORAN** contains artefacts from adjoining Fort of Magna, life-size figures displaying the armour, weapons and uniforms of soldiers, as well as audio-visual displays about the Roman soldier. Open mid Feb–mid Nov.

- **THIRWALL CASTLE** is a sinister tower constructed of stones from the wall and built in the 14thC to defend a gap against the Scots. Edward I is supposed to have slept here in 1306 on the way north to fight the Scots. Partly ruined in 1542, it was lived in until the 18thC.

- **FEATHERSTONE CASTLE** A large castellated mansion (private) is seen on the route. Built on the site of a castle constructed 800 years ago to guard the crossing over the South Tyne River, parts date from the 13thC, the tower from 1330.

- **HALTWHISTLE** is a busy little market town with a 13thC parish church, thought to have been founded by William the Lyon, King of Scotland in 1178. One of the best examples in the country of an Early English church, its spacious interior features a fine painted roof in the nave.

Long-Distance Walks
The Two Moors Way

The Two Moors Way traverses two of Britain's most popular National Parks – Dartmoor and Exmoor. The trail was officially opened in 1976 and four granite plaques at Ivybridge, Drewsteignton, Morchard Bishop and Lynmouth commemorate the occasion.

Though largely set against a backdrop of lonely moorland and big horizons, the Two Moors Way also takes the walker on delightful excursions into unspoilt valleys and along peaceful stretches of riverbank, providing a welcome alternative to the open country.

From Ivybridge the route heads north across Dartmoor, passing through the villages of Widecombe-in-the-Moor and Chagford, to the northern boundary of the Dartmoor National Park. Beyond it the Two Moors Way explores the rich, fertile farmland of mid-Devon before reaching the Exmoor National Park, near the famous beauty spot of Tarr Steps. The last leg samples some of Exmoor's loveliest valleys before descending into the village of Lynmouth on the seaside.

Take great care on the Two Moors Way. The route should not be attempted by novice walkers – except in stages. Much of the trail is hilly and, in places, can be wet and impassable after heavy rain, so walking boots and plenty of protective clothing are essential. Take a compass as well for the moorland sections. Accommodation can be found in many of the towns and villages along the way. Public transport serves the start and finish, and can also be found at several points on the route.

The route

The River Erme flows through the centre of Ivybridge and this charming little town, with its lines of colourful houses and cottages, is worth a closer look before beginning the Two Moors Way. After leaving Ivybridge, the walk makes for wild hostile moorland in the vicinity of the old Red Lake Tramway. From the disused track, constructed in 1910 to accommodate the Red Lake China Clay Works, there are splendid views in fine weather along the coast towards Plymouth and Cornwall. Along this stretch, too, there is a variety of prehistoric monuments, enclosures and cairns as well as a famous 2-mile- long (3 km) stone row. Beginning at a stone circle and extending to a cairn on Green Hill, it is the longest stone row on Dartmoor.

Further north, the route crosses a granite clapper bridge spanning the River Avon before passing close to the ruins of Keeble Martin's church, built in 1909 and named after the famous botantist who was also a clergyman. The remains of the church lie on the north bank of the river. Beyond the hamlet of Scorriton you reach the larger, most attractive

Essentials

Distance 103 miles/164 km
Start Ivybridge
Finish Lynmouth
Maps OS Landranger 180, 181, 191, 202; OS Outdoor Leisure 9, 28.
Guides include *Two Moors Way* published by Two Moors Way Association, available from Ramblers' Association. *The Two Moors Way* by James Roberts (Cicerone Press) and *The Two Moors Way* by John Macadam (Aurum Press).

village of Holme where the writer Charles Kingsley was born in 1819. North of here, the path descends into Cleave Wood and follows the riverbank to New Bridge. Thought to be 15thC, this landmark is understood to be the oldest road bridge on Dartmoor.

From this point the route climbs to Leigh Tor and then heads for Ponsworthy, a typical Dartmoor village, followed by famous Widecombe-in-the-Moor, chiefly associated with the song *Widecombe Fair*. After leaving the village, the Two Moors Way climbs to 1700 ft/518 m, the highest point on the Two Moors Way. This is Hamel Down – home to red grouse. Beyond Hamel Down Tor and Grimspound, where there are the remains of a Bronze Age community, the path heads west to Bennetts Cross, a 13thC guide post for the track between Tavistock and Chagford. 100 years ago this was a tin mining area with a maze of shafts and mine workings.

Crossing Chagford Common, the Two Moors Way passes through Yardworthy, with its Medieval farmhouse, before heading north-east along the Teign Valley to Chagford, a picturesque tourist village which was once a Stannary town. The 15thC Church of St Michael is said to have given R.D. Blackmore the inspiration for the wounding of Lorna by her father in his classic novel *Lorna Doone.*

The trail continues along the riverbank and then heads towards the granite edifice of Castle Drogo, perched 900 feet (272 m) above the valley. Owned by the National Trust and designed by Sir Edwin Lutyens for Julius Drewe of the Home and Colonial Stores, it was completed in 1930. The next objective on the walk is the charming village of Drewsteignton.

North of Drewsteignton the way crosses the A30, which signifies the northern boundary of the Dartmoor National Park. The route ahead is now over pleasantly rolling farmland – a landscape highlighted by its network of high hedgerows and deep red soil. Crossing several more main artery routes, the A3072 and the A377, the way then makes for the hilltop village of Morchard Bishop, where there are distant views over both Dartmoor and Exmoor. From here the route is again over undulating farmland until it arrives at the village of Witheridge, a conservation area set in the valley of the Little Dart River. At this point the way descends to the riverbank, heading east through the trees.

The next stretch is over high ground once more, with wide views in all directions. Beyond the conservation village of Knowstone, the route heads for the open expanse of Owlaborough Moor where buzzards may often be seen soaring through the skies. Crossing the A361, the way heads for West Anstey and soon reaches the southern boundary of the Exmoor National Park. The next stage is over open moorland towards Hawkridge. On the road again the way crosses Slade Bridge, below which the Dane's Brook runs, signifying the Devon/Somerset boundary. A stone's throw away, across a field, is the road into Hawkridge.

The next 2 miles (3 km) provide some of the prettiest scenery of all as the route heads for the banks of the River Barle. The most famous landmark at this stage of the walk is an ancient multiple clapper bridge known as Tarr Steps. Probably medieval, the steps have seventeen spans but it is not clear where exactly the stone slabs originated. The Two Moors Way continues along the banks of the Barle, with the river offering a host of delights. Walkers might even catch a glimpse of a red deer or an otter. If the river is high between Tarr Steps and Withypool, there is an alternative route over Withypool Hill. The village of Withypool includes a pub and youth hostel.

The trail keeps to the road for some time before crossing the Barle by Cow Castle, an Iron Age hillfort extending to nearly three acres. The route crosses the river at Cornham Ford before heading for the highest point on the Exmoor section. Further on, the path reaches the Hoar Oak Tree, representing the ancient Royal Forest boundary. The final stretch of the walk begins by following Cheriton Ridge.

Beyond Cheriton the path heads for Hillsford Bridge, following a route alongside the river. A short diversion here brings you to Watersmeet where the East Lyn River and Hoar Oak Water join forces. Returning to the Two Moors Way, the path zigzags across Myrtleberry Cleave and then descends very steeply into the village of Lynmouth. In 1952 a sudden storm hit the area and, with a terrible ferocity, pushed floodwater downriver into the village. Thirty people perished and Lynmouth was devastated. Today, thanks to civil engineering, even in full spate the river runs safely through the village. Lynmouth includes many attractions and is an ideal base for touring the Devon coast.

The Thames Path

The Thames is historically the most important river in Britain and has been used as a highway from early times. To stroll along its banks is surely the best way to appreciate it. The Thames Path, officially opened by the Countryside Commission in July 1996, is the only long distance national trail in the country to follow a river for its entire length. Some 13.5 million people live within its catchment area, and with numerous access points, frequent public transport services, a high standard of waymarking and many points of interest, not to say amusement, along the way, the Countryside Commission believes its long-term popularity is assured.

The user-friendly terrain and level, easy-going surface also enable walkers to tackle the route at any time of the year, though stretches of the riverbank can become wet and muddy after prolonged rain. More than 95 per cent of the trail currently follows the intended route, running beside the river, which begins life as a trickling stream in a Gloucestershire field near Cirencester. Despite problems over prohibited access in several places, the Thames Path has come a long way since the 1920s when the concept of providing public access along the length of the river was first mooted. Over the years, increasing demand by the public for recreation and access to the countryside led to the eventual designation of the route in 1989. Much of the Thames Path is set against an urban background, but even here there are many distinguished buildings and famous monuments to be seen, reflecting Britain's history and tradition; the rural stretches are plentiful, too, and will satisfy those who seek peace. The Thames Path, which frequently changes from one bank to the other and in London follows both banks simultaneously, can easily be completed in stages or as a two-week walking holiday.

The route

The setting for the source of the Thames is peaceful and pretty. A simple stone marks the spot where the river rises beneath an ancient ash tree and before long the Thames graduates to an infant river on its way to the Cotswold Water Park where gravel extraction has transformed the landscape into a vast network of lakes and pools. Cricklade lies further downstream and is the first town of any size to be found on the upper

Essentials

Distance 180 miles/288 km
Start Thames Head near Cirencester
Finish Thames Barrier, Woolwich
Maps Landranger series 163, 164, 174, 175 and 176
Guides *The Thames Path* by David Sharp, published by Aurum Press in association with the Countryside Commission.

Thames.

Beyond Cricklade the willow-fringed river runs through the village of Castle Eaton, a popular spot in high summer with an 18th century pub overlooking the water. Old Father Thames, still a fledgling at this point, meanders alongside the gardens of private houses towards the church, with its Victorian bell turret and spire, over on the right bank.

Lechlade is a delightful town of warm Cotswold

stone and it was here that stone for the dome of St Paul's Cathedral was loaded into waiting barges. Beyond the Trout Inn the Thames Path reaches Buscot weir and lock, one of the prettiest spots on this reach of the river. The Buscot estate is in the care of the National Trust and from the lock the great soaring spire of Lechlade church stands out on the horizon. A little further downstream the path crosses into Oxfordshire and close by at this point is Kelmscott Manor, open to the public at certain times of the year and once the summer home of William Morris, the 19th century writer, artist and craftsman. Morris died in 1896 and is buried in the village churchyard. The route now passes several famous crossings – Radcot Bridge, the delightfully named Tadpole Bridge and Tenfoot Bridge – before reaching a pretty ford at Duxford.

Near here, on the opposite bank of the river, is the tiny isolated community of Shifford. The church stands out clearly amid the meadows. Evidence of old earthworks indicates that Shifford was a place of some importance. Some sources suggest that King Alfred was supposed to have conducted one of the earliest English parliaments here. A little further downstream the trail reaches New Bridge, one of the river's most famous crossings. Two pubs guard the bridge, its old pointed arches prettily reflected in the water.

Further on the path reaches Bablock Hythe, known locally for its associations with the poet Matthew Arnold. His local walks included Bablock Hythe and the surrounding countryside and he made reference to these much- loved haunts in his *Scholar Gipsy*. The Thames runs close to Farmoor Reservoir at this point, a popular spot where fishing, sailing and bird watching regularly take place. Beyond Pinkhill Lock and the luxuriant curtain of Wytham Great Wood, stretching down to the water's edge, the river passes under the busy A34.

Just to the east of the main road lies the Trout Inn, a popular watering hole in the Oxford area and originally built as a hospice in the 12th century. Port Meadow, a vast expanse of ancient grazing land given by William the Conqueror to the burgesses of Oxford, provides teasing glimpses on the horizon of 'that sweet city with her dreaming spires'. Mink can sometimes be seen in the water on this stretch of the river and fishermen regularly line the banks. Folly Bridge was used by the 13thC friar Roger Bacon as an observatory. Beyond it the Thames skirts Christ Church Meadow, passing the point where it meets the River Cherwell.

South of Oxford the trail reaches the market town of Abingdon, its picturesque stretches of water alive with rivercraft. Now firmly in Oxfordshire, Abingdon used to be the county town of Berkshire. The nearby village of Clifton Hampden is famous for its historic thatched pub, the Barley Mow, which Jerome K. Jerome describes in his *Three Men in a Boat* as 'the quaintest, most old-world inn up the river.' From here the Thames Path follows a wide curve all the way to Day's Lock near Dorchester-on-Thames.

The Sinodun Hills, or Wittenham Clumps as they are more widely known, rise almost 400 ft/121 m above the Thames along this stretch. Castle Hill includes the earthworks of an Iron Age fort built to defend the river. Dorchester, on the north bank of the Thames, has a fascinating history. The Romans built a town here, though its ramparts are now only faintly identifiable, and in Saxon times it was the bishropric for Wessex and Mercia. The abbey, at the heart of Dorchester, dates back to the 12th century and the adjoining Gatehouse is now a museum.

Beyond Shillingford Bridge The Thames Path heads for Wallingford, exploring the heart of this historic town before continuing downstream towards the site of the old Littlestoke Ferry near Cholsey. At one time regular ferry services operated along the entire length of the Thames, but many of them were discontinued during the Second World War. A short diversion takes walkers along the A329 before the route returns to the riverbank at Moulsford. The villages of Streatley and Goring are the next objectives, the latter being on the Oxfordshire bank, the former in Berkshire. This stretch of the river is famous for the Goring Gap where, during the Ice Age, the Thames carved a new passage through the chalk hills. The Ridgeway long-distance trail crosses the river at this point, as does the Thames Path. The route keeps to the north bank as far as Whitchurch where it crosses back into Berkshire via a Victorian iron tollbridge distinguished by its white lattice architecture. This is Pangbourne which became a fashionable haunt for the rich and famous during the Edwardian era. Kenneth Grahame, who wrote *The Wind in the Willows* lived here. The path

The Thames at Strand-on-the-Green.

runs alongside Pangbourne Meadow, owned by the National Trust, and then heads for Mapledurham Lock where classic river illustrations by a local artist can be seen and a sign on the lock island informs you that London is 78.5 miles/126 km away.

From here it is an easy walk to Caversham Bridge on the outskirts of Reading. The trail skirts King's Meadow, crosses the famous Horseshoe footbridge at the mouth of the River Kennet and then meanders past Sonning and Shiplake to reach Henley – one of the river's most famous landmarks and much photographed, particularly from the towpath. The trail continues downstream, passing alongside the world renowned regatta course before arriving at Hambleden Lock, Mill and weir. This is also a famous river scene reproduced in thousands of pictures and photographs. The village of Hurley is one of the prettiest on the entire stretch of the river, its streets revealing many picturesque and historic buildings, including the remains of an old priory. There is also a picnic area on Hurley Lock Island. Further on is Bisham Abbey, venue for the Sports Council's National Recreation Centre.

The view of Marlow's soaring church spire and bridge over the weir is particularly memorable; soon the river runs along the foot of Winter Hill before reaching Cookham, the home of the controversial artist Stanley Spencer whose paintings include *The Last Supper*. The tradition of Swan Upping or counting takes place here. The river's approach to Maidenhead reveals glimpses of the Cliveden estate, probably most notably

associated with the Profumo scandal of the early 1960s. Today, the late 19th century house is run as a luxury hotel.

Beyond Boulter's Lock, Maidenhead Bridge, Bray and Dorney Reach the path reaches the Brocas, a renowned meadow adjacent to the Thames and part of Eton College since the early 16th century. A little further downstream is Windsor Bridge, which was pedestrianized in 1970. Erected in 1822, this has probably been a river crossing point for 800 years. The bridge is often crowded with tourists and on this stretch of the Thames there are impressive vistas of Windsor Castle, one of the river's most famous features and founded as a fortress by William the Conqueror. The castle's Round Tower, built by Henry II, is visible for miles around.

During the late 1950s, the exiled Duke of Windsor described the royal residence as follows: 'there is one place...which hardly changes at all, and that is Windsor Castle. Here is a palace essentially English in character. I take pleasure in the way it broods, with an air of comfortable benevolence, down over the homely town of Windsor, while to the south spreads the spacious Great Park, with the Long Walk stretching three miles through the soft, green English landscape and the meadows of the Home Park to the south, refreshed by the waters of the slowly winding Thames.'

Between Windsor and Datchet the path crosses to the north bank, as access to Home Park is prohibited. The meadows at Runnymeade include several memorials and it was here on wooded Magna Carta Island that King John signed the famous Magna Carta in 1215 – symbol of democracy and one of Britain's most historic events. The river's surroundings become increasingly more urban from now on, as the Thames Path heads for London. The river snakes through its suburbs, passing Staines, Chertsey, Shepperton and Walton-on-Thames before slicing through a maze of reservoirs. The next objective is Hampton Court Palace, its distinctive Tudor facade overlooking the river. At Kingston Bridge the path crosses to the south bank again, heading for Richmond and Teddington Lock.

Eel Pie Island near Twickenham harks back to the Victorian era, taking its name from the local pies which were a favourite with daytrippers. 17thC Ham House, owned by the National Trust, is nearby and worth a look when open. The delights of Kew await, with Strand-on-the-Green beyond on the north bank – one of the prettiest communities on this stretch of the Thames. Rows of picturesque cottages and elegant period houses directly overlook the river – some were once the home of fishermen. The City Barge pub is where the City Corporation once levied tolls on Thames barge traffic. Chiswick is famous for its Mall, where you walk alongside lines of riverside houses adorned with railings and balconies. Hammersmith has various Georgian homes situated close to its famous, lavishly decorated suspension bridge, constructed in 1887.

This reach of the river includes the course of the Oxford and Cambridge Boat Race, one of Britain's great sporting traditions. Oarsmen can often be seen sharpening their skills here. On the south bank notable features include the old Mortlake Brewery, while Chiswick Bridge and Barnes Bridge gracefully span the Thames.

Downstream lie many more classic river crossings – Putney Bridge and Wandsworth Bridge, followed by Battersea Bridge, Albert Bridge, Chelsea Bridge , Vauxhall Bridge and Lambeth Bridge. Ahead now is the Palace of Westminster, symbolizing the seat of government and the river's course through the heart of London. The river flows beneath Westminster Bridge and on towards the South Bank. The present Waterloo Bridge dates back to the beginning of the Second World War and from the riverbank here you can see St Paul's Cathedral, the BT Tower, the Savoy Hotel, the Temple – home of Britain's lawyers – and many other historic sites. The river passes under Blackfriars Bridge to reach Shakespeare's Globe Theatre, originally destroyed by fire in 1613 and faithfully recreated in the mid 1990s. By London Bridge is Southwark Cathedral, which dates back to the 13th century, was largely rebuilt in the 1890s and includes a Shakespeare monument.

Tower Bridge was built between 1886-94 and the view of the river between its Gothic twin towers is particularly memorable. The adjoining Tower of London has been both a prison and a royal palace and is also famous for Traitor's Gate. East of Tower Bridge the trail passes through Rotherhithe on its way to the Thames Barrier. Here, there are numerous reminders of how the industrial face of the river has changed in recent years, with the exuberant, post- modern architectural styles of today's Docklands seen at every turn.

The Port of London's history is described in words and pictures as you stroll along the Thames Path, helping to put this fascinating scene into context. During the 1950s a third of the total exports of the Commonwealth passed through London, making the port busier than ever before. However, by the 1960s and 70s this once bustling community was virtually redundant.

Now, with its new image of chic offices and luxury apartments, much of this eight square mile area has been transformed almost beyond recognition, and during the 1980s it became the largest construction site in Europe. The jewel in Docklands' crown is Canary Wharf, with its breathtaking 800 ft/243 m tower visible at different stages of the route. Further on, the path arrives at Greenwich, overlooked by the sumptuous Royal Naval College, designed by Christopher Wren and opened in 1705. It was here that Nelson's body lay in state. The fascinating Greenwich Foot Tunnel under the Thames bed links the north and south banks of the river.

The path cuts across an industrial landscape to conclude at the Thames Barrier – a suitably dramatic setting for the end of this spectacular walk. A plaque marks the spot where the Thames Path was officially opened, and nearby is an illustrated profile of the river journey, reflecting its many landmarks and historic features, etched into a concrete wall.

The Cleveland Way

The horseshoe-shaped Cleveland Way, officially opened in 1969 and Britain's second oldest national long-distance path, divides into two distinct halves. Beginning at Helmsley, one of Yorkshire's loveliest old market towns, the western half cuts across the bare, open expanses of the North York Moors – a world of snug villages, expansive heather moorland and dark legends. The Hambleton Hills and Cleveland range provide superb views as you cut across country. At Saltburn the trail reaches the sea, then marches with Yorkshire's magnificent coastline all the way to Filey, south of Scarborough. The route broadly follows the North York Moors National Park boundary.

The Cleveland Way is one of Britain's most spectacular long-distance trails. It is also a tough walk. Even those who like their hiking physically demanding will find it hard-going in places – but you are more than compensated by the breathtaking scenery and sense of space and freedom. A choice of accommodation, including several youth hostels, can be found along the way and a variety of public transport services enable walkers to complete the hike in stages. Part of the trail coincides with the Coast to Coast Path which was the brainchild of the legendary walker and walking guide writer Alfred Wainwright, spanning the width of England between St Bees on the Cumbrian coast and Robin Hood's Bay on the Yorkshire coast.

The route

From Helmsley, with its spacious market square of sturdy stone houses and cottages, the Cleveland Way skirts Duncombe Park before passing close to the remains of Rievaulx Abbey (pronounced Rivis), a stone's throw from the town to the west. The abbey was founded by Cistercian monks in 1131. The trail crosses the River Rye at this point and exploring this hidden valley leaves a lasting impression – whatever the season. Soon the walk leaves the sheltered valleys and wooded stretches, making for the scarp of Sutton Bank, one of the north-east's most famous landmarks. From here the views over the Vale of York are so wide and far-reaching, it is as if the whole of Yorkshire is spread out at your feet. Gormire Lake and the Hambleton Hills form part of this majestic scene, and

Essentials

Distance 100 miles/160 km
Start Helmsley
Finish Filey
Maps OS Landranger 93, 94, 99, 100 and 101; OS Outdoor Leisure 26 & 27.
Guides Several books including *The Cleveland Way* by Ian Sampson, published by Aurum Press in association with the Countryside Commission and Ordnance Survey.

gliders based at a nearby club can often be seen soaring overhead.

A short detour at this stage takes you to Roulston Scar where the figure of a horse can be seen carved into the hillside. This is the famous mid 19th century White Horse of Kilburn, the village being just below the hill.

From the A170 at Sutton Bank the trail heads north following the Hambleton Ridge up to a height of 1200 ft/365m. Cattle were once herded along this ancient drove road to the markets of central and southern England. Eventually you reach the village of Osmotherley, renowned as the starting point for the Lyke Wake Walk, a long-established 40-mile/64.3 km challenge route. The walk has to be completed in 24 hours in order to qualify for membership of the Lyke

Wake Club, formed many years ago by a local farmer.

Beginning on Scarth Wood Moor, the most westerly point of the Cleveland Hills, and finishing at Wyke Point near Ravenscar on the coast, the first official crossing of the Lyke Wake Walk was completed in 13 hours. Over the years hundreds of groups and organisations and thousands of people from all walks of life have successfully finished the route.

Joining forces with the Lyke Wake Walk for about 12 miles/19.3 km, the Cleveland Way now crosses some of the toughest and most gruelling moorland country anywhere in Britain. A chain of demanding ascents awaits the walker – culminating with Urra Moor to the east of the B1257 road. Then the two routes split – the Lyke Wake Walk continues in an easterly direction while the Cleveland Way swings north.

Kildale is the next village and beyond it the way reaches Captain Cook's monument on Easby Moor. The nearby village of Great Ayton is where Cook spent part of his childhood. North again towards Roseberry Topping, a distinctive peak soaring to 1,000 ft/305m and sometimes referred to as the Little Matterhorn. At this point the walk heads east, skirting the town of Guisborough by charting a course through Guisborough Woods. Negotiating the A171, the trail continues across country, eventually meeting the North Sea at Saltburn, a small resort which offers overnight accommodation. One of Britain's richest mineral and fossil coasts, this part of Yorkshire is a haven for geologists. The high cliffs are cut by bays and wooded 'wykes' and the beaches are strewn with jet and coiled ammonites.

The Cleveland Way follows the designated Heritage Coast from now on, and the sea views are particularly memorable, especially from the 600 ft/ Boulby cliffs, the highest point on England's east coast. Further on, the cliff path drops down to the picturesque fishing village of Staithes, where Captain Cook was employed as a grocer's boy. Steep cliffs, sturdy old cottages, a complex network of alleys and passages and a natural harbour setting give Staithes a timeless quality, though in summer it is a mecca for tourists.

The path heads down the coast, skirting Runswick Bay to reach Whitby – a jewel among Britain's fishing communities. The ruins of 13th century Whitby Abbey look down over the town, with Captain Cook's fine statue depicting the great man gazing out to sea. One of his most famous ships, *Endeavour*, was built here.

Whitby is synonymous with fishing and in Cook's day it was one of Britain's busiest and most important seaports. A host of local attractions keep the visitor and walker occupied for hours.

Robin Hood's Bay is chiefly associated with smuggling and its jumble of cottages huddled against the merciless forces of the sea leaves a lasting image in the mind. The way follows a rather isolated stretch of coast before reaching Scarborough, a nostalgic reminder for many visitors of the golden era of Britain's great seaside resorts. The town may look a little different today, but the familiar breezy promenades and the faded elegance of its grand hotels hark back to a different age. The late James Herriot, who wrote many books based on his experiences as a country vet in the Yorkshire Dales, was billeted here during the Second World War and had fond memories of the place.

The final leg of the walk is littered with various holiday developments. However, the dark rock of Filey Brigg and views of spectacular Flamborough Head provide a suitably dramatic touch as the trail draws to a close.

The Wealdway

The Wealdway explores some of England's prettiest pastoral and downland landscapes, opening a door on to the luxuriant hop gardens and orchards of the 'Garden of England'. From Gravesend, on the Thames estuary, the route crosses the broad sweep of the North Downs to the great Weald of Kent and Sussex, then makes for the glorious sandy heathland of the Ashdown Forest and the breezy expanses of the South Downs before culminating at Beachy Head on the Sussex coast.

The idea of a long-distance trail linking the Thames estuary and the English Channel was first mooted by the Ramblers' Association in the early 1970s. With support from the Countryside Commission, plus backing from local authorities in the south-east, the route was eventually established, one of its chief objectives being to take advantage of this great green swathe of diverse and fertile countryside.

With its crowded, ever expanding commuter towns and network of busy roads and motorways, this corner of England is not generally associated with gentle, unspoilt rural landscapes. But by following the Wealdway you are leaving the stresses of the late 20thC behind you and entering a secret, undiscovered world of downland pastures, dense woodland and greensand hills. In places the trail coincides with the Vanguard Way, a long distance path of 62 miles/99 km from East Croydon in South London to Seaford on the Sussex coast. The Wealdway is not particularly strenuous, and will appeal to those who enjoy an undemanding trek in gentle countryside. Inns, farmhouses and hotels offer accommodation along the way and Eastbourne, at the end of the walk, is on the main London/ Victoria railway.

The route

From Gravesend, which is also the starting point for the 160 mile/257 km Saxon Shore Way, following the south-east coast as far as Hastings in East Sussex, the Wealdway makes for Watling Street, famous as one of Britain's ancient Roman roads, before heading south to the hamlet of Nash Street, and on to the village of Sole Street. The Wealdway skirts Camer Country Park before carving a course across fields and through peaceful woodland. Soon the walker is deep in North Downs country – at this point a very pleasant mixture of thinly populated valleys and wooded knolls.

The hamlet of Luddesdowne was owned by Lewin, brother of King Harold in Saxon times. The Romans left their mark here too; fragments of pottery have been unearthed on the slopes above. Luddesdowne Court, which has been continuously occupied for 900 years, longer than any other house in Britain, includes a Norman dovecote and a Tudor chimney.

A very pleasant valley walk leads to the little Norman church at Dode – virtually all that remains of a once-sizeable village destroyed by the Black Death which swept across England with breathtaking ferocity in the mid 14th century. Soon the trail makes for the escarpment of the North Downs. The line of the North Downs Way and the Pilgrims Way can be seen heading west at this point. At the foot of the slopes lies Coldrum Long Barrow, a megalithic burial chamber enclosed by standing stones. The tomb was opened early this century and 22 skeletons were discovered.

South of the M20 motorway the route cuts through Mereworth Woods, where wild boar were once hunted, to reach the pretty village of West Peckham. The next stage of the walk involves a stretch beside the River Medway. The winding riverside path eventually brings you to Tonbridge; from the town centre the route continues by the river, following a section known as the 'straight mile' as far as the flood barrier. Beyond the hamlet of Haysden, the walk begins a long haul towards the ridges of the High Weald. Bidborough, where Sir Thomas More once lived, is the way's next objective.

Beyond the village lies the delightfully named Modest Corner, no more than a smattering of cottages. The church at nearby Speldhurst peeps into view now between the trees. The way soon enters Avery's Wood. With its multi-coloured mixed woodland and dazzling wild flowers, it is hard to believe this magical place is only a couple of miles from the centre of Royal Tunbridge Wells. Beyond the village of Fordcombe the trail heads for remote border country straddling the Kent/Sussex boundary, a rural 'no man's land' perfectly symbolized by its rich patchwork of fields and meadows.

Following the infant Medway briefly, the path then crosses the old Forest Row to Groombridge railway, now a linear country park, before plunging headlong into the 6000-acre Ashdown Forest. The Romans established a successful iron industry here and long before the invasion, prehistoric man hunted deep in the forest. Ashdown is the only surviving relic of the old Wealden Forest, much of which has long disappeared. A Royal Forest for 300 years, Ashdown represents the largest area of uncultivated land in south-east England. A.A. Milne, creator of the Winnie the Pooh, lived nearby and the walk makes for the oaks and beeches of Five Hundred Acre Wood – Hundred Acre Wood in Milne's stories.

South of the Ashdown Forest the trail eventually reaches Buxted Park and then cuts across country to Blackboys where there is a conveniently sited youth hostel. The name 'Blackboys' might be associated with local iron working and charcoal burning, though records indicate Richard Blakeboy was the village squire here during the 15th century.

Chiddingly church spire now rises against the South Downs. Inside the church is a monument to the Jefferay family, desecrated 200 years ago by those who believed that the effigy of Sir John Jefferay related to the notorious 'hanging Judge Jefferies' of 'Bloody Assize' fame.

Then it is a traipse across meadows to Hellingly, its churchyard prettily lined with cottages. Nearby Horselunges Manor has a moat. From Horsebridge, on the outskirts of Hailsham, the way makes for a famous river – the Cuckmere – and then the village of Arlington before aiming for the slopes of the South Downs. The salty tang of the sea on the breeze is a clue as to the close proximity of the Sussex coast.

Wilmington is famous for its Long Man, the largest chalk figure in England. The man is naked and clasped in each hand is a stave. His origin is unknown but some sources suggest he dates back to the Bronze Age. The Wealdway makes for his feet, then heads for the hamlet of Folkington. This section of the path offers some of the finest views on the entire route, with the low-lying Weald and the rolling green hills of the South Downs stretching to the horizon.

A sunken path leads the walker to the pretty village of Jevington, hidden in a fold of the downs. Coombe Hill, where farmers of the New Stone Age experimented with grain crops, is the next objective – and another fine viewpoint. The coast is visible from here.

The Wealdway officially ends by Beachy Head youth hostel on the A259, but most hikers follow the path to Beachy Head itself. The dramatic chalk cliffs and magnificent views of the sea make this is a spectacular setting for the conclusion of this immensely varied trek.

Essentials

Distance 82 miles/132 km

Start Gravesend

Finish: Eastbourne

Maps OS Landranger 177, 188, 198, 199

Guides *The Wealdway and the Vanguard Way* by Kev Reynolds, published by Cicerone Press. *The Wealdway* by Geoffrey King, published by RA Kent & Sussex areas and available from the Ramblers' Association National Office. The walk also appears in *Classic Walks in Southern England* by Kev Reynolds, published by Oxford Illustrated Press.

The Macmillan Way

The Macmillan Way, Britain's third longest path, was officially opened by Sir David Steel in April 1996 at Oakham in the old county of Rutland, recently reinstated having been abolished in 1974, as part of the national boundary changes.

The route, which was extended by 55 miles during 1997, now begins at Boston on the Lincolnshire Coast, and heads across country in a south-westerly direction, crossing several East Midland counties before threading through Warwickshire, Oxfordshire, Gloucestershire, Wiltshire and Somerset. Finally, the walk makes for Dorset, finishing at Chesil Beach on one of Britain's finest stretches of coastline.

The Macmillan is characterized by the familiar Cotswold stone of the oolitc limestone belt which extends all the way from South Yorkshire to Dorset. The route reflects the best of classic English scenery and is named after Douglas Macmillan who founded the organization now known as Cancer Relief Macmillan Fund. Macmillan grew up in the little Somerset market town of Castle Cary and used to walk to school at nearby Bruton every day. Both towns are on the route of the walk. The trail follows a chain of footpaths, byways and bridleways and some stretches of minor road. There are no difficult climbs and the walk, which will appeal to most age groups, can be completed in stages or as a two- to three-week holiday.

Incredibly, the Macmillan Way was devised by one man – Peter Titchmarsh – who spent more than two years developing the route, getting it waymarked, negotiating with landowners and writing an invaluable guidebook. One of his main objectives was to increase public awareness of the Cancer Relief Macmillan Fund and try to raise funds for this very important charity, which helps to improve the lives of cancer victims and their families.

The route

The trail begins in Boston, at the south door of St Botolph's Church. It skirts the Wash and crosses fenland before reaching Stamford. From here you make for the north shore of Rutland Water and then towards the neighbouring counties of Leicestershire and Northamptonshire. After following the old trackbed of a disused railway line, it makes for elegant 18thC Cottesbrooke Hall, thought to have provided the inspiration for Jane Austen's *Mansfield Park,* before reaching Althorp Park. This magnificent mansion, famous as the home of Earl Spencer, brother of Diana, Princess of Wales, and now her burial place, dates back to the 17th and 18thC and is open to the public at certain times of the year.

Further on, the way crosses the M1 motorway, followed by Watling Street – one of Britain's most famous Roman roads – and the Grand Union Canal, negotiating all three transport arteries in quick succession. At length, the route crosses another historic waterway – the Oxford Canal. Especially popular with boating enthusiasts, the canal took 20 years to complete and was eventually finished in 1790. Beginning near Coventry, it never extended south of Oxford, where it joins the Thames.

Farnborough Hall is the walk's next objective. The house is largely 18thC, and its delightful terraced walk is a notable feature. The battle of Edge Hill raged nearby. The Way now heads for classic Cotswold country and soon the trail is enclosed by sparkling landscapes of soft green hills dotted with honey-coloured villages. The route passes close to Stow-on-the-Wold before reaching Lower Slaughter. Many more miles of unbeatable Cotswold scenery are covered before coming to the old Thames and Severn Canal near the source of the River Thames. Bypassing the Gloucestershire town of Tetbury, the walk makes for the renowned 600-acre Westonbirt Arboretum where more than 13,000 trees form the centre-piece. Woodland walks and peaceful glades allow visitors to explore this delightful setting at their own pace.

Beyond Westonbirt the way heads south into Wiltshire, making for Castle Combe, one of the county's most visited places. Voted the prettiest village in England in 1962, Castle Combe has all the ingredients to make it a tourist's dream: a market cross, a fast-flowing stream in the main street, a medieval packhorse bridge and the remains of a Norman castle.

From Castle Combe the path follows the By Brook to Box. The setting for this village is a treat. There is a flavour of the Cotswolds about it, even a hint of the Derbyshire Dales, with its rolling fields, hills, drystone walls and picturesque stone cottages. Near the village is Box railway tunnel, one of Brunel's greatest engineering achievements. At the time it was built, it was the longest railway tunnel in the world and at one stage there were 4,000 men working on its construction.

Bradford-on-Avon is a jewel among the smaller towns of England and thankfully the Macmillan Way takes the visitor to its heart. Look out for the distinctive little Saxon church before beginning the next section of the walk, along a stretch of the Kennet & Avon Canal.

Crossing into Somerset, the route steers a course towards the eastern Mendips and the 1100-acre woodland of the Stourhead estate. Alfred's Tower is one of the walk's more intriguing landmarks; this triangular,

Essentials

Distance 235 miles/378km
Start Oakham, Rutland
Finish Chesil Beach, Dorset
Maps OS Landranger 141, 151, 152, 162, 163, 172, 173, 183, 194.
Guides *The Macmillan Way* by Peter Titchmarsh, published by The Macmillan Way Association, St Mary's Barn, Pillerton Priors, Warwick CV35 OPG. All publisher's profits on book sales are passed to the Cancer Relief Macmillan Fund. *The Macmillan Way Planner* (available from above address) includes information on accommodation, public transport, how to plan the walk.

windowless folly was built for the impressive view from the top, and to mark the spot where Alfred the Great erected his standard against Danish invaders in AD 879. There is a statue of Alfred depicted looking out over a landscape now cloaked with trees. The spire, hit by an aircraft in the Second World War, was replaced in the mid 1980s.

Alfred's Tower is also the starting point for the 28 mile/45 km Leland Trail which finishes at Ham Hill country park near Yeovil. The route is named after John Leland, the 16th century scholar and antiquarian who spent much of his time travelling the country on horseback. Leland was engaged by Henry VIII as keeper of the royal library, a post he held until 1530. Nearby are the famous landscape gardens at Stourhead, regarded as among the finest in the country.

Cadbury Castle, an 18-acre Iron Age hill fort guarded by ditches and banks, is synonymous with King Arthur's 'Camelot' and not far from this once- strategically important site is the Dorset border, representing the beginning of the final leg of the walk. The charming old town of Sherborne, famous for its historic abbey, is ideal for an overnight break. Then, it is on to stone-built Yetminster, the splendid park of Melbury and the charming village of Evershot. The way follows the River Frome south to Maiden Newton, the last few miles of the trail carving a delightful course across exposed downland.

Abbotsbury, with its thatched stone cottages and lonely chapel perched on the hill above the village, is much visited. From here the route heads for its terminus on the distinctive white shingle curve of Chesil Beach on Dorset's Heritage Coast, one of Britain's most isolated and beautiful stretches of seashore.

The Dales Way

*The Dales Way links two of Britain's most beautiful National Parks –
the Yorkshire Dales and the Lake District. Starting officially at Ilkley,
in brooding gritstone country, the way gradually heads up through
Wharfedale towards the spectacular limestone region of the western
Dales. Here, on the slow climb to Ribblehead, the surroundings
become increasingly more isolated, as the path traverses some of the
wildest moorland country in Britain.*

*Eventually you cross the M6 motorway, acting as a kind of border
between the magical scenery of the Yorkshire Dales and the awesome
beauty of the Lake District. The final leg of the walk is across
pleasant pastoral landscapes, with views across to the swelling green
foothills of Lakeland. The Dales Way finally comes to a halt at
Bowness on the shores of Lake Windermere.*

*An additional section between Leeds and Ilkley extends the walk by
about 19 miles/30.5km, providing those who live in the city's northern
outskirts with direct access to the route. Public transport serves the
start and finish of the walk, but there are somewhat limited services
in between. Several youth hostels and a range of accommodation are
available along the way.*

The route

Starting at the Marsden monument at the southern tip of Woodhouse Moor, otherwise known as Hyde Park, close to the university, the Dales Way cuts through the northern suburbs of Leeds before heading out of the city to neighbouring Bramhope. At this early stage, the trail joins forces with another long-distance path – the 70-mile/112-km Ebor Way, which begins at Helmsley on the southern edge of the North York Moors and finishes at Ilkley. Both routes journey through Caley Deer Park to Chevin Forest Park before climbing to the gritstone outcrops of the Chevin and Cow and Calf Rocks on the edge of Ilkley Moor.

From Ilkley Old Bridge, the way carves a path through Wharfedale to Bolton Abbey. With its timeless setting, on a sweeping curve of the Wharfe, this is one of Yorkshire's most famous and historic

Essentials

Distance 84 miles/135km
Start Ilkley
Finish Bowness-on-Windermere
Maps OS Landranger 97, 98, 104; OS Outdoor Leisure 2, 7,10, 30
Guides *The Dales Way* by Colin Speakman, published by Dalesman and also available from the Ramblers' Association National Office. *The Dales Way* by Terry Marsh, published by Cicerone Press. *The Dales Way* by Anthony Burton, published by Aurum Press in association with Ordnance Survey.

sites. North of here the path makes for the Strid, where the river dashes frantically through a narrow opening between trees and rocks. This is a beautiful spot – romantic and mysterious. A little further on, the path reaches the ruins of Barden Tower, which include a chapel and priest's house. The building was restored in the mid 17thC by the renowned Lady Anne Clifford.

The delightful village of Appletreewick was a prosperous community in Medieval times – mainly as a result of lead mining and sheep farming. Today, it attracts caravanners and walkers in search of peace and solitude among the hills and dales. Appletreewick's pretty name means 'dairy farm near an apple tree.'

Continuing upstream, the path crosses to the opposite bank via a suspension